Dependency and Socialism in the Modern Caribbean

Dependency and Socialism in the Modern Caribbean

Superpower Intervention in Guyana, Jamaica, and Grenada, 1970–1985

Euclid A. Rose

LEXINGTON BOOKS
Lanham • Boulder • New York • Oxford

LEXINGTON BOOKS

Published in the United States of America
by Lexington Books
A Member of the Rowman & Littlefield Publishing Group
4720 Boston Way, Lanham, Maryland 20706

PO Box 317
Oxford
OX2 9RU, UK

British Library Cataloguing in Publication Information Available

Library of Congress Control Number: 2002110353

ISBN 0-7391-0448-9 (cloth : alk. paper)

Printed in the United States of America

♾™ The paper used in this publication meets the minimum requirements of American
National Standard for Information Sciences—Permanence of Paper for Printed Library
Materials, ANSI/NISO Z39.48–1992.

Contents

Figures

Tables

Acronyms

ACLM	Antigua Caribbean Liberation Movement
ACP	Africa, Caribbean and Pacific
AID	Agency for International Development
ALCAN	Aluminum Company of Canada
ALCOA	Aluminum Company of America
AMC	Agricultural Marketing Corporation
API	Agency for Public Information
BGLU	British Guiana Labour Union
BITU	Bustamante Industrial Trade Union
BLP	Barbados Labour Party
CARICOM	Caribbean Common Market and Community
CARIFTA	Caribbean Free Trade Association
CBERA	Caribbean Basin Economic Recovery Act
CBI	Caribbean Basin Initiative
CCC	Committee of Concerned Citizens
CCWU	Clerical and Commercial Workers Union
CDB	Caribbean Development Bank
CDF	Capital Development Fund
CIA	Central Intelligence Agency
CIEC	Conference on International Economic Cooperation
CSA	Civil Service Association
DEMBA	Demerara Bauxite Company
ECDC	Economic Corporation among Developing Countries
EEC	European Economic Community
FCH	Feed, Clothe and House
FMS	Foreign Military Sales
G-77	Group of 77
GATT	General Agreement on Tariffs and Trade
GAWU	Guyana Agricultural Workers Union
GBA	Guyana Bar Association
GDF	Guyana Defense Force
GDP	Gross Domestic Product
GFLP	Grenada's Federated Labour Party

GHRA	Guyana Human Rights Association
GIWU	Guyana Industrial Workers Union
GMMWU	Grenada Mental and Manual Workers Union
GNP	Grenada National Party
GNP	Gross National Product
GPP	Grenada People's Party
GULP	Grenada United Labour Party
IBA	International Bauxite Association
ICSID	International Center - Settlement of Investment Disputes
IDB	Inter-American Development Bank
IMF	International Monetary Fund
ISI	Import-Substitution Industrialization
JAMAL	Jamaican Adult Literacy
JBC	Jamaican Broadcasting Corporation
JBI	Jamaican Bauxite Institute
JDB	Jamaican Development Bank
JDP	Jamaican Democratic Party
JEWEL	Joint Endeavour for Welfare, Education and Liberation
JIS	Jamaican Information Service
JLP	Jamaican Labour Party
JMB	Jamaican Mortgage Bank
JOS	Jamaican Omnibus Service
JWTU	Jamaican Workers and Tradesmen Union
LARR	Latin American Regional Report
LDCs	Less Developed Countries
LLDCs	Least of the Less Developed Countries
MACE	Movement for the Advancement of Community Effort
MAO	Movement Against Oppression
MAP	Movement for the Assemblies of the People
MAP	Military Assistance Program
MDCs	More Developed Countries
MNCs	Multi-National Corporations
MPLA	Movimento Popular de Libertacao de Angola
NACDA	National Cooperative Development Agency
NACLA	North American Congress on Latin America
NAM	Non-aligned Movement
NDP	National Democratic Party
NHT	National Housing Trust
NICs	Newly Industrialized Countries
NIEO	New International Economic Order
NJM	New Jewel Movement

NLF	National Labour Front
NPA	National Planning Agency
NWG	New World Group
NWU	National Workers Union
OAS	Organization of American States
OCCBA	Organization of Commonwealth Caribbean Bar Associations
OECS	Organization of Eastern Caribbean States
OPEC	Organization of Petroleum Exporting Countries
PAC	Political Affairs Committee
PDM	People's Democratic Movement
PNC	People's National Congress
PNP	People's National Party
PPM	People's Progressive Movement
PPP	People's Political Party (Jamaica)
PPP	People's Progressive Party (Guyana)
PR	Proportional Representation
PRG	People's Revolutionary Government
RGA	Representative Government Association
SEP	Special Employment Program
STC	State Trading Corporation
TLP	Trinidad Labour Party
TNCs	Trans-national Corporations
TUC	Trades Union Council
UF	United Force
UFOs	Unidentified Flying Objects
UN	United Nations
UNCTAD	United Nations Conference on Trade and Development
UNDP	United Nations Development Programme
UNECLA	United Nations Economic Commission for Latin America
UNIA	United Negro Improvement Association
UNIDO	United Nations Industrial Development Organization
UPP	United People's Party
USICA	United States International Communications Agency
USWA	United Steel Workers of America
WLP	Workers Liberation Party
WPA	Working People's Alliance
WPVP	Working People's Vanguard Party

Foreword

Dependency and Socialism in the Modern Caribbean is a brilliant analysis of the struggle to overcome dependency in the English-speaking Caribbean. The book is intellectually wide-ranging and depthful as to theoretical matters and empirical materials and impressively original. Euclid Rose's case study based on diminutive Guyana, Jamaica, and Grenada serves three important purposes. By adding to the meager storehouse of well-grounded scholarship on dependency, socialism, and superpower intervention in the modern Caribbean, his study underscores the great need for more high-quality research on that region and on small states generally. Moreover, his study generates insights which, if tested on a wide front in the Caribbean and elsewhere, should deepen our understanding of the issues of dependency, socialism, and superpower intervention in small state-big state relations and stimulate inquiry into more general questions—questions having to do, for example, with leadership and conflict, particularly in societies experiencing internal and external countervailing pressures, on the one hand, to effect change, and, on the other, to resist it. Finally, Euclid Rose's case study should help strengthen the link between Caribbean studies (and area studies generally) and the nomothetic social sciences—in the process, lending encouragement to sharing theoretical formulations and empirical data across the disciplines.

There is much evidence in *Dependency and Socialism in the Modern Caribbean* of its author's having acted upon a key axiom in social inquiry, i.e., that a science is cumulative. Building on the work of previous investigators of the Caribbean and of his contemporaries, Euclid Rose has succeeded in distilling new theoretical insights which should inspire future kindred research.

Doubtless that achievement owes in large measure to the author's having an insider's perspective and to his laudable critical faculty: Euclid Rose impresses us with his vast knowledge of the region in which it is imbedded, and with his skill in puncturing self-serving pretense, in whatever quarter. Indeed, he has proven himself an adept equal-opportunity critic, assigning wide responsibility for the region's poverty, underdevelopment, and dependency. The author's targets include high-sounding European imperialist powers which held back their Caribbean dependencies, failing to bequeath to them the tools and skills and habits of mind that would be needed for effectively dealing with modernism in all its aspects. Looming over the Caribbean of course is the United States superpower, whose beneficence and preachy moralizing cannot disguise its own acquisitive, heavy-handed, overreaching ways. The author underscores further that governing elites in the contemporary Caribbean are generally content to promote their narrow class interest, aligning it with the power of the ministates they command—all the while claiming, falsely, that their interest is congruent with that of the populations over whom they rule. Euclid Rose has a "good feel" for small plural societies, for their strengths and weaknesses, for what is right and wrong about them and their leaders.

It is worthy of note, too, that the language of *Dependency and Socialism in the Modern Caribbean* is felicitous. The book is an ambitious undertaking and a pleasure to read, and is sure to provoke debate among scholars.

Alvin Magid
State University of New York at Albany

Preface

Since the arrival of Columbus in the Caribbean over five centuries ago, the region has functioned as an adjunct of external economic interests, producing agricultural products or unprocessed minerals principally for export to Western Europe and North America. This event has generated considerable passion regarding the nature and consequences of this encounter between Europe and the West Indies. Because the territories of the Caribbean are where the European intrusion first occurred and where colonialism persisted the longest, they inevitably find themselves at the epicenter of great power struggles and momentous internal upheavals.

Like some other colonized areas, the Caribbean is an artificial society, in that the social fabric was created anew by European colonizers after the eradication of the indigenous population. In the process, the region was developed as an overseas economy for Western Europe and has since become extremely open and highly vulnerable to the international capitalist system. By virtue of their underdog and peripheral status, the territories of the Caribbean were compelled to function as exporters of raw materials and importers of manufactured goods. As the maxim goes, the Caribbean produces what it does not consume and consumes what it does not produce. The result is that the region remains heavily dependent on the core countries and the international capitalist system as it was five centuries ago.

For better or for worse, the continued inability of capitalism to lift the countries of the Caribbean out of the poverty and dependency that have characterized the postcolonial region has served as a powerful incentive that pushed a number of countries in search for alternative development strategies. Despite the enormous obstacles they encountered in an often hostile international environment and the considerable barriers they had to overcome to gain some control over their own economies and to assert some priorities not served by capitalism, several Caribbean countries, in the 1970s and early 1980s, embraced a variety of socialist policies or the so-called noncapitalist path to development. Although developed for Africa in the early sixties, the theory of the non-capitalist development quickly attracted quite a diverse array of politicians, parties, and organizations in the Caribbean, where it was recognized as a potentially powerful tool to limit the obstacles to the transformation to socialism. The objective was to move toward some form of a planned economic system to control the commanding heights of the economy, and reduce the region's extensive dependency on the developed countries.

Indeed, the decade of the seventies was a truly unique period during which the Caribbean underwent an in-depth exploration. In this period, the development strategies of Guyana, Jamaica, and Grenada were an out-growth of the socialist ideology to which the leaders had committed themselves and to which the state was given the leading role in managing the process of economic development. But owing to the prevailing structure of social, political, and economic organization typical of these countries, and the complex web of international relations of which they were a part, political survival depended heavily on a leader's willingness to serve the interests of a small but politically strategic minority. It also involved their impassioned and often unrequited commitment and dedication in the pursuit of noble political ideals, ideologies, and causes for which they seemed prepared to give their lives. The post-independence leaders made politically expedient decisions that foreclosed policy choices consistent with the satisfaction of collective needs and U.S. interests in the region. As a consequence, these countries experienced a series of political and economic crises, as they became the victims of disinvestment, massive U.S. sanctions and destabilization measures, not to mention a degree of mismanagement, corruption, and a shortage of appropriate expertise.

In Grenada, the collapse of the revolution and the elimination of one part of the socialist leadership by the other reinforced the image of the revolution as an unthinking animal devouring its young. The revolution went far beyond the country's importance as a microstate because it was the first coup d'etat carried out by a group of black English-speaking Caribbean leaders. The murder of Maurice Bishop, the regime's popular leader, and the collapse of the revolution in October 1983 have left an indelible scar on the image of Marxist-oriented socialism in the region. It presented to the U.S. the opportunity to reassert its hegemonic status by invading the island and overthrowing the government, which had already been shattered. The fact that the PNP regime in Jamaica conceded power on the basis of an electoral defeat in fair and free elections established a powerful precedent for an alternative possibility of radical social change coupled to a genuinely democratic process. This, however, was not the case in Guyana where the Burnham regime held power for almost three decades through patronage, rigged elections, and control of the coercive apparatus of the state.

It is not surprising, then, given the analysis of this study, that room for political maneuver and flexibility, which seemed to be available in the 1970s has been eroded or eliminated by deteriorating terms of trade, huge budget deficits, and growing debt burdens. Attempts at concerted actions to solve these problems and to rid the Caribbean of its external dependence have either petered out or yielded little, and neither have the recent U.S., the IMF, nor other multilateral incentives to arrest or reverse the economic deprivations affecting the poor has yielded much success.

Both dependency and modernization theories, which seek to explain and prescribe solutions to underdevelopment in the Global South have not provided adequate explanations to the current economic crisis facing the Caribbean. Equally true is the fact that socialist-oriented strategies or the noncapitalist path which, in the 1970s, have influenced a range of left-wing parties and governments in the Caribbean proved to be totally inappropriate to the contemporary realities of the region. Its very premise that the balance of forces in the world was shifting decisively toward socialism was seen as ludicrous, at best. Given the rapidity with which socialism has lost credibility in recent years in the Caribbean and elsewhere, it is perhaps safe to say that no clear alternatives, certainly from the left of the intellectual spectrum, have emerged to solve the region's problems.

While there is an element of overstatement in the presentation of each of these views, each in its own way contains some aspect of truth about the reality and nature of the current situation in the Caribbean. The issue, however, which has to be addressed is how to overcome or reduce the region's continued dependence on the United States and the other core capitalist countries. The study, beyond presenting a panoramic view of the socialist development strategies and U.S. interventionist policies in the Caribbean—in particular Guyana, Jamaica, and Grenada—assesses and evaluates the impact of dependency, which continues to have a lasting and devastating impact on the mainstream of political life in the region. This book resulted from my attempt to probe the linkages of dependency and socialism in the Caribbean, both at the theoretical and policy analysis levels. This, it is hoped, will not only enhance the literature on this issue, but also help us to understand the major obstacles to development in the Caribbean and prescribe solutions to improve the lives of the masses in the region.

Acknowledgments

Whatever positive contributions could be extracted from this study are due in no small measure to a number of dedicated and supportive people, whom a mere expression of thanks could never adequately convey its recipient's enormous contribution. Recognizing that much more is owed than is given, I wish to acknowledge indebtedness to the many leaders in the Caribbean who provided important documents and gave some of their valuable time for interviews and discussions on the main issues affecting the region. Most prominent among these are the late Michael Manley, Edward Seaga, and Percival Patterson of Jamaica; Desmond Hoyte, the late Cheddi Jagan, Janet Jagan, Brindley Benn, Hamilton Greene, Viola Burnham, Cammie Ramsaroop, Eusi Kwayana, and Rupert Roopnarine of Guyana; the late Eric Gairy, Bernard Coard, Kenrick Radix, and Mrs. Alimenta Bishop (mother of Maurice) of Grenada.

I am also very grateful for the encouragement and unfailing support that I have received from Professors Carlos Astiz, Erik Hoffmann, Alvin Magid, Gregory Nowell, Bruce Miroff and Secretary Eleanor Legieri of the University at Albany. Clive Thomas of the University of Guyana, the late George Beckford of the University of the West Indies, Daniel Salee and Everett Price of Concordia University contributed significantly to my thinking. I owe a special debt of gratitude to Dan Philip of the Black Coalition of Montreal for his encouragement and support throughout the project; to Miss Maxime Roberts of the Jamaican High Commission in Ottawa and Miss Pamela Ingleton of the Protocol Office in Jamaica, who helped to arrange my interviews in that country; and to Winston Courtney, Director of Prisons in Grenada who made it possible for me to interview Bernard Coard and the other members of the NJM at the Richmond Hill Prison.

Special appreciation to Martin Hayward, Jesse Goodman, and the rest of the editorial staff at Lexington Books, whose patience and understanding with my delays in completing the manuscript and whose support despite my transgressions went far beyond the call of duty; to Gail Trottier of the Political Science Department of Concordia University, who typed most of the manuscript; to Susan Kuebler of Siena

College Faculty Support Office, whose logistical assistance and expertise in computerized word processing were invaluable in preparing the final version of the manuscript; and to Patricia Beresford who allowed me to stay in her home in Guyana.

Finally, I want to thank those closest to me: Veronica, Reale, Trina, and Karen for their love, patience, and support for tolerating my frequent absences, even though their own lives were often totally disrupted by them. No one can atone for these neglects, but there is always the hope that the study merits it. Needless to say the failings of this work are entirely my responsibility.

Introduction

The Caribbean embraces some twenty-seven island and mainland territories, four major linguistic groups, and a kaleidoscope of races and culture. It has the highest level of fragmentation and balkanization in the world and this makes writing about the region as a whole a difficult task and the work of one author considerably more difficult in handling such a large number of different societies and nation-states within one volume without forfeiting any in-depth analysis. Yet another problem arises when one country such as Cuba develops in such a distinctively different direction from the others, that it becomes almost impossible to include them in a general analysis of the Caribbean. The fragmentation and balkanization of the Caribbean region was reinforced by colonialism and the imperialist activities of various European powers, including the migration of Europeans to the region, the destruction of the native populations and their culture, the growth of the slave trade and slavery, and the importation of indentured laborers mostly from India—all of which have contributed to the development of the region with little sense of internal cohesiveness. Each island and territory was administered in accordance with the practice of its particular imperial power which made little effort to foster a greater sense of unity amongst its colonial possessions in the region. As a consequence, all the territories of the region have developed distinct parochial and insular political cultures. Languages, religions, and political forms in the Caribbean largely reflect colonial experiences; insularity remains the most pervasive basis for identification in the region.

Another example of fragmentation occurred with the granting of political independence to the territories of the region after World War II. As in other areas of social life in the region, the decolonization process was uneven and, as a result, has divided the territories still further into three broad categories made up of (i) the twelve independent CARICOM states (table 1.1); as well as the other independent states of Haiti, the Dominican Republic, and Cuba; (ii) the semi-independent territories of Puerto Rico, the U.S. Virgin Islands, and the Netherlands Antilles, which is a federation of six separated Dutch islands; and (iii) the U.K. dependencies of Anguilla, the British Virgin Islands, Bermuda, Cayman Islands, Montserrat, the Turks and Caicos, and the French territories of Martinique, Guadeloupe, and French Guiana also considered the French overseas *departements,* which have legal rights to participate directly in national elections in France. The modern consequences of the natural and cultural fragmentation in the Caribbean are numerous underdeveloped independent states, whose existence and survival depend on aid, trade, investment, and technology from the developed countries and financial institutions of the Global North.

The English-speaking Caribbean, which is the primary focus of this study, comprised of sixteen island nations and two mainland territories, the one, Belize is situated in Central America, and the other is Guyana located in South America, are traditionally regarded as intrinsic parts of the Caribbean. This is based primarily on the shared ethnohistorical experience of the plantation economy and slavery, including the introduction into the region of large contingents of African slave populations from which the region's present Afro-Caribbean identity is derived. The diversity which characterizes the various Caribbean territories is evidenced in their respective geographic and demographic sizes and to the extent of their economic and political development. The smaller islands such as Montserrat and Grenada constitute a little over 100 square miles, while the largest is the mainland territory of Guyana with 83,000 square miles of the region's total land area of about 100,000 square miles. Similarly, there are striking population differences between the smaller and larger territories of the region. Anguilla, which declared its independence from the twin islands of St. Kitts and Nevis in 1967 has the smallest population of about 7,000 people, while Jamaica has the largest population of roughly 2.4 million of the region's total population of approximately 5.5 million. On the basis of the differences in levels of economic development, Barbados, Guyana, Jamaica, and Trinidad and Tobago are designated the more developed countries (MDCs) in the area and the rest are considered the less developed countries (LDCs). The latter three are rich in mineral resources such as bauxite-alumina and petroleum, and Barbados has a flourishing tourist industry. Together, MDCs account for U.S. $4.7 billion or 90 percent of the region's total gross domestic product (GDP) of U.S. $5.25 billion in 1995. The small size of the Commonwealth Caribbean countries and their far-flung location pose major obstacles to the economic development of the region.

The islands and territories of the Caribbean are located in a strategically significant area. Merchant and naval shipping from U.S. ports in the Gulf of Mexico, including the resupply of NATO during wartime cross narrow

Caribbean passages that constitute "choke points." The Caribbean Basin also links U.S. naval forces operating in the North Atlantic and South Atlantic areas and is an important source of many raw materials and minerals imported by the United States. Given its long history of colonialism and slavery, the Caribbean has been described as an artificial product of the exploits and rivalries of the major European colonial powers ever since the arrival of Columbus in the region in the late fifteenth and early sixteenth centuries. As a result, its connection with the international economic and political systems was made possible by this linkage and can be seen as both natural and historical. Consequently, the political and economic life of Caribbean peoples have been conditioned almost entirely by external forces, which dates back to the period of colonialism and slavery in the region. The anglophone Caribbean countries, for example, have developed political and economic institutions directly modelled after those inherited from Britain which, particularly after World War II, were influenced and controlled by the United States in what its policy makers claimed is part of its hemispheric and hegemonic responsibility.

The dependence of the Commonwealth Caribbean countries and their underdeveloped economies is deeply rooted in the political, economic, and social history of the region. Even the immutable factors of size can be understood only in the context of the colonial history which determined the way in which limited resources were misused and fragmentation of the region exacerbated. The result is that the Caribbean territories have emerged in the twentieth century with socioeconomic and political structures that are not easily adaptable to the needs of their populations and to the contemporary international economic system. Today's economic and social structure of the region is the direct legacy of the British mercantilist policy and development of sugar plantations based on slave labor from Africa. A direct consequence of this colonial heritage is that the islands and territories of the Commonwealth Caribbean have remained fragmented and dependent.

The political legacy of British colonialism in the Caribbean is indeed the institutionalization of a rather truncated form of democratic traditions based on the Westminster model with its inherent tendency to foster autocratic types of rule and to perpetuate colonial attitudes of subservience. Although theoretically the system is based on the legal framework of constitutional rule and a parliamentary system of government, in practice, democracy in the Caribbean has and continued to be controlled by what is known as vested interests, particularly those that are linked to foreign corporate capital. Such vested interests, for the most part, have displaced all pretences to the more egalitarian principles of political participation or popular representation in the region. This can be linked to the nineteenth-century British imposition of Crown Colony Government throughout the Caribbean, where colonial governors were given virtual arbitrary power over a nonelected legislative body whose goal was to ensure the general protection of British colonial policies and interests in the region. Barbados was the only island exempted from this type of rule.

Economically, the Caribbean is almost totally dependent on foreign corporate capital, aid, and technology, especially from the United States. This dependence, as stated throughout the text, is further compounded by a mono-culture development, which has effectively designated the territories of the region as primary producers of raw materials and consumers of manufactured goods to further the development of industries in Britain and its North American colonies. This occurred at a time when sugar replaced tobacco as the single most lucrative product in the Caribbean as a whole. The result of this mono-crop dependence with all its inherent characteristics is the failure today to develop a more diversified industrial base which could have significant positive implications for the overall economic development for the Caribbean region. This external oriented and mono-crop dependence on the part of the Caribbean economy actually laid the foundation for the development of the plantation economy system, which since the sixteenth century had intrinsically immersed the Caribbean within the international division of labor—a development that has left all the territories of the region underdeveloped and dependent on the outside world.

This is not to say that the plantation economy is a backward system or that it inhibits economic development. To the contrary, most of the literature on plantation economy suggests that it is an instrument of modernization in the sense that it opened up previously undeveloped countries and regions of the world resulting in the expanded production and the development of roads, ports, water supplies, communications, and health facilities. In spite of these positive factors, none of the plantation economies of the Caribbean or of the Global South is among the select group of advanced or developed countries. The plantation economy has left the countries of the Caribbean underdeveloped, dependent, and teetering on the edge of the international capitalist system. Their economies possessed limited natural resources and negligible industrial capacity. This, in part, explains why the territories of the region have always been considered by Britain as too small and too weak economically to sustain independence and become viable states within the contemporary international system. This, however, does not suggest that the countries of the Caribbean are physically unable to provide much of their own sustenance and basic needs for their populations. Rather, two factors militated against any prospect for sustained growth and self-sufficiency in the region. First, the islands and mainland territories were colonies, and whether placed in the Caribbean region or elsewhere, colonies were not permitted to become self-sufficient, only profitable outlets for the imperial powers. Second, just as the division and specialization of production was inherent in colonialism, so also was dependency, which has actually paralyzed the prospects for economic development in the Caribbean and other small Third World countries.

Notwithstanding the stranglehold dependency has on development in the Caribbean region, very little attempt has so far been made to systematically chronicle, analyze, and evaluate its impact on the modern Caribbean political economy. That dependency and all its inherent characteristics have been overlooked or ignored by Caribbean and other Third World social scientists reflect the paucity of literature on this important subject. But the paucity of literature on dependency in the modern Caribbean is not the only reason why this book is important. First, the significance of the dependency concept is that it constitutes the greatest irritant to development in the Caribbean. It also accurately locates the source of the problem and emphasizes the connections between the external penetration by the dominant powers and the internal domination of a country's political economy by local elites, and the impact of that interrelationship on peripheral societies. Secondly, at this crucial conjuncture of world developments, particularly the quickened pace of globalization, the leaders of the Caribbean need to critically assess the implications of interdependence and dependency on the region and strive for solutions to reduce their effects, despite their relatively disadvantageous position within a rather hostile and inhospitable global environment if they are to escape their underdog status in the international system.

In the anglophone Caribbean, socialism has been seen by the left as the only effective path to sustained growth for the region if it is to overcome its dependence on the world capitalist system and its dominant sponsor—the United States. Over the years, various efforts have been made by several Caribbean nations to break out of the confines of the world capitalist system and to embrace varieties of socialist philosophy. The experiences of Guyana in the 1970s and early 1980s, Jamaica in the 1970s, and Grenada between 1979 and 1983 are three distinct efforts in this direction, and they provide, in different ways, interesting analysis on the limits and potential of socialist policies in the region. Interlinked with the socialist ideals were the promise of greater economic independence, more decisive, locally controlled and inward-looking development policies, and greater local political autonomy, as well as dignity, and self-respect for the people. Implicit in the socialist promise was the democratic claim by some Caribbean leaders that socialist policies were more responsive and more accountable to the masses, provide extensive channels for mass political participation, and the achievement of a greater decentralization of political power.

The interest in socialist transformation and its promise had generated considerable attention from the left in the Caribbean because of the deeply rooted socioeconomic problems generated by the capitalist development in the region. Essentially, they include high levels of unemployment and under-employment; distressing poverty levels among the bottom 40 percent of the population; major reduction in prices and market demand for the region's exports; and extensive foreign ownership of key resources and capital. The region's weak production structures have led to its overdependence on a few mineral and primary products, such as bauxite, oil, sugar, bananas, foreign currency; enormous idle capacity in agriculture; and economic activity centered more on mercantilism than on local production. Moreover, its high reliance on imports has increased its external dependence and vulnerability to trade, financial, consumer, and fiscal trends in the international capitalist system. Also its technological dependence has meant that investments to improve its productive capacity would require foreign capital for its realization. Policies to address these problems should have the capacity to gain access to international resources, foreign capital, and overseas markets. Political and economic strategies of development cannot be inward looking only but should also have the capacity to extract resources from the international system, which would influence success or failure in the region's development efforts. Socialist development strategies mean very little if they cannot offer solutions to these deep-rooted problems over and above those offered by the capitalist model of development. The failure of socialist-oriented policies to offer real solutions to the dilemmas of dependency in the Caribbean has called into question the strong nature of Caribbean democracy and the capacity of the region's political system to accommodate other models of development other than the capitalist model.

This book, which attempts to examine, analyze, and explain the concept of dependency and socialist formulations in the Caribbean from a Caribbean perspective, is aimed at a fairly wide category of readers who, although not dependency or socialist theorists or specialists, nonetheless acknowledged that in order to comprehend the process, it is important to understand how dependency has evolved in the Caribbean and the various efforts to eradicate it. Because this book takes an original and objective approach to dependency in the Caribbean and the political changes that took place there during the 1970s and assesses their significance, most readers will find it intellectually stimulating to read and follow the discussion. As the title suggests, the book is essentially concerned with the constraints which dependency has placed on development in the region and the socialist-oriented policies advocated by the Caribbean left to rid the region from its subordinate and dependent position.

The reason for this is simple. Dependency theory provides a relevant explanatory framework for analyzing economic problems in the context of the conditions imposed by the contemporary international capitalist system. It will not recite the issues covered by Caribbean and other Third World dependency theorists. The focus is on the different strands and dimensions of Caribbean dependency which have not yet been fully examined by scholars. Neither have they examined the role of the domestic elite and ruling classes who continue to perpetuate their country's dependence on the developed nations in order to maintain their privileged status locally. The book therefore exhibits three crucial features: the first is to analyze the economic and noneconomic variables of dependency in the modern Caribbean and assess their impact and consequences on the peoples of the region. This will allow for the conceptualization of dependency in the context of the Caribbean, and to explain how it has been sustained and complemented by the international capitalist system with its asymmetrical distribution of power and wealth.

Second, we will examine and assess the socialist development strategies using Caribbean terminology to determine whether they constituted viable alternatives to the free market system. With the exception of Thomas (1988), and a few others, very little work has been done in this area. Our analysis of the political significance of socialist developments in the Caribbean is based on the distinct nationalistic characteristics and specific policy objectives adopted and implemented by Guyana, Jamaica, and Grenada. Third, it is our intention to rigorously examine the role played by the superpowers in the region during this highly volatile period of Cold War politics, particularly the United States efforts to destabilize the political economy of the leftist regimes in the region, including its military invasion of Grenada. The U.S. military and economic destablization of some Caribbean countries during the 1970s and 1980s are indeed reflections of the renewed attempt by a globally declining hegemon to reassert its international power and prestige. What this book is basically interested in, is the region's territories excessive economic dependence which began during the early period of colonialism nearly four centuries ago, and has since manifested into other noneconomic variables such as political, cultural, and psychological, all of which continue to inhibit many different aspects of human activity and development in the region despite its attainment of political independence and the implementation of capitalist reformist policies.

In the post-World War II period, many Caribbean countries have shifted production away from agricultural dependency to new sectors of petroleum, bauxite, tourism, and light manufacturing only to realize that these sectors have also been effectively penetrated by and dependent on foreign capital, hence the region's continued dependence on foreign resources. Dependency in the modern Caribbean is not a historical accident, but rather a result of the conscious effort by the developed countries to continue their domination and exploitation of peripheral societies.

The study, therefore, will not investigate the reasons surrounding the debate about the transition from capitalism to socialism in the Caribbean, which had been well documented in much of the existing literature on the region's development politics. We feel that the emphasis on the transition of socialism in the Caribbean is ill defined since it did not adequately deal with or address the complex issue of how the Caribbean left under a tight bipolar international system during the acute period of the Cold War, and given the region's location in what is regarded as being in the backyard of the world's most powerful hegemonic power—the United States—could be able to both obtain and consolidate state power as a necessary first step towards the ultimate realization of socialist transformation. Leftist ideologies in the region were nowhere close to the Marxist-Leninist tradition, but with leanings toward the egalitarian principles of Fabian socialism. The basic changes sought by the socialist regimes in the Caribbean were meant to influence the national political agenda and control the state apparatus ultimately for the attainment and consolidation of political power.

Although there exists an abundance of literature on dependency theory none has come close to addressing the different strands and dimensions of Caribbean dependency. The volume of literature on Caribbean dependency has been very abstract, dealing with highfalutin theories and formulas, and using irrelevant, rigid, and alien concepts in the tradition of liberal capitalism and Marxist socialism, with little or no mention of the day-to-day struggle of the average West Indian. This book offers new insights on dependency, socialism, and superpower intervention in the modern Caribbean. It presents a careful and comprehensive analysis of the political and economic changes that took place in the region and the results they produced. It suggests a new framework and analysis of dependency in the modern Caribbean that can provide readers with a concrete understanding of all its different features and the historical context within which it evolved, and how it continues to entrap the lives of the people. Dependency has become the chief obstacle to change and transformation of the modern Caribbean economy. This study differs from most others conceptually and analytically. It combines territories of enormous complexity, with both unifying and disintegrating tendencies, and links macro- and microanalyses to present a much clearer picture of the complexities of Caribbean dependency.

The theory around which this study is organized is meant to be general so that it can be applied to other examples of underdeveloped countries. The strands and dimensions of Caribbean dependency and the conclusions drawn from them, are not, of course, directly applicable to other regions, unless they are modified, but they should be useful in evaluating the degree to which the theory can contribute to the general understanding of dependency of peripheral societies and to what extent exogenous variables account for the outcome in light of all the various political, social, and economic factors that influence dependency in these societies.

Chapter 1 outlines the theoretical and analytical framework and defines the important concepts used throughout the text. It begins with information on the general nature of the political economy of the Caribbean in which we asserted that dependency in the modern Caribbean was not an accident, but rather a deliberate act on the part of European colonial powers, which over three centuries ago intentionally developed the region's economy for their benefit. Two major points are emphasized, the first is that the development of local politics and self-government in the Caribbean has reinforced the region's institutional dependence on the imperial power. Second, the postwar industrialization strategies were misguided principally because they increased competition among the states and that they were oriented toward profit making at any cost and not to the development of the region. The attraction of foreign investment by Caribbean governments had involved incentives that effectively reduced beneficial linkages with the economy and increased external dependence.

Chapter 2 provides an in-depth analysis of dependency in the modern Caribbean. The discussion draws heavily on existing dependency literature, which is extremely valid in identifying the international economic system as a central variable in underdevelopment, but suffers a major shortcoming in that it fails to point out that dependency relationships are maintained through a structure of internal elite control of the political apparatus of government. The chapter identifies and examines the distinctive strands of Caribbean dependency based on the historical, institutional, and structural approaches of New World Group (NWG). Although we concur with most of the NWG's assessments, we also recognized that the countries of the Caribbean are not dependent only because of their small size and limited resources. Rather, dependency has destroyed their national capacity to act as autonomous units because the power to exercise economic control and influence development resides in the advanced capitalist countries. In addition, the chapter broadens the concept of dependency in the modern Caribbean to include not only its economic and political variables, but also its cultural and psychological dimensions, which have negatively impacted the people of the region. It disagrees with the neo-Marxists' viewpoint that the region can escape its dependence on the core capitalist states only through a socialist revolution. Rather, we contend that no development strategy, neither capitalist nor socialist or any in-between model of development has so far been able to reduce dependency in the Caribbean and elsewhere.

Chapter 3 examines the postcolonial integration movements introduced to the Caribbean as a means to overcome the handicaps of small size, limited resources, and the dilemmas of dependency. The development of regional institutions such as the Caribbean Free Trade Association (CARIFTA), and its successor (CARICOM), was intended to buffer the economic effects of dependency created by the external oriented development strategies, which inserted the region's economy deeper into the internationalist capitalist system, thus making the elimination of dependency an unreachable goal. The chapter demonstrates that bilateral trade policies and ideological differences, particularly after the U.S. invasion of Grenada, coupled with persistence of dependency eroded the region's capacity to both implement policies geared toward regional economic cooperation, as well as its ability to organize a truly common economic system to bolster development and intraregional trade in the Caribbean.

Chapter 4 assesses the international challenges mounted by CARICOM states in international forums, such as the UN, the Non-aligned Movement, and the Group of 77 as a means of restructuring the international economic order to alleviate the problems associated with dependency in the Global South. It outlines the reasons that placed the territories of the Caribbean at the center of great power politics and the East-West conflict. It contends that the CARICOM states' participation in these forums and their efforts at South-South solidarity proved their determination to improve their underdog status and dependent position within the international environment.

Chapters 5, 6, and 7 are case studies of the different socialist strategies adopted by Guyana, Jamaica, and Grenada respectively. The discussion in these chapters focuses on the distinct policy objectives of the socialist framework in the region, which illustrates that politics took command of the economic forces and placed them in a direction that is either historically correct or designed to be used by the majority class. From this perspective, Caribbean socialism was seen as an escape route from over four centuries of imperialistic penetration, exploitation, and domination of the region. At the core of the socialist strategies was the consolidation of political power, state control of the economy, the development of an appropriate indigenous technology, mass mobilization, political awareness, class consciousness, and patronage.

In particular, chapter 5 analyzes the principal reasons for the adoption of cooperative socialism in Guyana. It was a novel ideology developed by the ruling party, the People's National Congress (PNC), which claimed that this approach was motivated by the concern for the plight of the poor or as Forbes Burnham puts it, "to make the small man a real man." We argued that the intent of cooperative socialism was tied to the consolidation of political power through an elaborate system of clientelism, political repression, and manipulation of the army and the police by the PNC regime. Patronage was employed directly against the opposition PPP itself to weaken its political effectiveness by co-opting many of its most capable and powerful leaders who controlled political resources of their own account. Clientelism also ensured the PNC loyalty and support of elites in control of the security, civil, and corporate branches of the state.

Chapter 6 focuses on the development of the concept of democratic socialism in Jamaica and its implications on the country's political economy during the 1970s. As an ideology, democratic socialism was a mixture of democratic and socialist principles as reflected in Prime Minister Manley's Fabian views of social equality for all Jamaicans. It emerged as a pattern of both international and domestic alliances to counter imperialism and U.S. hegemony in the Global South. It reveals that although democratic socialism was intended to lift the poor and the lower middle classes out of their poverty, it did not result in significant expansion of benefits in education, health care, and welfare, and was unable to meet the demands of urban masses. Instead, state expansionism justified programs that were directly beneficial to the middle classes and the capitalists, even though they were against Manley's socialist policies. The chapter explains that PNP's defeat at the polls in 1980 and the collapse of democratic socialism in Jamaica were in part due to U.S. destabilization policies and the alienation of the middle classes and the capitalists from the political process by the Manley administration.

Chapter 7 looks at the underlying reasons that led to the development of revolutionary socialism in Grenada and the traumatic way in which the revolution imploded. It documents, however briefly, the important gains made by the revolution in improving the economy, health care, education, and social welfare. This contrasted sharply with the existing literature in which many analysts vilified the revolution and condemned it as an outright political and economic failure. We advance the argument that the Grenadian economy was sound until mid-1982, when the regime was engulfed in an intense confrontation with the U.S. and had to divert resources to strengthen its armed forces in the event of an invasion. Although it is not categorically clear that this was responsible for the parallel political crises, there is evidence to support the claim that the economic crisis exacerbated the political crisis. This analysis differs from previous works by its systematic focus on the politics of the PRG and intense U.S. pressure that led to the demise of the revolution. The inescapable conclusion is that while U.S. destabilization policies might have had a negative impact on the economy and the PRG regime, it nonetheless cannot be accorded full blame for the internal power struggle that culminated in the murder of Prime Minister Bishop and the demise of revolutionary socialism in Grenada.

Chapter 8 addresses the implications of U.S.-led destabilization policies on Guyana, Jamaica, and Grenada during the 1970s and early 1980s. It provides insights into the distinctive elements of the destabilization process, not only its economic and political content, but also covert CIA activities, propaganda, negative press reports, diplomatic isolation, organized violence, and military exercises in the Caribbean. These policies were aimed directly at stalling the socialist revolutions in order to maintain the status quo, which means the continuation of the region's economic dependence on the United States and the international capitalist economy.

Chapter 9 summarizes the overall process of dependency, socialism, and superpower intervention in the Caribbean. It brings together the focus in the chapters to explain that the economy of the Caribbean and those of other small Third World countries are highly unlikely to be transformed or their dependency reduced by orthodox liberal or socialist economic policies within the existing international framework. The point being underscored in the chapter is that the international economic system has created formidable underdevelopment and dependency biases which cannot be overcome without the construction of a new international economic order based on equity and fairness. Micro- and ministates like those in the Caribbean region cannot develop autonomously of the world economic system because their fortunes are dictated by external developments beyond their control.

Although the data for this analysis draw extensively on both primary and secondary sources, much of the principal information was obtained through face-to-face interviews by the author with several heads of state, including Prime Ministers Michael Manley and Edward Seaga of Jamaica, Deputy Prime Minister of Grenada, Bernard Coard,[1] Prime Minister Eric Gairy of

Grenada, Presidents Cheddi Jagan, Janet Jagan, and Desmond Hoyte and Prime Minister Hamilton Greene of Guyana. Also confidential interviews were conducted with several individuals in sessions ranging from one hour to several hours. They included government ministers and senior officials of the member governments, opposition parties, representatives of the private and public sectors, individuals involved in radical political movements, and university professors. Because of the confidentiality under which these interviews were granted, these individuals are not identified, and to avoid tedious repetition of footnoting only primary and secondary sources are footnoted in the text.

Note

1. The interview with Bernard Coard was conducted at the Richmond Hill prison in Grenada where he and nine other senior members of the People's Revolutionary Movement (PRG) are serving life sentences for the murder of Prime Minister Bishop and five cabinet ministers in October 1983.

Chapter 1

The Development of the Political Economy
of the Caribbean

To the casual observer, the Caribbean basin has often been romanticized as a paradise and a mecca for tourists, drawn to the region by shimmering and crystalline waters, moderate winds, and benign temperatures ranging from 75°F to 90°F.[1] But lurking behind this visionary mask, nurtured by travel brochures with sanitized images of dashing buccaneers and romantic plantation life has always been the harsh reality of a brutal system of economic and political exploitation, both of the region and of the people associated with it. Characterized by the Trinidadian author V. S. Naipaul as the Third World's third world,[2] the English-speaking Caribbean is a conglomeration of former British colonies known collectively as the Commonwealth Caribbean or the (Caribbean Common Market and Community) CARICOM states whose ongoing struggle for socioeconomic development is seriously hampered by an unusual and indeed daunting combination of geopolitical and historical factors. These factors continue to have a negative impact on the development of the region's political economy as well as on the dynamics of its international relations with the developed countries. They have also contributed to the region's continued economic dependence on the international system and the core capitalist countries, especially the United States.

CARICOM is a direct descendant of the West Indies Federation that was created in 1958 and the Caribbean Free Trade Association (CARIFTA), founded in 1968. CARICOM's thirteen member-nations are Jamaica and Trinidad and Tobago, which achieved their independence in 1962; Guyana and Barbados, 1966; the Bahamas, 1973; Grenada, 1974; Dominica, 1978; St. Lucia and St. Vincent, 1979; Antigua and Belize, 1981; St. Kitts-Nevis, 1983; and Montserrat, which is still a colony of Britain.[3] Within these states is a heterogeneous mixture of nationalities, languages, and cultures whose racial and color groupings comprised of Amerindians, blacks, East Indians, mulattos, whites, and Asians. Despite the Caribbean cultural diversity, its shared history of colonialism, brutality and inhumanity of slavery, sugarcane plantations, and its common socioeconomic problems have given it a single identity. Most of the peoples of the Caribbean are descendants of slaves brought to the region from West Africa in the dark fetid holds of ships. The slave trade lasted for nearly four centuries and, although estimates vary, it involved the massive movement of no less than 13-15 million people, mostly Africans to the Caribbean region and North America.[4]

This colossal venture was principally undertaken by the major European colonial powers of Britain, France, Holland, and Portugal, all of whom held several slave bases in West Africa in order to monopolize the slave trade, both for their own possessions and for the sale of African slaves to the Spaniards.[5] Extreme brutality, physical hardship and in some cases bare survival and death characterized the slave experience on the plantations in which the plight of women, particularly the slave women, was horrific. These women suffered from the consequences of the sexual division of labor, from sexual advances of the slave owners and their sons on the plantation, and from the burdens of childbearing and child rearing. Many others traced their ancestry to the East Indians who came from India to the Caribbean as indentured servants to replace slave labor on the plantations. They too experienced physical pain and hardship and were exploited by the plantocracy class and the commercial and bureaucratic elite at what were essentially labor camps established initially by the Spanish and later by the Dutch, British, and the French. A daily routine of twelve to eighteen hours on the sugar plantations was the miserable fate of the indentured laborers.[6]

The colonial conquest of the Caribbean began in the 1500s and continued until the end of the Spanish-American War of 1898, when the United States defeated Spain and acquired effective control of the Spanish territories of Cuba, Puerto Rico, and the Dominican Republic.[7] Except for Spain, and the smaller European powers of Denmark, who sold the Virgin Islands to the U.S. in 1917 for $25 million, and Sweden, who held St. Barthelemy until 1877, all the original European colonial powers still have territories in the Caribbean.[8] The abolition of slavery in the West Indies in 1834 and the deterioration of the established order in the region shortly thereafter due to widespread riots and revolts, including the Morant Bay uprising in Jamaica in 1865, led to the introduction of limited self-rule in some of the territories of the region during the late 1860s. This laid the foundation for universal adult suffrage which was introduced in most Caribbean countries in the mid-twentieth century and beyond.

By this time the Caribbean economy was already fully integrated into the international capitalist system. Along with the other underdeveloped areas of Africa, Asia, and Latin America, the Caribbean was economically and politically dominated by the advanced industrialized countries of the Global North. Moreover, autonomous development of the region's productive forces was precluded because its pattern of resource use, production, exchange, and class relations were all mediated through the colonial office. The result was a systematic separation of domestic output from the patterns of consumption as indigenous resources were brought into use in the Caribbean almost exclusively at the dictate of capital accumulation in the core capitalist countries. What was actually consumed through the market was, by and large, imported and did not reflect the basic needs of the population in the region. According to William Demas, "The [Caribbean] countries have a common historical legacy: the sugar plantation, slavery, indentured labour, mono-cultural economies producing what they did not consume and consuming what they did not produce . . . and perhaps the longest period of external political dependence in any part of the world."[9] In addition, the lack of indigenous labor-oriented technology and the continued dependence of the Caribbean economy on only raw materials and a few primary products, such as sugar, bauxite, and petroleum have made the countries of the region extremely vulnerable to the influence of international trade,[10] which is a distinct characteristic of peripheral economies in the world capitalist system.

Needless to say, none of the various attempts of the last 150-odd years to diversify the Caribbean economy has succeeded in eradicating from the region the dependency syndrome so familiar throughout the Global South. These included (i) the establishment of a peasant agricultural sector to grow food and new export crops, such as cocoa, coffee, citrus, and spices; (ii) the development of light manufacturing, mineral, and tourist sectors; and (iii) the export of bauxite and petroleum to North America.[11] Thus, the Caribbean in the postwar period had in abundance all the problems usually associated with peripheral status within the global economy. The people of the region continue to suffer endemically from the effects of underdevelopment and dependency and their related problems: shortage of foreign currency, high population growth rates, weak and vulnerable structures of production, lack of development, high levels of foreign corporate capital and ownership, high unemployment, and ultimately rising discontent.[12] As our analysis of the Caribbean experience below shows, the stranglehold of dependency on the region's economy has remained to this very day and has continued to limit the possibility of development in the area.

The Development of Dependency in the Caribbean

Economic and political dependence in the Commonwealth Caribbean can be traced to the sixteenth century when the major European powers colonized territories of the region and incorporated them into the international capitalist system as plantation societies. In these plantation societies were European settlers who developed the land for the future of their children and built institutions to facilitate the development of their settlement. The European settlers, most of whom were absentee owners of land and capital, established institutions that perpetuated the exploitation of the region's resources and the labor of its people. They also appropriated the surplus generated mostly by African slave labor for the development of Europe and the British North American colonies, thus giving no thought to the long-term economic and political development of the Caribbean region and its people.

Within the plantation system there existed an inner dynamic which led to the creation of distinctive and very rigid social and political relationships. The populations of the various Caribbean territories were predominantly comprised of African slaves whose destinies, activities, and behavior were controlled by a small number of free white Europeans. In fact, economic and political power was vested in the plantocracy, merchants, professionals, and state functionaries to ensure the perpetual domination and exploitation of both the slaves and the structures of production. As a result, the plantation system was not only an agricultural scheme, but also became the basis for oppression of the region's inhabitants, underdevelopment, and dependency. This dependency, which had at its foundation a distinct economic element, subsequently manifested itself into relationships of political, cultural, and psychological dependency, which eventually became the dominant historical attribute of modern Caribbean societies.[13] It resulted primarily from the forcible ejection and, in some instances, the actual killing of large numbers of the native Taino-Arawak and Carib Indian populations by Europeans. Many others succumbed to small pox, whooping cough, and other deadly infectious diseases, to which they were not accustomed, but contracted from white Europeans. The killing off of the native population gave the European settlers a fresh start in the Caribbean region for, unlike some Asian countries such as India and Indonesia, they did not have to build on indestructible indigenous structures or preserve indigenous social, economic, and political systems. Sidney Mintz provides some insights into this phenomenon:

> The Caribbean colonies were not European imperial possessions erected upon massive indigenous bases in the area of declining great literate

civilizations as was true of India and Indonesia, they were not mere ports of trade, like Macao or Shanghai, where ancestral cultural hinterlands could remain surprisingly unaffected . . . they were not tribal mosaics, within which European colonizers carried on their exploitation . . . they were in fact, the oldest industrial colonies of the West outside Europe, manned entirely with introduced populations, and fitted to European needs with peculiar intensity and permissiveness.[14]

The decimation of the indigenous population and the destruction of their culture by Europeans had not only marginalized their simple communal life-style and economies, but also provided opportunities for the colonizers to create large plantations for the sole purpose of producing and exporting sugar and other single tropical items, such as tobacco, indigo for dyes, and cotton to the European metropolitan countries. Food and other basic items of consumption by the local population were imported from Europe and the New England colonies in North America. The extinction of most of the native population however, produced a shortage of labor in the Caribbean. White Europeans fleeing religious and political persecution in Europe were expected to work on the plantations but, as was the case, many of them could not withstand the heat of the sun and, as a result, died of exhaustion and others were, by and large, free or placed in indentured service.[15] As a result of these developments, the various Caribbean territories suddenly became dependent on the outside world for its food and other basic items because what was produced in the region was not for local consumption but material to be sold overseas for profit. Moreover, the plantation system in particular had to rely almost exclusively on the importation of labor, mostly black slaves from the West African coast. Thus, the slave trade, which had already begun in Africa as early as 1415, provided a solution to the labor shortage in the Caribbean for the next four hundred years.

Following emancipation in the Caribbean in the 1830s many of the newly freed slaves had refused to work for their former slave owners, preferred instead to establish an independent existence as far removed as possible from the brutality and inhumanity of the slave plantations. In the process, they established small farms on the mountainous regions of the various Caribbean territories or wherever they could find free land. The ex-slaves supplemented their income by working part-time on plantations for wages. As Mintz explains, the ex-slaves' rejection of the plantation system "represented a reaction to the plantation economy, a negative reflex to enslavement, mass production, mono-crop dependence, and metropolitan control. Though these peasants continued to work part-time on plantations for wages to eke out a living, their orientation was in fact antagonistic to the plantation rationale."[16] Their actions led to the importation of indentured laborers who were brought to the Caribbean as a substitute for slave labor between 1837 and 1917, mainly from India, but also from China, Madeira, Malta, Brazil, Europe, Mauritius, Africa, and other Caribbean territories.[17] Of the 750,000 East Indians who came from India, 234,205 were sent to Guyana, 144,000 to Trinidad and Tobago, 78,000 to the French territories of Martinique and Guadeloupe, 36,000 to Jamaica, 34,000 to Suriname, and various numbers under 5,000 to Grenada, St. Lucia, St. Vincent and St. Kitts.[18] The second most widely distributed immigrant population following emancipation were the Chinese who went to Jamaica, Trinidad and Tobago, and to Guyana, which received the largest number of over 14,000. Large numbers of Portuguese indentured laborers who were among the first group imported to the region went to Guyana and Trinidad and Tobago, again the great majority settled in Guyana.[19] The parcelling out of the indentured laborers in conjunction with the already settled African, white, colored, and indigenous population in the various Caribbean territories had severe political and cultural ramifications for the people of the region. It has left a legacy of volatile class and ethnic conflict, economic underdevelopment, and dependency in the region. The current racial and ethnic distribution of the English-Caribbean territories is reflected in table 1.1.

The societies in the Caribbean were defined by deeply divided social and political structure in which power was vested in a small group of white Europeans, comprised of the commercial and plantocracy class at the apex of the social and political hierarchy. This group exercised almost total control over the free Europeans at the intermediate level and over the vast majority of African slaves located at the bottom of the structure. Politically, the masses in the Caribbean were not permitted to take part in the political process since this was perhaps one of the ways for the small group of whites to maintain their dominance over the larger population during the post-emancipation period. The vast majority of the nonwhite population was socialized into a form of political dependency in that they were encouraged to support the existing institutions and the leaders who dominated them. Culturally, the situation in the region was not different before, during, or after emancipation, due largely to the fact that the bulk of the labor force was mostly blacks, who were uprooted from their accustomed environment in West Africa and inducted into one for which they had no prior knowledge or cultural preparation.

In the Caribbean, as elsewhere, slavery has destroyed most of the African institutions and norms and suppressed much of their religious beliefs

Table 1.1
Distribution of Ethnic Groups in the Anglophone Caribbean

Country	Percentages of Ethnic Groups				
	Africans	East Indians	Native Amerindians	Mixed	Chinese/ Europeans/ Others
Antigua	77.0	2.2	–	16.5	4.3
Bahamas	93.0	0.2	–	1.3	5.5
Barbados	80.5	0.3	–	3.2	16.0
Belize	39.7	2.1	9.5	40.7	8.0
Dominica	93.0	0.3	–	2.8	3.9
Grenada	93.0	1.0	–	1.1	4.9
Guyana	40.7	50.4	4.0	2.9	2.0
Jamaica	76.3	3.4	–	15.1	5.2
Montserrat*	94.0	–	–	2.5	3.5
St. Kitts-Nevis	94.0	–	–	3.8	2.2
St. Lucia	90.3	3.2	–	4.3	3.2
St. Vincent	93.0	1.1	–	3.3	2.6
Trinidad-Tobago	43.0	40.0	–	14.0	3.0

Source: CIA, *The World Fact Book,* Washington, D.C., 1990.
These states are members of the Caribbean Community and Common Market or CARICOM. *Montserrat is still a colony of Britain.

and practices as well as denied them the basic right to speak their mother language. Much of what became cultural values for the vast majority of African slaves in the Caribbean was imitated from their European colonial masters and leaders and passed on to succeeding generations. These savage acts have not only made the Afro-Caribbean people who are the descendants of African slaves almost totally dependent on the metropolitan powers of Europe and North America, but also relegated the entire region to a mere locus of production of raw materials and agricultural goods, and consumers of manufactured products which have contributed to the development of the Caribbean as an overseas economy for the metropolitan markets of Western Europe and North America.

The Caribbean as an Overseas Economy

The development of the Caribbean as an overseas economy for metropolitan Europe began in the mid-1600s when sugar was found to be more profitable than cotton, tobacco, and other tropical products. The demand in Europe for Caribbean sugar and its by-products, rum and molasses, reached its peak from approximately 1750 to 1775, and continued until about the 1870s.[20] During this period, the development of sugar plantations in the region by European settlers was rapid, as sugarcane cultivation was pursued to the exclusion of virtually all other productive activities. There was absolutely no alternative to the demand for sugarcane cultivation in the region. Marginal crops such as perennial fruits were not permitted by the planter class, even though the trees could have been left unattended on estate lands which would otherwise have remained idle. The majority of the planters were totally committed to the single-minded pursuit of sugarcane cultivation and production in the region. In the process, an extensive mono-crop agricultural export economy was developed and consolidated in many Caribbean territories.[21]

The process to cultivate and produce sugar in the Caribbean was complex; it involved technology and economic planning. For example, cultivating sugarcane required a detailed knowledge of the plant, various soil types, and land preparation. Extracting the sugar from the plant also involved fairly elaborate processes, from milling and crushing to filtering and crystallization to drying, bagging, and weighing.[22] This technology came from Shephardic Jews and the Dutch by way of northeastern Brazil. The Shephardic Jews and the Portuguese had been involved earlier in the manufacture and production of sugar, first in Iberia and in the Cape Verde Islands, and later in northeastern Brazil. The Dutch, during their occupation of Brazil from 1630 to 1654, acquired the skills to manufacture and produce sugar from the Shephardic Jews and the Portuguese. Driven out of Brazil in 1655, the Dutch and the Shephardic Jews transferred the technology to the three Guianas (British, French, and Dutch) and to the British West Indies.[23] Because the production of sugar was costly, the scale of operations had to be large in order for it to be profitable. The large-scale operations of sugar in the Caribbean were made possible by slave labor and because sugar was produced for sale to the rapidly expanding markets of Europe, the industry was, from the outset, exclusively export and profit oriented. The colonies were not only profitable to the planters but also made the Caribbean the most valuable part of the hemisphere for Europeans, particularly to the British Empire as they were developed to satisfy European consumption and economic needs. As Eric Williams writes: "the tiny sugar island [Barbados] was more valuable to Britain than Carolina, New England, New York, and Pennsylvania together. . . . Jamaica's external trade was larger than New England's, as far as Britain was concerned; Nevis was more important in the commercial firmament than New York; Antigua surpassed Carolina."[24]

Sugar production was at the heart of the trade circulation of Caribbean plantation products, which were interlinked with the movement of global inputs for the plantation in a complex shipping network often described as the "triangular trade." This classic three-way trade arrangement involved the shipping of manufactured goods from Europe to West Africa, the British West Indies and to North America, slaves from the West African coasts to the Caribbean to cultivate sugar, and finally, sugar and other tropical staples from the Caribbean to Great Britain and its North American colonies. This triangular trade arrangement, beyond transporting goods and people from one area to another, generated huge capital surpluses that richly rewarded its European colonizers. As Anthony Maingot has observed: "the Caribbean became a center of activity as direct sea mobility . . . was the key to empire and riches."[25] Most of the wealth accrued from the Caribbean sugarcane plantation triangular trading system contributed to the industrialization of Europe and the American colonies which, prior to the American Revolution of 1776, had supplied the bulk of the region's foodstuffs.

Even without economic integration in the form of a custom union or free trade areas, the British economy of the nineteenth century was in a real sense an Atlantic economy as a consequence of its investments in North American railways and factories. Again, Williams asserts that the capital accumulated from African slave labor and Caribbean sugar, and the exploitation of the plantation system greatly financed the industrialization of Western Europe and North America, as well as European imperial expansion into parts of Africa and Asia, and thus precluded economic and technological development in the region. In his own words:

> The slave trade kept the wheels of metropolitan industry turning; it stimulated navigation and shipbuilding and employed seamen; it raised fishing villages into flourishing cities; it gave sustenance to new industries based on the processing of colonial raw materials; it yielded large profits which were ploughed back into metropolitan industry; and finally, it gave rise to an unprecedented commerce in the West Indies and made the Caribbean territories among the most valuable colonies the world has ever known.[26]

Williams also pointed out that between 1714 and 1773 approximately 20 percent of Britain's imports came from the British West Indies and that 7 percent of Britain's total exports were absorbed by the region. Triangular trade accounted for 21 percent of British imports, 8 percent of exports, and 14 percent of external trade. For Williams the triangle trade arrangement was indeed sound politics, based on sound economics. Similarly, in 1945, a Royal Commission of Inquiry (*the Moyne Commission*) acknowledged the enormous wealth generated from Caribbean sugarcane plantations and the importance of the colonies to the British Empire.

> In the eighteenth century . . . the ownership of sugar estates in the West Indies was the main foundation of the fortunes of many wealthy British families. West Indian Colonies were regarded by the state-craft of the day as an asset of the first importance, hence the prominent part played by expeditions to the Caribbean in the naval warfare between France and Britain.[27]

Political scientist Gordon Lewis has argued that the linkage of the Caribbean plantation system to the European economy and international capitalism during this period caused it to become a capitalist institution. This was evident in its internal structure as well as its dependence as an institution on the world capitalist economy of which it was forcibly inserted. As Lewis put it, "it is vital to remember that . . . all of the Caribbean territories [have] from the beginning been forcibly incorporated into the world economic system and particularly that system in the form of Western capitalist core economies. That has meant a system of structural dependency."[28] It is from these early linkages that today's modern forms of Caribbean dependency grew. One of its main characteristics in the modern Caribbean was its bias towards the utilization of domestic resources in the production of primary exports and the widespread importation of food and other products, such as clothing, construction materials, and machinery for local consumption.

In addition, several factors lay behind the development of the Caribbean as an overseas economy of metropolitan Europe. First, plantation land has been considered a commodity of production by Europeans because monetary profit has been their overriding goal for its development. Second, the internal dynamics of the plantation system were controlled by a constellation of changing rules and restrictions imposed by the powers of Europe. Third, the demand and high prices for sugar in Europe and North America during the seventeenth, eighteenth, and early nineteenth centuries led to a substantial investment in equipment, technology, and skilled personnel from Europe, again with an eye towards profitability. Fourth, the plantation workforce was comprised mainly of slave labor from West Africa and slave masters from Europe. Fifth, the Caribbean economy was oriented towards serving the capital expansion requirements of Europe, and thus prevented internal development because surpluses were not ploughed back into the region's economy. Sixth, sugar and other tropical staples were produced for an impersonal overseas market in Europe. Seventh, the plantation system was a product of colonialism, slavery, and exploitation of the region's resources and its population, and European capital and enterprise integrated into a Caribbean setting.[29] As Sydney Mintz puts it: "Slave and proletarian together powered the imperial economic system that kept the one supplied with manacles and the other with sugar and rum, but neither had more than minimal influence over it."[30]

Furthermore, intense rivalries among the five major European powers, Britain, France, Spain, Portugal, and Holland, for Caribbean possessions, manifested themselves in an almost endless state of warfare for over three centuries after Columbus's arrival in the region in 1492. As Spanish power waned, a series of Anglo-French wars created an ever changing geopolitical map of the region that eventually stabilized in the 1800s. In the process, many territories changed hands several times. In all of the colonies, the planter class, through the control of capital, virtually monopolized political, economic, and social authority. The worker was at worst, a slave, and at best, a freed laborer in a system with a long authoritarian tradition. These factors, to say the least, not only affected directly the long-term development of the Caribbean, but also contributed to its development as an overseas economy for Europe's metropolitan market which, in turn, contributed to the region's external dependency on the very European powers. This is at the core of John Stuart Mill's famous dictum that in the nineteenth century the sugar colonies of the West Indies were not really economies separate from Britain in any meaningful sense but merely "the place where England finds it convenient to carry on the production of sugar, coffee, and a few other tropical commodities. . . . The trade of the West Indies is therefore hardly to be considered as external trade, but more resembles the traffic between town and country."[31]

In the early mercantilist period, an elaborate system for Caribbean sugar was enacted to protect the interest of the planter class in the region. The Navigation Acts introduced by the British in the mid-seventeenth century prohibited the refining of sugar in the Caribbean. Later, as Europe became industrialized, the capitalists of Britain campaigned for free trade, and this resulted in the passage of the Sugar Act in 1846, which abolished colonial preference for Caribbean sugar. The movement away from protectionist policies to free trade, and Britain's refusal to allow sugar to be refined in the Caribbean, created severe crises in the region. The Caribbean which had been the rich commercial prize of the European powers in the seventeenth and eighteenth centuries was in economic decline in the nineteenth century.[32]

By the mid-1880s, the European sugar market, which the Caribbean plantation system had created and sustained for more than two centuries, no longer needed its production of sugar. It was not that the demand for Caribbean sugar in Europe had decreased. Quite the opposite, the average adult in Britain was consuming more sugar than ever before because of the growing popularity of tea and coffee in the country at the time of industrialization.[33] Caribbean sugar had to face stiff competition derived mainly from the favoritism accorded to European beet sugar producers, especially those from Germany and France as well as cheaper sugar from India and Brazil. Moreover, the massive dumping of sugar substitutes on the world market by European beet farmers drastically lowered the price of sugar. In the face of these developments, British politicians and industrialists credited the low price for sugar on the world market to the practice of the free market system or laissez-faire economics whereas two centuries earlier they insisted on tariff protection to protect the planter class in the region.

These factors, combined with several others, both in and out of the region, made slavery and sugar productivity, which was already declining, less important to the rapidly industrializing Europe of the nineteenth century than it had been in the two previous centuries. This resulted in massive suffering among the majority black population in the area, not that they or their ancestors ever had prospered from their toil on the sugar plantations. The truth is that local economic alternatives were limited to the mostly black population due to the fact that the imperial powers built infrastructures designed to service the colonial trading system only. Roads, railways, and communication lines, for instance, linked plantations and mines with ports, thus bypassing population centers in the interior of the countries. The drainage and irrigation systems were developed solely for the cultivation of sugarcane, and vast agricultural lands were converted from the production of staple foods for domestic consumption to cash crops that were exported to Europe for profit. Without a domestic manufacturing base of its own, the Caribbean region and its inhabitants had to depend on the revenues earned from a few exports in order to purchase expensive consumer goods imports. And although some natives were incorporated into the colonial bureaucracy, they were, for the most part, given few opportunities to learn entrepreneurial skills. As a whole, these various policies adopted by the colonial powers were basically designed to perpetuate their domination and thus reinforced the region's economic and production structures into those of metropolitan Europe. Attempts to redress these issues led to development and growth of local politics and the mobilization of the Caribbean masses against the colonial system.

The Development of Local Politics in the Caribbean

In the Caribbean, resistance against colonial rule began in the 1920s with major demands, especially among the black middle classes, for racial equity in the civil services, for more democracy through relaxation of the voting franchise, and for constitutional reform aimed at giving broader powers to natives on the islands.[34] These pent-up aspirations by the local population for more political freedom, combined with reduced wages, lower prices for the region's principal export commodities on the world market, planter bankruptcies, increased taxes, and fewer jobs during the Great Depression decade of the 1930s contributed considerably to angry working class protests and widespread rebellion and revolt throughout the former British West Indies. The first two outbreaks occurred in Trinidad between May and July 1934; and in St. Kitts in January 1935, when unemployed sugar workers occupied estates owned by absentee white proprietors. These were only two cases among several as the wave of violence spread over the next three to four years to Jamaica in May 1935 and again in May and June 1938; on several sugar estates in Guyana between September and October 1935 and in February 1939; St Vincent in October 1935; and in Barbados in July 1937. During the riots, 29 persons were killed and more than 115 wounded.[35]

These events reflected a general political awakening of the Caribbean people, mostly blacks, after a century of continued servitude following the abolition of slavery in the region. In the wake of the disturbances, a new pattern of politics emerged in the region that led to demands for greater measures of political freedom and better wages and working conditions for the working class. Consequently, a number of trade unions, such as the Industrial Trades Union in Jamaica, the Oil-field Workers Trade Union in Trinidad and Tobago, the Barbados Workers Union, the Guyana Labour Union, and similar unions elsewhere in the Caribbean emerged and became the collective bargaining agents for the overwhelming majority of workers in the region. These unions were led by some of the region's most prominent lawyers, labor leaders, and politicians like Norman Manley and Alexander Bustamante of Jamaica; Grantley Adams and Errol Barrow of Barbados; Eric

Williams of Trinidad and Tobago; Eric Gairy of Grenada; and Forbes Burnham and Cheddi Jagan of Guyana, all of whom later became prime ministers and presidents of their respective countries after independence.

From the trade union movement emerged several labor-oriented political parties in the region, which quickly established close ties with the British Labour Party as they advocated independence for the region. Britain's policy by this time was to gradually grant universal adult suffrage to its West Indian colonies. The process began in 1944, when universal adult suffrage was granted to Jamaica by the British colonial office, and after the Second World War, to Trinidad and Tobago in 1946, and to Barbados in 1951. In Guyana, elections to the Legislative Council had been permitted since 1943, but income and property qualifications were not removed until 1952. The pace of these constitutional advances was dictated by Britain, which took on the character of another generous concession by the imperial power, rather than make it appear as a victory on the part of the leaders of the region.

In the meantime, new union-party alliances sprang up in the much smaller Leeward and Windward Islands under leaders such as Eric Gairy of Grenada, Robert Bradshaw of St. Kitts, Vere Bird of Antigua, and Ebenezer Joshua of St. Vincent. Slightly different situations developed in Trinidad and Tobago and Guyana, the two Caribbean territories whose populations are more or less divided between blacks and East Indians. In Trinidad and Tobago, party politics at the national level became organized only in 1956, when the People's National Movement (PNM) under the leadership of Dr. Eric Williams established itself as the island's leading nationalist party. The PNM grip on power lasted until 1986 in an unbroken tenure of rule. In Guyana, the People's Progressive Party (PPP) led by the Marxist Dr. Cheddi Jagan emerged as the dominant political party in the country. It captured both the East Indian and black votes and won the 1953 elections, the first to be held under universal suffrage.[36] Although political changes in the region were rapid and momentous during this period compared with more than three-and-a-half centuries of plantation oppression and domination of the masses, it still, however, took public protest and violence, in some cases, to end colonial rule in the Caribbean.

Institutional Dependence of the Caribbean

The institutional dependence of the Caribbean countries and territories upon Britain was evidenced by their parliamentary systems of government based on the Westminster model.[37] Following their independence, all the

English-speaking Caribbean states have remained members of the British Commonwealth of Nations, which recognizes the British Crown as the association's symbol and whose principal function is to provide economic assistance and diplomatic support to its member states, particularly to the smaller islands. The reason being the decolonization process in the region that began after World War II had involved no national liberation struggles. As a result, the identity of the English-speaking Caribbean nations continued to be strongly linked by their cultural, economic, and political ties to Great Britain. Despite attempts by Guyana, Jamaica, and Grenada to implement socialist-oriented development strategies during the 1970s and early 1980s, these countries have maintained a pro-Western position and a free market economy. Their initial decision to accept the status quo amounted to a rejection of Third World non-alignment and the leftist ideology sought by some Afro-Asian states in favor of the inherited institutions and ideas of British colonialism. Their choice also rested heavily on the geopolitical considerations of the region, given its close proximity to the United States.

Constrained by their small size, both in population and in physical area, and a dependent economy in a tight bipolar international system controlled by the two superpowers, the U.S. and the former USSR during the Cold War period, as well as being under the intimidating shadow of an overbearing United States, the countries of the Caribbean were not in a position to experiment with anti-status quo ideology. Moreover, because of the gradual and peaceful nature of the decolonization process in the region (except in Guyana where the period from 1961 to 1963 was marked by racial conflicts, and riots), the cultural and psychological dependency instilled by the British on the region prevented the development of the type of deep resentment against the colonizers that produced ideological and nationalistic militancy.[38] The attainment of political independence did not improve the economies of the Caribbean or reduce unemployment and dependency. In fact, in all of the Caribbean countries the same marks of the plantation system exist in varying degrees, such as economic and political fragmentation, underdevelopment, and dependency. Attempts to correct these problems have contributed to the implementation of the postwar development strategy of industrialization by postcolonial Caribbean governments.

Industrialization in the Caribbean

In the anglophone Caribbean, postwar industrialization was a formal commitment by the various governments and the colonial office to promote economic growth and development in the region. The thinking behind this strategy was simple. It was based upon the belief that a coherent industrial development strategy for the region as a whole could lead to economies of large-scale production for a wider market, promote greater rationalization and specialization in the existing industries and, above all, the establishment of industries that would utilize the region's labor and natural resources and technology. The ultimate goal was to create a sustainable economy in the Caribbean better able to withstand the pressures of dependence on the international economic system and the advanced industrialized countries.

Development strategies in the Caribbean in particular, and the Global South in general, have followed a rough historical progression. The British government, after the Second World War, discouraged and even forbade the development of manufacturing industries in the Caribbean and other British territories. The reasons were twofold. First, these industries might compete with British products on the international market, and second, the territories of the Caribbean were not endowed with the resources needed to sustain a manufacturing sector. The latter view dates back to the 1890s when the West Indian Royal Commission asserted that in the Commonwealth Caribbean, "there was no prospect for manufactured industries being established on any considerable scale."[39] The Moyne Commission, established by the Crown in the 1940s to investigate the causes of the widespread revolt and rebellion throughout the then British West Indies reconfirmed this view. The official view was that the small size, requisite skills, and resource configuration of the territories, coupled with the racial and cultural characteristics of their populations, militated inexorably against the development of manufacturing industries in the region.

The Commission further asserted that the Caribbean region was not an area where manufacturing would have a comparative advantage and that its destiny lies in the deepening of its traditional specialization in the production of agricultural staples and raw materials.[40] The Commission conceded that certain products, such as cement, could be manufactured in the region only if British firms were persuaded to participate, but it maintained that West Indian governments should not be involved in speculative industrial enterprise.[41] These views were principally based on colonial policies which were specifically designed to perpetuate colonial domination and dependence and, as such, were opposed to the interests of the masses in the Caribbean. By and large, the planter class and absentee owners of land and foreign capital in the region were invariably the main beneficiaries of these policies, which many Caribbean policy makers accepted almost without question or consideration in the contemporary period. Thus, in the Caribbean, industrialization and diversification of economic activities as well as the structural transformation of the region's production forces were virtually ruled out by those policy makers.

The disruption of traditional supplies during World War II, however, stimulated the growth of an embryonic industrial sector in the Caribbean in areas such as mining, manufacturing, construction, and food production. In spite of these developments, official British policy maintained that industrial development in the Caribbean was not viable. This viewpoint, combined with nationalist denunciations of the British colonial system on the grounds that it stifled economic growth and development in the Caribbean, led many to believe that industrialization was possible in the region under the right circumstances. Thus, in the late 1950s, a number of Caribbean countries began to develop a manufacturing sector based upon a strategy known as industrialization by invitation. This strategy was first adopted as a necessity by the colonial government and then, after its early success in Puerto Rico, as a matter of conscious choice by the newly independent countries of the Caribbean.

Industrialization by Invitation

Initially proposed by the West Indian (St. Lucian born) economist and nobel laureate, the late Sir Arthur Lewis, industrialization by invitation was the Commonwealth Caribbean version of Puerto Rico's "Operation Bootstrap" model of economic development. It was first embraced by the Four Powers Commission that emerged from the Anglo-American Caribbean Commission originally established by the U.S. and Britain in the early 1940s and later joined by France and Holland to establish a regional approach to solve the basic problems in the Caribbean at a time when most of the colonial powers were beginning their gradual withdrawal from the region. This strategy of industrialization by invitation derives from the notion that a scarcity of capital, skills, and technology in developing countries make it imperative to attract foreign investment which was sought principally in the sectors of light manufacturing mainly for import substitution and production for export. This approach to development has sometimes been called the "diffusionist" or "trickle down" approach, which means that the economic benefits from the industrial sectors would spread throughout the entire society which will be transformed by the diffusion of these effects and economic development will have occurred.

Lewis's primary concern was with the creation of full employment in the area. His strategy was based principally on the region's underdevelopment and long-standing role as primary commodity producers, and the theory of comparative advantage.[42] He was of the firm opinion that agriculture was incapable of providing enough jobs for the region's growing population let alone sustained development in the area, and that industrialization would remove the surplus labor off the agricultural sector, thus making it more efficient. He believed that rapid industrialization would establish the basis for the emergence of genuinely national economies in the Caribbean, and that it would be strategic in internalizing the dynamic of the growth process and compensate for the region's relatively high birthrate. In his own words: "The case for rapid industrialization in the West Indies rests chiefly on over population. The islands already carry a larger population than agriculture can absorb, and populations are growing at rates of 1.5 to 2.0 percent per annum. It is therefore, urgent to create new opportunities for employment off the land."[43]

Lewis saw the industrialization as playing a pivotal role in transforming the Caribbean economy not as an alternative to agricultural diversification and development, but as its complement, which would provide new jobs and absorb the surplus labor off the land.[44] The failure to recognize this aspect of Lewis's development strategy led to the serious neglect of agriculture in the region. Industrialization by invitation, which was aimed at replacing the plantation economy and at overcoming the increasing unemployment and dependency it had generated in the region, was established within the framework of dependent capitalist development, based strictly on private corporate capital controlled by a dynamic class of industrialists who would utilize the surplus to develop the region's economy. Lewis also insisted on labor intensive industries and a regional approach to Caribbean industrialization because of size and limited resources. In his view, "the policy which seems to offer most hope of permanent success is for the Islands to follow in the footsteps of other agricultural countries in industrialization. . . . No other policy seems to offer such permanent prospects as the development of local industries."[45]

In theory as well as in practice, industrialization by invitation was meant to attract both local and foreign private capital to the Caribbean countries through generous tax incentives, most of which were earmarked for the latter. These comprised: (i) state provision of basic infrastructure services such as harbors, airports, roads, telecommunications, and electricity; (ii) tariffs and quota restrictions on imports to protect local goods against foreign competition; (iii) income tax holidays for new investment or for those expanding their operations; (iv) state-supported training facilities for the local workforce in the form of technical institutes and universities; (v) access to the region's raw materials, low wage rates, and the existence of a stable political and labor climate; and (vi) the adjustment of income and property taxes to provide accelerated depreciation allowances to firms that invested locally. The last exemption was meant to correct any imbalances that might have occurred in the long run as a result of foreign investment in specific economic sectors.[46]

Lewis believed that once the English-speaking Caribbean countries had succeeded in attracting foreign investors to the region, unemployment would reduce, wages would gradually increase, foreign exchange levels would rise, and linkages with the local economy would be established.[47] By the early 1960s, the four MDCs and some of the LDCs in the region had established the institutional and legal apparatus to accommodate the industrialization development strategy. At the same time, foreign capital responded to the request of the governments and flowed into the region in massive quantities, bringing with it a number of highly visible light manufacturing industries, which catered primarily to the export market. Thus, in the beginning, Lewis's strategy of industrialization appeared to have been successful in that it contributed to some economic growth in the MDCs of the region in the form of industrial development, a substantial increase in per capita income, and a rise of approximately 15 percent of GDP in Jamaica, 16 percent in the case of Trinidad and Tobago, and 9 percent and 13 percent for Barbados and Guyana respectively.[48] However, a careful appraisal of the strategy reveals that the smaller Caribbean islands were not as fortunate as the four MDCs in that they were generally less successful in attracting substantial foreign private capital to promote industrialization.

The success of the four MDCs with this development strategy did not, however, lead to a substantial reduction of the endemic unemployment and dependency in the region, which in fact increased in the 1970s as a result of the decline of agriculture.[49] Industralization by invitation generated a series of negative results mainly because most of the industries developed during this period were principally in the mining sector and were capital intensive rather than labor intensive. This was contrary to Lewis's industrialization strategy which focused mostly on labor intensive industries to absorb the high rates of unemployment in the region. The situation was compounded by social conditions derived from an increase in migration from the rural areas to the cities in the hopes of obtaining employment, and consequent urban concentration, and by social and political tensions caused by greater unemployment in the region in the mid- to late 1960s.[50]

In Trinidad and Tobago, the development strategy contributed to the establishment of approximately 100 industries, mostly U.S. subsidiaries and the creation of fewer than 5,000 new jobs between 1950 and 1965, while its labor force grew by almost 100,000 people, thus increasing the island's unemployment rate from 6 to 15 percent during the fifteen-year period.[51] Over the same period, the strategy created more than 150 new industries and 9,000 jobs in Jamaica, but this did not reduce the country's unemployment since its labor force was increasing at the rate of 20,000 people a year. The reality is the reduction of unemployment and underemployment, which had been the main factors behind Lewis's thinking, was much higher than that which had existed at the commencement of the industrialization strategy. One reason is that the capital intensive industries absorbed only between one-tenth and one-eighth of the labor force increase in the region.[52] This means that they were unsuited to the special needs of the labor surplus economies of the Caribbean, to which they had been introduced.

Furthermore, the region's economies had failed to capture, as Lewis had hoped, a greater share in the gains from technology because the MNCs centralized their research and development efforts in the home country. This inhibited the creation of linkages between local firms and local research institutions. The technology utilized by most of the industries was limited to assembling imported components which had required the use of an ordinary screwdriver. This precluded the development of indigenous technology based on the use of local skills and resources and thus reinforced the region's dependence on imported technology. In addition, strict patent rights and licensing rules were enforced, and maintenance and replacement of equipment as well as innovation were regulated by foreign corporations. The result was that the value created locally by these products was so low that they strengthened the manufacturing sector and increased the region's dependence on foreign capital. Also, the new industries extensive reliance on external decisions prevented the development of close linkages with the rest of the local economy.

In most of the Caribbean territories, the primary source of income and foreign exchange came from agriculture which, in the 1970s, continued to employ 33 percent of the region's labor force, with 50 percent of agricultural workers employed in the growing of sugar and bananas mainly for export.[53] By imitating Puerto Rico's Operation Bootstrap development strategy, the governments of the English-speaking Caribbean ignored that island's close relationship with the United States and its privileged access to U.S. markets. The Caribbean countries that adopted the industrialization by invitation strategy had to compete with each other to attract foreign capital. In this sense, the strategy undermined the move towards regional integration, which it had intended to promote in the first place, by reducing the region's dependence on foreign markets and foreign imports. Also, the new industries of tourism, mining, and manufacturing have incorporated many of the features of the plantation society. The heavy reliance of these new sectors on foreign technology, capital, enterprise, raw materials and components, and the consequent transfer of surpluses from the region into foreign banks or luxury lifestyles in Europe and North America rather than ploughing some back into the domestic economy have significantly increased the region's dependence on the very metropolitan sources of domination it was ostensibly trying to eliminate in its endless pursuit of self-government and economic development. As Rex Nettleford explains:

> Caribbean life as evidenced in the various territories continues against the background of persistent forces seeking to perpetuate the domination of metropolitan Europe . . . within the context of the old style plantation system not only in terms of economic dependency but also in terms of an abiding Eurocentrism which put everything European in a place of eminence and things of indigenous (i.e., native born and bred) or African origin in a lesser place.[54]

The limited success of industrialization by invitation and the high degree of external dependence it created in the economies of the Caribbean were further intensified by the import-substitution industrialization development strategy. Initially developed by members of the UN Economic Commission for Latin America (ECLA), import-substitution industrialization (ISI) was first introduced to Latin America in the 1950s and later in the Caribbean. Its goals were to internalize the process of productivity in the region, which was the basic ingredient of economic growth; provide an escape route for the countries to reduce their high reliance and dependency upon foreign imports and technology; and at the same time establish industries to produce goods which traditionally have been imported, particularly from Europe and North America. "Industrialisation was the only alternative for the periphery, the principal means at the disposal of these countries of obtaining a share of the benefits of technical progress and of progressively raising the standard of living of the masses."[55] This strategy was premised on the achievement of national autonomy through state control and planning of the economy under a middle class comprised of intellectuals and industrialists. This meant the development of economic and political policies designed to restrict foreign interests. To this end, the Caribbean governments increased tariffs on foreign imports and provided financial assistance to nurture the local industries. In addition, local currencies were intentionally kept overvalued to keep the price low for imported products such as oil and capital goods for the industries. Wages were increased and so was social spending so as to encourage the growth of a domestic market for the goods produced by ISI industries.

Under ISI, a number of new industries were established and more goods were produced and marketed in the region, but the industrialization process was organized around the use of foreign imports and technology. The use of local resources was negligible and most of the equipment needed in the manufacturing process had to be imported. Furthermore, the most profitable ISI industries such as food processing and the manufacturing of home care products and garments were owned by foreigners, who siphoned most of the profits back to their home countries. Most of the products manufactured by the ISI industries could not compete with the higher quality and lower prices of foreign manufactured goods. Production processes of the new industries were confined to markets that concentrated on the consumption requirements of a small group of urban elite in the region. This group's desire for foreign products led to a substantial increase of imported goods, which exhausted these markets. In the end, ISI proved to be very import intensive, thus making the availability of foreign exchange a critical factor in the region's development. Also, government subsidies to the industries and high social spending increased the already high budget deficits in all the countries of the Caribbean. At the same time, extensive foreign borrowing by governments, the repatriation of profits by the MNCs, and the discouragement of exports due largely to overvalued currencies increased the external debt, despite the substitution of domestically produced goods for imports. This, along with the high prices associated with inefficiency and bureaucratic mismanagement and red tape contributed to severe inflationary pressures in the Caribbean.

Despite some improvement in the region's productive structure, both ISI and industrialization by invitation have failed to structurally transform the Caribbean economy and society. Some of the reasons for the failure can be attributed to natural variables such as the region's small size and limited resources, but the major problem was that foreign investors invested no more of their capital in the Caribbean than was necessary to be awarded the tax incentives and other government generous subsidies. A second reason was that Lewis was rather shortsighted to suggest that the surplus generated would be automatically ploughed back into the domestic economy to the point where unemployment and underdevelopment would be completely eradicated. By focusing almost exclusively on local demand for agricultural products, Lewis seriously underestimated the role of international trade and the region's dependence on foreign capital. This capital, once invested, was biased towards a particular sector and led to the misallocation of resources in the region and marginalized the local business class. The pattern of industrial growth developed in the Caribbean region during the tenure of the post-World War II development strategy is summarized by the Commonwealth Regional Secretariat, the administrative arm of CARICOM:

> The rapid growth of the manufacturing sector which has taken place in the last decade or two in the four independent countries has been accompanied by certain undesirable features; too heavy a dependence on foreign capital, foreign technology and foreign inputs (that is, raw materials and components); the excessive capital intensity (and therefore the limited impact on employment) of the foreign technologies used; the creation of insufficient linkages between this sector and other sectors of the economy (particularly agriculture); a drain abroad of profits, dividends, interest, royalties, licence fees and management charges because of heavy dependence on foreign capital and foreign enterprise; and insufficient expansion of exports of manufactures to countries in the outside world—a very important objective for small countries such as those in the Caribbean.[56]

Political Independence

During the 1960s, political independence aroused expectations of economic and social improvements in the anglophone Caribbean, just as it transferred to its leaders the awesome responsibility of meeting such aspirations. For awhile, it looked as though the English-speaking countries of the Caribbean were indeed making the transition from preindustrialism and colonialism to become modern, developed nations. This was due largely to the post-World War II development strategies which, in the beginning, had contributed to a substantial increase in the mining, manufacturing, banking, and tourism industries. For the majority of West Indians the 1960s was a buoyant period and a time of prosperity, vision, and hope. The habits of slavery were cast aside for a new dignity and the hope for a bright future in the region.

A decade later, these expectations gave way to rising frustrations as the development strategies failed to transform the region's economy from its plantation inheritance and thus reduced its excessive dependence on the developed countries of the Global North. The result was that the newly independent countries of the Caribbean were among those directly affected by the vagaries of the international economic order and by the process of globalization, both of which had been created by the United States and the developed countries of Western Europe. In this period, the countries of the

Caribbean experienced a general economic decline due mostly to falling prices and lower demands on the world market for their commodity exports; burgeoning debts to cover enormous trade and budget deficits; high interest rates; and double digit inflation imported from the core capitalist countries through dependency relationships.[57] The economic situation in the Caribbean was made worse by the international production crisis of the 1970s, which produced unemployment rates between 20 and 35 percent; and exchange and balance-of-payment problems that led to foreign debts in the 1970s of $41 million for the Bahamas; $60 million each for Barbados and Grenada; $430 million for Guyana, $417 million for Trinidad and Tobago, and a little over $1 billion for Jamaica.[58]

The growth of the economies of the Caribbean were further undermined in 1973, when the Organization of Petroleum Exporting Countries (OPEC) quadrupled the price of oil and imposed an embargo against countries that supported Israel in the Yom Kippur War. Despite some degree of success to diversify the Caribbean economy during the 1960s, in the 1970s most of the countries of the Caribbean found themselves teetering on the margins of the international capitalist economy. This was not a purely economic failure but a social one as well. Distribution of income in the region was notoriously uneven both between countries and within states where it was, and still is, a common Caribbean occurrence to find affluent suburbs and sordid shanty towns in close proximity. Across the Caribbean, notwithstanding its political fragmentation, the twin scourges of underdevelopment and dependency have continued unabated with little or no signs of an economic turn around in the early 1970s. This scenario has not only baffled the leaders of the region, but increasingly, it came to be seen that the development and expansion of the region's economy had been fuelled by, and dependent on, external inputs, such as foreign capital, technology, and perhaps decision making mainly from the industialized countries.

These were not unrelated events. In fact, during the 1970s, the Common-wealth Caribbean Secretariat claimed that the economies of the Caribbean represented a continuous and probably irreversible situation of the centuries-old pattern of West Indian economy: growth without development; growth generated from outside rather than within; growth accompanied by acute imbalances and distortions; growth without the full possible use of the region's land capacity, manpower, entrepreneurial and natural resources; growth based on foreign expertise rather than indigenous technology; and growth accompanied by foreign consumption patterns.[59] Added to these were several serious weaknesses in the structure of the political economy of the countries of the Caribbean. First, the agricultural sector which produced food basically for domestic consumption had been (and continues to be) in poor shape in all CARICOM states. This was partly due to the contracting nature of the agriculture in most of the countries, and the growing demand for food imports to sustain the tourist industry, which relied heavily on foreign tastes. Second, since World War II, manufacturing and tourism which had become the two main growth sectors in the region's economies were based on the external dependence of products, an outflow of dividends and profits to the metropolitan areas, and the lack of effective linkages between these and other sectors of the economy. Ironically, all of these deficiencies resulted partly from subsidies and tax incentives offered by the various Caribbean governments to foreign corporations in order to encourage investment in the region so as to improve their economies and reduce unemployment and dependency. Third, as already indicated, most of the industries established in the area were based upon the assembly of imported products, which for the most part did not penetrate foreign markets. These failures have had an adverse impact on the Caribbean economies which remained fragmented, underdeveloped, and dependent on foreign input. The region continues to suffer from growing inequalities among its social groups, and from rapid population growth rates which had been brought about by a substantial decline in the death rate through marginal improvements in health care and social welfare programs.[60]

Compounding the situation were the new radical groups that sprang up in the Caribbean region and spurred interest in models of modernization and development other than the traditional free enterprise system. Among them were the New Jewel Movement in Grenada (NJM), the Working People's Alliance (WPA) party in Guyana, the Movement for National Liberation (MONALI) in Barbados, the Workers Liberation Party (WLP) in Jamaica, the Antigua Caribbean Liberation Movement (ACLM), and the New Beginning Movement (NBM) in Trinidad and Tobago. These radical movements were anti-imperialist and antiestablishment. Their principal objective was to eliminate the legacies of racism, economic dependence, and oppression of the Caribbean people and to take control of the multinational corporations which maintained their leverage over the region's economy. Their focus on a new socialist framework for the social, political, and economic develop-ment of the Caribbean were perceived by Washington as anti-status quo ideology which would endanger U.S. interests in the region.

The difference between these new organizations and those of the 1950s was the former basic shift from "laborism" as the basis of their demands for change. In the earlier period the prototype for political radicalism in the English-speaking Caribbean was rooted in anticolonial sentiments. The emphasis on unionism and the welfare state embedded in the principles of Fabian socialism offered the new intelligentsia a practical way of fusing nationalist aspirations with the Westminster model, especially after the 1968 Rodney riots in Jamaica, and the black power uprisings in Trinidad and Tobago in 1970.[61] Set apart by a generation gap from the entrenched old guard of West Indian political leaders that represented the postcolonial political system, this new and much younger group with their own power ambitions were particularly concerned with the lack of control over the mode of production in the region. They articulated policies that favored new development strategies that fell generally within the framework of a socialist or a noncapitalist path of development. Their thinking generally was that the Caribbean governments had to negotiate better terms of agreement for themselves in their dealings with the international economic system and the developed countries, and that the state and not the local bourgeoisie must assume responsibility for executing that task.

The radicalization of the Caribbean political environment was highly influenced by international tendencies related to Cold War conflicts between the superpowers, Third World economic nationalism, the growth of non-alignment and the widespread discontent reflected in the grassroots movements that embraced Rastafarianism (discussed in chapter six) or some kind of black Caribbean nationalism as expressed in the black power movement which originated in the United States during the 1960s. In the U.S. the goal of the black power movement was to counter white racism and promote and strengthen black culture and identity within the predominant white American society. In the Caribbean, the black power movement was based essentially on a combination of black culture, racial nationalism, and antiestablishment. Its proponents were especially concerned with the plight of the poor and the powerless, inequality among the various social groups, youth unemployment, imperialism, and the region's heavy dependence on the core states and the international capitalist system.

Caribbean political activist and historian Walter Rodney redefined the concept of black power and set it more firmly within an economic frame-work of the Caribbean which recognized both imperialism and dependency as two key elements conditioning the lives and prospects of the masses in the Caribbean. Rodney defined black power as "a movement and an ideology springing from the reality of oppression of black peoples by whites within the imperialist world as a whole."[62] Explaining that the entire West Indies had always been a part of the white European capitalist society, oppressed and exploited at each stage of its history from colonialism and slavery to emancipation and beyond, Rodney unequivocally asserted that the black power movement in the Caribbean in the contemporary period is tied to three principal objectives: (i) the need for the Caribbean countries and people to break with imperialism, which is historically white racism; (ii) the need for blacks in the region to assume both economic and political power; and (iii) the need for West Indian societies to be culturally constructed in the image of blacks.[63] Recognizing the process of class formation and the racial types and mixtures found in the Caribbean, Rodney made it clear that he regarded blacks as people of either African or Indian origin and was prepared to invite the other groups to support the black power cause. In this sense, black power was not racially intolerant, but merely meant to ensure that the black man had real power over his own destiny. Rodney's articulation of black power expressed both global and local critiques of class rule and transcended the barriers which hitherto had prevented the alliance of radical intellectuals and the militant unemployed youth. It also reconciled the previously estranged ideologies of socialism and cultural nationalism in the Caribbean. In his own words:

> The moment that power is equitably distributed among several ethnic groups, then the very relevance of making the distinction between groups will be lost. What we most object to is the current image of a multiracial society living in harmony—this is a myth designed to justify the exploitation suffered by the blackest of our population, at the hands of the lighter skinned groups. . . . Black Power must proclaim [the Caribbean] is a black society . . . and we will treat all other groups in the society on that understanding—they can have the basic rights of all individuals but no privileges to exploit Africans as has been the pattern during slavery and ever since.[64]

It was within this context that the young intelligentsia pressured the various governments of the region, particularly the leaders of the four MDCs to either expropriate or nationalize the foreign corporations in order to gain control of the commanding heights of the economy. But as the global economic crisis intensified in the early 1970s, the countries of the Caribbean were faced with huge import bills which they were unable to pay because of lower earnings from commodity exports and light manufactured products. The result was that balance of payments drastically deteriorated, budget deficits skyrocketed, foreign exchange reserves fell to dangerously low levels, and governments all across the region faced serious financial and economic problems. The failure of the Caribbean economy to achieve self-sustained economic growth and overcome its dependence on the developed countries has been due to its import dependent character, which required more foreign exchange than it actually generated, and the creation of capital intensive industries which exacerbated the problem of unemployment in the region.

The conjunction of these economic problems was, for the most part, beyond the managerial capacity of the political leadership of the traditional conservative governments that predominated in the Caribbean. The leaders of the Caribbean were not sure if the legacy of colonialism and its related problems—dependency and underdevelopment—could ever be overcome in the region, but they quickly realized that politically the problems associated with underdevelopment and dependency could not be ignored much longer. They also knew that if they were to maintain their grip on power they would have to find other means to secure greater economic independence for their respective countries. They were aware that by the mid-1970s, the national strategies of economic development seemed to have exhausted all their possibilities. The global recession, the oil crisis, and calls for a new international economic order or to reform the existing one by the Global South countries had interacted with local developments in the various territories of the region to produce an environment that led to even greater penetration and domination of the region's economy by foreign capitalist enterprises.

These developments have not only made the Caribbean a net importer of food and consumer goods, but created the conditions for the ideological takeover of the region by a particularly radical nationalism which, in turn, had contributed to the emergence of a new form of political struggle and the proliferation of mass social movements that promoted some type of new development strategies in a number of countries.[65] These harsh realities were recognized by the leaders of the Caribbean who took the radical view that because political independence and the region's dependency on foreign capital were not reconcilable under the existing international conditions, the latter had to be changed. Many of them became increasingly dubious of the Western capitalist system because of its failure to improve the region's economy and alleviate its unemployment, poverty, and dependency and began to search around for new strategies of economic development and new models of political organization to replace the inherited Westminster type of government. The search was made more urgent by the weak performance of manufacturing in the region on which so much hope was pinned.

While no clear pattern or no clear direction of change emerged from the search, the consensus, however, was to move to the left of the political spectrum to reject in some way the status quo which had prevailed in the Caribbean prior to and after independence. For some Caribbean leaders, Cuba offered a socialist development strategy as opposed to the capitalist system that was seen to have exacerbated inequity not only in the region but also in the Global South and Global North countries as a whole. It was quite evident that Cuba's command type economy, modelled after the former Soviet Union and the Eastern European countries, had generated excessive dependence on the USSR, had a large and inefficient bureaucracy, and a shortage of essential consumer items due to the emphasis on heavy industry. The economy had also failed to insulate the island against the problems caused by lower world prices and demand for raw materials and agricultural commodities, particularly sugar. Moreover, the Castro regime's focus on labor mobilization and moral incentives rather than merit led to the over-estimation of high production targets for the island's sugar, tobacco, and other agricultural products, which were not met and which had contributed to the growth of inefficiency, poor work habits, lack of motivation, and anti-social behavior. These glaring problems which originated from Cuba's socialist model of development did not deter the leaders of the Common-wealth Caribbean. Most of them were still impressed with Cuba's relative technological advancement and high economic growth rates, broad success in areas of health, education, and housing, experience in land reform and agricultural production, low levels of unemployment, the example of social and political rewards of a mobilized society, a disciplined army and Cuban workforce, and the revolutionary convictions of Castro and his unwavering commitment to socialism.[66]

In the early 1970s, state participation in the national economy increased in some Caribbean countries as a result of greater interest by the political elite to achieve more control of their country's economy and their propensity to implement socioeconomic and political development models with distinct nationalistic features. This was particularly true of Guyana, Jamaica, and Grenada which, despite their close ties to Britain, the United States, Canada, and other Western countries, embarked on socialist development strategies aimed at eliminating their heavy dependence on the region's traditional partners, mono-cultural system, and the international capitalist system. The socialist strategies were based on a trisector economic structure of state, private, and cooperative which, according to the leaders, was more suited to the needs of the region than the capitalist model of development. These developments, while challenging U.S. hegemonic status in the Caribbean, led to a series of unsettling political developments that unfolded in the 1970s and forced a number of countries, particularly the United States and the Soviet Union, to take notice of the widespread political instability and the ideological changes taking place in the region. The Caribbean had suddenly become an international arena in which superpower rivalries, competing merits of alternative ideologies and models of development, as well as the ambitions of individual leaders were fought out. Despite their eagerness to adopt the socialist model of development, no development strategy, neither socialist nor capitalist, has brought any real progress towards eliminating or reducing dependency in the Caribbean. In reality the opposite had occurred despite the advent of trade unions, political parties, universal suffrage, and political independence. In fact, little has changed in the region's persistent underdevelopment and dependent relationship, which continues in the contemporary period of globalization.

Notes

1. John Macpherson, *Caribbean Lands: A Geography of the West Indies*, 3rd ed. (London: Longmans, 1973), 6.

2. V. S. Naipaul, *The Middle Passage* (New York: Macmillan Press, 1963).

3. Anthony Payne, *The International Crisis in the Caribbean* (London: Croom Helm, 1984), 4; Clive Y. Thomas, *The Poor and the Powerless: Economic Policy and Change in the Caribbean* (New York: Monthly Review Press, 1988), 4.

4. Thomas, *The Poor and the Powerless*, 20.

5. Ibid., 12-21.

6. Ibid., 34-35; Leo A. Despres, *Cultural Pluralism and Nationalist Politics in British Guyana* (Chicago: Rand McNally, 1967), 54-56.

7. D. Anderson, *Geopolitics of the Caribbean: Ministates in a Wider World* (New York: Praeger Publishers, 1984), 3-57; Bartlow J. Martin, *U.S. Policy in the Caribbean* (Boulder, Colo.: Westview Press, 1978), 14-16.

8. Thomas, *The Poor and the Powerless*, 17; Anderson, *Geopolitics of the Caribbean*, 94.

9. Cited in H. Michael Erisman, *The Caribbean Challenge: U.S. Policy in a Volatile Region* (Boulder, Colo.: Westview Press, 1984), 187.

10. Thomas, *The Poor and the Powerless*, 40.

11. Commonwealth Caribbean Regional Secretariat, *From Carifta to Caribbean Community* (Georgetown, Guyana, 1972), 14.

12. Ibid., 14.

13. George L. Beckford, *Persistent Poverty: Underdevelopment in Plantation Economies of the Third World* (London: Oxford University Press, 1972), 1-52.

14. Sidney W. Mintz, "The Caribbean as a Socio-Cultural Area," in *Peoples and Cultures of the Caribbean: An Anthropological Reader*, ed. M. M. Horowitz (New York: Natural History Press, 1971), 36.

15. Thomas, *The Poor and the Powerless*, 14.

16. Cited in Beckford, *Persistent Poverty*, 22.

17. Thomas, *The Poor and the Powerless*, 34.

18. David A. Waddell, *The West Indies and the Guianas* (Englewood Cliffs, N. J.: Prentice Hall, 1967), 87; Thomas, *The Poor and the Powerless*, 34-35.

19. Despres, *Cultural Pluralism, 72;* Percy Hintzen, *The Costs of Regime Survival: Racial Mobilization, Elite Domination, and Control of the State in Guyana and Trinidad* (Cambridge: Cambridge University Press, 1989), 26-27.

20. Waddell, *The West Indies and the Guianas,* 41.

21. Thomas, *The Poor and the Powerless*, 22-25.

22. Ibid., 22.

23. R. B. Sheridan, *Sugar and Slavery: An Economic History in the British West Indies, 1623-1775* (Baltimore: Johns Hopkins University Press, 1973), 12.

24. Eric Williams, *From Columbus to Castro: The History of the Caribbean, 1492-1969* (London: Andre Deutsch, 1970), 123.

25. Anthony P. Maingot, "Caribbean International Relations," in *The Modern Caribbean,* ed. F. W. Knight and C. A. Palmer (Chapel Hill: University of North Carolina Press, 1989), 259.

26. Williams, *From Columbus to Castro*, 148.

27. West Indian Royal Commission, *Report of the West Indian Royal Commission* (London: HMSO, CMD 6607, 6608, 1945), 4.

28. Gordon K. Lewis, *Grenada: The Jewel Despoiled* (Baltimore: Johns Hopkins University Press), 149.

29. Beckford, *Persistent Poverty*, 5-13.

30. Sidney W. Mintz, *Sweetness and Power: The Place of Sugar in Modern History* (New York: Viking Press, 1985), 184.

31. Mill, John Stuart, *Principles of Political Economy with some of their applications to Social Philosophy* (London: Longmans, 1878), 454-55.

32. Williams, *From Columbus to Castro,*165.

33. Sheridan, *Sugar and Slavery*, 27-29.

34. Williams, *From Columbus to Castro*, 470.

35. Williams, *From Columbus to Castro*, 473-474; Thomas, *The Poor and the Powerless*, 47-48.

36. For a general discussion on race politics in Guyana, see Cheddi Jagan 1966; Forbes Burnham 1970; Despres 1967; Lutchman 1974; Spinner 1984; Hintzen 1989; for Trinidad and Tobago, see Ryan 1972, J E. Greene 1974; Stone 1972; Bahadoorsingh 1968, 1971.

37. In the Commonwealth Caribbean, exceptions to the Westminster Parliamentary model can be found in the Cooperative Republic of Guyana and in Trinidad and Tobago, which became a republic in the late 1980s. In Grenada, the adoption of revolutionary socialism for a short period was a paradoxical case where the governor who was the titular head of state coexisted with the New Jewel socialist regime.

38. J. Braveboy-Wagner, "The Politics of Developmentalism: U.S. Policy toward Jamaica," in *The Caribbean Challenge: U.S. Policy in a Volatile Region* (Boulder, Colo.: Westview, 1984), ed. H. Michael Erisman, 166, 176.

39. West Indian Royal Commission, *Report of the West Indian Royal*

Commission (London: HMSO, CMD 8655, 1897), 2; Thomas, *The Poor and the Powerless*, 76.

40. *Report of the West Indian Royal Commission,* 443.

41. Norman Girvan, "The Development of Dependency in the Caribbean and Latin America: Review and Comparison," *Social and Economic Studies* 22 (1973): 2-3.

42. W. Arthur Lewis, "The Industrialization of the British West Indies," *Caribbean Economic Review* no. 2 (1950): 1.

43. Ibid., 7.

44. Andres Serbin, *Caribbean Geopolitics: Toward Security through Peace?* (Boulder, Colo.: Lynne Rienner Publishers, 1990), 16-18; Thomas, *The Poor and the Powerless*, 81-82; Clive Y. Thomas, "From Colony to State Capitalism: Alternative Paths to Development in the Caribbean," *Transition* no. 5 (1982): 7-8.

45. W. Arthur Lewis, *Labour in the West Indies: The Birth of the Workers' Movement* (London: Fabian Society, 1939), 44.

46. Tom Barry et al., *The Other Side of Paradise: Foreign Control in the Caribbean* (New York: Grove Press, 1984), 55-58.

47. Jay Mandle, "Ideologies of Development," *Transition* 2, no. 1 (1979): 40-47; Commonwealth Caribbean Regional Secretariat, *From Carifta to Caribbean Community*, 10.

48. Payne, *The International Crisis in the Caribbean*, 7-10.

49. Thomas, "From Colony to State Capitalism," 11.

50. Kenneth Boodhoo, "The Economic Dimension of U.S.-Caribbean Policy," in *The Caribbean Challenge*, ed. H. Michael Erisman, 80.

51. Thomas, *The Poor and the Powerless*, 90-91.

52. Ibid., 92; Anthony Payne and Paul Sutton, *Dependency under Challenge: The Political Economy of the Commonwealth Caribbean* (Manchester, England: Manchester University Press, 1984), 136.

53. Serbin, *Caribbean Geopolitics*, 17.

54. Rex M. Nettleford, *Caribbean Cultural Identity* (Kingston, Jamaica: Institute of Jamaica, 1978), 3.

55. Raul Prebisch, *The Economic Development of Latin America and Its Problems* (New York: United Nations, Department of Social and Economic Affairs, 1950), 2.

56. Commonwealth Caribbean Regional Secretariat, *From Carifta to Caribbean Community*, 12.

57. Ibid., 14.

58. International Development Bank Annual Report, 1979.

59. Anthony Payne, Paul K. Sutton, and Tony Thorndike, *Grenada: Revolution and Invasion* (London: Croom Helm, 1984), intro.

60. Thomas, *The Poor and the Powerless*, 184.

61. J. Edward Greene, "The Ideological and Idiosyncratic Aspects of U.S.-Caribbean Relations," in *The Caribbean Challenge*, ed. H. Michael Erisman, 38-40.

62. Walter Rodney, *The Groundings with My Brothers* (London: MacGibbon

and Kee, 1969), 24.

63. Ibid., 28.

64. Ibid., 29-30. For a full discussion of the black power movement in the Caribbean, see Rodney, *Groundings with My Brothers*.

65. Serbin, *Caribbean Geopolitics*, 18.

66. J. Braveboy-Wagner, "The Politics of Developmentalism," in *The Caribbean Challenge*, ed. H. Michael Erisman, 167.

Chapter 2

Dependency in the Caribbean

A distinctive feature of dependency in the Commonwealth Caribbean has been the legacy of the plantation economy created primarily by European capital, the exploitation of the region's soil and its people, and African slave labor. Insofar as it was possible, all economic activities in the region were geared toward the production of sugar and food for Europe's expanding working classes, and raw materials for its industries, while almost everything else, including commodities for local consumption were imported from the metropolitan centers of Europe and North America. Characterized by the highest degree of economic dependence, the economies of the anglophone Caribbean countries were, from the beginning, ruthlessly exploited to benefit European colonizers. According to the Trinidadian economist Lloyd Best and the Canadian economist Kari Levitt, economic dependence is the term applied generally to a situation where the growth of income of a country was substantially, if not entirely, dependent on external factors, such as exports, imports, capital, and technology.[1] Other Caribbean economists, however, viewed dependency in the region not only as an external datum, but as a condition in which the interplay of internal economic, social, and political forces were impacted by factors which, while functioning within each country's economic system, were determined by external forces.[2] From this perspective dependency theory explains underdevelopment in the Caribbean as a consequence of outside economic and political influences that have relegated the territories of the region to a subordinate and often exploited status in the contemporary international capitalist system.

Dependency theory emerged partly out of frustration on the part of some Latin American countries in their inability to improve their economic situation to reach levels of development similar to those of the developed countries of Western Europe and North America. It was subsequently diffused to the Caribbean where it had a major influence on the thinking of economic underdevelopment and dependency of the region. Its intellectual roots can be traced to three principal sources: classical Marxist writings on imperialism, especially by Lenin and his followers; the publication in the postcolonial period, mainly by Third World scholars and politicians, of such concepts as neocolonialism and neoimperialism; and the work of various Latin American scholars and economists associated with the United Nations Economic Commission for Latin America (ECLA). The last group, often called the Prebisch school (after its leading proponent, Raul Prebisch), was initially the most influential in advancing the Latin American concept of dependency theory, which attributed the development of underdevelopment to the historical expansion of the capitalist system that effectively penetrated even the apparently most isolated sectors of underdeveloped societies. This group defined dependency basically as the uneven development inherent in, and promoted by, the international capitalist structure and espoused solutions geared toward more state intervention in the domestic economy, import substitution, diversification of Third World exports, regional integration, and greater emphasis on economic nationalism as opposed to free trade in North-South economic relations.

During the 1960s much of the work produced by West Indian scholars on the political economy of the Caribbean had been conducted within the broad framework of dependency theory. In this, the anglophone Caribbean countries are not in any way unique, for dependency thinking and the problems associated with it, in general, had dominated the study of society, politics, and economics in the Global South countries. Its diverse intellectual background has not only denied it the claim of a unified theory, but has enabled a wide range of social scientists, for the most part, radical in conviction, to explore fully the concept of dependency and its historical link to underdevelopment in the Global South. In this way, dependency theory has over the years contributed considerably to the development and understanding of the political economy of the Caribbean, Africa, Asia, and other peripheral areas of the earth. The formulation of Caribbean dependency is remarkably similar to the classic definitions offered by the Latin American dependency theorists, particularly Theotonio Dos Santos, whose much cited definition of dependency is:

> A situation in which the economy of certain countries is conditioned by the development and expansion of another economy to which the former is subjected. The relation of interdependence between two or more economies, and between these and world trade, assumes the form of dependence when some countries (the dominant ones) can expand and be self-sustaining, while other countries (the dependent ones) can do this only

as a reflection of that expansion, which can have either a positive or negative effect on their immediate development.[3]

Dependency Tradition in the Caribbean

Economic dependency has a particularly long history in the Caribbean. It began in the sixteenth century when the major European powers established themselves as powerful metropolitan centers for overturning the traditional beliefs and customs of indigenous communal societies and installing a new system of production based on forced labor (slavery and indenture) which had a tremendous impact on the people of the region. The European colonial powers not only colonized and dominated the territories of the Caribbean but also inserted their economies into the international economic system as sugarcane plantation societies, producers of raw materials, cheap and free labor, and as outlets for their financial surpluses. In the modern period, dependency has manifested itself in foreign ownership of the key resources, the mode of operation of multinational corporations, the widespread use of inappropriate technology, the existence of capital intensive industries, the parlous state of domestic agriculture, the austere lending policies of the IMF-World Bank group, and a host of other widely known symptoms that are linked to underdevelopment in the region. Thus, in the post-World War II period, dependency and underdevelopment emerged as the dominant feature of the structure and functioning of the Caribbean economy.[4]

Over the years, many Caribbean scholars have viewed dependency as an inherent component of the international economic order that was deliberately established and is maintained in the contemporary period by the developed countries' multinational corporations to facilitate their systematic pillaging of the Caribbean and the periphery as a whole. Norman Girvan, in particular, has unequivocally stated that foreign corporations have promoted economic underdevelopment in the Caribbean. This viewpoint is in sharp contrast to that generally held by modernization theorists that foreign investments were instrumental in helping developing countries modernize their economic system.[5] Like Girvan, Clive Thomas, Lloyd Best, and Havelock Brewster, to name a few, have remained skeptical and even contemptuous of solutions limited to economic reforms as advocated by modernization theorists. The economists claimed that the problems associated with underdevelopment and dependency are to be found in the broader configurations of power at both the national and global levels. This is nothing new since power is wielded by the advanced developed countries who benefit at the expense of peripheral societies, where underdevelopment and dependency are perpetuated as their natural resources and other forms of wealth continued to be exploited to underwrite both the developed countries' high standards of living and their prospects for future growth. The Caribbean economists went beyond the purely economic ties involved in dependency and underdevelopment and sought explanations of the paradigm in terms of sociopolitical dynamics operative within the developed and developing countries and also at the level of their international linkages. This is clearly a rejection of modernization theory which argued that traditional societies like those in the Caribbean entering the development path must pass through various stages by means of the operation of the free market system before they can be fully developed similar to the advanced countries of the West.

The New World Group

The dilemmas of dependency and underdevelopment were first discussed in the Commonwealth Caribbean in the early 1960s by a number of economists from the New World Group (NWG) at the University of the West Indies (UWI), Kingston, Jamaica. Founded in Georgetown, Guyana, in 1962, the NWG was a loosely knit group of Caribbean intellectuals whose aim was to develop an indigenous development strategy to correct some of the problems encountered by industrialization by invitation and to overcome or reduce the region's dependence on external sources. Central to the Group's analysis of the causes of underdevelopment and dependency in the region is the concept of the plantation economy.[6] Some of its most prominent members were George Beckford, Lloyd Best, Havelock Brewster, William Demas, Arthur Lewis, Alister McIntyre, Norman Girvan, and Clive Thomas. Like that of other dependency theorists, their work was strongly influenced by the Raul Prebisch school and especially from the writings of Andre Gunder Frank and Karl Marx.

Comprised mainly of neo-Marxists, non-Marxists, and structuralists, the NWG associates identified five principal reasons for Caribbean dependence: (i) the stagnation and decline of agriculture in the region, which implied a slow growth in agricultural exports and a rapid increase and dependence of food and consumer goods imports; (ii) the high commodity concentration and dependence on a single or limited number of export products, such as sugar, bananas, citrus, tourism, and bauxite; (iii) the high degree of foreign ownership in industry and the dominant role played by foreign capital; (iv) the growing fiscal deficit, due to the stagnation of the traditional mining or the agricultural export sector which resulted in a huge public debt for most Caribbean countries by the late 1960s; and (v) high levels of unemployment, ranging from 10 to 30 percent of the labor force.[7] This highlighted the fact that the development strategy of industrialization by invitation pursued by the various Caribbean governments during the first decade of their political independence was a failure. It was criticized by the NWG associates for increasing the region's unemployment rate and undermining its economy.

The NWG stressed the dependence of the Caribbean economy on the rest of the world for markets and supplies, transfers of income and capital, banking and financial services, business and technical skills, and even for ideas about themselves.[8] For example, in his analysis of the structure of Caribbean economies, Havelock Brewster has observed that although there had been some developments in the mining and industry sectors, these have been achieved within the framework of an economic organization similar to that of the sugar plantation system in the region. He quantitatively illustrated the definition of economic dependence as a lack of capacity to manipulate the operative elements of an economic system in such a way that there is no internal dynamic to govern the functioning of the economic system.[9] He and other Caribbean scholars have contended that even though the brutal system of colonialism and slavery that dominated life on the Caribbean plantation for two-and-a-half centuries is gone, the region's economies unfortunately have been unable to break the bonds of the legacy of the plantation economy, and are today even more dependent on the U.S. As Barry, Wood, and Preusch explain:

> Caribbean politicians have made a show of confronting the colonizers, but only rarely has local leadership seriously considered the possibility of breaking out of the plantation economy. Many have sidled up to the United States the new foreign overseer of the plantation, which has dispatched its development agents, agricultural experts, and investors to ensure U. S. command of agricultural development in the Caribbean.[10]

At the beginning of the 1970s, the income of most Caribbean territories was derived mainly from agricultural products such as sugar, rice, bananas, citrus fruits, spices, agriculture, and more recently marijuana, particularly from Jamaica. Agriculture continued to be the major employer of the labor force in the region.[11] The gravity of the unemployment situation, especially as it affects young people, and the region's increased dependence on foreign goods were the two most explosive problems facing Caribbean leaders.[12] Across the Caribbean, notwithstanding its political fragmentation, economic dependence and the lack of development remained the outstanding feature of the social and political scene in the region in this period. The degree to which the Caribbean economies depend on the rest of the world to maintain and increase internal levels of employment, output, capital, and technology is captured by Alister McIntyre, who said:

> West Indian territories are . . . still regarded as outstanding examples of dependent economies. They are heavily dependent on the rest of the world for markets for their production, they import the wide variety of the goods which they require, and they rely on other countries for transfers of income and capital, for banking and financial services, for business and technical skills, and even for ideas about themselves.[13]

In the Caribbean there exists a major contradiction between political development and economic reality. The achievement of independence by the four larger countries during the 1960s bound their economies more to the international economic system. Again, as McIntyre argued, one of the more striking features of the West Indian development is that the progress made towards political independence during the 1960s has not been accompanied by parallel advances in the economic field.[14] Implicit in this viewpoint is the idea that economic dependence in the Caribbean was an undesirable state of affairs that ought to be overcome in order for political independence to be meaningful. The NWG economists advocated solutions that emphasized changes in the region's internal production structures, which gave rise to the mechanisms of dependence; and the institutional structures, principally the multinational corporations, which underlie and reinforce the mechanism of dependence. The focus on the structural and institutional method is viewed as the two most important characteristics of the revolution in economic thought in the Caribbean in the mid-1960s.

These developments spawned a serious and conscious effort by some NWG associates to attempt to develop an authentic indigenous economic strategy with the objective of improving the economy of the Caribbean and reducing its external dependence. Explicitly or implicitly, Caribbean scholars as well as politicians and government officials have often been inclined to conceptualize many of the region's socioeconomic problems and much of its future development prospects in terms of dependency. However, like their ECLA counterparts and other dependency theorists elsewhere, the NWG has not spoken as a unified body, gravitating instead into schools of thought with their own distinctive discourses and theoretical nuances. Their attempts to diagnose, interpret, and provide solutions to the causes of underdevelopment and dependency in the Commonwealth Caribbean resulted in three different strands of modern Caribbean dependency: the non-Marxist, the neo-Marxist, and the structuralist, all of which warrant separate attention.

Strands of Caribbean Dependency

The Non-Marxist Strand

The first strand of dependency theory within the NWG was advanced by William Demas's 1965 influential work on *The Economics of Development in Small Countries with Special Reference to the Caribbean*. Essentially, Demas saw the need to develop both a theoretical and practical approach to explain the failure of Caribbean countries to transform their economies to achieve self-sustained growth, eliminate or reduce high unemployment, and significantly reduce the region's persistent underdevelopment and structural dependence from the legacies of the past. His work was inspired largely by Sir Arthur Lewis who explained the region's development problems largely in terms of natural variables, such as size, limited resources configuration, limited market size, problems of economies of scale, the lack of a dynamic and well-motivated entrepreneurial class, and other inherent characteristics of these societies.[15]

This pessimistic and somewhat deterministic viewpoint by Lewis of the English-speaking Caribbean nations is even more pronounced in the work of Demas who maintained that the question of size is very relevant to the character of, if not to the possibility of achieving structural transformation, and that self-sustaining growth is possible only in a large continental type economy such as the United States. According to Demas, "Self-sustained growth . . . which includes not only structural transformation but dependence on domestic savings and on domestically generated poles of growth is more likely to be achieved in large self-contained continental economy such as the U.S.A. . . . than in small countries [where] the degree of self-sustenance of the growth process is less because of external dependence."[16] Demas also asserted that small size, defined in terms of both area and population, severely constrained the process of import-substitution industrialization and other development strategies in the Caribbean and thus removed the option of balanced economic growth in the region. The smallness of the domestic market and limited resources means that the countries of the Caribbean must of necessity exchange the products of their few specialized resources against a great variety of imported goods to meet the consumption needs of their domestic population. The economist contends that this process is common in nearly all underdeveloped countries with few primary resources. But the situation in the Caribbean is explosive mainly because the region's heavy dependence on foreign capital, foreign aid, and technology has limited its capacity to transform its production structures to sustain its development. As Demas writes:

The economies [of the Caribbean] are very dependent, not only structurally in the sense that there is a high ratio of foreign trade to Gross Domestic Product, but also in that there is great reliance on foreign private capital inflows and foreign aid, there is little financial and monetary autonomy, and there are still important gaps in the domestic financial structure. It is quite obvious that the size of a country in this sense imposes certain constraints on the pattern of growth and hence on the character and degree to which such growth can be self-sustaining.[17]

Demas's appraisal of the Caribbean economy fits well with Alister McIntyre's explanation that structural dependence is the dependence that arises out of the size and structure of a country's economy which cannot be changed.[18] The problems resulting from the convergence of the colonial structures of domination and size versus viability considerations of the Caribbean region in general were articulated by Demas, who lamented the fact that,

many people in the region . . . hold pessimistic and deterministic positions regarding our prospects for any degree of effective independence vis-à-vis the outside world. They believe that we are doomed to abject subordination because of our small and in some cases minuscule size, and because of our long colonial history as mere political, economic, military, and cultural appendages of the metropolitan countries. They consider that we can only be specks of dust . . . impotent, unable to control our destiny, imitative rather than innovative and inevitably subject to the decisions, and indeed the whims, of outside countries, nearly all of whom are much larger and much more powerful than we.[19]

The view that economic dependence in the Caribbean is conditioned by some natural variables such as size and limited resources, and was therefore inescapable to some degree, generated a powerful influence over economic thought in the region, especially among non-Marxists. This group contends that the Caribbean countries' dependence on the core capitalist states could be reduced not by asserting greater autonomy from the developed states, but rather by integrating themselves more thoroughly into the international economic system. Although this strategy does not necessarily suggest a blueprint for economic development in the Caribbean and elsewhere, it does seem clear that the nature of the international economic system does not preclude the possibility of development for all Global South countries. The non-Marxists, particularly Demas, were convinced that Caribbean economic integration with neighboring underdeveloped countries as well as those outside of the region would not only promote industrial growth, but would make possible a strategy of development based on import substitution rather than export creation, thus resulting in a less dependent pattern of development in the region.[20] Demas stressed that the integration of large and small economies would generate more domestically financial capital for the latter. Largely, as a result of the work of Demas, McIntyre, and other Caribbean non-Marxists, regional economic integration replaced the post-World War II industrialization strategies as the development model in the Caribbean in the late 1960s. But as discussed in chapter 3, it did not reduce the region's economic dependence on external sources.

The Neo-Marxist Strand

The second strand of Caribbean dependency theorists originated from the neo-Marxist school, whose analysis of the Caribbean political economy in terms of dependency developed relatively late. Two reasons accounted for such late development of Marxism in the region. First, Marxism had no roots in the Caribbean either as a basis of intellectual commitment, teachings, or of political practice. With the exception of the Marxist People's Progressive Party (PPP) in Guyana founded by Cheddi and Janet Jagan in 1950, Marxist political parties have historically been unsuccessful in the Caribbean region and moreover, the study of Marxism was not part of the British colonial educational system there. The study of Marxist philosophy in the region began slowly at the University of the West Indies in the mid- to late 1960s, which originated as an overseas college of the University of London.

Second, the Marxist doctrine came from secondary sources principally from the writings of Andre Gunder Frank, which were generally translated into English too late to have much impact on the formative period of the Caribbean plantation economy school. As a consequence, neo-Marxism has not been able to penetrate the Caribbean as a prolific form of analysis of dependency and underdevelopment in the region. Nevertheless, it has highlighted some of the major failings of the theoretical assumptions of the non-Marxist group by presenting a much broader version of dependency in the Commonwealth Caribbean in particular and the Global South in general. Its principal exponent has been Dr. Clive Thomas, one of the founders of the New World Group and a Guyanese economist who directs Developmental Studies at the University of Guyana.

In analyzing the political economy of the Caribbean, Thomas moved beyond both the natural variable approach of Demas, McIntyre, and other non-Marxists, and the structuralist framework advanced by Beckford, Best, Levitt, and Girvan. Thomas's analysis of underdevelopment and dependency in the modern Caribbean focused on the legacy of colonialism, slavery, the exploitation of Caribbean land and its people by the major European colonial powers, and the disparities in political power between the developed and underdeveloped states. It drew extensively from the works of Paul Baran and Andre Gunder Frank, and claimed that contemporary underdevelopment and dependence are in large part the historical product of past and continuing economic and other relations between the underdeveloped countries and the developed metropolitan countries. Thomas contends that these relations are an essential part of the international structure and that the development of the international capitalist system on a global scale has resulted in power disparities, asymmetrical relationships, underdevelopment, and dependency of peripheral societies on the core states.

According to Thomas and the other neo-Marxists, this dynamic gave rise to the reality that the development of underdevelopment in the periphery resulted directly from the dialectical process of the internationalization of the capitalist system.[21] European powers used their political domination to create and enforce an international division of labor that made the Caribbean and other Global South countries providers of raw materials, cheap labor, and consumers of manufactured goods.[22] He claims that by the middle of the eighteenth century, the economic preconditions of capitalism—the spread of money economy, the primitive accumulation of commercial, the level of technology, and the network of trade—had spread to such an extent over large parts of the world that Western Europe's early lead in the development of industrial capitalism was not of truly decisive proportions. Rather, it was made decisive and indisputable by plunder, slavery, colonial conquest, and exploitation, which accompanied European expansion in and penetration of peripheral societies. The establishment of colonial territories was a formal expression of industrial expansion and development in Western Europe and underdevelopment of colonial territories. In other words, as Thomas puts it, "European development generated the underdevelopment of the rest of the world by destroying those indigenous social forces which otherwise might have led to the transformation of their pre-capitalist modes of production."[23]

The long-term consequence of these brutal and deliberate acts was that the productive forces of the countries of the Caribbean and elsewhere were detached almost permanently from their roots in the domestic market and therefore were no longer responsive to the consumption needs of the local population. This has contributed considerably to the lack of development and the structural dependence experienced by almost all underdeveloped countries, including those in the Caribbean. In identifying what were to him the two most important features of structural dependence, underdevelopment and the economic backwardness of the process of production evident in the Caribbean as well as in other small Third World countries, Thomas said "on the one hand, the lack of an organic link, rooted in an indigenous science and technology, between the pattern and growth of domestic resource use and the pattern and growth of domestic demand, and, on the other, the divergence between domestic demand and the needs of the broad mass of the population."[24] This can be blamed on the historical legacy of traditional trade and investment patterns and colonialism which allowed for very little linkage between the different elements of the region's economy. The result of this is that external dependence constitutes a major obstacle to self-sustained growth and development in the Caribbean. The importance of this process to the current debate of underdevelopment and dependency is expressed by Havelock Brewster:

> Economic dependence may be defined as a lack of capacity to manipulate the operative elements of an economic system. Such a situation is characterized by an absence of interdependence between the economic functions of a system. This lack of interdependence implies that the system has no internal dynamic which could enable it to function as independent, autonomous entity.[25]

The neo-Marxists claimed the these structural weaknesses have caused the economies of the Caribbean to exhibit a pattern of consumption that did not represent the needs of the region's population and a pattern of production geared to neither domestic consumption nor domestic needs. They insisted that the structural dependence, which was historically created by European colonialism and imperialism, continues to exist in the Caribbean in the modern era despite the establishment of light manufacturing industries in the region, the emergence of new export sectors, and the high national growth rates they generated. It is manifest in the operations of subsidiaries of multinational corporations in the principal export sectors, the banking and financial system, tourism, the widespread use of inappropriate capital-intensive technology, the perilous state of the region's agriculture, which has declined considerably in the post-independence era, and a host of other widely known symptoms indicative of underdevelopment in the Caribbean.[26] These external factors have not only precluded economic development in the Caribbean and increased its dependency, but continue to produce growing misery and poverty among the poor masses. In addition, they are supported by the local elite and capitalists who continue to benefit from the region's present structures of under-development and dependency. "The principal beneficiaries of dependence in the South would be a compradore class who benefited from their privileged ties with the North, whether they be political or economic, and who acted as the local agents of imperialism."[27]

Like other neo-Marxists, Thomas's analysis of dependency in the modern Caribbean also has a distinctly political element. The economist did not only describe the historical origins and contemporary economic consequences of the globalization of capitalism, but also tried to explain the political under-pinnings of the present conjuncture of production relations and productive forces in peripheral societies. Thomas pointed to the failure of an indigenous capitalist class to create its own local material base for self-reproduction in the Caribbean and other small societies with limited market size, and to the dominant social classes who continue to benefit immensely from the present structures of underdevelopment and dependency in the region. The persistent nature of dependency and underdevelopment in the Caribbean led Thomas to conclude that a comprehensive socialist strategy and indigenous capital were the only viable alternative to transform the productive forces and liberate the political and social order in the region.[28] He warned that if the present neocolonial system persists, the region's economy will continue to be a dependent by-product of developments in the core capitalist states. The neo-Marxist claimed that the neocolonial structures that currently exist in the Caribbean countries have and continue to rely on a high dependence on foreign inputs, to encourage the export of a few primary products, and to neglect positive measures for import-substitution, even where a country may have a variety of resources and the domestic market.[29]

The neo-Marxist approach by Clive Thomas and the neo-Marxist school of dependency represented a useful step beyond the natural variable viewpoint in the sense that it introduced a greater awareness of class and politics to the interpretation of dependency in the modern Caribbean. It presented the whole phenomenon more aptly in the global context of European colonialism and expansion and the development of the world capitalist system.

The Structuralist Strand

The third strand of Caribbean dependency emerged in the late 1960s in response to attempts by the non-Marxists to internalize the growth process and the persistent external dependence of the region's economy. Advocates of this strand claimed that the theoretical focus on natural variables such as small size, limited natural resources, and overpopulation by the neo-Marxist school as the primary source of modern dependency in the Caribbean downplayed the role and consequences of dependent capitalist development, imperialism, and other external factors that continue to dominate the region's economy. Such an approach, the structuralists argued, ignored, for the most part, the historical circumstances under which the territories of the Caribbean were initially developed as an overseas economy for the metropolitan markets of Western Europe and later North America. They also contend that the non-Marxists overlooked the fact that colonialism, slavery, and the massive inflow of foreign capital and technology have left the economies of the Caribbean geared more toward the needs of European and North American markets than to the domestic needs of their own societies. They pointed out that the countries of the Caribbean have and continue to trade more with the developed countries than they do amongst themselves, despite the creation of CARICOM. This set of economic relationships have outlived colonialism in the region.

In addressing the causes of dependency in the Caribbean, structuralists such as Lloyd Best shifted the responsibility away from natural variables to societal factors, and focused on institutions and the historical development of the Caribbean as an overseas economy for the metropolitan powers. Best asserted that the natural variable theory of Caribbean dependency advanced principally by the non-Marxists suffers from certain theoretical and empirical defects in their analysis that the small size of Caribbean economies and domestic markets have inherently limited their structural transformation. He argued that by focusing on natural variables, the non-Marxists missed the role played by foreign corporate capital, technology, and decision making in undermining development of Caribbean economies. Not only did they fail to analyze the impact of external forces on domestic accumulation, but their analysis ignored completely the social relations and conflicts that existed between different classes. Smallness is merely the physical context in which social relations are established and the mode of production is organized, but becomes a major problem especially when small economies are inserted into the international capitalist economy and pursue the same goals as the industrialized countries.[30]

Best and Levitt not only refuted the natural variable concept but contend that the Caribbean countries are dependent not only in the sense that they are small in size and population and have open-type economies, which render them vulnerable to external economic influences. Rather, dependency has destroyed their national capacity to act as an autonomous unit because the power to exercise economic control and influence employment, prices, and development are controlled by the core capitalist countries. The structuralists also blamed the region's external structural dependence on transnational corporations, which continue to play an important role in structuring the patterns of demand and consumption in the Caribbean through production and advertising of products designed for metropolitan markets, which they argued have reinforced the transfer of foreign tastes which may be alien to the culture of the region. This has created a further impetus to increase the region's dependence through a greater demand for foreign products rather than those indigenously produced.

In focusing on continental economies, the structuralists are of the firm opinion that the larger countries are not automatically better placed to exploit their resource endowments than the small countries, and that there is a path of innovation which could lead to the fullest structural transformation of small economies such as those in the Caribbean. They insisted that the particular experiences and resources of a particular group of people in a particular area would lead them both to express qualitatively different sets as well as different orderings of preferences from others, and also to devise different means for achieving their goals. They also claimed that it is to the advantage of the imperialists to keep wages low and not to reinvest surpluses into the Caribbean economy in order to impoverish the people, reap huge profits, and deepen the region's economic dependence. Best in particular has stressed that it is inherent in the structure of multinational corporations which operate in the Caribbean to see that the region's economy remained fragmented, unintegrated, underdeveloped, and dependent.[31] In this way they can continue to exploit the region's resources and its people and capitalize on the generous tax incentives provided by the various governments. For Best and Levitt, and the other structuralists, these factors proved that the crucial obstacles to transform the economic, social, and productive structures of the Caribbean lie in the nature of its economic institutions, exploitative relationships, and the pattern of tastes and technology, and not in natural variables, as argued by the non-Marxist group. The necessary implications for self-sustained growth in the Caribbean region could be a reorganization of the institutions to permit a transformation of the structure of the productive forces, the development of appropriate indigenous technology, and the establishment of social goals and preferences conducive to the needs of West Indians.[32] What the analysis presented by Best and Levitt and the other structuralists seeks to convey is not to ignore the natural variable concept, but a genuine interpretation of the material dynamics that contributed to dependency and underdevelopment of the Caribbean and other small economies. It is based on the region's long history of colonial rule and slave institutions such as the plantation, multinational corporations, and alliances with independent states and the international capitalist system.

Although the analysis offered by the NWG associates represents a major advance in Caribbean scholarship, it nevertheless suffers from a number of limitations, which related mainly to the structuralist methodology. Best, in particular, criticized the non-Marxists and the neo-Marxists for their use of irrelevant, rigid, and alien definitions of both liberal capitalism and Marxist socialism instead of Caribbean formulas and concepts to explain dependency in the region. According to the structuralists, the tendency by the non-Marxists to focus on the exceptional living standards enjoyed by the people of the Caribbean relative to those in other small Third World societies had virtually ignored the reality of class and politics in their analysis. They did not address the changing political and economic interests which permitted the structures of plantation economy to survive in the Caribbean in the post-colonial period without radical transformation.

Table 2.1 shows the historical, institutional, and structural experiences of the Commonwealth Caribbean and Latin America. Although the structural method was common in both regions, it was nonetheless most pronounced in the English-speaking Caribbean as evident by the adverse consequences to national growth and development and of the operations of multinational corporations in the mining and manufacturing sectors. Therefore, it was not surprising that proposals by some associates of the NWG (neo-Marxists and structuralists) for structural reform in the region in the 1960s and 1970s emphasized the need to change or reform the internal production structures and institutional forms, to initiate the development of a national economic system in order to eliminate or overcome dependency in the region.

Despite their many analytical approaches and ideological differences, the issues raised by the theorists concerning the transformation of the region's economy, and the nature and extent of dependency, underdevelopment, and fragmentation in the region cannot be properly understood without an understanding of the structure and function of the plantation economy, and how the system has evolved, preserved, and strengthened in the period prior to and after emancipation.

Plantation Economy

Initially developed by Caribbean economist Lloyd Best and Canadian Kari Levitt, the theory of plantation economy represented the most sophisticated Caribbean version of Latin American structuralist view of dependency.[33] It is also one of the main strands of dependency in the modern Caribbean in that it attempted to quash the natural variable theory advocated by non-Marxist theorists. The theory of plantation economy consists of a historical and structural analysis of the evolution of the plantation system in the Caribbean

Table 2.1
Historical, Institutional, and Structural Experience of
the Commonwealth Caribbean and Latin America

Period	1600-1850	1850-1930	After 1930
System	Mercantilism (Protectionist)	Liberalism (Free trade)	New Mercantilism (Global Trade)
Latin America	Colonial Export Economy	Externally Oriented Development	Internally Oriented Development
Commonwealth Caribbean	Pure Plantation Economy	Plantation Economy Modified	Plantation Economy Further Modified

Source: C. Furtado, "Development and Stagnation in Latin America: A Structural Approach," *Studies in Comparative International Development* 1, no. 11, 1965; Lloyd Best and Kari Levitt 1969; Oswaldo Sunkel, "National Development Policy and External Dependence in Latin America," *Journal of Development Studies* no. 1, October 1969.

from the early seventeenth century to the modern period. In analyzing the long-term development of Caribbean dependency, Best and Levitt stressed that their primary interest lay in isolating the institutional structures and constraints which the contemporary economy has inherited from the plantation legacy. The economists suggest that the different stages in the evolution of the Caribbean plantation economy should be viewed in the "contemporary perspective of successive layers of inherited structures and mechanisms which condition the possibilities of transformation of the present economy."[34] They posited that the classical plantation economy of the slave era and its modern variants have functioned as a mechanism for locking the various territories of the Caribbean into a series of dependency relationships with a shifting cast of European metropolitan powers and the United States. The economists explained that the theory of the plantation economy "is the study of the character of the plantation sector and its relation both with the outside world and with the domestic economy which provides essential insights into the mechanisms of Caribbean economy."[35] They claimed that the development of the plantation economy was effected initially by political association, but was maintained by the operations of the predominant economic institutions, which typically were subsidiaries or affiliates of metropolitan enterprises.[36] The authors' work was strongly influenced by members of the NWG who, in studying the modern forms of dependency and underdevelopment in the Caribbean, observed that sugar cultivation was pursued to the exclusion of all other production activities in the region.

> The Sugar Industry has traditionally been, and remains today, the main prop of the colonial economy. The character and structure of the economy and society have been moulded to suit its needs. It has always been foreign-owned and run, dependent on foreign capital, skill and on imperially protected (formerly and informerly) markets, it has been, until recently, the main influence on public policy. . . . The structure of production (i.e., the limited importance of production for domestic consumption) and the structure of demand (i.e., the overwhelming importance of demand for imports) can all be explained in terms of the history of the sugar industry.[37]

Along with Best and Levitt, George Beckford advanced the thesis that plantation economy refers to those countries of the world where the internal and external dimensions of the plantation system dominate the country's economic, social, and political structure and its relations with the rest of the world.[38] The plantation economy can be identified by considerations such as its share of national economic aggregates in the region, its contribution to national employment, income, government revenues, and foreign exchange earnings; its effects on social and political structure; and the psychological impact on the minds and outlook of the local population. Beckford contends that underdevelopment in plantation economies in the Caribbean and elsewhere, and development in metropolitan countries are aspects of the same phenomenon and that the emergence of the vertically integrated plantation enterprise has served to preserve the character of the slave plantation system with little or no structural change in the local economies.[39]

By definition, the plantation economy was a dependent economy that resulted from Caribbean land, African slave labor, and European capital. As a settlement, plantation institutions brought together enterprise, capital, and labor from various parts of the world into the Caribbean where land was free and available for production of a particular staple. In the process a system of authority and control was vested in the institution. As Lloyd Best explains:

> Where land [was] free to be used for subsistence production, the recruitment of labour exclusively for export production imposes a need for total economic institutions so as to encompass the entire existence of the work force. The plantation which admits virtually no distinction between

organization and society and chattel slavery which deprives workers of all civil rights including the right to property, together furnish an ideal framework.[40]

The plantation economy theory developed by Best and Levitt illustrates, by and large, this pattern of dependence has remained intact with little structural change in the region's economy in the contemporary era. The economists identified three broad phases of the historical development of the plantation economy in the Commonwealth Caribbean: (i) Pure Plantation Economy, 1600-1838; (ii) Plantation Economy Modified, 1838-1938; and (iii) Plantation Economy Further Modified, 1938 to the present.[41] It is worthy to note that this economy was developed as a hinterland of exploitation as opposed to a hinterland of settlement such as what was established on the American mainland.

Pure Plantation Economy

The pure plantation economy phase covered the period from about 1600 to the abolition of slavery in the British West Indies in 1838. It originated from the old mercantilism period which began with European exploration and colonization of the Caribbean at the end of the fifteenth century. It is a crucial and decisive period for the region in that it established the framework for the development of the Caribbean as an overseas economy of distant metropolitan powers where most, if not all, of the decisions concerning the territories of the region were made. Imperialism, mercantilism, and slavery ensured that the income generated from plantation production served to promote industrialization and development in the metropolitan countries.[42] As a consequence, dependence on outside forces was instituted into the Caribbean plantation economy from the very outset. Apart from land, all the requirements of the plantation economy were imported. The metropolitan powers provided organization, capital, transport, supplies, markets, and even brought slave labor from West Africa.

This phase of the pure plantation economy was characterized by the establishment of slave-based plantation institutions for production of export staples. The economies did not experience any considerable or sustained relief from their dependence on the export staple. The local economy was composed entirely of the plantation sector with no internal interdependence. Each plantation operated as an independent unit that was linked to a metropolitan Merchant House through a joint-stock trading company, and as a result, each secured its supplies from and disposed of its output through its own particular metropolitan agent. As a result, there was no structural interdependence within the pure plantation economy system, either between production units or between production and consumption units. Lloyd Best outlines the process:

> The characteristic . . . of the slave plantation economy is really a segmental economy consisting of a number of firms, each of which is a self-sufficient unit almost completely independent of the rest of the economy. . . . The slave plantation economy was such that it created only subsistence income for the residents of the plantation . . . and it could not generate spread effects for economic development in the [region] because of the almost total absence of linkages outside of the unit itself. [43]

This limitation relegated the Caribbean to the mere locus of production—a kind of production that did not compete with the metropolitan countries. In fact, it helped to produce food for Europe's expanding working classes and raw materials for its industries.

Conceived as part of the metropolitan economy, where all the profits of expansion were accumulated, pure plantation economy was without a doubt a highly successful and profitable enterprise for its European colonizers in its foundational period. On the other hand, it laid the foundation for the region's underdevelopment and economic dependence and its subordinate position within the international division of labor. Pure plantation economy formed the matrix from which successive modifications derived and from which dependency in the modern Caribbean evolved. As Best and Levitt and other Caribbean plantation theorists have observed, the basic mechanisms of plantation economy continue to operate in the Caribbean, albeit with some important changes in its characteristics.[44]

Plantation Economy Modified

In the first half of the nineteenth century, Best and Levitt contended that adjustments were forced upon the plantation economic system. The period was characterized by two principal modifications: the abolition of slavery and the removal of imperial preference for sugar (the main plantation staple in the Commonwealth Caribbean) by Britain as it entered the free trade era. These developments led to other adjustments, most notably the emergence of a local peasantry class comprised mostly of former black slaves on non-plantation land; and a new wave of indentured servants mainly from India to work on the plantations. The ex-slaves did not have any other skill or training apart from tilling the soil. Not only were the ex-slaves in conflict with the planter class for land, but they also competed for other resources, especially farming equipment, credit, marketing facilities, and domestic infrastructure. Their efforts were constantly thwarted by the merchants and bankers who had control of the finances, and by government policies which supported and preserved the plantation sector despite its growth-inhibiting nature on development in the Caribbean.[45]

The peasant sector was believed to have geared its production primarily towards the domestic market, thereby stimulating the local economy and, at the same time, generating development in plantation societies. On the other hand, the plantation sector with its overwhelming export orientation, catered mostly to the consumption needs of the metropolitan countries and, as such contributed to growth and development outside the region. Thus, the limited development which some of these plantation economies experienced in the postemancipation period can be attributed to the growth and dynamism of the peasant sector. As was the case, the expansion of the peasantry and of domestic agriculture in the Caribbean territories was ultimately checked by the dominance of the plantation sector, which discouraged the development of domestic agriculture and light manufacturing industry in the region.

Although the Caribbean plantation economy modified period might have had a much greater internal dynamic as a result of peasant agriculture, nonetheless, the essentials of the pattern of development characteristic of the pure plantation economy phase continued unabated, and genuinely economic transformation remained an illusion.[46] One reason for this is that very little income was available to the residents from plantation production and the plantation could not have provided the impetus for Caribbean development. This observation of the plantation system is well supported by Beckford who explained that "the dynamic for economic development in the Caribbean is therefore not within the plantation sector but outside of it. Economic progress in the plantation colony can come only from the efforts outside the direct orbit of the slave plantation. The plantation unit was organized principally to produce an export staple and almost all its resources were deployed to that end."[47] This yields the conclusion that the development of the peasantry and by extension the development of the Caribbean economy were seriously constrained and undermined by the plantation sector by virtue of its systematic domination of land, capital, labor, and other resources in the plantation economy, and by rules defined by the city of London. Plantation economy's modified phase corresponded with the period of the North Atlantic industrial revolution and ended with the slide of commodity prices and the collapse of the world economy in the 1930s.

Plantation Economy Further Modified

The period since 1938 was marked by other modifications in the plantation economy system, which generated an unprecedented level of dependence on foreign capital, technology, managerial, and administrative skills, as well as active government intervention in the Caribbean economy. The multinational corporations, particularly American enterprises, replaced British firms as the principal agencies of metropolitan investment in the region in the postwar period. Perceived as agencies of industrialization and modernization, the entry of multinational corporations into the Caribbean was facilitated by generous tax incentives and subsidies from the various governments in the region. Thus active government in the Caribbean turned out to mean active support for foreign private capital and technology. Apart from the traditional plantation sector, the Plantation Economy Further Modified period also witnessed the emergence of new, high value, export commodities such as bauxite from Guyana and Jamaica, petroleum from Trinidad and Tobago, and light manufacturing, tourism, and banking in Barbados and in the rest of the region.

Consequently, in the modern Caribbean, many of the old mercantilist features characteristic of the early phase of the pure plantation economy are again reproduced through foreign investment by multinational corporations, which combined organization, capital, technology, and entrepreneurial skills into a single unit. They also exhibited a high degree of vertical integration, which has served to preserve the character of the slave plantation system as an appendage of the metropolitan overseas economy. The result is that the Caribbean economy in the modern era has become more firmly entrenched into the orbit of the developed countries' economies and the internationalist capitalist system. The MNC's active involvement in the forward integration process from importation and distribution of goods to branch plant assembly is actually one of the principal characteristics of the new mercantilism and dependency in the modern Caribbean in the postwar period. Ida Greaves has posited that because of its character, "the plantation has been associated with most political and international developments of modern times: mercantilism and free trade; slavery and independence; capitalism and imperialism."[48] It is in this context that Beckford, Best, and Levitt have argued that the MNCs are no different from the joint-stock trading companies during the pure plantation economy phase. Both continue to dominate the Caribbean economy and have served just as effectively in plundering resources from the region, thereby deepening the process of underdevelopment and dependency and limiting the possibilities of transforming the economic and social structures in the area. Andrew Axline explains that the policies of the MNCs

were naturally conceived in the corporate interest of the larger countries and
were contradictory of the national economic interest of the region. "These
companies," Axline says,

> restricted exports to certain markets both within and outside the region in
> order to avoid competition with other subsidiaries of the same company,
> they inhibited the development of the local capital market by reinvesting
> savings in the same activity or remitting profits to the head office, and they
> distorted the relative cost of factors of production through transfer pricing.
> . . . The transnational enterprise provided very strong linkages between the
> host economy and the economy of the country of origin thus creating a
> situation of vertical integration with the metropolitan centre and
> disintegration in the national or regional economy by the failure to create
> forward and backward linkages. It contributed to unemployment by
> utilizing highly capital-intensive technologies adapted to the country of
> origin, but inappropriate to the labour surplus situation of the Caribbean.[49]

Once again and with even greater force, the Caribbean has become part
of the overseas economy of the metropolitan economic system through the
multinational corporations, thus creating the era of new mercantilism in the
region. Best and Levitt put it well when they said that the plantation system
has opened the region's economies to foreign investment of all kinds, not
just for plantation activity, but also in manufacturing, mining, and service
activities, which are of the same general nature as the plantation.[50] Levitt
highlights the characteristics of the new mercantilism in the Caribbean.

> In the new mercantilism, as in the old, the corporation based in the
> metropole directly exercises the entrepreneurial function and collects a
> venture profit from its investment. It organises the collection or extraction
> of the raw material staple required in the metropolis and supplies the
> hinterland with manufactured goods, whether produced at home or on site
> in the host country.[51]

The historical, institutional, and structural methods employed by Best
and Levitt represent a useful analysis of the processes of the Caribbean
plantation economy. It has shed much light on the incompleteness of change
in the region's plantation system, which according to the economists as well
as members of the NWG, has not only created underdeveloped structures in
the Caribbean, but also conditioned adversely the subsequent evolution of
the economies where it predominated. They located the region's dependence
and underdevelopment in the nature of the plantation economy and, in the
contemporary period, to the domination, penetration, and exploitation of the

region's natural resources by multinational corporations and their agents. Best and Levitt concluded that at best, multinational corporations could produce economic growth in the Caribbean, but not genuine economic transformation of the region's structures. While the structural characteristics of the plantation economy have, over the years, contributed to economic growth, they have also contributed to the dynamic process of dependency and underdevelopment because of the foreign ownership and high import content of plantation investment. Similarly, Beckford claimed that although the countries of the Caribbean have attained constitutional independence, the plantation system with all its inherent characteristics still dominates the lives of the Caribbean people in fundamental ways. It has left them with a legacy of economic, political, cultural, and indeed even psychological dependence on the outside world.[52]

This explanation of dependency in the modern Caribbean and lack of development differs from those put forth by modernization theorists and the non-Marxists who explained Caribbean underdevelopment and dependency in terms of natural variables. The analysis of Beckford, Best, and Levitt portrayed the Caribbean economies with a high degree of external structural dependence and a lack of internal structural interdependence between many of the most important elements of the region's economy.

The approaches discussed in this section focused primarily on the effects of economic dependence in retarding the potential growth and development of the forces of production in the Caribbean. While in each country the material dynamic has actually been the same, the cultural and psychological dimensions of dependency in the Caribbean have differed to some degree and have not been examined. In addition to economic dependency, political, cultural, and psychological dependence have influenced the behavior of groups and individuals in every society; and these noneconomic variables are important in determining the pattern of underdevelopment or development. It is to these dimensions of dependency we now turn in seeking to explain their constraints on the people of the Caribbean.

Dimensions of Caribbean Dependency

Broadly speaking, there has been a general tendency, especially on the part of scholars in the Caribbean and elsewhere, to treat dependency almost exclusively as an economic phenomenon. Such an approach does not, however, sufficiently take into account the fact that there exists a considerable interface between the economic, political, and cultural subsystems of any society, including those of the Caribbean. The approach also ignored the development process of dependency in the Caribbean and its continuing deep penetration of and impact on the region's inhabitants and subsystems by external forces. The penetration and domination of the region's sub-systems and its people by the European powers and by the growing strength and influence of the United States mean that the territories of the Caribbean have succumbed to a position of comprehensive dependency. According to Lowenthal, this occurs when the three major subsystems of a society—the economic, the political, and the cultural—are all dominated by a foreign country,[53] thus resulting in the total loss of effective sovereignty and the incorporation of these penetrated societies such as those in the Caribbean into an informal empire. Michael Erisman captures the process:

> When a nation has been penetrated . . . the role of foreigners is not limited to merely exerting exogenous influence. Instead, they are intimately involved in another society's internal decision-making processes, with such participation being accepted, whether willingly or not, by important elements within the target country's elites and sometimes even by its population at large. . . . that the extent of such interventions will inevitably vary, being confined in some cases to one issue-area (e.g., economic affairs) while in other instances it will be much more pervasive and thus have a multidimensional effect. . . . The most rudimentary . . . or . . . first phase form of dependency occurs when a metropole's meddling is restricted to a single policy area. At the other extreme lies comprehensive dependency, which results when all the major subsystems of a developing nation have been penetrated and consequently it assumes the posture of a prototype (or pure) peripheral society.[54]

Economic Dependency

Basically, economic dependency is the most salient feature of core-periphery relationship, which in the Caribbean experience is the residue of colonialism and the external control of the region's economy through unequal terms of trade, unrestricted private investment, and aid with strings attached from the core capitalist nations. The end result has always been the same—the external control of the Caribbean economies has been deliberately created in order to facilitate the systematic pillaging and plunder of the region and other small Third World economies. Caribbean economic dependence has not only retarded growth in the region, but has also resulted in the continuing foreign penetration and domination of the countries' economies and its people. George Beckford was one of the first Caribbean dependency theorists to vigorously pursue this line of reasoning, asserting that external control of the region's economies has left their inhabitants existing in the most wretched conditions of poverty in that it has created considerable high unemployment and underdevelopment in the area.[55] Other Caribbean dependency theorists have concluded that very little can be done to reduce the structural inequalities between core and peripheral states short of a complete overhaul of the international economic system. Cal Clark aptly explains the consequences of dependency on small states:

> The exploitation and particularly the distortion and retardation of the dependent economy which *dependencia* theory sees as integral to dependence should result in a widening of the capabilities between the dominant and subordinate states; so that their structural inequality should increase over time. . . . Even when economic concessions are used to augment dependence for political purposes, it would be a rare center of power that would be foolhardy enough not to turn off the spigot long before any significant change occurred in the structural inequalities between the dominant and dependent partners. Thus, under normal conditions dependence should increase the dyadic structural inequalities between the dominant and dependent partners.[56]

This situation has produced a subservient relationship, which in turn has led to sporadic or uneven economic growth, inequitable distributions of income and wealth, and foreign domination and control of certain sectors of the economies of the Caribbean and other underdeveloped regions of the world. Once such a symbiotic relationship is well established, political power defined here as the capacity to determine the allocation of vital resources and values in a society as well as the responsibility to make major economic decisions, which is normally considered to be the prerogative of a country's government, is to a great extent exercised by the dominant metropolitan powers. The dominant powers materially benefit from this state of affairs and therefore will not hesitate to offer aid to those elites in the dependent countries who are co-opted to serve as local agents for, or junior partners of, foreign capital interests and perpetuate their country's economic dependence in order to preserve their privileged status in their home country. Bruce Moon explains how the process works: "the incorporation of a national elite into an internationalized bourgeoisie produces decisionmakers who, owing not only to the economic interests they share with American elites through economic transactions but also to their shared values and perspectives, produce policy virtually indistinguishable from that which would be generated by American elites."[57] In other words, elites from the dominant country will participate directly and authoritatively in both the internal and external affairs of the dependent country through actions taken jointly with members from the latter. In this context, political dependence has emerged as the natural corollary to economic dependence.

Political Dependency
   In general, political dependence is based on the common belief that within an asymmetrical relationship between states, the economically power-ful and dominant states can extract favorable foreign-policy concessions from their dependent and less powerful economic partners, by virtue of their influence, economic and military power. Political dependence has routinely affected the general foreign policy choices of many Third World countries, including those in the Caribbean (Cuba being the exception), causing them in most cases to pursue policy initiatives in international affairs and other forums that closely parallel and strongly support the preferences of the metropolitan powers to which they are linked. In the Caribbean it is the United States that wields such power, principally because of its influence and hegemonic status in the Western hemisphere and its capacity to effectively use the carrot-and-stick tactics to reward states that agreed to its demands and to threaten those with the specter of serious retribution should they refuse to comply.
   In some instances foreign policy consensus is achieved from informal bargaining between the core and the periphery countries, and in other cases, it involved the crude manipulation and coercion to the point where the perceptions of values and attitudes of the dependent countries are translated into foreign policies that are often virtually indistinguishable from the core countries. Biddle and Stephens explain the phenomenon: "The empirical correlation between the foreign policy choices of dependent states and the preferences of the core states is best seen as the result not of bargaining within asymmetrical power relationship but rather as the result of an historical process of dependency which shaped and formed the views of the policy making elites in the dependent states to conform to the preferences of decision-making elites in the core nations."[58]
   This has often been the experience of the Caribbean countries where foreign governments, especially the United States, assumed a much more direct role in establishing not only an international and national code of conduct for the countries of the region, but also deciding who should govern. Over the years the U. S. has resorted to a series of covert operations and in some cases open military interventions in several Caribbean and Latin American states as a means to topple recalcitrant regimes or to prevent radical nationalists and leftist parties from taking control of state power. This

is particularly true of U. S. interventions in the Dominican Republic in 1965, Chile in 1973, Grenada in 1983, and Panama in 1989. In all four cases the U.S. intervened and installed new governments sympathetic to its policies and interests in the region. Although the territories of the Caribbean may have achieved political independence, which they have displayed in international forums such as the United Nations, and in Third World movements such as the Group of 77 and Non-Alignment, in reality most if not all are seriously deficient in areas of effective foreign policy sovereignty, despite the creation of CARICOM to coordinate their foreign policy initiatives.

The Caribbean countries loss of control over certain, and often important, aspects of their domestic and foreign policy decision making apparatus in addition to their dependent position and underdog status within the global hierarchical system mean that they are not truly autonomous as a political or economic entity. Thus, political and economic dependency of the Caribbean has created an environment favorable to the long-term development of cultural dependency in the region.

Cultural Dependency

By its very nature, cultural dependency in the Commonwealth Caribbean is regarded as the emulation of the metropolitan countries, particularly the United States culture, attitudes, and values, the ideology underlying its organizational and institutional structures, and indeed its entire lavish lifestyle by the people of the Caribbean. This has occurred mainly because the socialization processes of the Caribbean have been extensively penetrated and shaped by the dominant European colonial powers and the United States. Thus, the region's people, who have been deliberately forced into these foreign social and cultural systems, have little or no desire to maintain a distinct national or Caribbean identity. Rather, many have adopted the American way of life while others are Westernized in accordance with British social and cultural values. As a consequence of these developments, foreign influences continue to penetrate and dominate not only the economic and political subsystems of the Caribbean, but also the hearts and minds of its people, hence their culture, who, generally speaking, have been conditioned by and succumbed to the media (television, radio, newspapers, magazines, and Internet services) to regard their own biological structure, behavior, social habits, culture, and last, but not least, their education, as inferior to those of North Americans and Europeans. This is a rather sad state of affairs for many West Indians whose hope is to one day land on the shores of the United States or Canada.

Cultural dependency in the modern Caribbean is also directly related to the postwar development of tourism and its associated industry, again by foreign capital, which has built up false hopes for the people of the region with its benign form of interaction between tourists and the local residents. Apart from government ministries and agencies, and local owners of the tourism industry, favorable sentiment about tourism in the Caribbean is not easy to find. Tourism has defined Caribbean culture in that it has encouraged the integration of peoples through the interchange of ideas, drinking and eating habits, and styles of clothing. With the exception of a few groups such as the native Indians and the Rastafarian movement in the region, the vast majority of West Indians emulate the North American lifestyle. The wining and dining of Caribbean tourists on mostly foreign and not local menus have deepened the region's economic dependence, chiefly on the United States. This has culturally and psychologically damaged the minds of the people because of unrealistic promises of a new and higher standard of living for them. As Barry, Wood, and Preusch explain: "Caribbean tourists generally have come not to share the local culture, ambience, and cuisine, but to model the island communities in the image of themselves and their own foreign culture. Caribbean parents complain that their children grow up with values of a consumer and disco culture that are especially inappropriate for such underdeveloped societies."[59] Similarly, University of the West Indies sociologist Rex Nettleford has remarked that "everything which has been done in that industry has been done for someone else and never for us. Instead of building our house and decorating it for our selves and having our visitors welcome to share it with us, we have decided to put up monstrosities which we think they would want."[60]

Cultural dependency has not only conditioned the Caribbean people to act and think inferior, but also has succeeded in making the entire region where culture does not exist in its own right or as a distinct value, but as a blend of American, British, and West Indian values, where commodities and ideas are all imported, where success only can be measured by outsiders, and where failures are accepted more or less as the norm rather than the exception. Cultural dependency in the Caribbean can be traced directly to colonialism and to the brutal and inhuman system of slavery in which race was instituted into the mode of production and the mode of exchange. It was race that determined whether or not a poor laborer would eventually rise on the social ladder. The systematic subordination of the African race has degraded them as inferior human beings, and eroded their culture to the extent that many of them were unable to discern between the European culture and their own. The slaves were brainwashed into accepting their culture as being inferior to the European culture. This negative attitude has been reinforced in the modern era by neocolonialism and passed on to succeeding generations of blacks. In discussing cultural neocolonialism in the Caribbean, Lowenthal has argued that "new forms of dependency reinforce old colonial habits. Political, economic, and cultural constraints are intimately inter linked, commercial ties lead to strategic accommodations, cultural dependency stems from overseas economic dominance. Submission to external cultural criteria is the inevitable concomitant of West Indian political and economic dependence."[61]

In the most depressing terms, the maturity of cultural dependency in the Caribbean has conditioned much of the population to accept their inferior status and problems associated with dependency and underdevelopment as a normal state of affairs in the region. West Indians in general are unaware that culture dependence exists because of its subtlety and, as a result, are not able to make distinctions regarding significant changes in the status quo. Thus, the subordinate position in which the former British West Indian colonies and their inhabitants found themselves at the turn of the new century was not an accident, but the conscious effort of the economic and political forces of the developed countries and by the cultural and sociological consequences of those forces. This has produced a symbiotic relationship of dominance and dependence which, over the years, has contributed to the development of psychological dependency in the Commonwealth Caribbean.

Psychological Dependency

In the Caribbean, psychological dependency can be defined as a deep-seated and ideological attachment to the socioeconomic, cultural, and political institutions of Britain by the people of the region. It is viewed by Caribbean scholars as the passive acceptance of an inferior position by West Indians relative to the more powerful, and the adoption of European and American values, preferences, and consumption patterns. This attitude of lack of pride, patriotism, and cultural identity is derived largely from the length and totality of the imperial experience suffered by generations of West Indians who were forcibly brought to the region over three hundred and fifty years ago as slaves and subsequently stripped of their individual rights and all cultural identity within the framework of colonial domination. Being black and a slave in such a society at the time was an absolute curse. The penalty was not only intense backbreaking toil on the plantation and contempt, but also a loss of one's name, language, education, religion, identity, social affiliations, and habits. The slave population was socialized into becoming docile, passive, and obedient as well as being dependent on the slave master who determined the life or death of a slave. Race was the basis of this caste system that placed the African slaves at the bottom of the social, economic, and political structures of society. This subordinate and inferior cultural experience was passed on to future generations of blacks in the Caribbean and elsewhere.

These early developments have not only disrupted the cultural life of the Caribbean people but also generated a powerful sense of inadequacy and a lack of self-determination and false hopes, which rendered them the most colonized of all peoples in the world. Frantz Fanon summarizes the colonial experience of the slaves in telling terms:

> Colonial domination, because it is total and tends to oversimplify . . . manages to disrupt in spectacular fashion the cultural life of a conquered people. . . . Every effort is made to bring the colonized person to admit the inferiority of his culture which has been transformed into instinctive patterns of behaviour, to recognize the unreality of his nation, and, in the extreme, the confused and imperfect character of his own biological structure.[62]

The indictment does not end here, for the legacies of the past as reflected in a continuous state of inferiority resulting from sociological factors are even more pernicious. Among the sociological legacies of colonial domination are the destruction of the family as an institution and hence the social fabric; the ethos of dependency and patronage engendered by the slave system, thereby depriving the black masses of their dignity, security, and self-respect; and basic human rights, and the undermining of the material, social, and spiritual advancement of the majority black population. What emerged over time was a Caribbean population that lacked motivation, self-confidence, and self-reliance. So all-pervading was the influence of the colonial system that it conditioned, and still does, the behavior of the masses in the region and stigmatized their culture and language. In true Caribbean spirit, the late Eric Williams explains the consequences and impact of centuries of imperial rule on the Caribbean people today:

> A too long history of colonialism seems to have crippled Caribbean self-confidence and Caribbean self-reliance, and a vicious circle has been set up: psychological dependence leads to an ever-growing economic and cultural dependence on the outside world. Fragmentation is intensified in the process. And the greater degree of dependence and fragmentation further reduces local self-confidence.[63]

Like cultural dependency, psychological dependence in the Caribbean is also directly linked to colonialism, slavery, and the hierarchical nature of the plantation economy in which the contemporary sociocultural structure of the region is derived. Compulsion and coercion were the means for the owners of the plantations to secure their adequate labor supplies, and in the acquisition of this labor the racial inferiority of blacks became the moral justification of slavery and indentureship. As Andrew Axline has observed:

> The centralized control of the plantation economy and its direct dependence on the home country has created in these societies a deep-seated psychological dependence on the outside world in general and the mother country in particular, which continues as an important influence today. This psychological dependence of a hierarchical social structure based upon race is a legacy of colonialism which was not changed by flag independence, and which plays an important role in the contemporary political life of the Caribbean.[64]

Caribbean psychological dependence is also evident in the constitutional arrangements inherited from colonialism and developed in quite different political and historical circumstances in the region that have not only conditioned the people to accept their subordinate position, but also helped disguise it by way of constitutional legitimacy. This inferiority feeling still exists among many West Indians who continue to believe and accept the Westminster model of parliamentary democracy to be the only proper way political activity and thought should be conducted in the Caribbean and consequently distrust any alternative constitutional framework or arrangements designed by their governments to suit their particular needs and circumstances of the country. "Whatever its shortcomings, the British political system demon-strated a persuasive power representing itself as the best of which man is capable. In the English-speaking Caribbean, this was to become increasingly accepted as axiomatic."[65] So great was the hold of this belief over most of the population that virtually every prominent personality in the Caribbean region subscribed to it.

However, a careful analysis of the Westminster model, with its notion of democracy and orderly constitutional advance, was based on the premise that the masses at the time were incapable of self-rule, and that the Colonial Office would be the trustee of their economic, political, and social interest. This was not just a scheme, for it had long-term consequences on most of the Caribbean population. Bequeathed to the region by Britain, the Westminster parliamentary system with its inherent tendency to foster autocratic types of rule would inevitably exclude the masses from real political power, and this exclusion was neither accidental nor shortsighted, as some have argued, but fully in accordance with the long-term interest of the colonial power to perpetuate its dominance. The perpetuation of colonial attitudes and subservience among West Indians has served to sustain the deep-rooted prejudices, culture, and values planted by the slave experience and nourished by colonialism. It is in this particular way that the system has contributed to psychological dependency in the region.

Psychological dependence in the Caribbean has been deepened by the tourist industry in which the appetite for foreign tastes, values, culture, and preferences predominate, and where anything produced locally is viewed as being inferior. This is due largely to the foreign-oriented policies promoted by the governments to lure tourists to the Caribbean region and the high import content of food and beverages served to them, as well as to transport them both into and within the region. Moreover, the local population, which is predominantly black has always been portrayed as menial, servile, inferior, and willing to inculcate the habits of the overwhelmingly white North American and European tourists who frequent the area. The issue of racial inferiority, for better or for worse, has long pervaded the Caribbean; it was an integral component of the slave-based plantation societies imposed by European imperialism, and has continued to be an important aspect of the social fabric in the region in the postcolonial period.

Tourism has caused far-reaching damage to the Caribbean psyche by rewarding obsequious behavior with employment and tipping and by withholding those rewards from, and thereby effectively punishing, those West Indians who lack the talent for servile behavior.[66] Speaking of the servility promoted by the tourism industry, Caribbean journalist Alister Hughes said: "We made special efforts to maintain the image. But nobody warned us of the danger and, in the interest of attracting tourist dollar, we overdid the effort and offered more than service. We offered servility. We acted in the worst sense of the word, as unspoiled natives of the Caribbean isles, and in the process developed an inferiority complex."[67] Commenting on some of the worst aspects of the tourist industry and the psychological dependence it has created on the people of the Caribbean, Demas said: "We welcome foreigners, we ape foreigners, we give away our national patrimony for a pittance to foreigners and, what is worse, we vie among ourselves in doing all these things. It is a state of psychological, cultural, and intellectual dependence on the outside world."[68]

The conclusion is simple. The impact of colonialism upon the Caribbean was not only formative, but it set in motion an important and enduring contradiction between a legacy of political fragmentation on the one hand,

and economic uniformity, on the other. Different legal and political systems were established in different languages and within different cultures. The British colonial system of governance was mostly autocratic; local legislative councils, where they existed at the time, had little or no power to formulate or shape policy or even maintain their culture. The European powers, in general, made very little, if any, effort to unite the colonies in the region.

By contrast, the economic impact was similar across the entire region, comprised mainly of a plantation economy and slave labor, and exporting a single cash crop—sugar—in largely unprocessed form to the metropolitan markets. Malcolm Cross said that this type of Caribbean uniformity resided in the fact that "all the countries of the region have either had to, or still have to, come to terms with the uniquely New World experience of being dependent suppliers of tropical primary products for Western European or North American markets."[69] It was this colonial legacy that led Caribbean academics and politicians to conceptualize most of the region's problems and much of its future prospects for development in terms of dependency. Although dependency theory provided a useful framework for understanding the region's problems, most Caribbean scholars differed widely over the appropriate solution that could eliminate the region's underdevelopment and dependent position. Some favored inwardly directed development strategies that emphasized production for the domestic and regional markets only. This meant a curtailment of economic ties with their traditional trading partners through high protectionist barriers designed to bolster the domestic industry. Others advocated some form of collective bargaining strategy, whereby the CARICOM states would pool their resources and join with other Third World nations to demand reforms in the international economic system. This had some leverage on the superpowers struggle for global preeminence during the Cold War era, but died when the Cold War ended in 1991.

Still others have contended that the Caribbean can escape its dependence upon the core capitalist countries only through a socialist revolution. Such a strategy involved the elimination of private capital and the development of nonexploitative economic relations with the socialist states. This strategy ignored the region's historical ties with the West, the role of technology and capital, and the region's subordinate position in the global economy. To that end, a good number of Caribbean dependency theorists placed emphasis on indigenous framework of development, but nowhere did indigenous models of development work well or as expected. At the very best, they were highly problematic and, at worst, they were a downright failure. Carl Stone summed up the dilemma of development faced by Caribbean governments when he said, "no development strategy has worked for the countries of the

Caribbean. Neither capitalist or socialist or any in-between models of development offered any easy road to transformation or any easy escape route from the economic stagnation that beset the region."[70] In spite of these differences, the theorists nevertheless have maintained that dependency continued to impose sharp limits on development in the region and has made economic growth and industrialization an almost impossible goal for the countries and people of the Caribbean.

Notes

1. Lloyd Best and Kari Levitt, "Character of Caribbean Economy," in *Caribbean Economy: Dependence and Backwardness*, ed. George L. Beckford (Kingston, Jamaica: The Herald Ltd., 1975), 34-60.

2. For excellent analyses of dependency in the Caribbean, see Havelock Brewster, "Economic Dependence: A Quantitative Interpretation," *Social and Economic Studies* 22 (1973); Norman Girvan, "The Development of Dependency Economics in the Caribbean and Latin America: Review and Comparison," *Social and Economic Studies* 22 (1973): 1-33; Dudley Seers, *Dependency Theory: A Critical Reassessment* (London: Frances Pinter Publishers, 1981); Clive Y. Thomas, *Dependence and Transformation: The Economics of the Transition to Socialism* (New York: Monthly Review Press, 1974).

3. Theotonio Dos Santos, "The Structure of Dependence," *American Economic Review* 60 (May 1970): 231.

4. Some well-known definitions of dependency can be found in Andre Gunder Frank, *Development and Underdevelopment in Latin America* (New York: Monthly Review Press, 1968); James D. Cockcroft, Andre Gunder Frank, and Dale L. Thompson, eds., *Dependence and Underdevelopment* (New York: Doubleday, 1972); Ronald Chilcote and Joel Edelstein, ed., *Latin America: The Struggle with Dependency and Beyond* (New York: John Wiley and Sons, 1980); Fernando Cardoso, "The Consumption of Dependency Theory in the United States," *Latin America Research Review* 12, no. 3 (1977); Fernando Cardoso and Enzo Faletto, *Dependency and Development in Latin America* (Berkely: University of California Press, 1979).

5. Norman Girvan, *Foreign Capital and Economic Underdevelopment in Jamaica* (Kingston, Jamaica: Institute of Social and Economic Research ISER, 1971).

6. Brewster, "Economic Dependence," 39.

7. William G. Demas, "The Caribbean and the New International Economic Order," 20, no. 3 (1978): 242. Also see Girvan, "The Development of Dependency Economics"; Thomas, *Dependence and Transformation*; and Brewster, "Economic Dependence."

8. Alister McIntyre, "Some Issues of Trade Policy in the West Indies," in *Readings in the Political Economy of the Caribbean,* ed. Norman Girvan and Owen Jefferson (Kingston, Jamaica: New World Group, 1972), 165; Girvan, "The Development of Dependency Economics"; and Havelock Brewster and Clive Thomas, *The Dynamics of West Indian Economic Integration* (Kingston, Jamaica: ISER, University of the West Indies, Institute [UWI], 1967).

9. Havelock Brewster, "Economic Dependence," 39, 91. Also see Alister McIntyre, *Current Problems of Economic Integration: The Effects of Reverse Preferences on Trade among Developing Countries* (New York: United Nations, 1974); and McIntyre, "Some Issues of Trade Policy," 165.

10. Tom Barry, Beth Wood, and Deb Preusch, *The Other Side of Paradise: Foreign Control in the Caribbean* (New York: Grove Press, 1984), 27-28.

11. Armando Lopez Coll, *La Colaboracion y la Integracion Economicas en el Caribe* (Havana: Editorial de Ciencias Sociales, 1983), 56.

12. The Caribbean Group of Experts, *The Caribbean Community in the 1980s* (Georgetown, Guyana: CARICOM, 1981), 41-42.

13. Alister McIntyre, "Decolonization and Trade Policy in the West Indies," paper presented to the Conference of Caribbean Scholars, Jamaica, April 1964.

14. Ibid.

15. W. Arthur Lewis, "The Industrialization of the British West Indies," *Caribbean Economic Review* no. 2 (1950): 1-61.

16. William G. Demas, *The Economics of Development in Small Countries with Special Reference to the Caribbean* (Montreal: McGill University Press, 1965), 32, 91.

17. Demas, *The Economics of Development in Small Countries,* 22, 115.

18. McIntyre, "Some Issues of Trade Policy in the West Indies," 166.

19. William G. Demas, "Consolidating Our Independence: The Major Challenge for the West Indies," lecture at the Institute of International Relations, University of the West Indies, St. Agustine, Trinidad, 1975, 12.

20. Demas, *The Economics of Development in Small Countries,* 35-36.

21. Thomas, *Dependence and Transformation,* 50.

22. Ibid., 58.

23. Ibid., 58.

24. Ibid., 59.

25. Brewster, "Economic Dependence," 90.

26. Clive Y. Thomas, "Monetary and Financial Arrangements in a Dependent Monetary Economy," *ISER,* UWI (1964); Norman Girvan, "The Caribbean Bauxite Industry," *ISER,* UWI (1967); Thomas, *Dependence and Transformation.*

27. Thomas D. Lairson and David Skidmore, *International Political Economy: The Struggle for Power and Wealth,* 2 ed. (New York: Harcourt Brace College Publishers, 1997), 228.

28. Thomas, *Dependence and Transformation,* 116-17.

29. Clive Y. Thomas, *The Poor and the Powerless: Economic Policy and Change in Caribbean* (New York: Monthly Review Press, 1988).

30. Lloyd Best, "Size and Survival," in *Readings in the Political Economy of the Caribbean*, ed. Girvan and Jefferson.

31. Ibid.

32. Lloyd Best and Kari Levitt, *Externally Propelled Industrialization and Growth in the Caribbean* (Montreal: Mimeo, 1969), 34-35.

33. Ibid., 12.

34. Ibid., 12.

35. Ibid., 12-13.

36. Ibid.; George Beckford, *Persistent Poverty: Underdevelopment in Plantation Economies of the Third World* (New York: Oxford University Press, 1972), 30-52.

37. New World Associates, "The Long-term Economic, Political, and Cultural Programme for Guyana," in *Readings in the Political Economy of the Caribbean,* ed. Girvan and Jefferson, 244.

38. Beckford, *Persistent Poverty*, 12.

39. Ibid., 5-13.

40. Lloyd Best, "Outlines of a Model of Pure Plantation Economy," *Social and Economic Studies* (September 1968): 287.

41. Best and Levitt, *Externally Propelled Industrialization*, 23-25.

42. Eric Williams, *Capitalism and Slavery* (London: Andre Deutsch, 1964).

43. Best, "Outlines of a Model of Pure Plantation Economy," 308.

44. Best and Levitt, *Externally Propelled Industrialization*; Beckford, *Persistent Poverty.*

45. Beckford, *Persistent Poverty,* 42-46.

46. Best and Levitt, *Externally Propelled Industrialization*, 24.

47. Beckford, *Persistent Poverty*, 45, 47.

48. Ida C. Greaves, "Plantations in World Economy," in *Plantation Systems of the New World* (Washington, D.C.: Pan American Union 1959), 14.

49. W. Andrew Axline, *Caribbean Integration: The Politics of Regionalism* (New York: Nichols, 1979), 143.

50. Lloyd Best and Kari Levitt, *Studies in Caribbean Economy*, vol. 1 (Kingston, Jamaica: ISER, UWI, 1974).

51. Kari Levitt, "Old Mercantilism and the New," *Social and Economic Studies* 12, no. 4 (1970): 471.

52. Beckford, *Persistent Poverty,* xxiv-5. The distinction between "constitutional" and "political" independence is one that is important to recognize. The former refers to symbols and trappings of independence—flags, anthems, a seat in the UN, and of course constitutions. Real political independence derives from the ability and power to control and manipulate the environment for the benefit of the people of the independent state. It derives in large measure from the degree of control of the economic resources of the country. From this definition, it means that only the developed countries are truly politically independent, while some measure of independence exists in the less developed countries.

53. David Lowenthal, *West Indian Societies* (New York: Oxford University Press, 1972).

54. H. Michael Erisman, *Pursuing Post-Dependency Politics: South-South Relations in the Caribbean* (Boulder, Colo.: Lynne Rienner, 1992), 38. For more details regarding the concept and dynamics of penetrated societies, see James N. Rosenau, "Pre-Theories and Theories of Foreign Policy," in *Approaches to Comparative and International Politics*, ed. Barry Farrell. (Evanston, Il.: Northwestern University Press, 1966).

55. Beckford, *Persistent Poverty*, xxii.

56. Cal Clark, "The Process of Dependence and Dependence Reversal," paper presented at the Conference of the International Studies Association, Los Angeles, March 1980, 9-10.

57. Bruce E. Moon, "Consensus or Compliance? Foreign Policy Change and External Dependence," *International Organization* 39, no. 2 (1985): 297-329.

58. William J. Biddle and John D. Stephens, "Dependency and Foreign Policy: Theory and Practice in Jamaica," paper presented at the Conference of the Latin American Studies Association, Boston, October 1986, 2-3.

59. Barry, Wood, and Preusch, *The Other Side of Paradise*, 87.

60. Rex M. Nettleford, *Caribbean Cultural Identity* (Kingston, Jamaica: Institute of Jamaica, 1978).

61. Lowenthal, *West Indian Societies*, 233, 245.

62. Frantz Fanon, *The Wretched of the Earth* (New York: Grove, 1961), 236.

63. Eric Williams, *From Columbus to Castro: The History of the Caribbean 1492-1969,* (London: Andre Deutsch, 1970), 502.

64. Axline, *Caribbean Integration,* 69.

65. Michael Manley, *Jamaica: Struggle in the Periphery* (Oxford: Oxford University Press, 1972), 31.

66. Barry, Wood, and Preusch, *The Other Side of Paradise*, 87.

67. Alister Hughes, "National Inferiority," Kingston, Jamaica, *Sunday Gleaner*, 30 June 1974, 10.

68. William G. Demas, "Consolidating Our Independence," 17. Also cited in Barry, Wood, and Preusch, *The Other Side of Paradise*, 87.

69. Malcolm Cross, *Urbanization and Urban Growth in the Caribbean* (Cambridge: Cambridge University Press, 1979), 5.

70. Carl Stone, "Whither Caribbean Socialism? Reflections on Jamaica, Grenada, and Guyana," in *The Troubled and Troubling Caribbean*, ed. Roy Glasgow and Winston Langley (Ontario, Canada: Edwin Mellen Press, 1989), 144.

Chapter 3

The Struggle to Overcome Dependency in the Caribbean through Integration

In the 1950s and 1960s orthodox thinking about economic development has been challenged by Latin American *dependencia* theorists and their focus on the dependent relationship of the Global South countries as a major factor in their underdevelopment.[1] The position of underdeveloped countries in the global economy and the structure of their national economies is perceived as being strongly influenced and conditioned by their interaction with the capitalist metropolitan economies. Thus, underdevelopment in the Global South is seen as the result of the process of economic development of the Global North. As two advocates of dependency theory put it: "Both development and underdevelopment are aspects of the same phenomenon, both are historically simultaneous, both are linked functionally and, therefore, interact and condition each other mutually."[2] The dominant thrust of dependency thinking in Latin America and the Caribbean during the 1950s and early 1960s was articulated by Sir Arthur Lewis and Raul Prebisch, whose nearly simultaneous publication of works had a tremendous impact on the political economy of both regions.

As indicated already, the present international economic structure was established during the period of colonialism and is perpetuated through the current policies of international trade, aid, finance, and investment. During the period of colonial rule the Global South countries were integrated into the metropolitan economic system as primary producers of raw materials for either domestic consumption or for processing overseas. As a result, these territories became the site of extensive extractive activities or plantation production for export to the metropolitan countries on terms dictated by them. The economic structure, which to a large degree still characterizes the English-speaking Caribbean today, was not the result of free market forces working on the basis of comparative advantage, but rather the conscious political decisions taken by the European colonial powers to advance their own economic advantage.[3] These acts resulted in an economic structure characterized by a large proportion of national income and employment based in the primary sector with exports concentrated in a single or very few products sold on the world market under very unstable conditions. This has contributed to the worsening of the terms of trade, wide fluctuations and shortages of foreign exchange needed for economic growth and development planning, and an exacerbation between the masses and the ruling elite. These social-economic differences originated in the colonial era and still persist today in the Caribbean.

This dependency relationship is seen by many Caribbean economists as the direct result of foreign penetration, exploitation, and domination of Third World societies. Thus, certain factors such as limited economic size, lack of natural resources and foreign capital, overpopulation, and low productivity, which have been traditionally regarded as immutable variables of the development capability of Third World countries, are rather constraints that derived from dependency. It should be noted that limits of economic size reflect the fact that a large portion of the population is virtually excluded from the economy and thus have limited purchasing power. Lack of natural resources could be attributed to the misuse of available resources to meet the needs of the metropolitan markets; overpopulation means surplus labor due to capital intensive industries; and low productivity is the direct legacy of the slave economy. This is not to deny that certain climatic and topographical conditions pose serious obstacles to development in the Caribbean and the Global South in general, but simply to illustrate that these factors can often be traced to the condition of dependency.

Since World War II, dependency in the Caribbean and other Global South countries has taken a new form as a result of the expansion of the world capitalist system mainly through the mechanism of direct foreign investment and the institutional manifestation of transnational corporations, and more recently, by the quickened pace of the process of globalization. The former has been encouraged by policies of investment incentives on the part of Caribbean governments in their pursuit of economic development based on the strategy of industrialization by invitation. This policy has had some success in a number of countries, whose growth in terms of real GDP has been improved along with an increase in their per capita national income recorded at the aggregate level. There were visible results in the mining sector with bauxite in Guyana and Jamaica, and petroleum in Trinidad and Tobago, and in the development of the manufacturing sectors in Jamaica and Trinidad and Tobago, and light industry in Barbados. Partly as a result of this development strategy, these countries ranked among the most developed of the Global South countries based on the measurement of per capita GDP. These positive indicators do not, however, suggest that development in the sense of structural transformation of the region's economy has occurred; to the contrary, this has not been the case in most countries. One reason is that the enterprises created were vertically integrated with the parent company and were capital intensive and, as a result, produced few spread effects in the secondary and tertiary sectors of the economies. This, along with transfer pricing between subsidiaries of the same parent company as well as licensing fees, has reduced foreign exchange earnings and hence public savings in the host countries.

In spite of the success, it quickly became apparent to economists and politicians in the Caribbean that the industrialization by invitation strategy had failed to achieve two of the major goals, the reduction of unemployment and the creation of an internal dynamic of growth in the region's economy. These appraisals led economists to the idea that the economic dependence of the Caribbean was a major obstacle to economic development—a concept that began to play a major role in the politics of the Caribbean in the 1960s, a full decade later than in Latin America. This can partly be explained by the trade preference accorded to Caribbean agricultural exports by Britain in the 1940s and 1950s, which cushioned the territories from some of the effects of the export instability experienced in Latin America during this period.[4] Economic dependence, as seen in this period by some Caribbean scholars, including Demas and McIntyre, was a concept that was specifically related to the size of the national economy, its internal structure, and the particular economic policies pursued by the governments of the region. The Caribbean economy was described by them as being dependent on the rest of the world for supplies and resources of all kinds in order to function. This description of Caribbean economic dependence is explained in Alister McIntyre's 1964 essay on the decolonization process and trade policy in the Caribbean, where he stressed that the size and structure of the region's economy has severely constrained its development and increased its dependence on extra-regional sources. He distinguishes between structural and functional dependence, claiming that the latter arises as a result of the particular policies chosen and can therefore be avoided if alternative policies are pursued, while the former is the act of nature.[5]

The emphasis on structural and functional dependence is expressed in Brewster and Thomas's extensive study on Caribbean economic integration published in 1967 as part of the studies commissioned by the University of the West Indies for the August 1967 meeting in Guyana. It contributed to the

development of a region-wide free trade policy of economic integration for
the Caribbean. It was believed that through integration the limitation of size
and resource problems could be reduced by the creation of a single regional
economy and the establishment of regional institutions through which
policies could be developed to bring about structural transformation within
the expanded opportunities of the regional economy. It was also apparent
that trade diversification could contribute to import substitution on a regional
level, and that trade creation was undesirable since it meant the destruction
through competition of existing productive capacity in the region. Further, it
was recognized that this approach to Caribbean economic integration should
not be limited to regional trade liberalization but should include the
integration of production within the region and provision for government
intervention through a direct regional economic policy. Regional economic
integration, thus conceived, offered a solution to the failure of the post-
World War II industrialization strategies to make a significant contribution
to development of the Caribbean economy by attacking the dual problem of
structural and functional dependence.

But dependency in the Caribbean was thought to have been related to the
trade relationship between the territories of the region and the metropolitan
countries, and was defined subsequently in terms of the region's external
structural relationships within the international political economy. This
dependence is reflected not only in the pattern of trade, but also in the high
degree of foreign control of the Caribbean economies. Until recently, the
principal resources and industrial enterprises in the Caribbean were largely
owned and controlled by foreigners. The export of petroleum, bauxite, and
agricultural products in recent times, while providing some national income,
has not contributed greatly to the region's employment, and has undermined
the development of domestic agriculture, creating a dependence on imported
foodstuffs. This has made the region's economic and political viability an
elusive goal.

Regional Integration of the Caribbean

During the mid- to late 1960s, regional economic integration replaced
industrialization by invitation as the principal development model in the
Caribbean. It was conceived fundamentally as a mechanism for correcting
the economic woes that had beset the territories of the Caribbean during the
first decade of their independence and to overcome the handicaps of small
size, limited resource base, economic fragmentation, and the region's

extensive dependence on foreign sources. It was a formal commitment by the territories of the region to undertake to promote a process of industrial development which could lead to the expansion of more production links within the area. Basically, it involves the coordination of policies and the pooling of local resources and markets by the governments of the region in order to achieve as a group a higher level of socioeconomic development that would not be attained if they continue to operate individually. At the time, the various governments were under severe pressure to reduce the high levels of unemployment and underemployment and to improve their national economy by reducing its external dependence. In these circumstances, the integration movement seemed to most Caribbean governments to be the best strategy to move the region's industrial development to the next phase, since each of the alternatives available to them involved some degree of economic dependence.

Theoretically, this process of regional economic integration is achieved and accelerated if it is accompanied by a certain degree of political union whereby participating Caribbean states delegate the authority to make some choices regarding the allocation of values and resources to collective decision-making bodies operating at the regional level. In practice, however, this has not always been an easy choice. The eastern Caribbean islands usually have been extremely reluctant to surrender any of their sovereignty to regional institutions, choosing instead some form of policy coordination as a mere exercise of unity. Regional economic integration has provided a possible means for Caribbean and other developing states to address the size-versus-viability problem, dependency issues, and to increase their bargaining power in relation to the developed countries. Andrew Axline has contended that, "The principal political objective of underdeveloped countries involved in regional integration schemes is development itself, the betterment of economic and social conditions and a redressing of the unequal relationship between the industrialized countries and themselves with respect to the distribution of economic and political power in the international system."[6]

Serious thoughts on Caribbean integration first came to the forefront of political thinking in the region principally as a result of the pro-integrationist William Demas's implicit message of collective self-reliance, which derived initially from the fact that the newly independent nations in the region were beginning to feel the effects of self-government. Demas in 1965 published an original and highly influential analysis on the condition of the Commonwealth Caribbean economy in which he points to three important weaknesses in the post-World War II pattern of industrial growth in the region. One is the level of unemployment and underemployment, which had been the primary consideration behind Lewis's industrial strategy, was still very high and increased instead of decreased during the period of industrialization by invitation. Second, the high wage rates paid to workers in the manufacturing sector not only increased the price of labor in the urban areas, but also encouraged people to leave their low-paid agricultural employment for better paying jobs in the cities. This led to a major decline in agricultural products throughout the region. Third, most of the imported technology used in the industrial sector had turned out to be highly capital intensive rather than labor intensive and unsuited to the special needs of the region's labor surplus economies into which it had been introduced. Demas also noted that the use of local resources in the process of industrialization had been negligible and that investors repatriated the surplus generated from the capitalist sector to their home country instead of reinvesting in the domestic economy. In addition, most of the industries that had been created performed only final assembly operations and, as a result, had failed to establish close linkages with other sectors of the local economy. Combined, these factors have not only contributed to the marginalization of the Caribbean economy, but also reinforced its dependence on the metropolitan countries.

He was convinced that the economic integration of the Caribbean would not only promote industrial growth by making possible the elimination of excess capacity in existing manufacturing industry, but also, and more important, by stimulating investment in new manufacturing industries, which would become economically feasible for the first time in the region due to the expanded market. He however stressed that "integration may often not remove the necessity to seek export markets outside the region,"[7] but the key to the strategy of economic integration was the pursuit of import substitution on a regional basis. He asserts that "the creation of an economic region can mean that the development pattern for the region as a whole can approximate more to import substitution—although from the point of view of individual member countries there will still be a large volume of exports to and imports from other member countries."[8]

Demas's thinking was based on the belief that integration would generate the conditions and incentives for greater interisland trade, attract foreign investment, improve the size of the market, and encourage economies of large-scale production. It would also reduce tariffs and, in the long run, establish a free trade area in the region that would then provide incentives for developmental projects by both local and foreign investors. The objective was to enhance the status of Caribbean countries as trading partners in the broader international economic system. Regional integration, according to Demas, would promote trade and greater rationalization and specialization in different branches of existing industries in the Caribbean and, above all, lead to the establishment of regional industrial complexes or integration industries utilizing fully the natural and technological resources of the entire region.[9] The aim was to create a much stronger and more deeply integrated Caribbean society to speed up the development process and to eradicate, at the very least, the region's economic dependence on the developed countries and the international economic system. Axline has argued that "Regional [economic] integration was conceived as a means to provide a larger market, increasing the attractiveness for foreign investment and thus accelerating the development process. It is an approach to development primarily oriented to the trade aspects of integration and principally concerned with the size of markets."[10]

The growing sentiment among the Caribbean leaders at the time was that some form of collaboration was needed to stimulate economic development and to minimize the region's external dependence. They were particularly concerned about the relatively sparse volume of interisland trade caused by tariff barriers, market prospects for their primary products, and continued preferential trading ties with Great Britain, in light of its application to join the European Economic Community (EEC) and its likely abandonment of the region's preference. They were also alarmed by the closure of emigration outlets to Britain, the United States, and Canada, since migration has always contributed considerably to Caribbean overpopulation prior to and after independence. Other obstacles to Caribbean development were inadequate intraregional transportation and communication systems, the perpetuation of traditional trade patterns, with the territories of the region locked into a disadvantaged position of trading low-cost raw materials and commodities, such as sugar for expensive finished products produced by the industrialized countries.[11] Anthony Bryan explains that as the postcolonial process evolved,

> the dichotomy between political independence and the reality of economic dependence emerged. As had been happening almost a decade earlier in Latin America, the concern [in the Caribbean] was now directed toward external dependency and the need for regional economic integration as a means of accelerating economic development and minimizing this dependency.[12]

Initial steps toward Caribbean integration or federation were cautious, but they were first advanced along this line, with a long-term view at some form of political and economic union among the territories of the region. This idea had been repeatedly proposed by the various royal commissions that had visited the region since the late nineteenth century and was based on the belief that each territory's capacity to survive and perhaps protect and promote its interests globally is enhanced by operating through a union such as the West Indies Federation.

The West Indies Federation

Historically, the difficulties inherent in the tiny and dispersed Caribbean islands led to the formation of a number of cooperation experiments in the region, among them a federation of the Leeward Islands in 1674 and a Common Council in 1871. The fact that the islands were geographically isolated from each other and the lack of a functioning communications network worked against these efforts to integrate the islands and territories of the region. The first attempt to establish a Caribbean common market came during the postwar period when the West Indies Federation was founded at the instigation of Great Britain in 1958. The idea of a federation received strong support from local labor unions, political parties, and the business community, which advocated greater autonomy and political independence for the territories of the region.

The emerging political elite envisioned a federation that would ensure a more stable and developed democratic process, a wider scope for political action, and greater possibilities for implementing the appropriate economic policies to remedy the region's social and economic ills. Economically, the federation was geared towards the expansion of the regional market with the aim to stimulate economic growth and development in each Caribbean territory through various forms of cooperation. As a political union, the federation would have included territories as distant from each other as Jamaica and Guyana, and would serve as an entity for consolidating national sentiments to oppose any outside force threatening the survival of the territories, and to enhance their bargaining power within the general framework of the inter-national system.

But during the period of colonialism, the English-speaking Caribbean territories enjoyed, in general, very little communication among themselves and, in particular, negligible political or economic interaction. Thus, when the British created the federation among its former Caribbean colonies (the Bahamas, British Honduras, and Guyana excluded), partly to avoid granting full independence to a number of seemingly nonviable microstates, West Indians, who had lived in semi-isolation and had more in common with the city of London than among themselves, frowned at the idea. The federation was formed at the time when Britain was clearly exhausted by its extensive involvement in World War II, and by a rapidly disintegrating empire, found it difficult to deal with so many small territories that were about to gain their political independence. It was conceived as a means to better manage the British colonies in the Caribbean and keep them within the economic and political orbit of Britain. As Gordon Lewis has observed:

> British opinion . . . throughout viewed federation, not as a vehicle for self-government, but, overwhelmingly, as a problem of colonial administrative convenience. Examination of the voluminous documentation of that opinion in Westminster debates, royal commission reports, Colonial Office memoranda and the published correspondence between the Colonial Secretary and individual West Indian governors shows that the most persistently recurring reason evoked in support of federation was the greater economy and the improved administrative efficiency it was supposed federation would bring about.[13]

Opponents to the federation, including the late Cheddi Jagan of Guyana, claimed that it was doomed from the very beginning for these reasons. First, the imperial power plans to integrate the Caribbean territories from above, taking into account the ruling-class interests and not those of the masses, the limited participation by the masses in promoting and supporting the idea of federation, the lack of information of this idea by organizations other than the ruling political parties, and the ideological dependence of the political elite on Britain could not overcome the obstacles posed by divisions and deeply rooted island loyalties. Second, during the late 1950s, the federation was no longer viewed as a necessary route to political independence since Barbados, Jamaica, Guyana, and Trinidad and Tobago had already achieved internal self-rule and partial autonomy from Britain. Finally, Jagan was opposed to the idea that the ultimate executive authority rested with the governor general who was appointed by the British Crown and who had primary jurisdiction over defense, foreign relations, and financial affairs. Anyway, the leaders of the smaller islands were enthusiastic supporters of the West Indies Federation, where it seemed to provide greater and faster access to independence.[14]

Four years after the founding of the federation, differences among the members in terms of territorial and physical size and economic and political autonomy, imbalances in political representation and financial contributions by the smaller and larger states, and contradictions arising from state versus federal interests contributed to its demise. For instance, interisland acrimony among its ten members, Antigua, Barbados, Dominica, Grenada, Jamaica, Montserrat, St. Kitts Nevis-Anguilla, St. Lucia, St. Vincent, and Trinidad and Tobago, clouded the decision about the location of the federation's head-quarters. Jamaicans and Trinidadians had wanted the headquarters in their respective countries, and residents from each of the smaller states considered their own islands an ideal compromise. Jamaicans were disgruntled that the federation's cabinet was eventually seated in Port of Spain, the capital of Trinidad and Tobago. Most were opposed to the idea that their government had to lower its extremely high tariffs and open its markets to other members of the federation, particularly Trinidad and Tobago, which already had the lowest import duties in the area. In a national referendum held in September 1961, Jamaicans voted against further membership in the federation and instead for independence. Among the many reasons were the alienation of the vast majority of Jamaicans from the negotiation process which allowed the opposition to suggest that Jamaica was being forced by the British to shoulder the financial burden of the smaller Caribbean states and that the benefits derived from its newfound wealth (bauxite and tourism) would be diverted away from the Jamaican masses to subsidize the poorer islands.[15] Less than a year later, Trinidad and Tobago's Prime Minister Eric Williams's famous comment that "one from ten leaves nought" finally led to the official dissolution of the federation on April 2, 1962.[16] Thomas explains that the West Indies Federation collapsed,

> because it was conceived essentially as a colonial arrangement to protect colonial interests. This however, was introduced at a time when the masses were on a strong offensive against colonialism and the petty-bourgeois leadership of the period had already been committed to the struggle for constitutional independence. . . . The petty-bourgeois leadership were against colonialism and colonial arrangements.[17]

Despite an awareness of the need to deal with the spectre of dependency in the region, the West Indies Federation, from its inception, did not display any significant capacity to transform this perception into policy and reality since none of its members were independent states during this period. Their goal within the federation was to deal with the problem of external control and the attainment of formal independence. From the Caribbean leaders' perspective, the process of decolonization had to be completed before they were in a position to elevate the struggle against dependency at the international level. Even so, the power structure of the federation itself militated against any dependency initiatives because the governor general who represented the interest of the colonial office had complete jurisdiction over its members' external relations as well as the authority to block any legislation by member states. Given this authority, the federation could not serve effectively as a platform to combat dependency in the Caribbean, especially any attacks against imperialism that might be targeted at British interests or those of its allies. Had the Caribbean countries actually become independent within the framework of a strong regional union, the size and limited resource problem might have been less severe and their degree of vulnerability to dependency may have been reduced. Also, in tackling the problem of regional political association first, the federation erred in that it ignored the lessons of history, which suggest that the chances of successful integration in a community are enhanced when its economic interests are established ahead of time. The collapse of the federation, however, increased awareness on the part of the four largest Caribbean countries of the need to develop a viable regional economic union to improve intraregional trade and to stimulate economic growth in order to minimize the prospects of the external dependence and improve the overall well-being of the Caribbean people.

Caribbean Free Trade Association

Regional economic integration was revived in the Caribbean in the mid-1960s at the initiative of Guyana which led to the creation of CARIFTA. It was the first genuine step in the direction of integrating the Commonwealth Caribbean countries. Guyana's interest in Caribbean integration was based largely on the racial division of the country between East Indians and blacks, the latter being in the minority. At the time, the PNC government support came from the black population, therefore a politically integrated Caribbean would provide the basis necessary for immigration and settlement of persons in Guyana from the other predominantly black Caribbean states and thus increased the black population as well as support for the PNC regime.

Modelled directly upon Demas's thinking, CARIFTA began as a modest free trade agreement among Antigua, Barbados, and Guyana in December 1965. Three years later, on May 1, 1968, the treaty became official, and within three months, was expanded to include the original ten members of the ill-fated West Indies Federation. Belize joined in 1974 and the Bahamas in 1983. CARIFTA's expansion was made possible through the West Indies Associated States (WISA) Council of Ministers, which had been established in 1966 among the islands of Antigua, Dominica, Grenada, Montserrat, St. Kitts-Nevis, St. Lucia, and St. Vincent, which in April 1968 became the Eastern Caribbean Common Market (ECCM).[18] Unlike the West Indies Federation, which was primarily a political union, CARIFTA was essentially devoted to economic matters of mutual concern. Its charter was drawn up and ratified at the August 1967 Caribbean Heads of Government Conference meeting in Georgetown, Guyana.

Using the existing Antigua-Barbados-Guyana model, it was agreed that CARIFTA's main thrust was to promote intraregional commerce among the countries of the Commonwealth Caribbean through the mechanism of a free trade regime that was guided by these general principles: (i) the elimination of import duties and quotas in intraregional commerce; (ii) the establishment of a Caribbean Bank to help provide funds for development, particularly for infrastructure in the agricultural and tourism sectors; and (iii) organization of the institutional mechanisms (e.g., a regional secretariat) necessary to assure smooth and efficient management of its programs.[19]

As a free trade regime, CARIFTA succeeded in liberalizing the bulk of intraregional trade, thereby extending the size of the region's markets to accommodate its various light manufacturing industries. Data obtained from the Economic Commission for Latin America revealed that between 1967 and 1974 the value of intraregional trade of all CARICOM states increased from U.S. $44 to $224 million, while the share of intra-CARIFTA exports in total regional exports rose from 6 percent to 7.2 percent over the period. This represents an annual average increase of over 16 percent, compared to less than 5 percent before the establishment of CARIFTA.[20] These increases, it should be noted, were measured in current prices at the time and reflected a higher rate of inflation, especially the effect of the precipitous rise in oil prices at the end of 1973. In this period, the region's trade was dominated by the four larger countries, with 34 percent of manufactured goods from Trinidad and Tobago, 49 percent from Jamaica, 40 percent from Barbados, and 66 percent from Guyana were exported to other CARIFTA countries.[21] Together, these countries accounted for 96 percent of Caribbean exports and 90 percent of its imports in 1974.[22]

Despite these impressive achievements, weaknesses within CARIFTA's trade regime surfaced as early as 1971, particularly in the manufacturing sector. The use of local materials in the production of manufactured goods among its members was relatively small and, as a result, yielded very little benefit to the exporting countries. In part, this was due to the fact that the CARIFTA Agreement had what was known as the Basic Material List. This system conferred local origin on a number of products which, even though not produced in the region were deemed to be of regional origin for the purpose of the "value-added criterion" whereby 50 percent of a product's value had to be created in the region for it to qualify and to be treated as a local product.[23] These materials were needed essentially to sustain the light manufacturing industries that had been established by earlier development strategies. This deficiency in the region's trading arrangement was taken over by CARIFTA's successor, CARICOM, and was eventually phased out in 1981. Consequently, Demas and other architects of the trade regime admitted that a great deal of intra-Caribbean trade "from a strictly economic point of view may not be all that beneficial to the member countries who are exporting."[24]

Some of the weaknesses exhibited by CARIFTA stemmed from the fact that it was neither a customs union nor a common market, but merely a free-trade arrangement. It did not require the territories of the region to have uniform external trade arrangements and did not promote a common market for the other factors of production, such as labor and capital. In essence, CARIFTA was a modest approach into the realm of multilateral cooperation in the sense that it achieved a minimum level or degree of integration among its members. Its efforts were concentrated almost exclusively on the more limited goal of breaking down the barriers to intraregional trade. It lacked any effective means to ensure a reasonably and equitable distribution of benefits derived from the cooperation between the region's four larger states and the smaller islands. For instance, the Caribbean Development Bank, which was created in 1970 to support the association's activities and to raise cheap investment capital to help the smaller islands whose narrow resource base precluded them from raising money outside the region, was not a formal CARIFTA institution.[25] This shortcoming by CARIFTA is illustrated by the fact that the share of the region's commerce controlled by Barbados, Guyana, Jamaica, and Trinidad and Tobago increased from 60 percent in 1967 to 69 percent in 1971. During this same period trade among the smaller islands declined from 1.9 percent to 1.4 percent of the total trade activity within the CARIFTA area.[26] Commenting on the fundamental nature of CARIFTA and its inability to address these problems, Axline says that:

> CARIFTA involved the elimination of barriers on products traded within the region. It did not free the movement of other factors of production (labour and capital) and thus was not a common market. It did not have a common external tariff and thus was not even a customs union. Although [its] proponents had recognized the problem of inequitable distribution of benefits . . . there were no major distributive measures included. There were a number of provisions affecting the LDCs in such a way as to alter favourably the relationship between the costs and benefits of their participation, but most of them were opting out or escaping clause mechanisms which aimed to reduce costs rather than provide benefits.[27]

In the final analysis, CARIFTA was not an ambitious blueprint for regional economic integration of the Caribbean. Its failure to confront the issue of establishing a common external tariff to safeguard the region's trade, to integrate its members, and to renegotiate their economic relations with the advanced developed countries were indications that the organization was not particularly concerned with developing or enhancing the region's bargaining power vis-à-vis the countries of the Global North within the international system. Furthermore, its inability to utilize the human and natural resources of certain countries in the Caribbean to overcome the deficiencies of others could not generate economic growth in the area. Its ill-fated attempts to integrate regional production removed the collective self-reliance strategy as an option among its members and precluded any serious efforts to accelerate economic growth and development in order to reduce or eliminate the region's high levels of dependency on foreign products. Andrew Axline has stated that "CARIFTA represented a minimal form of regional integration, without major compensatory and corrective mechanisms to counter unequal distribution of gains and polarization, or measures to reduce dependence."[28]

The disillusionment with its track record, combined with the sentiment among practically all the leaders of the Commonwealth Caribbean for a common external tariff and a free zone area, triggered an ongoing debate about the need to deepen the integration process and establish mechanisms to reduce its dependency. This was perhaps the main driving force behind the leaders to explore new efforts of collaboration that eventually produced CARICOM.

Caribbean Common Market and Community

During the early 1970s, several factors converged to produce a much more ambitious integrated movement in the Caribbean. The initial impulse was to replace CARIFTA's modest free trade regime with a more ambitious one that would eventually lead to the creation of a common market revolving around a comprehensive system of uniform external tariffs and mechanisms to help in the fair distribution of benefits to the LDCs of the region. The leaders of the Caribbean felt that CARIFTA, with all its flaws, had served its purpose and, therefore, it was time to move the integration process to the next plateau. The crucial government negotiations in this process occurred in three Council of Ministers Conferences in Dominica in July 1972, in Trinidad and Tobago in October 1972, and in Guyana in April 1973, as well as two parallel Heads of Government meetings in Trinidad and Tobago and

Guyana in the same period. The latter became known as the Georgetown Accord. Among the main topics of discussion were the harmonization of fiscal investment incentives, especially those applying to countries outside the region, regional allocation of new industries, and a unified Caribbean approach to negotiations with the EC.

There was also a growing concern on the part of many Caribbean leaders about the effects of postcolonial dependency on the region's economy. As Britain was about to join the European Common Market (ECM), practically all the leaders of the Commonwealth Caribbean countries faced the daunting task of maintaining their privileged access to the English market and of redefining their relations, not only with Britain, but also with the Western European countries. Individually, the Caribbean countries' small size and limited economic influence had historically placed them in a position of considerable weakness to negotiate with Britain. This had made them highly susceptible to the divide-and-conquer tactics. A collective approach, while obviously preferable, was hindered by the fact that there was no existing organizational structure in place to negotiate on behalf of the Caribbean states. CARIFTA was not suited to that task, given the fact that it was authorized to establish and manage a regional free-trade regime and not to function as an agent for collective bargaining with countries outside the region. In addition, the governments of the Commonwealth Caribbean had to face up to the need to advance the integration movement to new and higher levels if the socioeconomic well-being of the region was not to be adversely affected.

The importance of regional integration that gave birth to CARICOM on July 4, 1973, was institutionally expressed with the signing of the Treaty of Chaguaramas in Trinidad by the leaders of Barbados, Guyana, Jamaica, and Trinidad-Tobago. It provided for CARICOM to be operative on August 1, 1973, and the Eastern Caribbean states to become members no later than May 1, 1974. The exception is the Bahamas who became a member in July 1983. CARICOM constituted a major step forward in the development of the integration process in the Caribbean and has achieved such objectives as the establishment of the Caribbean Investment Corporation and incorporated some of the special interest of the smaller islands, such as the harmonization of fiscal incentives to industry and the avoidance of double taxation.

The principal economic objective of CARICOM has been to increase the size of the Caribbean market in order to encourage new investment and the growth of profitable industries. The leaders of the CARICOM nations felt industrialization by import substitution would only succeed if there was one large region market. CARICOM created a common market that liberalized trade with little or no import duties or tariffs on regional trade between its members. It also set up a high tariff wall to protect Caribbean manufacturers from competing goods produced outside the region. Besides implementing the regional common market, CARICOM was authorized by its members to support institutions and projects that improved the region's infrastructure and encouraged new private and public investment.

These goals, among its many provisions, were incorporated in its charter and embraced three broad areas of cooperation: (i) the establishment of a common market for the purposes of trade and economic cooperation, based not only on free trade as in the CARIFTA agreement, but also with a common external tariff, the commitment to the progressive removal of non-tariff barriers to trade, and the harmonization of fiscal incentives. While the treaty made no explicit arrangements for the free movement of labor and capital, in practice, some restrictions were placed on intraregional migration of both people and money to shield the LDCs of the region from having their local investment resources and their most skilled workers siphoned off by better opportunities available in the larger Caribbean countries. Furthermore, CARICOM's uniform external tariff coexisted with a common external tariff arrangement of smaller islands which operated in CARICOM through a joint initiative in the form of the ECCM; (ii) the expansion of functional areas of cooperation based on a number of interministerial committees in the fields of health, education, finance, labor, agriculture, communications, air and sea transportation, energy and mining, science and technology, and natural resources, as well as the cooperation to develop production and distribution structures for food and industry throughout the region. There is also a provision in the charter for ad hoc cooperation in matters such as law, information, and women's affairs; and (iii) the coordination of foreign policy among the independent states of the Caribbean. This provision is unique in integration arrangements for no other regional integration group in the Western hemisphere had ever before formally incorporated a specific requirement to coordinate foreign policy on such a wide range of issues.[29] The regional integration plan formulated by CARICOM was, in many ways, designed to establish a framework for the region's economic development and to reduce its dependence on the developed countries. Axline has argued that "One of the reasons that the idea of regional planning is so highly charged politically is that it implies measures of a distributive nature and measures to reduce dependence."[30]

CARICOM has coordinated the region's foreign policy in a number of areas, including the protection of the Eastern Caribbean islands in the inter-national environment, especially from the threat of mercenary invasion; the declaration and commitment to make the Caribbean region a zone of peace; regional support for the view that ideological pluralism is an irreversible fact of international relations; a joint condemnation of U.S. destablization policy that was directed towards Jamaica and the Manley regime and the Burnham government in Guyana during the 1970s; regional support for Guyana and Belize in their border disputes with Venezuela and Guatemala respectively; and a unified critical reaction to the limited perspective of the Caribbean Basin Initiative. Anthony Bryan highlights the foreign policy success of CARICOM:

> [T]he member states of CARICOM have successfully coordinated their policies at forums such as the ACP [African, Caribbean Pacific Group], the UN, the OAS [Organization of American States]. Similarly, there have been coordinated positions on specific issues, such as the normalization of relations with Cuba, the Panama Canal, the Law of the Sea, Southern Africa, and the territorial claims facing Guyana and Belize (coming respectively from Venezuela and Guatemala). They have also consulted on matters such as the Caribbean Basin Initiative and regional security.[31]

The idea of making foreign policy coordination a central feature of the CARICOM treaty grew out of the region's earlier experiences of negotiating with the European Economic Community (EEC). This led to the creation of the African-Caribbean-Pacific group (ACP), a new agreement to replace the Canada-West Indies Agreement of 1925, and the Law of the Sea treaties. These experiences showed the strength of collective bargaining that asserted the region's independence and the right to pursue a Caribbean identity through fraternal relations with all Caribbean nations thereby ending the United States isolation of Cuba in the region. Despite their ideological differences that have made it difficult to attain consensus, the CARICOM states formal incorporation of the principle of a united international front within the context of an association dedicated to promoting development on a regional scale clearly implied that CARICOM intended to function as a mechanism for initiating and implementing collective bargaining between its members and other states at the global level.

The reduction of Caribbean dependence on external markets was part and parcel of the organization's first two goals, which were primarily oriented toward increasing the prospects of its members to diversify their North-South linkages, and by assisting the efforts of the CARICOM group as a whole to establish solid economic and political ties that extend well beyond their trading partners, particularly Britain and the United States that have traditionally dominated the region. The ultimate goal was to push back as far as possible the constraining socioeconomic and political boundaries within which the CARICOM states must operate. This does not mean a total expulsion of the CARICOM states association with their trading partners, but rather certain aspects of their international economic transactions that took place primarily within the context of a dependency relationship were shifted outside of that framework. This approach, it was argued, would weaken the continued penetration and domination of CARICOM economies by the metropolitan powers, expand their connections with a broad cross section of industrialized countries and, in the end, eradicate or reduce their economic dependence. This line of reasoning was pursued by Demas who explained the possible benefits of diversification.

> Our degree of economic and other forms of effective independence is likely to be increased by a much greater geographical diversification of our trade and economic relationships than is now the case. . . . This issue of geographical (and therefore geopolitical) diversification . . . is fundamental. . . . It literally increases our options and degrees of freedom and can greatly reduce our trade and economic dependence.[32]

Diversification also presented an opportunity for CARICOM members to embrace the principle of collective action and to be able to deal effectively with the more powerful economic blocs created in part by the process and structures of globalization, which have since dominated the international capitalist economy. CARICOM's foreign policy component was conceived as a means for its members to acquire the political will and the bargaining power necessary to renegotiate at least some of the terms of their relationship with the developed countries, especially with Britain and the United States in light of emerging global and regional trading blocs. In addressing this issue Guyana's former president, Desmond Hoyte said,

> a pervasive feature of international relations today is the politics of economic regionalism, which derives from the emergence of powerful economic blocs in the world. . . . I think the inference to be drawn from all these developments is quite clear; we must avoid the temptation of believing that we can act individually even to protect our individual national interests. Huge economic groupings are going to dominate the world economy and there will be no place for countries that try to go it alone. Certainly the member states of CARICOM cannot face the powerful groupings individually. We have to combine our forces to obtain maximum leverage in any negotiations with them.[33]

The institutions of CARICOM are intergovernmental in nature, with none of the aspects of a supranational structure like the European Union (EU). CARICOM's structure is schematically illustrated in figure 3.1. It comprised three principal organs of authority and influence and a number of institutions, associated institutions, regional bodies, agencies, and subsidiary committees. Its principal organs are the Heads of Government Conferences (HGC), the Common Market Council of Ministers, and the Caribbean Community Secretariat (CCS). The HGC have the overall responsibility for the development of the integration movement, the mandate to sign treaties on CARICOM's behalf, and for overseeing relations with other international organizations. It is the highest decision-making body, where each member country has one vote, and unanimity is required to pass binding resolutions. The Council of Ministers is primarily responsible for supervising the operations of the organization and developing agenda items for consideration by the heads of state at their annual meetings. The Caribbean Community Secretariat acts on the authority of member states and the intergovernmental institutions of the Community and the Common Market. It is the principal administrative arm of CARICOM. It operates under the normal rule of international institutions such as the United Nations in that its personnel may neither seek nor accept instructions from any national government and their actions must serve the interest of the Community rather than the parochial concerns of its members.[34] According to Axline, the Secretariat

> has become the most dynamic element in the process of Caribbean integration. Drawing upon the expertise of the Secretariat, studies have been undertaken and policies designed which have provided the basis for inter-governmental negotiations and the adoption of integrative measures. The Secretariat, in fostering an ideology of integration, has provided a communications link among the various forces in the region, including intellectuals, the private sector, and member governments. . . . The Secretariat has also participated in missions to various countries in order to develop support for compromises on the adoption of regional policies. The Secretariat represents the vanguard of the Caribbean integration movement by attempting to build a regional consensus around measures which will constitute an integration scheme likely to contribute to the development of the region.[35]

With the inauguration of CARICOM, most of the governments of the Caribbean leaders had hoped that the integration movement would create the necessary infrastructure for future economic development that would help eliminate the size and limited resources problems which have stifled growth and increased dependency in the modern Caribbean. While coordination has generally been effective on some major regional and international issues, including its participation within the ACP group, the UN, the Organization of American States (OAS), and other international forums, and in relation to specific matters such as the region's relations with Cuba, and Guyana and Belize's territorial conflicts with Venezuela and Guatemala respectively, its efforts to integrate the area's economy met with little success that threatened the very survival of the organization. Some of its problems originated from the bilateral economic arrangements between individual CARICOM states and the developed countries. CARICOM's tariff rules also made it difficult to identify components that were and were not produced in the region, and its loose regulations allowed the promotion of finishing touch industries that reinforced external control and dependence rather than economic growth and development.[36]

Compounding the situation were the severe economic difficulties faced by the countries of the Caribbean which were severely hit with the full force of the international economic crisis following a dramatic increase in the price of petroleum and in the prices of other essential regional imports in 1973 and 1974. This came at a time when CARICOM countries had already begun to experience acute economic difficulties in the form of unprecedented inflationary pressures. The impact of these developments on the economies of the CARICOM states and other non-oil producing developing countries was, with few exceptions, disastrous. Not only did they result in a significant increase in the value of the imports of these states relative to their exports earnings, thereby adversely affecting their terms of trade, but there were also deteriorating balance of payments and government finances. In the early 1980s, imports from outside the region constituted more than 90 per cent of total imports to the CARICOM states. To some extent, the shock of external price increases was cushioned in Trinidad and Tobago as a result of its petroleum and natural gas resources. But economic conditions in Guyana, Jamaica, and the smaller islands had reached alarming proportions in 1977, and by 1978 these countries were in, or had approached a state of, total financial and fiscal bankruptcy due to increased budgetary and balance of payment deficits. The Jamaican government, for example, was forced to introduce a stabilization economic program involving some very austere financial and fiscal measures prescribed by the IMF-World Bank group as a condition of obtaining IMF balance of payment support.

In the wake of their respective economic crises, Guyana and Jamaica had to adjust their economies through import restrictions on both global and CARICOM products as a means of reducing their individual external debt,

Figure 3.1
Institutional Organization of the Caribbean Community

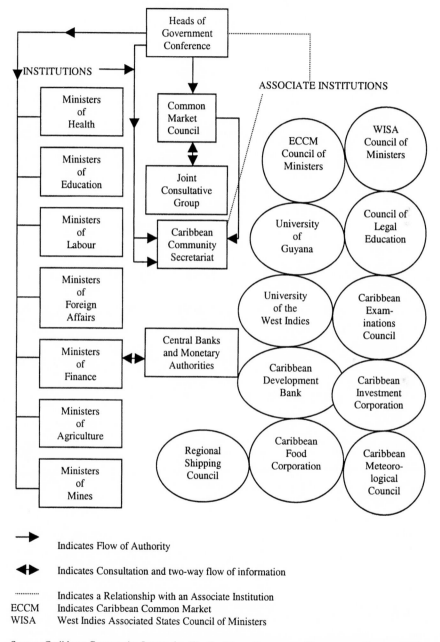

→ Indicates Flow of Authority

◄► Indicates Consultation and two-way flow of information

·········· Indicates a Relationship with an Associate Institution
ECCM   Indicates Caribbean Common Market
WISA   West Indies Associated States Council of Ministers

Source: Caribbean Community Secretariat, *The Caribbean Community* (Georgetown, Guyana: 1973)

a practice that put further strain on the Caribbean integration movement. By the early 1980s Jamaica's imports from CARICOM member countries had been reduced by almost 50 percent while the figure for Guyana was over 60 percent during the same period. The exchange rates of these countries depreciated as their economic difficulties increased, thus forcing them to devalue their currencies. Between 1977 and 1984, the Jamaican dollar fell from U.S. $1.1 to $0.20, and the Guyana dollar decreased from U.S. $0.39 in 1980 to $0.24 in 1984. These developments provoked antagonism throughout the region. Trinidad and Tobago, which suffered a trade deficit in the early 1980s, retaliated by restricting imports from the region into its markets. It, along with Barbados, introduced a system of import licensing which required approval for all foreign exchange, including those within CARICOM as a result of lower oil revenues. To make matters worse, in early 1983, CARICOM's trade system, the Community Multilateral Clearing Facility, collapsed as it reached the $100 million limit to its credit granting powers, with over $90 million indebted to Guyana, which was not repaid because of that country's financial difficulties.[37]

While each of these factors had an adverse effect on intraregional trade, the problem is the continued weakness and vulnerability of the Caribbean economy to external economic adversities and the consequent fragility of integration arrangements, especially the free-trade regime, which has been the hub of the CARICOM treaty. CARICOM's failure to create a regional economy and to control and direct the flow of foreign investment has left the economies of the region unintegrated and in the control of foreign enterprises. Each country still produces what its population does not consume and consumes what it does not produce. Most Caribbean countries have stronger connections to the United States, Britain, and Canada than to each other. Also, CARICOM's industrialization program opened the region's market to penetration by a larger group of foreign investors who benefited immensely from the expanded market, which further entrenched the region's dependent position within the international capitalist economy. Intraregional trade has not increased since the creation of CARICOM. Regional trade as a percent of total trade grew about 3 percent to 11 percent between 1967 and 1973 and then fell by 4 percent of total trade by the mid-1970s. In absolute terms, however, intraregional trade rose from U.S. $47 million in imports in 1967 to approximately U.S. $330 by 1980, but declined by 26 percent between 1981 and 1985, from U.S. $456 to U.S. $335.[38]

In addition, after nearly three decades of regional integration, the less-developed members of CARICOM still lag economically behind the four more developed nations of the region. One reason is that foreign corporate capital flowed to the larger countries, which increased their dominance in regional affairs and the further polarization of the Caribbean. The lack of unity among CARICOM members could not have been demonstrated more clearly than by major events. The first was Prime Minister Eric Williams's, of Trinidad and Tobago, displeasure at the other Caribbean countries' refusal to support the Trinidadian owned British West Indian Airways (BWIA) as the region's principal airline, and his frustration and inability to set up a joint aluminum project with Guyana and Jamaica. The project had involved the building of two aluminum smelters, one in Guyana and the other in Trinidad and Tobago, which was viewed as a major step towards the integration of regional production. The smelters were to use the bauxite resources from Jamaica and Guyana, natural gas from Trinidad and Tobago, and Guyana's hydroelectricity to power the smelters in their respective countries. The project was abandoned when in the midst of a protracted negotiation with Guyana and Jamaica, the Jamaican government announced that it had agreed to supply Venezuela with large quantities of bauxite and aluminum to help increase that country's smelter capacity. A frustrated Williams announced his government's withdrawal from the joint venture in bitter words. "My friends," he said to members of his ruling People's National Movement party at a convention, "one man can only take so much, and I have had enough. To smelt or not to smelt, no big thing as there is no shortage of claims on our natural gas."[39] Williams was even more pessimistic at the future prospects of the Caribbean integration process when he asserted that "it is now clear beyond any possibility of doubt that Caribbean integration will not be achieved in the foreseeable future and that the reality is continued Caribbean disunity and even perhaps the reaffirmation of colonialism."[40]

The second event was when several CARICOM states collaborated with the United States and invaded the tiny island of Grenada in October 1983. The invasion caused tension between Guyana and Trinidad and Tobago, who condemned it, and Jamaica, Barbados, and Dominica, the three U. S. allies in the region, who supported it. For awhile, relations between Jamaica and Barbados and the other two MDCs of the region, Guyana and Trinidad and Tobago, were severely strained by the invasion. The latter two countries felt that Jamaica and Barbados had again demonstrated a greater loyalty to the United States than they had to the Caribbean. Anthony Payne spelled out the ill feelings generated from the invasion.

> [T]he damage done . . . to Caribbean integration was enormous. It was, after all, not only that the region disagreed over what to do in Grenada . . . but that the invading states deliberately connived to conceal their

intentions from their remaining CARICOM partners—Trinidad, Guyana, Belize, and the Bahamas. Unfortunately the other leaders, especially [Trinidad's] George Chambers and Forbes Burnham, the president of Guyana, felt that they had been made to look foolish.[41]

Although this specific incident revolved around ideological and security questions rather than socioeconomic issues that usually dominate the dependency discussion, it clearly illustrates the political ill will that can have a spillover effect into other dimensions of CARICOM relations, thereby making any kind of joint venture in the Caribbean more difficult and the reduction of the region's dependency less attainable. The extent of the division of opinion which the invasion generated in the Commonwealth Caribbean was such that bilateral relations between the region's countries became strained so much so that diplomatic ties between Barbados and Trinidad and Tobago were severed for awhile.

Functional cooperation, despite its success in establishing important new regional institutions, including the Caribbean News Agency (CANA), a regional secondary school examination system, and a technical assistance program to assist the smaller states, was undermined as several countries sought their own services, particularly in air transportation. Also, the Eastern Caribbean governments pursued their own collaborative goals through the ECCM, which officially became the OECS in 1981. As a result of these economic and political differences, the Heads of Government Conferences of CARICOM, normally an annual event, have since the invasion of Grenada carefully avoided discussing any controversial foreign policy issues.

CARICOM is said to have represented a major step forward in regional integration movement and the liberalization of trade in the Caribbean for several reasons. It established a Caribbean common market for the protection of regionally produced goods, a common external tariff, the harmonization of national economic policies in areas such as fiscal incentives to industry, and the development of the region's natural resources. It supported a number of institutions in the region, including the University of the West Indies, the Caribbean Development Bank, the Caribbean Food Corporation marketing and distribution arrangement, and the West Indies Shipping Corporation.[42] It also prepared its member countries to adopt a common position on major international issues and a united front in their dealings with the metropolitan countries which control the international system. This was apparent in their negotiations with the EEC that resulted in several Lome Conventions since 1975.[43]

In spite of these notable achievements, CARICOM has had some major setbacks, both within and outside the region in developing an integrated Caribbean economy. One reason was that interregional trade wars and bilateral alliances with the U.S., Canada, and other developed countries constituted the dog-eat-dog mentality that has characterized CARICOM relations since the early 1980s. Clive Thomas has indicated that "The politics of regional integration has disappeared from the agenda of most Caribbean leaders. It is as if we have forgotten that no single territory can have a future on its own."[44] Second, the worldwide economic crisis in 1974 created a situation which put further strain on the integration movement. Inflation, which was high in 1972 accelerated even more, and the global energy crisis which saw a fourfold increase in the price of oil had severely ruptured the economies of CARICOM states. These developments, combined with the high degree of foreign control of the Caribbean economies and the underdevelopment of agriculture, have served to immobilize CARICOM's efforts to industrialize the region and, in the end, prolonged its dependency on the outside world. Caribbean integration policy must attempt to mitigate the effects of foreign direct investment and the activities of multinational corporations if they are to reduce their external dependence.

Notes

1. W. Andrew Axline, *Caribbean Integration: The Politics of Regionalism* (New York: Nichols, 1979).

2. J. Samuel Valenzuela and Arturo Valenzuela, "Modernization and Dependency: Alternative Perspectives in the Study of Latin American Underdevelopment," in *From Dependency to Development: Strategies to Overcome Underdevelopment and Inequality*, ed. Heraldo Munoz (Boulder, Colo.: Westview Press, 1981), 25.

3. This is historically documented in the Caribbean by Eric Williams, *From Columbus to Castro: The History of the Caribbean 1492-1969* (London: Andre Deutsch, 1970). See also Eric Williams, *Capitalism and Slavery* (Chapel Hill: University of North Carolina Press, 1944).

4. For a comparative view of the development of thinking on this topic in the Caribbean see Norman Girvan, "The Development of Dependency Economics in the Caribbean and Latin America: Review and Comparison," *Social and Economic Studies* 22 (March 1973): 1-33.

5. Alister McIntyre, "Some Issues of Trade Policy in the West Indies," in *Readings in the Political Economy of the Caribbean*, ed. Norman Girvan and Owen Jefferson (Kingston, Jamaica: New World, 1972), 165-83.

6. Axline, *Caribbean Integration,* 8.

7. William G. Demas, *The Economics of Development in Small Countries with Special Reference to the Caribbean* (Montreal: McGill University Press, 1965), 88.

8. Ibid., 88.

9. William G. Demas, "The Political Economy of the English-Speaking Caribbean: A Summary View" (Port of Spain, Trinidad: Caribbean Ecumenical Consultation, Study Paper no. 4, 1971). See also Vernon Mulchansingh, "CARIFTA: New Horizons in the West Indies, University of the West Indies, Department of Geography," Occasional Publications no. 3 (1968).

10. Axline, *Caribbean Integration,* 11.

11. Caribbean Community Secretariat, *The Caribbean Community: A Guide* (Georgetown, Guyana, 1973), 34-36.

12. Anthony Bryan, "The CARICOM and Latin American Integration Experiences: Observations on Theoretical Origins and Comparative Performance," in *Ten Years of CARICOM* (Washington, D.C.: Inter-American Development Bank, 1984), 75.

13. Gordon K. Lewis, *The Growth of the Modern West Indies* (London: Macgibbon and Lee, 1969), 345. See also Clive Y. Thomas, "On Formulating a Marxist Theory of Economic Integration," *Transition* 1, no. 1 (1978): 59-71; Clive Y. Thomas, "Neo-Colonialism and Caribbean Integration," in *Contemporary International Relations in the Caribbean,* ed. B. Ince (Trinidad: University of the West Indies, Institute of International Relations, 1979).

14. R. Greenwood and S. Hamber, *Development and Decolonization* (London: Macmillan, 1980), 87; Isaac Dookhan, *A Post Emancipation History of the West Indies* (London: Collins, 1982).

15. Clive Y. Thomas, *The Poor and the Powerless: Economic Policy and Change in the Caribbean* (New York: Monthly Review Press, 1988; R. Hart, "Trade Unionism in the English-Speaking Caribbean: The Formative Years and the Caribbean Labour Congress," *Contemporary Caribbean: A Sociological Reader,* ed. Susan Craig, Trinidad: vol. 2 (1982).

16. Thomas, *The Poor and the Powerless,* 306.

17. Thomas, "Neo-Colonialism and Caribbean Integration," 285. For a good summary of the origin and disintegration of the West Indies Federation see Thomas 1988; 1979; and H. Michael Erisman, *Pursuing Post Dependency Politics: South-South Relations in the Caribbean* (Boulder, Colo.: Lynne Rienner, 1992).

18. Although they became members of CARIFTA, the Eastern Caribbean states (WISA) continued to pursue their economic activities within the ECCM. Therefore, within the twelve-nation free trade area established by CARIFTA, the seven ECCM states operated as a subregional common market. For details regarding the complex relationships between these various Caribbean groups, see Axline, *Caribbean Integration,* 83-102.

19. Axline, *Caribbean Integration;* Thomas, *The Poor and the Powerless.*

20. Economic Commission for Latin America, "The Impact of the Caribbean Free Trade Association (CARIFTA)," *Economic Bulletin for Latin America*

XV111(1973): 144.

21. Ibid.

22. Sidney E. Chernick, *The Commonwealth Caribbean: The Integration Experience* (Baltimore: Johns Hopkins University Press, 1978), 30.

23. Agreement establishing CARIFTA, Georgetown, Guyana, 1968. Schedule 11 (Appendix of the Treaty) lists the products which were to be treated as having been produced in the Caribbean, irrespective of where they have been actually produced. For more on this discussion, see Thomas, *The Poor and the Powerless*, 312-15.

24. W. G. Demas, "The Caribbean Community and the Caribbean Development Bank," speech delivered at a Seminar on Management in the Caribbean, Port of Spain, Trinidad, December 2, 1975, 5.

25. Thomas, *The Poor and the Powerless*, 307-10.

26. Economic Commission for Latin America, *The Caribbean Integration Programme, 1968-1972*, Port-of-Spain, Trinidad, 1973, 19.

27. Axline, *Caribbean Integration*, 89.

28. Ibid., 89.

29. Lloyd Searwar, "Joint Conduct of External Political Relations and Its Effect on the Integration Process," paper presented to Inter-American Bank Seminar, Barbados, on the theme "Ten Years of Caricom," Washington, D.C.: *Inter-American Development Bank,* 1984.

30. Axline, *Caribbean Integration*, 75.

31. Bryan, "The CARICOM and Latin American Integration," 87.

32. William Demas, " Consolidating Our Independence: The Major Challenge for the West Indies," Lecture Series, University of the West Indies, Institute of International Relations, Trinidad (1986): 23.

33. Desmond Hoyte, "Making the Quantum Leap: Imperatives, Opportunities, and Challenges for CARICOM," *Caribbean Affairs* 2, no. 2 (April-June 1989): 55-56.

34. Axline, *Caribbean Integration*, 77-78; Erisman, *Pursuing Post Dependency Politics*, 74.

35. Axline, *Caribbean Integration*, 78.

36. Thomas, *The Poor and the Powerless*, 315-22.

37. Ibid., 310-13.

38. Ibid., 312.

39. *Trinidad Guardian,* June 16, 1975.

40. Eric Williams's speech to the Fifteenth Annual Convention of the PNM, cited in Thomas, *The Poor and the Powerless*, 323.

41. Anthony Payne, "Whither CARICOM? The Performance and Prospects of Caribbean Integration in the 1980s," *International Journal* 40, no. 2 (Spring 1985): 222.

42. Tom Barry, Beth Wood, and Deb Preusch, *The Other Side of Paradise: Foreign Control in the Caribbean* (New York: Grove, 1984).

43. The roots of first Lome Convention in 1975 can be traced to Britain's

decision in the late 1960s to join the European Community (EC), which has been subsequently renegotiated every five years (Lome II, 1980, Lome III, 1985, Lome IV, 1990, and Lome V, 1995). It provides duty-free access to the EC for practically all ACP goods, as well as commerce, financial, and technical aid and industrial cooperation to ACP member nations. For a full discussion on the Lome agreements, see H. Michael Erisman, *Pursuing Post Dependency Politics,* 91-100.

44. Clive Y. Thomas, *Caribbean Contact* (July 1983).

Chapter 4

International Challenge to Dependency by CARICOM States

The societies that constitute what is called CARICOM were first drawn into the international economic system long before the common usage of such concepts as world economy, underdevelopment, and dependency by social scientists. Christopher Columbus's voyage to the New World at the end of the fifteenth century brought the Caribbean into Europe's orbit as its first over- seas outpost. The European powers colonized the region and transformed its landscapes and populations to produce staples, mainly sugarcane that could not be cultivated in Europe. For the next two-and-a-half centuries (1600-1850), the Caribbean economy was harnessed to produce goods specifically for the metropolitan markets of Europe. Since then, the territories of the Caribbean have been closely linked with the European, and more recently the North American-centered world capitalist system. As a consequence, the economy of the Caribbean has been directly and indirectly affected by the advances and retreats, swings in commodity prices, and the resultant booms and busts that are characteristic of the international capitalist system.

Political independence provided the CARICOM countries with the opportunity to make their own foreign policy. This marked the beginning of a process that was expected to lead to the development of their economies within the international capitalist system. But by the end of the 1960s, no CARICOM member state had possessed in any great measure the attributes generally considered necessary to sustain an active foreign policy over any length of time and none of them had any real power to contest forcefully policies at the international level. The primary reason being their small size and limited natural resources as well as their economic dependence on the Global North countries and the contemporary international economic system.

Indeed, the achievement of political independence was not accompanied by material progress in the Commonwealth Caribbean. The leaders' earliest preoccupations were with political forms of government, external relations, and socioeconomic development. The European colonial powers which, in the postwar era conceded political independence to the CARICOM states except the island of Montserrat, and virtually the entire colonized world quickly joined with the United States and put in place new economic and political institutional structures to ensure their continued global domination, control, and survival of the contemporary international system. Four such institutions, the United Nations, the International Monetary Fund (IMF), the International Bank for Reconstruction and Development (IBRD), and the General Agreement on Tariffs and Trade (GATT) were established in 1944 at the Bretton Woods conference under the aegis of the United States.

The IMF was created ostensibly to manage the global monetary system, but soon changed its role and began providing loans to Latin America and the newly independent countries of Asia, Africa, and the Caribbean in order to help them meet problems regarding budget deficits, balance of payments, and the development of their economies so as to reduce their high levels of unemployment. The IBRD, popularly known as the World Bank, provides development capital in the form of loans to the less developed countries that cannot obtain investment capital from private banks and other sources at reasonable terms. From the very beginning, both institutions were heavily influenced and dominated by the United States who provided about one-third of their funds. The terms of trade created by GATT in the early postwar period continued to favor manufactured goods from the developed nations over primary products and raw materials from the Caribbean and other Global South countries.[1] On the other hand, the United Nations remains an enigma in that its basic principle of sovereign equality is not applied throughout the organization. The developing countries do not have any say in the Security Council, which has veto power over most of the UN's operations.

These global institutions established the liberal framework within which the economies of the Caribbean and the Global South in general, resting on fragile economic and political foundations and locked into a world system hostile to change, were to seek economic development. Most, if not all the leaders of the Caribbean (and the Global South) were aware that the world economic structures established by the United States and the other imperial powers work substantially to the advantage of the developed countries with technological and military superiority and market and financial control. They were also aware that the possibility for a greater share of the world's wealth and prosperity and the reduction of their economic dependence on the core capitalist countries lay in their capacity to align themselves with the other developing countries in order to strengthen their bargaining power and hence restructure the international economic system.

Bargaining power as James Caporaso explains is the power to control the outcome of specific events.[2] The capacity to do this is perhaps the most critical test of whether the Global South countries are in a strong position to negotiate better terms of their relationships with the metropolitan powers to which they are traditionally subordinate. Occasionally, the developing states possess quite an unusual bargaining power at the international realm because the developed nations are strategically dependent on them for raw materials, minerals, and cheap labor for their continued prosperity and future growth.

In practice, however, it has been extremely difficult for the developing countries to capitalize on the weakness of the developed countries. The reason being their small size and limited resources have caused them to be perceived both theoretically and certainly in the eyes of the great powers as objects of control. Thus, the Third World countries' attempt to obtain and exercise bargaining power in a tight military and strategic bipolar world during the Cold War era could not have been easily achieved. Rather, East-West struggle had placed the CARICOM states at the center of great power politics within an international environment that provided political space only for the world's two principal actors—the United States and the former Soviet Union. This situation, however, was not new to the CARICOM states, for they were first placed at the center of great power politics during their long history of colonialism.

CARICOM States at the Center of Great Power Politics

Since the arrival of Columbus in the Caribbean, a number of factors have profoundly influenced the basic configuration and dynamics of the region's various territories' interactions with other areas of the world. The region's long history of colonialism and slavery, its physical fragmentation, the assimilation of peoples of different cultures and from all regions of the world into the Caribbean, and its recent strategic and economic importance to the United States have, in many respects, made it a unique subsystem within the contemporary international system. The Caribbean is unique in that most of its indigenous peoples, the Carib and Arawak Indians, did not survive the brutality and inhumanity of colonialism and slavery due to the genocide, plunder, and unspeakable barbarism that took place in that period. Those who did survive the horror were forcibly placed into servitude by European settlers who not only destroyed their culture and communal way of life, but also the societies and means of production. The European colonizers created new structures exclusively within the colonial matrix, each of which was a product of English, Spanish, French, and Dutch colonizers. The Caribbean uniqueness also stems from the fact that the region constitutes the largest concentration in the world of small underdeveloped and dependent islands and territories that are to a fairly significant degree regionally integrated and have maintained the democratic institutions based on the Westminster model of parliamentary government inherited from Great Britain. In supporting this viewpoint, Jamaica's former prime minister, Edward Seaga, has remarked that "nowhere else in the world, does a conglomeration of parliamentary democracies exist as it does in the Caribbean."[3]

Historically, the West Indies (and the entire Caribbean Basin) have been recognized as one of the major crossroads of the world. The region has long been considered a geographical receptacle in the sense that through it and into it have flowed a variety of goods, food items, technology, cultural influences, people, and ideas from Western Europe, North America, Africa, Latin America, and to a somewhat lesser extent, the Near East and the Far East. The crossroad concept is also derived from the fact that for three centuries (1550-1850), the Caribbean Basin in general, and the CARICOM region in particular, have been the primary objects of intense competition and conflict among the great powers of Europe. At the core of these centuries' old struggle was a wild scramble for Caribbean land and slaves from West Africa, especially for the cultivation of sugar on large plantations which, for the most part, generated enormous wealth for the European organizers. This was illustrated vividly by the Dutch exchange in 1667 of New York City and most of New York state for the sugar producing territory of Suriname.[4] The prosperity of sugarcane cultivation in the Caribbean was also evidenced by the fact that England at one time displayed a willingness to trade Canada to France for the two sugar-rich French islands of Martinique and Guadeloupe. According to Michael Erisman, "the primary function of the plantation societies the European colonial powers established in the Caribbean was, of course, to generate wealth that would be transferred to the home country through a variety of mechanisms."[5] Similarly, in a series of influential works on plantation economies, plantation theorists Lloyd Best (1967, 1968), Lloyd Best and Kari Levitt (1974, 1975), and George Beckford (1972) have argued that the plantation was a highly capitalistic enterprise and its character was such that it created enormous wealth for the metropolitan powers of Europe from the sixteenth to the eighteenth centuries and provided only subsistence living for its inhabitants.

By the middle of the nineteenth century, European preeminence in the Caribbean began to decline and was gradually displaced by the growing power and enormous influence of the United States, who sees the region as being in its backyard.[6] The expansion of the U.S. into the Caribbean region in the early twentieth century was considered part of a global imperialist framework. The European powers, particularly Britain, France, and Germany had, by this time, annexed large parts of Africa and East Asia that were not as yet colonized. After the Spanish-American War of 1898, the United States stood alone as the supreme and hegemonic imperial power in the Caribbean in the presence of a number of small European colonies that were devastated by intracontinental wars. The war was said to have marked the beginning of a new United States imperialism that led to the expansion of U.S. power not only in the Caribbean, but also in the Pacific region, notably Guam, the Philippines, and Hawaii.

These acts placed the territories of the Caribbean at the center of great power politics and rivalry and was also part of the United States effort to buttress its economic interests in the region with military force because of Germany's imperial designs to annex parts of Latin America and the Caribbean during the First World War.[7] Robert Gilpin asserts that U. S. expansion in the Caribbean region was in some ways part of the British accommodation with its former rivals in other parts of the world, not only the Americans in the Caribbean, but also the Japanese in the northern Pacific region, and the French in the Mediterranean, in order to allow Britain to counter the growing German military threat in Eastern and Central Europe.[8]

This approach to U.S. policy toward Latin America and the Caribbean dates back to the Monroe Doctrine of 1823 when the United States warned the European powers, then in the full flood of their imperialist expansion, to stay out of the American continent. It also assured the European powers that it will not interfere in their or the Latin American countries internal affairs. The Monroe Doctrine was essentially a blend of national self-interest, a realistic recognition of the status quo, and a declaration of U. S. economic and political interest in the region. The doctrine is one of the earliest and most explicit declarations of hegemonic intent, later to become the sphere of influence politics in twentieth-century Cold War struggle. Although it speaks of the acceptance of the status quo and clearly indicates an intent not to interfere in the affairs of countries, it, however, provided the rationale for countless interventions by the United States into the affairs of several Latin American and Caribbean countries, most notably Mexico, Columbia, ending with the creation of Panama and the Panama Canal, Cuba, Nicaragua, Haiti, Honduras, the Dominican Republic, Chile, Panama, and Grenada during the rest of the nineteenth and twentieth centuries. Despite being a latecomer to the struggle for Caribbean influence, the United States had, at the turn of the twentieth century, developed substantial economic, political, and strategic interests in the region. Efforts by the U.S. to control these interests and to prevent the spread of communism in the area intensified during the height of the Cold War and have placed the Caribbean at the center of great power politics between the superpowers.

Economic Interests

Economically, U.S. interest in the Caribbean revolved around markets for its products, the extraction of the region's natural resources by U.S. corporations, and the U.S. reliance on the region for key primary products. Since the early 1950s, U.S. private investment in the Caribbean, which stood $1.526 billion displaced British investment at $637 million, and Canadian investment at $431 million.[9] The bulk of U.S. financial investments were in the mining sector, such as petroleum in Trinidad and Tobago, and bauxite in Guyana and Jamaica, while British investments were concentrated mostly in the agricultural sector. The list of U.S. enterprises operating in the region at the time includes over 800 corporations, compared with only eighty-five British companies.[10] During the 1970s, the number of foreign-owned companies in the region actually declined as some of them were nationalized by various Caribbean governments

The Caribbean is also the fourth largest market for U.S. products, after Canada, Japan, and the European Union, accounting for 14 percent and 11 percent respectively of its exports to and imports from the region.[11] Almost 85 percent of its bauxite imports and 70 percent of its petroleum, the two resources that are strategically vital to the economic prosperity of the United States, come from the Caribbean. In addition, the region's refineries account nearly for 83 percent of residual fuel imports to the U.S. In peacetime, 44 percent of total foreign cargo and 45 percent of all crude oil imports to the United States cross the Caribbean Sea.[12] Besides, there are reserves of other less strategic resources, such as nickel, cobalt, manganese, and gold that are important to the U.S. market. The availability of these minerals and products so close to the U.S. mainland is undoubtedly a convenience that has made the Caribbean a magnet for U.S. private investment which, over the years, has yielded tremendous profits for its multinational corporations. Data obtained by Carl Stone have revealed that the total outflow of profits as a percentage of total U.S. foreign private investment inflows in the four largest Caribbean countries between 1973 and 1977 ranged from 55 percent in Barbados to 340 percent in Guyana and Jamaica respectively, with 200 percent for Trinidad and Tobago.[13] Stone's data are consistent with the claims made by many Caribbean and Third World social scientists that the profit margins for foreign investors in the Caribbean tend to be extremely high and at times exorbitant.

Strategic Interests

Strategically, in the eyes of many American policy makers and analysts, the Caribbean Basin constitutes the vulnerable southern flank of the land mass of the United States. Its proximity to the United States mainland, its major underwater lines of communication and surveillance facilities in the Eastern Caribbean sea, and its vital maritime route for a whole range of valuable raw materials and commodities coming to the U.S. from the region as well as for all sea vessels passing through the Panama Canal, have placed the Caribbean in a strategic position in U.S. security interest. The U.S. must be guaranteed access to the region's raw materials, trade and investment opportunities, the production of crude oil in Mexico and Venezuela, and transportation routes not only to protect its security interests and communications lines with its North Atlantic allies, but also to ensure its continued prosperity and global superpower status.[14] For example, the U.S. Navy's Atlantic Undersea Test and Evaluation facilities in the Bahamas are crucial to the development of American antisubmarine warfare capabilities.

Although it can be argued that the advent of nuclear weapons has made the Caribbean and other areas of the world less strategic, militarily, the region is still important to the United States because of its military bases in Puerto Rico, Guantánamo Bay, and its deepwater passage to Europe. In a protracted conventional conflict, it is estimated that 50 percent of all NATO supplies would cross the Caribbean Sea, and a large portion of the United States troop reinforcements will use the gulf ports in the region en route to Europe. On the basis of these factors the Caribbean Basin has been accorded top strategic and military priority within the context of U.S. strategic and security interest and as a function of its hemispheric hegemony and its superpower status.[15] To quote Sheila Harden:

> Put at its most extreme, one element of nuclear strategy envisages an East-West war beginning with a land battle of limited duration in Europe. It is argued that if such a land battle is to remain non-nuclear for an acceptable period, then material and supplies must be able to pass swiftly and unimpeded from the United States through the deep water channels between the Caribbean islands to Europe.[16]

Political Interests

U.S. political interests in the Caribbean continue to be linked to the fact that it possessed two semi-colonies in the region, Puerto Rico and the U.S. Virgin Islands, but extended well beyond this consideration to a concern with the political direction of the entire region and the Western hemisphere. Since the proclamation of the Monroe Doctrine, the U.S. has regarded itself as the leader of the Western Hemisphere, and was viewed as such by other world powers. Its great power status is, to a large degree, dependent upon its ability to maintain and demonstrate control over the region. This, in effect, involved compliance from the region's political elite.[17]

During the Cold War, it was assumed in Washington that any weakening of U.S. political control in the Caribbean and Latin America would have reduced the Soviet's perception of U.S. strength, weakened U.S. leadership among its allies in Asia, Europe, and in NATO, and seriously undermined its credibility among developing nations. On this basis, several administrations have interfered in the internal political affairs of almost all the countries of the Caribbean in order to maintain the U.S. status, both as a hegemon and a superpower, and to prevent the spread of communism in the region. The U.S. government was also preoccupied in securing and promoting pro-American governments in the Caribbean, which could then be viewed as political stability in the region. In times of conflict or crisis, the United States has intervened, militarily and by other means in the region in order to ensure the outcome it desired.[18] Thus, the presence of the communist regime in Cuba, just ninety miles from the tip of the Florida coast, is still viewed by the U.S. as an undeniable and highly visible breach of hemispheric solidarity. Ever since Fidel Castro and his July 26 movement seized power in Cuba on January 1, 1959, every U.S. president, from John Kennedy to Bill Clinton, has either increased or maintained the level of U.S. economic and diplomatic sanctions against the communist regime. To the extent that the United States seems unable to protect its interests in the Caribbean region, the credibility of its commitments elsewhere, and its status as the only global superpower may erode. J. Agnew has argued that the Caribbean region's peripheral status had been reinforced as it became an economic appendage to the newly emerging core economy of the United States in the post-World War II era.[19]

The incorporation of the Caribbean into the U.S.-Soviet superpower rivalry came at a time when all of the territories of the region were in dire economic straits as they remained fragmented and heavily dependent on the United States and the international capitalist system it sponsored. Since then the Caribbean has suffered further identity problems as it continued to live in the superpower shadow of its giant northern neighbor. These factors, along with the intense ideological confrontation as manifested by the global Cold War, the Cuban missile crisis, and the adoption of socialist-oriented policies by the Caribbean left, brought the region directly under U.S. dominance and at the crossroad of superpower politics during the 1970s. The end result of this and other struggles in the region has always been the same, that is, the Caribbean countries have and continue to be objects of foreign domination, and the region's history has, to a great extent, consequently been written in terms of its incorporation, first into the various European colonial empires, and second, into the United States sphere of influence. This legacy has had a profound impact on current perceptions concerning the basic dynamics of the relationship between CARICOM members and other countries as well as their international relations with the developed countries.

In spite of being at the center of great power politics, the CARICOM states, in contrast to many other Global South countries, have often managed to achieve some degree of cooperation in their foreign policies, which have bestowed upon the region a distinct international character. This represents a rather rare phenomenon of a concrete example of small developing nations attempting to influence and if possible change the structure and dynamics of the existing international economic order. The newly independent countries of the Global South have progressively argued that they were born into an international system with rules they had no voice in creating. According to Paul Sutton, the Commonwealth Caribbean

> has been defined from without as a collective unit at the same time as a collective self-identity has developed from within, the one fortuitously reinforcing the other in respect of the pursuit of tangible interests in the international system. This has established a presence for the region in international politics in the 1980s which it did not possess in 1970 and which in the future it may be hoped to yield economic returns so far denied.[20]

Although political will and shared visions have, at least, proven in the past to be indispensable elements of success, the CARICOM countries must confront the problem that their small size and limited resource base have translated into high levels of external dependency and vulnerability whereby they are highly likely to be adversely affected by changes within the general structure of their external ties. In these circumstances, their dealings with the more developed countries could result in a zero-sum game in which all the significant benefits are monopolized by a few rich and powerful states. Such asymmetrical relationships, which cannot always be avoided in today's global interdependence, continue to threaten the viability and survival of small Third World countries such as those in the Caribbean within the general framework of the international system. The point to be made here is that within an asymmetrical relationship, the economically dominant country can extract favorable foreign policy concessions from its dependent economic partner by virtue of the power levers it has at its disposal.

Viability of CARICOM States

Individually or collectively, the CARICOM states are indeed small by international standards and norms as reflected in the population data in table 4.1. Defined in terms of physical area, population, or both, most small countries are generally weak both militarily and economically or are not considered as viable entities within the contemporary international system; the exceptional cases are demonstrated by the experiences of such small states as Norway,

Table 4.1
Classification of States by Population

Population	Group	Category
Under 100,000	A	Micro States
100,000–500,000	B	Mini States
500,000 –1 million	C	Small States
1–5 million	D	Small to Medium States
5–25 million	E	Medium States
25–50 million	F	Medium to Large States
50–100 million	G	Large States
100–200 million	H	Extra Large States
200 million +	I	Super Large States

Israel, Luxembourg, and Singapore, to name a few. However, as shown in table 4.2, in the CARICOM region there exists not just small states but also mini- and microstates, the exception being Guyana, Jamaica, and Trinidad and Tobago. The CARICOM states' small size and meagre populations have produced such inherent liabilities as the lack of a local market capable of supporting a modern, diversified domestic economy and very high per capita costs for public services and the development or maintenance of a viable socioeconomic infrastructure. Most of the small countries do not have the financial resource base or technology to attract and retain high-quality administrators, managers, engineers, and other skilled personnel from other countries, particularly from the developed ones. In fact, there continues to be high migration levels of some of the most healthy and highly qualified West Indians to the United States, Canada, and Britain. Burton Benedict has studied migration flows from developing to developed countries and has pithily remarked that the lack of economic opportunities in developing states, increased demand for manufactured goods, the spread of education resulting in higher economic and social aspirations, rapid increases in population growth rates, and the increase of information about opportunities and excitement in the developed countries have all been factors inducing emigration from small territories such as those in the Caribbean to the industrialized countries. Most of the migrants are in their twenties and thirties, usually drawn from the working population, and are often the most healthy and qualified.[21] This has over the years seriously affected the development or lack thereof in the Caribbean and other small developing countries.

Compounding the situation is the fact that most CARICOM states are not particularly well endowed with the type of natural resources that today are normally considered by economists of diverse persuasions to have a high development potential in a globalized world economy. The only exceptions are Guyana and Jamaica, which are major producers of sugar and high grade bauxite-alumina, and Trinidad and Tobago, which has significant reserves of oil and natural gas. During the 1970s, however, both Guyana and Jamaica suffered serious economic and financial problems partly because of their socialist-oriented development strategies, which led to overspending and mismanagement in the public sector, the steep drop in the price of bauxite-alumina, sugar, and other raw products, and the dramatic rise in the price of crude oil and manufactured goods on the world market. Similar economic and financial problems were also encountered by Trinidad and Tobago in the 1980s when the price of petroleum fell significantly on the world market.

As evident in their track record dating back to colonialism and more recently, since their attainment of political independence, the CARICOM states' size and resource problems have placed a powerful and independent constraint on their socioeconomic and political decision-making processes, which continue to adversely affect their economic growth and development within the existing international economic system. The consequence is that the economies of the Caribbean have remained highly dependent on the outside world for capital and technology. However, the CARICOM countries are not alone in this unfortunate situation. In his book, *Small States in World Markets,* Peter Katzenstein contends that several small European countries have faced similar problems like those experienced by CARICOM member states in their dealings with the international system.

> The import dependence of the small European states makes them . . . open to influences from the international economy. . . . This dependence, both on the import of modern investment goods and the export of more traditional consumer goods, reinforces imbalances in the economic structures of the small European states. For the small European states, economic change is a fact of life. They have not chosen it, it is thrust upon them. These states, because of their small size, are very dependent on world markets.[22]

The problems derived from small size and limited resources have raised several questions concerning the actual long-term survival of the CARICOM states and other small Global South countries. Will they continue to bear the scars associated with foreign control, domination, and dependency of their economic and political systems? Contrary to Naipaul's characterization of the Caribbean as the Third World's third world, the socioeconomic picture of the CARICOM states is not that bleak as compared with other developing countries. Measured by certain global life quality indices, living standards and the quality of life in general are much higher in the Caribbean than in many other developing countries, and they are not as underdeveloped as their Caribbean neighbor, Haiti, which is the poorest and the least developed country in the Western hemisphere. In particular, the figures on literary rates, life spans, immunization against deadly diseases, and infant mortality attest to the fact that the educational and health care services available in the Caribbean surpass Third World standards. Moreover, population growth rates in the region are not rising as fast as in other Global South countries and the per capita income figures for several CARICOM countries are also fairly good. For example, in the Bahamas the per capita income during the 1980s was U.S. $11,036; Barbados, $5,965; Trinidad and Tobago, $3,183; and Jamaica, $1,103. The data clearly indicate that the overall living standards in the CARICOM countries are relatively higher than in almost all of Africa and most of Asia, where the average annual income is approximately U.S. $1,000.[23]

But beyond these high performance areas there exist serious weaknesses in the region's economy and production infrastructures. The data in table 4.3 show more than half of the CARICOM countries have experienced zero or negative real per capita growth rates during the 1970s and the situation did not improve in the 1980s or in the 1990s and beyond. Beset by drastic price reductions in international markets for their commodity exports and increased costs for manufactured goods as well as cost to cover their trade and budget deficits, the economies of most CARICOM countries floundered as their productivity declined, aggravated by double digit inflation and chronic unemployment and underemployment rates that were at times as high as 40 to 50 percent.[24] With the exception of Trinidad and Tobago[25] and a few other CARICOM states for which data is not available, all the other anglophone Caribbean countries had a deficit on their current accounts between 1972 and 1982 (see table 4.4). This actually limited the CARICOM states' ability to respond individually or collectively to international issues, such as the North-South dimensions of the region's relations in which underdevelopment and dependency have emerged as major concerns, but were often ignored or deemed unimportant by the developed and more powerful nations of the Global North.

This approach is consistent with the realist school of thought as well as proponents of the Cold War whose goal was to make a clear distinction between high politics (military and security related issues) and low politics (internationally linked aspects of social and economic development), with the former generally being viewed as dominating or structuring the overall environment in which the latter operates. As a result, Caribbean dependency and other social welfare issues that generally fall into the second category represented low priority items in the realist power politics approach to international relations in the Caribbean and elsewhere during the Cold War period. The realist scenario to Cold War politics, which has been embraced by many scholars and analysts of foreign policy, provides little in the way of encouragement to the small CARICOM countries, who like their counterparts elsewhere continue to be the inevitable victims of the global hierarchy of nations created by power differentials between the superpowers, both of whom were locked in a major power struggle for global preeminence during the Cold War. Their primary goal was to tip the balance of global power decisively in one or the other's favor almost at any cost. Thus the interests of CARICOM and other Global South countries were marginalized during this period.

Unlike some other countries in the Global South, particularly those in Asia and Africa that were able to capitalize on the paranoia of the United States and the former Soviet Union to draw as many countries as possible into their respective sphere of influence during the Cold War period, the CARICOM states were not as fortunate to play one superpower against the other. Rather, they fell victim to the classic Cold War conflict or high politics, with some similarities to the historical dynamics that propelled them into great power politics by the European powers over centuries ago. Since the early nineteenth century, the United States has always considered the Caribbean Basin vital to its security interests whereby it could enforce its law, its concept of acceptable socioeconomic and political order, and its code of international conduct on the countries of the Caribbean. This was particularly true of the Soviet Union, who did not tolerate any challenges to

Table 4.2
Grouping of CARICOM States

Group	Countries	Population	Population (per square mile)	Area (square miles)
A	Montserrat	12,467	275	40
	St. Kitts-Nevis	53,157	510	103
	Antigua-Barbuda	75,726	441	170
	Dominica	84,854	286	290
	Grenada	97,135	857	133
B	St. Vincent	126,646	840	250
	St. Lucia	153,646	521	238
	Belize	219,737	7	8,867
	Bahamas	246,491	46	4,404
	Barbados	262,688	1,657	166
C	Guyana	797,649	4	83,000
D	Trinidad & Tobago	1,334,639	465	1,980
	Jamaica	2,441,396	521	4,244

Source: *World Fact Book*, Electronic version, Washington, D.C., 1990.

Table 4.3
Annual Real Per Capita Rate of Change
in CARICOM States 1970-1979

Countries	GNP
Antigua-Barbuda	-2.6
Bahamas	-4.7
Barbados	2.1
Belize	4.1
Dominica	-3.2
Grenada	-2.3
Guyana	0.0
Jamaica	-3.7
Montserrat	3.8
St. Kitts-Nevis	1.3
St. Lucia	2.8
St. Vincent	-1.7
Trinidad and Tobago	4.5

Source: *World Bank Atlas*, Washington, D.C., 1982, 20

Table 4.4
Balance on Current Account of CARICOM States (U.S. millions)

Country	1972	1974	1976	1978	1980	1982
Antigua-Barbuda	–	–	-1.0	-2.00	-22.90	-42.40
Bahamas	n/a	n/a	-0.8	-1.35	-4.76	-11.30
Barbados	-43.3	-47.8	-64.20	-31.30	-25.70	-35.60
Belize	n/a	-0.5	-1.10	-1.90	-3.20	-9.78
Dominica	–	–	-1.10	-1.30	-14.70	-7.65
Grenada	–	-0.2	-0.27	0.30	-0.64	-16.77
Guyana	-16.3	-10.7	-142.80	-29.60	-127.80	-142.40
Jamaica	-196.7	-91.9	-302.60	-50.00	-166.00	-403.40
Montserrat*	n/a	n/a	n/a	n/a	n/a	n/a
St. Kitts-Nevis*	n/a	n/a	n/a	n/a	n/a	n/a
St. Lucia	–	-3.6	-5.40	-23.00	-33.10	-24.09
St. Vincent	–	-1.1	-2.20	2.70	-5.10	-6.30
Trinidad-Tobago	-123.9	266.3	255.40	42.70	397.00	283.00

Source: *International Financial Statistics Yearbook*, Washington, D.C., 1984
*Data Not Available

its authority, especially in areas it considered critical to its national security interests as epitomized by its 1956 Hungarian and 1968 Czechoslovakian interventions.

The superpowers' dominance of the international system made it very difficult for countries located in an area considered by one of them to fall within its sphere of influence to pursue their own independent foreign policy agendas. The unrelenting pressure applied to some CARICOM countries over the years by various U.S. administrations to conform to the dictates of Washington has limited them from developing an effective foreign policy to influence the structure and dynamics, not only of their regional subsystem, but also the international system as a whole. The recent military interventions in Grenada in October 1983 and in Panama in December 1989 by the Reagan and Bush administrations respectively are two of the many blatant cases of such strong arm tactics by the United States. These constraints have had a profound and negative impact on the region's international relations, particularly with countries other than their traditional metropolitan partners.

Individually, the CARICOM countries have not been successful in their attempts to acquire and exercise bargaining power in the global system or to pursue policies at the international level aimed at overcoming or reducing their high dependence on the developed countries. At one time, regional integration of the Caribbean which seemed to have been the ideal solution to the region's small size and limited resources has failed to achieve a truly integrated and less dependent regional economy. To overcome this problem, the CARICOM countries, particularly Guyana, Jamaica, and Trinidad and Tobago expanded their relations to large multilateral organizations such as the Non-aligned Movement (NAM) and the Group of 77 (G-77). These two organizations provided a credible capacity for joint diplomatic and political action and original responses to the peculiar situation of small and weak countries in international politics. Because of these movements the CARICOM countries were able to increase their bargaining power and evolve their foreign policy goals toward a shared Third World critique of the structures of the existing international economic order, economic disparities between North and South, and the dependency of the latter on the former.

CARICOM's Role in the NAM

In 1955, twenty-nine independent Asian and African countries met in the Indonesian resort city of Bandung to formulate a strategy to end colonialism. Six years later, the leaders of twenty-five of the twenty-nine states assembled in Belgrade, Yugoslavia, and created the Non-Aligned Movement (NAM), a political coalition whose membership increased to over 125 countries by the early 1980s. Their goal was to avoid entrapment in Cold War politics, promote Third World unity, and to reject the idea that they had to be associated with either superpower in the East-West conflict. Instead, the members of the NAM embraced the principle of non-alignment, which stressed sovereign equality, economic development, decolonization, and a distinctive Third World political identity. As part of that identity, the Global South countries would not be passively neutral in international affairs but would become active in their own independent way in a bipolar zero-sum contest. The NAM was also committed to the broad principles of global peace and Third World solidarity on various international issues, including the establishment of a new international economic order.

By the early 1970s, the NAM broadened its focus to include such issues as poverty, underdevelopment, and the growing economic dependence of the newly independent countries of the Global South on the Global North. This provided an augur for future protests against their subordinate status in the international system. For over a decade the coalition of more than 100 states has argued that the structure of the current international economic order perpetuated underdevelopment and dependency in Third World countries, inhibiting their development and causing them to become poorer. As one Third World spokesperson put it: "A poverty curtain has descended right across the face of the world, dividing it materially and philosophically into two different worlds, two separate planets, two unequal humanities—one embarrassingly rich and the other desperately poor."[26] This belief grew out of the basic assumption that the present international economic system is amoral because it emerged from a history of colonialism and imperialist domination and that its essential features had been consolidated at a time when most of the Global South countries were adjuncts of the developed world. The inequities of the contemporary international system and the need for radical and fundamental changes in its basic structure were intensified by the rapid changes in the global economy during the 1970s, especially with the devaluation of the American dollar in 1971 which subsequently resulted in the virtual collapse of the Bretton Woods system, and the global economic recession.

These difficulties were compounded by high levels of unemployment and spiralling inflation both of which contributed to significant increases in the price of essential food supplies and manufactured products. The conventional economic wisdom based on Keynesian economic principles which had sustained the postwar international economic system had never experienced such a rapid succession of changes and thus seemed incapable of explaining this new economic activity in a period of crisis. This has not only impacted the economies of the Caribbean but also the non-oil-producing Third World nations, and contributed to a significant increase in the value of their imports relative to their export earnings and their external debt.

Frustrated by their inability to reduce their dependence on the developed countries and to develop their economies within the established rules and structures of the international economic order, some CARICOM countries became increasingly committed to the NAM in their search for alternatives. This was exemplified by their extensive participation in the NAM, especially during the 1973 summit held in Algiers which in many respects represented a response to their efforts to rid themselves from the triple evils of poverty, underdevelopment, and dependency.

The basic administrative structure of the NAM is shown in figure 4.1. Its most important event is its summit conference of heads of state which occurs once every three years and is usually attended by most of its prominent members. The NAM's routine work occurs within the framework of the foreign ministers' conferences and its Coordinating Bureau. The foreign ministers of all member states would meet prior to every summit to set the agenda and to finalize the details of specific resolutions for discussion by the non-aligned leaders. Participants of the Coordinating Bureau are chosen to serve three-year terms on the basis of their geographical location whereby approximately 48 percent of the seats are allocated to Africa, 32 percent to Asia, 16 percent to Latin America, and 4 percent to Europe.[27]

As indicated in table 4.5 there was little participation by the CARICOM countries in the NAM during the 1960s. The reason being most of them were preoccupied with attaining political independence or establishing regional organizations to strengthen intra-Caribbean trade and cooperation as a means of eradicating their dependency on extra-regional powers. The focus on regional integration was therefore understandable and quite natural for most small nations, such as those in the Caribbean not to become heavily involved in the larger arenas until some degree of regional cohesion has been achieved. This approach is consistent with the CARICOM and other small Third World states whose small size and limited resource problems often placed them in a potentially disadvantageous position as individual actors on the international scene.

As early as 1970, Guyana and Jamaica, and to a somewhat lesser extent, Trinidad and Tobago, became active participants in non-aligned affairs. Their objective was to broaden the economic dimensions of the Caribbean and to intensify the North-South issue, both of which were directly related to the region's dependent and subordinate status in international politics. By joining the NAM, the CARICOM countries sought economic and political collaboration with other Global South nations in order to acquire some input in effecting changes in the existing international economic order. Most of the leaders of the English-speaking Caribbean viewed economic development in the region as inextricably linked to that of other Global South countries, and that the region's commitment to diversify its economic relations could reduce its dependence on the metropolitan powers. This was premised on the ideals of self-reliance and sovereignty, two of the founding principles of the Non-Aligned Movement. The theme of self-reliance was prominently associated with Tanzania's Julius Nyerere's implied strategy of autonomous socialist development free of foreign capital and superpower influence. This approach was based on direct Global South initiatives to reclaim control over their own resources and to exercise complete sovereignty in the economic realm. The essential idea behind self-reliance, in other words, is to capitalize on and enhance the collective capabilities of the developing countries to

Figure 4.1
Organizational Structure of the Non-Aligned Movement

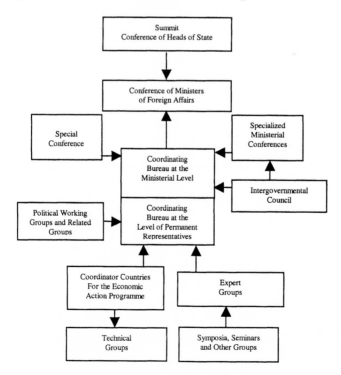

Table 4.5
CARICOM States in the Non-Aligned Movement

Year	Summit	Full Members	Permanent Observers
1961	Belgrade Summit	0	0
1964	Cairo Summit	0	Jamaica Trinidad and Tobago
1970	Lusaka Summit	Guyana Jamaica Trinidad and Tobago	Barbados
1973	Algiers Summit	Guyana Jamaica Trinidad and Tobago	Barbados Grenada
1976	Colombo Summit*	Guyana Jamaica Trinidad and Tobago	Barbados Grenada
1979	Havana Summit*	Grenada Guyana Jamaica Trinidad and Tobago	Barbados Dominica St. Lucia
1983	New Delhi Summit	Bahamas Barbados Belize Grenada Guyana Jamaica St. Lucia Trinidad and Tobago	Antigua and Barbuda Dominica

Sources: Richard L. Jackson, *The Nonaligned, the U.N., and the Superpowers* (New York: Praeger, 1983, 279-83); Odette Jankowitsch and Karl P. Sauvant, "The Initiating Role of the Nonaligned Countries" in *Changing Priorities on the International Agenda: The New International Economic Order,* ed. Karl Sauvant (New York: Pergamon, 1981, 44-48). *Belize was given special consultive status.

overcome the specific deficiencies of the others and vice versa. Collective self-reliance also focused on the bargaining power of peripheral societies in pursuit of a common agenda in their negotiations with the core countries. The creation of the NAM provided the basis for collective self-reliance and for neutrality among the countries of the South. It was considered as a third force in world affairs to enable the CARICOM and other Global South countries to avoid choosing between the East and the West (that is, between communism and capitalism) because of the deep-rooted fear that one form of superpower domination might simply be replaced by another. From this perspective, the NAM was established as a vehicle to allow the Global South countries to remain neutral in the East-West conflict and to acquire the bargaining power required to sustain their effective sovereignty within the international order.[28] In Manley's own words:

> People in the West are put in a position where they are pressured to choose between one system or the other, between God and the Devil . . . economic, financial, technological, political and psychological—pressure is maintained on developing countries, particularly in the Western hemisphere, to choose. Not to be with the West is to be against God. To be with the East could certainly reveal an alignment with the Devil . . . most Third World people do not wish to be with either the West or East for a variety of reasons. To have to be with one or the other might involve a surrender of the very sovereignty, which had been missing for so long and struggled for so hard.[29]

He was convinced of the necessity for the Third World to find a new path of development that would reflect the cultural pattern and historical experience, and the need and expectations of the masses in the region. He was strongly against the imperialist forces, which he claimed have reduced two-thirds of humankind to a peripheral status in political, economic, and even in social terms. It did not make sense to Manley and many other Third World leaders to remain part of the very system that not only conquered, enslaved, traded, and exploited the peoples of the Global South, but even now nurtured the deformities from which they continued to suffer. Manley believed that the NAM presented the best political hope for the development of a third force in world affairs to end the degree, the scale, the ruthlessness, and the completeness of economic exploitation and dependency which bear the scars of this imperialism. It is only through united action that the Global South countries can aspire to reduce their dependence, create economic viability, and give true meaning to their political independence. Neither capitalism, which has been the experience of all citizens of the Global South nor communism in the Marxist-Leninist tradition, which developed in Russia and spread to Eastern Europe and China, had offered any prospect of real economic progress to the developing countries.[30]

This was the rationale for CARICOM's presence in the NAM, which was felt in a major way when all of its members except Montserrat (which is still not an independent state and was not eligible to join) became full members or permanent observers of the movement at the time of the New Delhi Summit in 1983 (see table 4.5). Prior to and during this period, both Guyana and Jamaica articulated policies in support of the NAM and in defending the interest of the Third World in general and the Caribbean region in particular.

Guyana's Role in the NAM

Guyana's entry into the NAM during the height of the East-West tension was motivated by a number of factors, including the desire to remain truly independent and to join in solidarity with its CARICOM and Global South counterparts to develop a common economic strategy based on collective self-reliance and sovereignty to improve their economies and control their own resources. Its goal was to change the dependent pattern of integration of the economies of the CARICOM and other Third World countries in the international economic system and to help build an economic power base in order to substantially reduce CARICOM and the Global South's dependence on the industrialized countries of the Global North. The non-aligned countries were predominantly producers of raw materials and, with the exception of OPEC members, have traditionally been at the mercy of the industrialized capitalist countries and international institutions such as GATT, now the World Trade Organization (WTO), to sell their products on the world market at reasonable prices. On the political front, Guyana had envisioned a Third World collaboration that would lead to the strengthening of South-South cooperation and increased the South's bargaining position vis-à-vis the developed countries. Guyana's leader Forbes Burnham has remarked that meaningful cooperation between the CARICOM states and members of the non-aligned movement at various levels, specifically through the creation of international producer cartels such as OPEC and the International Bauxite Association (IBA), is meant to strengthen their bargaining position in their dealings with the developed countries. He cited CARICOM's successful participation in various Lomé negotiations as an example of the region's bargaining power vis-à-vis the members of the

European Union (EU). He claimed that the NAM was not hostile to the major powers; rather it sought to mobilize its members in their own political and economic interests.[31] In outlining the reasons for Guyana's membership in the NAM, Burnham said:

> [O]ur central philosophy of self-reliance and our dedication to self-reliance . . . largely inspires our membership of the Non-Aligned Movement and the role we are playing therein. Like our colleagues in that Movement, we want to be truly independent, politically and economically, like them we do not want to be pawns in the game between the major powers and blocs; like them we reject satellite status, like them we aim at owning, controlling and developing our resources for our own benefit.[32]

The fundamental idea behind the concept of self-reliance advocated by Guyana was based on more balanced growth which will serve to satisfy the basic socioeconomic needs of the poor in the Global South, the eradication of the existing inequitable patterns of core-periphery relations, the vertical diversification of trade toward the modern countries in Eastern Europe, and horizontally toward other developing nations. This multilateral approach has become the norm of most Global South countries seeking a solution to their economic dependence on the core capitalist countries.

Soon after becoming a member of the NAM in 1969, Guyana assumed a high profile when it obtained a seat on the Coordinating Bureau and more so when it hosted the Foreign Ministers' Conference in 1972. The Bureau is one of the organization's primary nerve centers in that it is responsible for monitoring the work of those countries that coordinated the various aspects of the movement's Action Programme for Economic Cooperation, which grew out of the 1972 Foreign Ministers' Conference in Guyana. It emphasized cooperation and self-reliance both in and among developing countries, [33] and denounced the practices and activities of multinational corporations that have violated the sovereignty of Third World countries, and characterized economic threats and pressure by these corporations as an act of aggression against the developing countries.[34] The spirit of self-reliance was expressed by several leaders of the non-aligned movement:

> Non-aligned countries emphatically affirm that the complete exercise of permanent sovereignty over their natural resources and the direct control of strategic economic activities . . . are vital to economic independence. They . . . agree to grant their un-stinging support to other developing countries which are struggling for the full and effective control of their natural resources and those strategic economic activities under foreign control.[35]

At the Foreign Ministers' Conference, Guyana was appointed to serve as the principal coordinator country in the critical areas of trade, transportation, and industry. In this capacity, Guyana emerged as the leading advocate of Third World unity and economic cooperation not only within the NAM, but in other international forums, such as the UN and the Group of 77, where it took a radical position against imperialism and the existing international economic system. Guyana's overall political orientation at the conference reflected the influence of the non-aligned radicals. By maintaining its seat in the bureau, Guyana was able to exercise influence over a wide range of functional areas, including the promotion of trade and economic cooperation among developing countries.[36] It mounted a vigorous campaign against the core capitalist countries in order to forge a change in their policy towards the Global South as a whole. What emerged from the Georgetown conference was a strategy based on a more radical conception of collective self-reliance which laid the foundation for more effective pressure on the developed countries on North-South negotiations. Shortly after, the NAM began to operate at the more fundamental level and radicalized policies as component parts of a collective policy of self-reliance. As Lloyd Searwar explains:

> Several students of the Movement have held that this conference led to its revitalitation and to an important addition to its agendas, namely, the programme of collective self-reliance as outlined in the Georgetown Action Programme of Economic Cooperation among Nonaligned and other Developing Countries (ECDC). This was, in fact, the first programme of ECDC adopted by the developing world. It is indisputable that the hosting of this conference earned Guyana a major leadership role [in the NAM].[37]

Subsequently, Guyana was appointed to serve on the NAM's Working Groups at the UN that dealt with the Solidarity Fund for the Reconstruction of war-torn areas in Asia and Africa, especially in Vietnam and Laos; the Solidarity Fund for the Liberation of Southern Africa and Cyprus; and non-interference in the internal affairs of states.[38] In August 1977, Guyana hosted the first ministerial meeting of non-aligned countries designed to promote horizontal cooperation among the (ACP) members. It was argued that the promotion of horizontal cooperation among ACP member countries could directly affect the basis of power in the international economic system and thus change the present pattern of the dependency relationship that existed between the developed and developing countries. Guyana also hosted the August 1978 meeting of representatives of major producers' associations, where it advocated the creation of a Council of Producers' Associations and more raw materials producer associations like OPEC, and a body to examine the effects of private foreign investment in developing countries.[39]

In keeping with its commitment to promote cooperation among the countries of the Global South, Guyana urged members of the Coordinating Bureau of the NAM to go beyond the formation of producers' associations and to develop a comprehensive industrial strategy based on the utilization of their natural resources and for the renewal of negotiations between the developed and developing countries. Guyana also chaired the Economic Committee of the Non-aligned Foreign Ministers' Conference in Belgrade in June 1978 which adopted a number of important resolutions that were relevant to the discussions on dependency issues and the need for structural change in the international economic system. At the June 1979 meeting of the Coordinating Bureau in Colombo, Guyana called on the non-aligned nations to develop programs of economic cooperation and mutual assistance, and as a means for the Global South countries to strengthen their bargaining power in their negotiations with the developed countries.[40] It also called on OPEC members at a meeting of a select group of countries in August 1979 to reduce the price of crude oil for non-oil-producing developing countries in an effort to shore up Third World solidarity. It warned OPEC that unless prices for crude oil were reduced in general, increased price of manufactured goods and other products from the developed countries and the depreciation in the value of their currencies and double digit inflation would continue, with serious consequences for the developing economies of most Global South countries.

Guyana's active role in the NAM continued in the 1980s as a direct result of its involvement in the debate over a New World Information Order (NWIO) aimed at providing information to the developed countries. It was elected vice-chairman at the First Conference of Non-aligned Information Ministers in Djakarta, Indonesia, in January 1984 to formulate plans in support of the developing countries' stance on various NWIO issues.[41] In addition, the Guyana government instituted a program called Third World Lectures at the University of Guyana in which Third World leaders and other prominent individuals were invited annually to lecture and discuss relevant issues regarding structural changes in the NIEO. The initiatives taken by Guyana at the various NAM conferences were important in setting the agenda for subsequent discussions on similar issues within the movement. Guyana's active participation in the movement was indicative of its commitment to strengthen Third World unity and cooperation, restructure the existing international economic order, and reduce CARICOM and the

Global South's dependency on the developed countries, particularly the United States.

Jamaica's Role in the NAM

In 1968, Jamaica, under the leadership of Prime Minister Hugh Shearer and the conservative Jamaican Labour Party (JLP), joined the NAM, but unlike Guyana, did not take an active role in the movement. In the first four years of its membership, Jamaica was reluctant to support, advocate, or promote policies within the NAM it felt were incompatible with United States policy in the Caribbean. Rather, the JLP government had preferred to maintain Jamaica's traditional role not only in the Caribbean but also in international arenas. This situation changed dramatically in 1972 with the election of Michael Manley and the democratic socialist People's National Party (PNP) to office. As a socialist, Prime Minister Manley's goal was to take Jamaica out of the traditional orbit of the U.S. and make its presence felt in both the Third World and in international circles. In less that a year after coming to power, Manley disengaged Jamaica from what he called the "slavish obedience to the U.S. and the countries of the NATO alliance merely because we were weak and dependent. . . . The Non-Alignment seemed to us our natural and proper home, and that way we headed."[42] Manley was strongly opposed to any infringement upon the sovereignty of small states by the larger nations. Despite U.S. objections, Manley aligned himself with Fidel Castro and the Cuban-led radical wing of the NAM and became a prominent advocate of a new, just, and equitable international order at the Non-aligned Summit meeting in Algiers in 1973. At that meeting, he urged members of the movement to review the policies of the international economic system and to develop a comprehensive strategy to eliminate the brutal disparities and inequalities between the developed and developing nations. He unveiled a plan that called for the creation of a Third World fund to be undertaken by the more prosperous non-aligned countries, especially those in OPEC with large reserves of petrodollars, in order to help the less fortunate states reduce significantly their external debt and their economic dependence on the developed nations and Western financial institutions.

Jamaica's active involvement in the NAM pushed the movement toward a much more assertive and in some respects confrontational position toward the developed countries on socioeconomic-related issues. Manley's harsh rhetoric regarding the existing international economic system was evident in his support of the NAM declaration which stated that "the poverty of the developing nations and their economic dependence . . . constitute a structural weakness in the present world economic order," and that "the persistence of an inequitable world economic system inherited from the colonial past . . . poses insurmountable difficulties in breaking the bondage of poverty."[43]

Manley called on the non-aligned countries to work closely together to develop a common strategy to effect change in the international economic system since it cannot be changed by the mere application of logic, reason, or rhetoric, but rather by collective action on the part of the developing states. Such radical moves by Manley had quite a lot to do with his earlier support of Caribbean regional integration and his personal commitment and struggle to put an end to the unfair treatment accorded to Jamaica and other Caribbean countries and the Global South in general by the Global North. Manley's radical position, according to Winston Langley, derived from a

> strategy [that] was twofold: gained increased power needed to deal with industrial states by forming regional groupings and, in a broader thrust, pursue the development of a common economic policy among Third World states. In other words, the power Jamaica needs to improve its bargaining position versus developed states can, in part, be found through regional ties with the Caribbean; and the power of the latter can, in turn, be enhanced by a broader collaboration with the rest of the Third World.[44]

Indeed, Jamaica's national experiences have had considerable significance in shaping policies at the NAM, particularly in 1973 when it agreed to serve as a coordinator for the movement's ECDC Active Programme with regard to the role of Women in Development and Tourism. The latter is believed to be a major contributor to foreign exchange for Jamaica and the other Caribbean islands, despite various estimates which showed that 81 cents out of every tourist dollar finds its way back to the United States and the other developed countries.[45] As a coordinator of the ECDC, Jamaica increased its international stature and respect for its principled positions against the developed countries and for Caribbean unity and solidarity with the other NAM members. Jamaica's activist approach was also evident when it participated in two of the United Nations Work Groups on Southern Africa and United Nations Affairs and became the principal spokesman in support of the self-determination of Third World nations throughout the world. At this and other non-aligned summits held in the 1970s, Manley urged NAM members to support the wars of liberation in Africa, Third World demand for fundamental structural change in the existing international economic order, and an end to U.S. economic sanctions against and isolation of Cuba,

Nicaragua, and other Global South countries. At the 1973 Algiers summit, Manley supported Algeria's position for a reduction of East-West tension, the emergence of a multipolar world in place of the postwar bipolar order, and an end to colonial wars and imperialist aggression.

This argument found its way into the final declaration of the summit, which reiterated that "peace is far from being assured in all parts of the world and that as long as colonial wars, apartheid, imperialist aggression, alien domination, foreign occupation, power politics, economic exploitation and plunder prevail, peace will be limited in principle and scope."[46] Manley also praised the socialist bloc for their alliance with the non-aligned nations and claimed that they have always assisted liberation struggles and, at the time, represented a crucial element in the balance of forces needed to neutralize the raw power of economic imperialism. Manley's anti-imperialist rhetoric provoked considerable controversy among the traditional developing countries, since it sought to deal with important international socioeconomic and political issues outside the general framework of the United Nations General Assembly. Such radical departure from traditional Caribbean conservative politics by Manley was based on the experience of economic exploitation and domination of the economies of the Third World, including the Caribbean by the industrial powers. It was Prime Minister Manley's belief that a more equitable distribution of the world's resources between the Global North and the Global South countries would ensure that the latter economies become less dependent on the former. As he put it:

> We had a clear choice to make: did we believe in the world as we found it, favouring a close, subservient alliance with the U.S.? Or did we make common cause with the Non-Aligned Movement and work for changes in the world's economic system in a principled way? . . . The Non-Aligned Movement had tremendous significance for us. Its underlying philosophy was exactly compatible with the position to which we were led by our own experience. Its anti-imperialist ethos were consistent with our interpretation of the past and our perspective for the future. [It] . . . presented our best political hope for the development of a third force in world affairs.[47]

During the early 1980s, Jamaica's high profile and active participation in the NAM was drastically reduced by the conservative Edward Seaga who, upon assuming power as prime minister in October 1980, reversed most of the country's foreign policy positions and transformed the island into one of America's most trustworthy Caribbean allies. Like Hugh Shearer, Seaga not only refused to take part in Third World and international affairs, but also undermined the influence Cuba, Guyana, and other radical elements in the

Caribbean had acquired in the NAM during the 1970s. This was evident in the conflicts that arose between Guyana and Jamaica when the latter claimed that Cuba was a surrogate of the former Soviet Union and tried to expunge it from the region. Seaga also blamed the collapse of Jamaica's economy on Manley's ill-fated socialist policies. But while Seaga was in the process of reversing Jamaica's leading role in the NAM and in international forums, Grenada, under Maurice Bishop's New Jewel socialist government, was making a concerted effort to exert influence in the NAM and the G-77 until its self-destruction in October 1983. The other members of CARICOM were committed in principle to the goals and objectives of the non-aligned movement even though none of them as individuals have played an active role or function collectively as a highly assertive regional group. Such inaction by some CARICOM countries in the NAM and other Global South organizations has had significant implications for the region's dependency politics.

The abrupt end of the Cold War and the East-West rivalry in 1991, however, eroded much of the bargaining leverage the NAM had provided the Global South countries. The way the East-West rivalry ended with the values and systems of the West vindicated and triumphant, undermined the very basis of the non-aligned movement, which had adopted as its foundation a moral neutrality between the two superpowers.[48] Although the original justification of the NAM no longer exists, efforts to lift the Global South countries out of their dependent and subordinate position continue, and the ideals envisaged by its founders in 1961 remain unchanged. This was evident at the movement's eleventh conference held in Colombia in 1995 where its leaders asserted that "When the Nonaligned Movement began, it was inspired by one motive—that developing countries could take decisions and positions in international politics depending on their own interests and not according to one or the other of the superpowers. This continues to be valid."[49]

Despite the limited influence of the NAM in the 1990s, the CARICOM countries' involvement in the movement should not be seen mainly as an attempt to obtain immediate material rewards for each country, but rather as a commitment to enhance Third World unity. CARICOM's affiliation with the NAM was intended to serve notice to the developed countries that its members have redefined their international relations to include South-South economic cooperation and are to be taken seriously in their pursuit to restructure the international economic order, reduce their dependency, and achieve full and effective sovereignty. Since its creation, the non-aligned movement has been for the most part specifically oriented towards

promoting Third World solidarity on matters of general principle and policy.
It has built Third World consensus and cohesion on dependency issues,
which have been advanced by other institutions, particularly the G-77. This
division of activities is explained by Leelananda de Silva.

> [The NAM] is primarily concerned with the organization of a counter-
> vailing power within the Third World and the creation of conditions for
> organic unity within it, and the [G-77] is concerned more with the
> utilization of this strength and power in the external dimension of
> negotiations with the North, especially within UNCTAD, and in the
> improvement of international markets for trade in commodities, capital,
> technology, labour, and so on.[50]

CARICOM's Role in the Group of 77

The Group of 77, which in the first place is a misnomer since its members
had increased to approximately 125 countries by the mid-1980s, emerged out
of the first UN Conference on Trade and Development (UNCTAD) in 1964.
UNCTAD is now a permanent member of the UN family of organizations
through which the Global South countries could address their economic
interests concerning development and dependency issues. It became the forerunner of several later conferences that focused on various aspects of the
dependency relations between the world's rich and poor states. Created as an
international forum to promote the economic interests of the developing
countries and to negotiate North-South issues, including the need for radical
changes in the existing international economic order, the G-77 subsequently
expanded its role to coordinate the activities of the United Nations Industrial
Development Organization (UNIDO), the IMF-World Bank group, and the
UN operations in New York. Established in 1966 by the UN, UNIDO's role
was to encourage development in the Third World in an effort to combat the
problems of dependency and underdevelopment in the Global South.

Perceived by most CARICOM countries as being less politicized and
less confrontational than the NAM and more oriented towards concrete
solutions to developmental and dependency issues, Jamaica and Trinidad
and Tobago were the first two CARICOM countries to join its ranks. Several
other CARICOM countries became members of the G-77 shortly after they
had achieved their independence. But it was Guyana and Jamaica who
assumed and maintained a vanguard role within the G-77, with Trinidad and
Tobago also maintaining a fairly high profile. This was due mostly to their

commitment to reduce the region's dependence, which propelled them to the forefront in promoting economic and political cooperation among Third World countries.

The CARICOM countries' active participation within the group began in 1973 at the NAM summit in Algiers, when they joined with other NAM countries and called for a New International Economic Order (NIEO). The goal of the G-77 was to correct the economic imbalances created by the old order, which many in the Global South viewed as an instrument of their continued oppression and subordination in the global environment. The demand for a new international economic order resulted from the resolution adopted at the Sixth Special Session of the UN General Assembly and was "based on equity, sovereign equality, interdependence, common interest, and cooperation among all states irrespective of their economic and social systems which shall correct inequalities and redress existing injustices, and make it possible to eliminate the widening gap between the developed and the developing countries."[51]

The developing countries were in fact demanding an active, full, and equal participation in the formulation and application of all decisions that concern the international community. The declaration in itself provided the conceptual framework for a fundamental restructuring of all international economic relations and became, as it were, the guiding principles of the developing countries in their approach to North-South negotiations and their quest to overcome dependency. In a word, the principles embodied in the declaration summarized the major demands the Global South countries had constantly elaborated since the founding of the G-77. The point to be made here is that these countries considered the existing international economic order as unjust and outmoded as the colonial order from which it originated. It puts the command of the global economy in the hands of a minority of highly developed states who determine by themselves the distribution of the world resources as a function of their own hierarchy of needs.

Given the crisis in the global economy in the early 1970s (anterior to the oil price increases), which had its most severe consequences on the Global South economies, the CARICOM leaders judged that the moment was ripe for them to articulate forcefully their conception of the policies necessary to break the vicious cycle of poverty, underdevelopment, and dependency in the Caribbean. The CARICOM countries, particularly Guyana and Jamaica, embraced the Global South coalition and followed in their recent practice of coupling a declaration with an action program as had been done in the NAM. The G-77, like the NAM, converged to promote collective diplomacy and increased the effectiveness and solidarity of the developing countries.

Guyana and the G-77

In its capacity as coordinator of the Trade, Transport, and Industry sector of the NAM Action Programme for Economic Cooperation, Guyana assumed a leading role on economic cooperation among the Global South countries. In this particular role it was responsible for drafting proposals on the subject and discussing them both formally and informally with the G-77 member states and the developed countries. Supported by CARICOM members and other developing countries, Guyana succeeded in establishing a UN Special Programme and a Special Fund designed to provide financial assistance on a short-term basis to Third World countries whose economies were most seriously affected (MSA) by the international economic crisis. As

Figure 4.2
Organizational Structure of the Group of 77

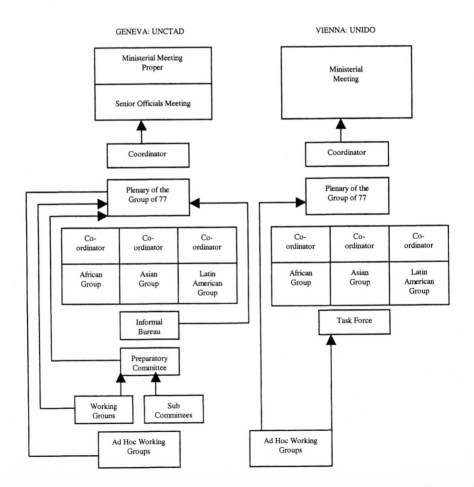

it turned out, Guyana itself was subsequently designated an MSA country and, as a result, benefited from the UN Special Fund it had helped to create.

Guyana's prominence within the movement was enhanced in 1975 when it hosted the Commonwealth Finance Ministers' Meeting of the G-77. At the meeting a Group of Experts was appointed to develop a comprehensive program of practical measures aimed at alleviating the problem of poverty and deprivation in developing countries, reducing the poverty gap between the rich and poor nations, and establishing rules for the creation of an NIEO. Headed by Alister McIntyre, then the Secretary General of CARICOM, the Group asserted that "the developed countries, especially those with balance of payments surpluses, are well placed to take a lead in supporting the efforts of developing countries by direct measures and, indirectly, through policies aimed at generating greater strength in the world economy."[52]

Mainly because of its active involvement in the negotiation of economic issues in the United Nations and other international forums, Guyana was elected Vice-chairman of Negotiating Group IV, a subgroup within UNCTAD that dealt with the problems of the least developed, landlocked, and island developing countries. It also chaired the Drafting Group appointed by the Conference on ECDC, whose function was to ensure the preservation of a cooperative relationship between the initiatives of the NAM and those of the Group of 77 by emphasizing their mutually supportive character to the developing nations. The reason was to prevent internal conflicts between the two groups from dominating future meetings. The conflicts arose because some NAM members were opposed to the idea that their own program on ECDC, endorsed at the summit level, was being subordinated to the more moderate proposals of the G-77, which were adopted at the ministerial level.

At the Commonwealth Prime Ministers' Conference held in Kingston, Jamaica, in 1975, Forbes Burnham again elaborated on the need for a new world order and urged members of the G-77 to adopt an integrated and comprehensive development program to eliminate the disparities and inequalities between the rich and the poor countries instead of a piecemeal reconstruction of the existing international order. As he emphasized, "it will not do to deceive ourselves about the nature of the task which must be attempted. We must embark on building a new [world] order. It is not a task involving the repair, renovation, or piecemeal reconstruction of the old order."[53] Guyana's influence were also evident during the fourth Ministerial Meeting of the G-77 in Arusha, Tanzania, in January 1979. At this meeting, Guyana led the discussion on some major Global South issues, such as economic development and political cooperation among the G-77 countries.

In recognition of its strong commitment to Third World affairs, Guyana was nominated by the Latin American contingent and was elected Chairman of Negotiating Group Two, whose purview included such issues as international trade, manufacturing, technology, and shipping. The work of this Group was particularly important for the CARICOM states mainly because it addressed the special preferential trade arrangements of the Caribbean and other ACP countries established under the Lomé Convention in which Guyana and Jamaica played an active role in the negotiations with the EEC. Guyana's activism within the G-77 framework continued into the 1980s when Forbes Burnham was one of thirteen Third World leaders invited by the United States to attend the highly publicized North-South summit held in Cancun, Mexico, in October 1981. There the group of thirteen expressed their continued solidarity with the aspirations of other Global South states to restructure the international economic order.

But aside from offering some specific aid commitments, the United States barely addressed the issues raised by the group of thirteen regarding debt reduction, international trade, and the restructuring of the NIEO. The Reagan administration was not persuaded to make a firm commitment to reopen the dialog on North-South issues. Its actions appeared suspiciously like an attempt to buy the group off—a ploy the Global South delegation did not appreciate. Frustrated by the U.S. meaningless participation, Burnham called on the developing countries to abandon the negotiating process and to focus their efforts on promoting collective self-reliance as a means to end their dependency and redefine their status and role in the global community. This involved the exercise of sovereignty over their natural resources and the diversification of trade away from the traditional metropolitan countries.

Guyana's active participation in the G-77 during the 1970s and 1980s was derived largely from its traditionally active role in global politics, its involvement in the negotiation of North-South issues at the UN, the NAM and the Lomé Conventions, as well as its track record as the host of a number of international conferences. To these must be added Guyana's commitment to the principles of sovereign equality and self-determination, self-reliance, Global South solidarity, as well as its support of the socialist bloc, Cuba, and China.

Jamaica's Participation in the G-77

Jamaica's rapid emergence as one of the most active CARICOM countries in the G-77 during the 1970s can, to a large extent, be traced directly to Manley's personal belief that only a new international economic order would enable the poor countries to have a substantially greater share of the world's wealth. Prime Minister Manley was convinced that Western imperialism had to be confronted in order to end the extremely high levels of dependency, underdevelopment, and poverty in most of the Global South countries. It also stemmed from his socialist background and the PNP membership in the Socialist International, a fraternal body to which are affiliated socialist, social democratic, and labor parties of Europe and elsewhere.

Accordingly, at the UNCTAD IV, which was held in Nairobi, Kenya, in May 1976, Jamaica was elected Chairman of the G-77 and played a crucial role in negotiating the platform adopted by the Group at its Ministerial meeting in Manila in February 1977. The election was partly due to the prominent role played by the Jamaican government permanent representative in Geneva prior to UNCTAD IV, and to the activist policies pursued by the Manley government in the field of international economic relations.[54] As chairman, Jamaica was instrumental in the shaping of policies aimed at restructuring the economic and social sectors of the United Nations system. It also refined and expanded the North-South negotiating agenda which had a major impact on the Conference on International Economic Cooperation (CIEC) proceedings that had begun in Paris. Jamaica was also elected the co-ordinating country for UNCTAD IV, which placed it at the very center of the complex North-South dialog that focused primarily on Third World unity and the possibility of improving the dependent and subordinate position of developing economies. As Manley explicitly puts it:

> It is only through united action that the Third World can hope to reduce its dependence, create economic viability and give meaning to its independence . . . there can be no compromise in the struggle for a new international economic order and the task of building Third World unity. To us . . . the East-West struggle was secondary, that it was our duty to avoid its entanglements and our duty to resist hegemonic pressures wherever and by whomever it was exerted.[55]

Perhaps Jamaica's most important foray in the G-77 was in 1976 when it was chosen as one of nineteen states from the Global South to negotiate on behalf of the G-77 with a group of eight Western developed countries at the CIEC in Paris. The negotiations lasted for eighteen months, from January 1976 to June 1977.[56] The CIEC was the result of efforts by the developed countries, particularly France, to transfer the discussion on North-South issues from the United Nations to a more limited forum in order to escape the overwhelming control exercised by the developing countries in the UN General Assembly by virtue of its democratic nature where each country has one vote. Jamaica's presence at the Paris conference, in a sense, not only ensured a Caribbean perspective on North-South issues, but also the small developing countries in general, since it was the smallest country in terms of both population and physical size.

Because of their explicit linkage to the G-77, the Group of Nineteen capitalized upon the developed countries diplomatic investment in the CIEC while at the same time reaffirmed their own status as part of the larger Third World coalition. They established the negotiating agenda, which provided for four separate commissions, each of which was cochaired by a developed and a developing country to ensure fairness and consensus. The CIEC was organized specifically for the developed and developing countries to discuss and hopefully reach agreement on four main items: energy; raw materials; finance; and development—all of which were linked to the critique of the existing international economic order.[57] The basic premise for these ground rules was that the Group of Nineteen wanted to provide a new approach to problems that had previously defied solutions in the UN and other global forums. It agreed that no single issue could be solved satisfactorily without an overall political commitment to development in the Global South. While no definite issue was precluded by these rules, nothing was assured either, but the Third World delegation had hoped that the talks would lead to major structural changes in the existing international economic order that would bolster development in the South and reduce its dependency on the North. This, however, was exactly the opposite of what the U.S. wanted. Robert Mortimer provides some insights into the format:

> The prompt consolidation of the Group of 19 and its explicit association with the Group of 77 established the political ground rules of the Paris Conference. The developing states were committed to a bloc strategy and insisted upon the integration of CIEC into the total environment of North-South politics. This strategy was designed to maintain the cohesion of the larger coalition as the more important long-term instrument. These early moves made it evident that the success of the conference depended upon the satisfaction of the major grievances of the developed world.[58]

After several tense negotiating sessions, the CIEC did not produce any significant results beyond a semi-formal agreement to establish a Common Fund of one billion dollars to aid the most destitute countries in the Global South, and a pledge to increase the level of development aid and technical assistance to those countries. It did not provide solutions to the problems that were at the heart of the developing countries demands: debt reduction and the restructuring of the existing world order, which were aimed at reducing the traditional power and influence of the core countries.[59] The developing countries have stated that while some progress had been made at the CIEC, most of the proposals for structural changes in the international economic system have not been agreed upon. The developed countries, on the other hand, highlighted the spirit of cooperation in which the whole conference took place and the failure to reach agreement only on certain aspects of energy cooperation.[60]

These contrasting views summed up the distance that still separates the Global North and the Global South, the former concerned essentially with energy and the latter with development issues. Because of the stalemate, the CARICOM and other Global South countries have agreed to move future North-South negotiations on the establishment of the NIEO and other major issues back to the UN rather than in limited forums outside it.

Concurrent with the high-visibility appearances by Jamaica and Guyana, Trinidad and Tobago actively participated on several issue areas in the G-77 permanent UNCTAD working groups. It was appointed spokesman of the group on problems facing small island developing states, an issue in which the CARICOM countries, Trinidad and Tobago in particular, had taken a special interest in view of their insular character.[61]

It appears that CARICOM's interests have been well represented in most of the major dependency initiatives undertaken by the Non-aligned Movement and the Group of 77, although only Guyana, Jamaica, Trinidad and Tobago, and a few other CARICOM countries have in many instances been directly or indirectly involved. Such limited participation did not restrict the G-77 or the NAM's exposure to all the different views that might have existed in the Caribbean because foreign policy coordination is one of CARICOM's core principles. Therefore, the few CARICOM countries that participated in the activities of the NAM and the G-77 transmitted the concerns of the region as a whole. In terms of dependency, CARICOM was from the beginning conceived as a vehicle for the Caribbean countries to acquire greater political space and ultimately to assert their collective bargaining power in their dealings with the developed countries of the Global North.

The role of the CARICOM countries in the negotiations on the NIEO represented an interesting example of the capacity of small developing states to influence and shape international politics and to make a contribution to the dialog on change in the international system. The role of Guyana and Jamaica has been specially referenced because of their activist stance in international affairs and their efforts to reduce or eradicate CARICOM and the Global South dependence. Leaders like Forbes Burnham and Michael

Manley marched the CARICOM region into global politics and embraced the struggles of other Global South nations through the Group of 77 and the NAM. Clear positions of support were articulated for Third World demands for a new international economic order, an end to apartheid in South Africa, respect of sovereignty and self-determination, the establishment of closer ties with the socialist bloc, and an end to dominance and dependence of Global South countries by the Global North.

Although progress has been extremely slow in this area, CARICOM, nevertheless acquired substantial bargaining power at the very highest global level of North-South politics in its attempt to reduce the region's dependency on the developed countries and to exercise a predominant influence in a globalized world economy. It succeeded in shifting the focus away from the East-West conflict to the more pressing issues of dependency, development, and poverty. But during the tense Cold War period, these issues were not an affront to the social conscience of the international community. They were considered low politics and were recognized only to the extent that they provided a breeding ground for communism in the Caribbean and elsewhere.

The rise of the Third World coalition and its demands for a new world order are largely demands upon the United States, which has and continues to be the principal beneficiary of the prevailing global economic system and, as a consequence, must assume a major responsibility for the Global South's high levels of poverty, underdevelopment, and dependency as well as the quality of North-South relations. As the only true global superpower in the twenty-first century, the United States must make choices about the kind of global economic system it wishes to have. To be sure, the issue of global poverty is of great moral significance, but as indicated earlier, the international system is amoral. These choices, therefore, must include the values of fairness and equity, that is, some conception of a just international economic order. In international politics, however, most of the decisions are determined by assessments of power, thus the success of the Third World coalition depends on the amount of power it can bring to bear on the United States and the other developed countries. Solidarity within the Global South is not a novel form of state behavior but rather a source of greater power which has been achieved, but not enough as yet to force major concessions by the developed countries.

Notes

1. Michael Manley, *Jamaica: Struggle in the Periphery* (London: Andre

Deutsch, 1982), 61.

2. James A. Caporaso, "Introduction to the Special Issue of International Organization on Dependence and Dependency in the Global System," *International Organization* 32, no. 1 (Winter 1978): 4.

3. Abraham F. Lowenthal, "The Insular Caribbean as a Crucial Test for U.S. Policy," in *The Caribbean Challenge: U.S. Policy in a Volatile Region*, ed. H. Michael Erisman (Boulder, Colo.: Westview Press, 1984), 187.

4. Adolphe W. Roberts, *The Caribbean: The Story of Our Sea of Destiny* (Indianapolis: Bobbs-Merrill, 1940), 179.

5. H. Michael Erisman, *Pursuing Postdependency Politics: South-South Relations in the Caribbean* (Boulder, Colo.: Lynne Rienner, 1992), 2.

6. Richard Millett, "Imperialism, Intervention and Exploitation: The Historical Context of International Relations in the Caribbean," in *The Restless Caribbean: Changing Patterns of International Relations*, ed. Richard Millett and Marvin W. Will (New York: Praeger, 1979), 3-11.

7. R. H. Collin, *Theodore Roosevelt's Caribbean: The Panama Canal, the Monroe Doctrine, and the Latin American Context* (Baton Rouge: Louisiana State University Press, 1990), 69-70.

8. Robert Gilpin, *War and Change in World Politics* (Cambridge: Cambridge University Press, 1981), 196-97.

9. Andres Serbin, *Caribbean Geopolitics: Toward Security through Peace* (Boulder, Colo.: Lynne Rienner, 1990).

10. Ibid.

11. James R. Greene and Brent Scowcroft, *Western Interests and U.S. Policy Options in the Caribbean Basin: Report on the Atlantic Council's Working Group on the Caribbean Basin* (Boston: Oelgeschlager, Gunn and Hain, 1984).

12. Serbin, *Caribbean Geopolitics*, 6-7.

13. Carl Stone, *Power in the Caribbean Basin: A Comparative Study of Political Economy* (Philadelphia: Institute for the Study of Human Issues, 1986), 106. For more on U.S. economic interests in the Caribbean, see Kenneth Boodhoo, "The Economic Dimensions of U.S. Caribbean Policy," in *Caribbean Challenge: U.S. Policy in a Volatile Region,* ed. Michael Erisman (Boulder, Colo.: Westview, 1984.

14. Anthony J. Payne, *The International Crisis in the Caribbean* (London: Croom Helm, 1984), 35-38.

15. For excellent accounts of U.S. strategic interests in the Caribbean, see Andres Serbin, *Caribbean Geopolitics*; Gary P. Lewis, "Prospect for a Regional Security System in the Eastern Caribbean," *Millennium* (1986); Dion Phillips, "The Increasing Emphasis on Security and Defence in the Eastern Caribbean," in *Militarization in the Non-Hispanic Caribbean*, ed. Alma Young and Dion Phillips (Boulder, Colo.: Lynne Rienner, 1986); David Simmons, "Militarization in the Caribbean: Concerns for National and Regional Security," *International Journal* 40 (1985); and James R. Greene and Brent Scowcroft, *Western Interests and U.S. Policy Options in the Caribbean Basin.*

16. Sheila Harden, *Small Is Dangerous: Microstates in a Macro World* (London: Frances Pinter, 1985), 149.

17. Payne, *The International Crisis*, 35-36.

18. Ibid.

19. J. Agnew, *The United States in the World Economy: A Regional Geography* (Cambridge: Cambridge University Press, 1987), 13-15.

20. Paul Sutton, "Living with Dependency in the Commonwealth Caribbean," in *Dependency under Challenge: The Political Economy of the Commonwealth Caribbean,* ed. Anthony Payne and Paul Sutton (Manchester: Manchester University Press, 1984), 287.

21. Burton Benedict, *Problems of Small Territories* (London: Athlone Press, University of London, 1967), 6.

22. Peter J. Katzenstein, *Small States in World Markets: Industrial Policy in Europe* (Ithaca, N.Y.: Cornell University Press, 1985), 24, 82, 85.

23. *World Development Report* (New York: Oxford University Press, 1994).

24. For the most current information on economic conditions in the CARICOM region, see *Latin American Regional Reports: The Caribbean; Caribbean Insight;* and *Caribbean Business,* all of which are published locally and in London.

25. The primary reason for the striking difference between Trinidad and Tobago and the rest of the CARICOM states at the time was the former accumulated wealth from oil and natural gas. While the dramatic rise in the price of oil shook the economies of the other Caribbean countries in the 1970s, Trinidad and Tobago enjoyed a period of unprecedented economic growth, and was able to extend loans to a number of CARICOM states.

26. Mahbub ul Haq, *The Poverty Curtain* (New York: Columbia University Press, 1976), xv.

27. Erisman, *Pursuing Postdependency Politics*, 75.

28. Manley, *Jamaica: Struggle in the Periphery*, 65-66.

29. Ibid., 63-64.

30. Ibid., 63-64, 106.

31. Forbes Burnham, *Breakthrough* (Georgetown: Guyana Printers, 1973), 31.

32. Ibid., 31.

33. Robert A. Mortimer, *The Third World Coalition in International Politics* (New York: Praeger, 1980).

34. Odette Jankowitsch and Karl P. Sauvant, eds., *The Third World without Superpowers: The Collected Documents of the Non-Aligned Countries* (Dobbs Ferry, N.Y.: Oceana, 1978), 447.

35. Ibid., 450.

36. Among the range of functional areas that the coordinating countries to promote Third World cooperation are international cooperation for development; trade, transport, and industry; financial and monetary cooperation; scientific and technological development; research and information systems; telecommunications; social welfare policies; food and agriculture; fisheries; tourism; role of women in development; and control of transnational corporations, to name a few.

37. Lloyd Searwar, "Non-Alignment as a Viable Alternative for Regional Cooperation," paper presented at a Seminar on Geopolitical Change in the Caribbean in the 1980s, Georgetown, Guyana, March 1982, 7.

38. Erisman, *Pursuing Postdependency Politics*, 77.

39. Dennis Benn, "The Commonwealth Caribbean," in *Dependency under Challenge*, 259-79.

40. Ibid.

41. For details concerning the NWIO issue, see Anthony Smith, *The Geopolitics of Information: How Western Culture Dominates the World* (New York: Oxford University Press, 1980); and Thomas L. McPhail, *Electronic Colonialism: The Future of International Broadcasting and Communication* (Beverly Hills, Calif.: Space Publications, 1981).

42. Manley, *Jamaica*, 68.

43. Jankowitsch and Sauvant, *The Third World without Superpowers,* 85.

44. Winston E. Langley, "From Manley to Seaga: Changes in Jamaican Foreign Policy," *Transition* 8 (1983): 5.

45. Tom Barry, Beth Wood, and Deb Preusch, *The Other Side of Paradise: Foreign Control in the Caribbean* (New York: Grove Press, 1984), 85.

46. Jankowitsch and Sauvant, *The Third World without Superpowers,* 193.

47. Manley, *Jamaica*, 59, 67, 106.

48. Shahram Chubin, "Southern Perspectives on World Order," in *The Global Agenda,* 8 ed. Charles W. Kegley, Jr., and Eugene R. Wittkopf (New York: McGraw-Hill, 1998), 208-20.

49. Charles W. Kegley, Jr., and Eugene R. Wittkopf, *World Politics: Trend and Transformation*, ed. (New York: McGraw-Hill, 2001), 156.

50. Leelananda de Silva, "The Non-Aligned Movement: Its Economic Organization and NIEO Perspectives," in *The Challenge of South-South Cooperation*, ed. Brenda Palvic, Raul R. Uranga, Boris Cizelj, and Marjan Svetlicic (Boulder, Colo.: Westview, 1983), 76.

51. Alfred George Moss and Harry N. M. Winton, eds., *A New International Economic Order, Selected Documents 1945-1975* (New York: UNITAR, 1978), 891-900.

52. *Towards a New International Economic Order* (Final Report by a Commonwealth Experts' Group, Commonwealth Secretariat, London, 1977), 11.

53. Forbes Burnham, *In the Cause of Humanity* (Georgetown: Guyana Printers, 1975), 13.

54. Benn, "The Commonwealth Caribbean," 267.

55. Manley, *Jamaica*, 106.

56. Erisman, *Pursuing Postdependency Politics,* 85-86; Benn, "The Commonwealth Caribbean," 270-71.

57. Mortimer, *The Third World Coalition,* 95-109; Erisman, *Pursuing Postdependency Politics,* 80-87.

58. Mortimer, *The Third World Coalition,* 102.

59. Benn, "The Commonwealth Caribbean," 271-72; Erisman, *Pursuing*

Postdependency Politics, 86.

60. *Department of State Bulletin* 76, no. 1982 (June 20, 1977).

61. Benn, "The Commonwealth Caribbean," 268; Ensman, *Post Dependency Politics*, 87.

Chapter 5

Guyana: The Adoption of Cooperative Socialism

After more than three centuries of colonial rule, Guyana attained its political independence from Britain on May 26, 1966, following a turbulent political struggle against the British government during the 1950s and early 1960s.[1] As the only English-speaking country in South America, Guyana attracted worldwide attention on October 9, 1953, when the British government of Sir Winston Churchill, acting on the advice of the governor, Sir Alfred Savage, suspended the country's new constitution and removed the PPP government of Cheddi Jagan from office. As a result, various interpretations of Guyana's development as well as its political affairs have focused on events during 1953 and after, with the view that relatively little had occurred in the earlier period.

While the rapid emergence of the PPP in 1950 to a position of strength and prominence is of considerable significance to the country, colonialism, slavery, and the system of indentured immigrant labor have also, to a large extent, shaped Guyana's political and economic direction. Equally important is the fact that the PPP activities, apart from being the first nationalist movement in the country to pose a serious and consistent challenge and threat to British imperial rule, were directly responsible for the decision of the British government to suspend the constitution. This act set in motion forces that were instrumental in defining the future pattern of political developments in Guyana, and contributed its fair share to the problems with which the country was subsequently, and is now, confronted. It was perhaps the root causes for the subsequent division of the national movement and the socioeconomic polarization in Guyana on racial lines.

Guyana embarked on the road to independence in extremely difficult circumstances, some far more challenging than those of its Commonwealth Caribbean neighbors, and with keen awareness that the mere attainment of political independence was insufficient for the achievement of meaningful economic change in the country. This, in effect, resulted in the development of new strategies designed to reduce Guyana's economic dependence on the core capitalist countries and forged a new order in international politics. In this regard, the range of activities that occurred during the People's National Congress (PNC) government of Forbes Burnham under the novel label of cooperative socialism is relevant. The significance of the development of the first cooperative republic in the world have, by and large, educed world-wide interest among academics, politicians, and the citizens of other states, particularly those in the Caribbean. Part of the reason for this notoriety was that few accepted the PNC regime's claim to be motivated by concern for the poor as genuine, particularly since there was increasing evidence to support the widely accepted view that the regime existed through the use of force and fraudulent elections. Furthermore, most of the measures and policies developed and adopted under the concept of cooperative socialism by the Burnham regime between 1970 and 1985 represented a marked departure from the general direction of its counterparts in the anglophone Caribbean, and from those advocated a decade earlier by the PNC leadership itself, or by the Marxist PPP.

The Colonial Setting

Colonialism, slavery, sugar plantations, and English masters are some of the elements of Guyana's history that it shares with its Caribbean neighbors, especially those of the English-speaking region. What sets Guyana apart is its relative size and its three major geographical zones. First, the country's coastal plain, although just two to ten miles in width, stretches almost two hundred and seventy miles along the Atlantic Ocean. This narrow strip of land, which is below sea level, had historically been the main agricultural region. It is approximately 4 percent of the total land area of the country and houses about 90 percent of the population. Second, in the southwestern part of the country lies the main savannah area which is enclosed by forests, and is primarily used by native Amerindians for fishing and cattle grazing. Third, Guyana's most fertile land area reaches deep into the interior of the South American continent, an uncharted roadless land of vast savannahs, thick jungles, and majestic waterfalls. This huge portion of undeveloped land constitutes approximately four-fifths of all of Guyana's territory and is considered to have large reserves of minerals, including bauxite, manganese, gold, and diamonds. Most Guyanese nationals usually refer to this dense uninhabited forest area as the "bush."[2]

Guyana's present-day structure is largely fashioned by its colonial past, which began as an early Dutch trading outlet in 1621.[3] Under Dutch rule the territory was divided into three colonies and named after the rivers which made natural boundaries and are today the three counties: Essequibo to the west, Demerara to the center, and Berbice to the east. The country has since maintained a characteristic Dutch outlook, with its orderliness, the masterly system of dams, dikes, and canals, and its distinctive architecture. Its second largest city still bears the Dutch name of New Amsterdam, while its capital city, Georgetown, is named after King George of Great Britain, the country that ruled Guyana as a colony from 1814 to 1966.

The abolition of slavery in the Caribbean in 1834 was perhaps the greatest single factor responsible for social and economic change in the country. The two most immediate effects of emancipation were the economic ruin for dozens of white planters and the emergence of a free black peasantry in Guyana. Most of the ex-slaves, after a four-year transitional period of apprenticeship or semi-slavery, fled the brutal hardships of the sugarcane plantations to establish their own villages and cooperative farms rather than to remain subjected to white European overseers. A good number of them gravitated to the urban centers in search of employment in factories. In view of the resulting shortage of labor on the sugar plantations, the few blacks who chose to remain, demanded and received relatively high wages from the white planters, most of whom were forced to compete for the scarce labor that was available at the time.[4]

In order to meet the labor shortage in the country and to avert what appeared to the planters to be total ruin, indentured labor was introduced as a substitute for slave labor on the plantations. As shown in table 5.1, most of the indentured laborers were brought in between 1835 and 1917.[5] In India, famine, drought, and strict social stratification enabled the British agents for the sugar companies to lure East Indians into leaving their homes in the rural villages to undertake the long journey by boat to the West Indies. By the end of the nineteenth century, the sugar plantation laborers consisted mainly of East Indians who, apart from blacks, proved to be the most suitable and enduring group of people for estate work. Thus, India became the principal source of indentured labor supply, and immigration from other sources was not encouraged. The treatment accorded to the East Indians on their arrival in Guyana and in the Caribbean was quite different from that of the African slaves in some significant respects. In order to delineate the difference between the indenture system and the institution of chattel slavery, it is necessary to digress briefly. But much has been written on the subject of slavery in the region that little needs to be said here.[6]

Suffice to say that in theory, if not always in practice, the indentured laborers had certain rights. The East Indians were allowed to return to their homeland after the completion of their two-year contracts. Related to this was the right to retain as much of their culture as they desired, including the continued use of their language, the maintenance of their family structures, religious practices, and the ritual observances pertaining to marriage as long as these customs did not interfere with the work routine on the plantations. Unlike the slaves, the indentured laborers were not considered pieces of property but instruments of production in the sense that while their labor was bought and used, their persons were not owned by the planter and therefore could not be sold, as was the situation with African slaves. In a word, the indentured laborers were bondsmen, little better off than the slaves they had replaced in British Guiana and the Caribbean.

In Guyana, as elsewhere, black slaves were systematically deprived and disposed of their language and culture. They were forced to undergo a period of "deculturization" which, in essence, means the removal of those behavior patterns regarded as inimical to the proper performance of their duties. They were also forced to adopt the culture of their white European masters, which included language, religion, and Western customs and practices. At best, chattel slavery has left an indelible mark on blacks, the immediate effect was that, generally speaking, they became more receptive than the East Indians to European culture, habits and lifestyle. Thus, while the indentured system allowed the continuity of the East Indian culture in the rural areas of Guyana where most of the plantations are located, the institution of slavery stripped blacks of theirs. These and subsequent degrading conditions encountered by blacks during slavery have resulted in the existence of very few vestiges of African culture in Guyana and the Caribbean as a whole.

Africans not only left the plantations, but rural life altogether and have since dominated the urban working-class occupations of mining, civil servants, especially the police and military organizations, while the East Indians have become the dominant group in the peasantry. A number of upwardly mobile East Indians who, owing to discriminatory practices in employment by the Colonial Office, became professionals and owners of small and medium size business. This means that the two racial groups are not only occupationally, but also geographically, segregated, which not only helps to preserve the separate cultures but impedes social mixing as well.[7] Political scientist Percy Hintzen has hinted that the segregation of the two dominant ethnic groups in Guyana prevented the emergence of an interracial political alliance among the lower classes, despite a common experience of severe and extreme economic hardship on the plantations.[8]

Table 5.1
Number of Indentured Laborers in Guyana: 1835-1917

Country of Origin	Date of Immigration	No. of Immigrants	Percentage of Total
India	1838-1917	238,960	69.9
Madeira, Azores, Cape Verde	1835-1882	31,628	9.2
Malta	1839	208	0.1
Brazil	1841	617	0.2
Sierra Leone	1841	404	0.1
China	1853-1912	14,189	4.2
West Indies	1835-1917	42,562	12.4
Africa	1838-1865	13,355	3.9
United States	1840-1841	70	0.0
Total		**341,993**	**100.0**

Source: Raymond T. Smith, *British Guyana* (London: Oxford University Press, 1962), 42-44.

Thus, while the city of Georgetown is distinguished by the majestic St. George's Cathedral, the minarets of Moslem mosques and the domes of Hindu temples rise high above the East Indian villages in the rural areas of Guyana. The country's multiracial population of approximately 750,000 people is a product of its colonial past. The census data shown in table 5.2 reveal that the population is divided into six ethnic groups: the two largest are the East Indians or Indo-Guyanese, who constituted slightly under 50 percent of the total population in 1993, and Afro-Guyanese or blacks who account for 36 percent. The other four ethnic groups are the Amerindians, Portuguese, Chinese, and whites. The Amerindians are the only indigenous people, most of whom remained almost completely socially, culturally, and geographically isolated despite intense efforts by the Burnham government to integrate them into the rest of the Guyanese society. All the other groups were brought to Guyana as a result of European colonial expansion in the Caribbean. The mixed or colored race (mulattos), which is 7 percent of the country's population, is not considered a racial group. On the basis of status, this group was located just below the whites during colonialism. Many were employed as middle level functionaries in the government and in the private sector while others could be found among the local professionals. Recently, the coloreds have become less distinctive as a group and have developed a common identity with the upwardly mobile black middle class. There is agreement among scholars that the organic disruption and emasculation of the East Indians and Africans from their feudal cultural heritage in India and Africa respectively have, in the modern period, given rise to the radical anti-colonial nationalist struggle, which laid the foundation for the development of party politics in Guyana.

The Rise of Nationalist Movements in Guyana

In Guyana, the nationalist period began with labor mobilization during the 1920s, but it was not until after World War II that a truly comprehensive nationalist movement emerged. The delay was due largely to a weak and politically unorganized middle class who, because of its economic success, was not prepared to challenge the colonial status quo, thus making the thrust of nationalist movement weaker in Guyana than in the rest of the Caribbean. Labor mobilization, which was widespread in the Caribbean during the 1930s, emerged in Guyana not from the middle-class leadership, but from the lower ranks of the British Guiana Labour Union (BGLU) founded in 1919. The middle class was content to focus on material and social welfare issues rather than on political power and political representation.

At the same time, the situation on the estates was very authoritarian and very paternalistic. For the most part, the sugar barons controlled the finance of the colony and exercised supreme power over a population, even though nominally free after 1833, that had virtually no political say in the affairs of the colony. Development of any kind, even the building of roads and health and educational facilities, was sacrificed to the interests of sugar cultivation and production. The refusal by the planter class to improve the poor working conditions on the plantations subsequently exploded into widespread strikes and riots not only in Guyana, but also in several other colonies in the West Indies. The extent and severity of the labor unrest and the economic and social dislocation of the masses were investigated by a Royal Commission which, by and large, recommended far-reaching constitutional and social reforms in the colony that provided for a gradual approach to the transfer of political power to local politicians elected under universal adult suffrage and, eventually, to political independence.[9]

During the early 1940s constitutional reforms were implemented in British Guiana, but they were more the result of the British government's initiative in responding to nationalist pressures from the rest of the English-speaking Caribbean than of any demands made by the middle-class leadership in the colony. Although the reforms led to an increase in the number of elected seats in the country's Legislative Council in 1943, nonetheless, their effects were minimal. For one thing, the reforms were not based on universal suffrage, but on a franchise qualified by property and income and, as such, the interests of the masses were not represented. For another, most of the local politicians and trade union leaders were co-opted by British colonial officials who made every effort to demobilize and thwart the political ambitions of the lower classes. The middle-class support of British interests and the status quo in Guyana resulted in the lost of their legitimacy as leaders and, as was quite evident, Britain's decision to delay universal adult suffrage in the country until 1953.[10]

The absence of a middle-class leadership and a nationalist movement was primarily responsible for the lack of ideological direction which eventually paved the way for radical leadership, national mobilization, and intensive ideological thrust that made possible the transition in Guyana from colony to an independent state in 1966, and to a Cooperative Socialist Republic in 1970. Initially, the leadership came in the person of Cheddi Jagan, an East Indian son of a sugar estate foreman, who after completing his studies at Howard and Northwestern Universities in the United States returned to British Guiana in 1943 as a dentist and with his American-born wife, Janet Rosenberg.[11] The Jagans and several other middle-class radicals and intellectuals formed the Political Affairs Committee (PAC)—a quasi-political organization based on Marxist-Leninist ideology and principles. Membership in the PAC comprised largely of overseas-trained Guyanese intellectuals and professionals who were inspired by the radicalism of British Labour Party politics, Marxism, and Mahatma Gandhi's political struggle in India, while abroad.

In 1945, Jagan founded the Guiana Industrial Workers Union (GIWU) as a radical alternative to the traditionally conservative trade unions in the country, particularly the Man Power Citizens Association (MPCA), which at the time represented East Indian workers on the sugar plantations. Although

Table 5.2
Population by Race in Guyana

Race	1960 Number %	1970 Number %	1980 Number %	1993 Number %
Blacks	183,950 (32.8)	218,401 (31.2)	231,330 (30.5)	255,617 (35.6)
East Indians	267,797 (47.8)	362,736 (51.8)	389,760 (51.4)	355,092 (49.5)
Amerindians	25,453 (4.5)	34,302 (4.9)	39,867 (5.3)	48,859 (6.8)
Whites	3,217 (0.6)	2,186 (0.3)	770 (0.1)	4,651 (0.6)
Portuguese	8,415 (1.5)	5,998 (0.9)	3,266 (0.4)	252 (0.0)
Chinese	4,074 (0.7)	3,042 (0.5)	1,842 (0.2)	2,433 (0.3)
Mixed or Colored	67,191 (12.0)	72,317 (10.3)	83,763 (11.0)	50,554 (7.0)
Not Stated	233 (0.0)	502 (0.1)	8,021 (1.1)	000 (0.0)
Total	560,330 (100.0)	699,844 (100.0)	758,619 (100.0)	717,458 (100.0)

Source: Guyana Bureau of Statistics, Georgetown, 1960 Census, vol. 2, table 5; 1970 Census, vol. 7, table 1; 1980 Census, table 7.2; and *Guyana Statistical Bulletin*, March 1994 for 1993.

the GIWU was much more popular than the MPCA among sugar workers, it never managed to win bargaining rights for them until the 1970s. As leader of both the PAC and the GIWU, Jagan at age 29 was the youngest member to be elected to Guyana's Legislative Council in 1947.[12] His radicalism and willingness to confront the pillars of authority in support of the rights of East Indian workers on the plantation were a huge success for the GIWU, and became the basis for political mobilization that translated into demands for political representation and political independence for Guyana.[13]

In mid-1950, Cheddi and Janet Jagan were joined by Forbes Burnham, a young black lawyer who had returned from England as a Guyana Scholar (a scholarship awarded annually by the British to the top student in Guyana). Burnham immediately joined the PAC and with Cheddi and Janet Jagan founded the People's Progressive Party later that year. As coleaders of the PPP, both Jagan and Burnham united blacks and Indians, sugar workers, rice workers, and city workers and, in the process, had created a powerful multiethnic nationalist movement firmly rooted in middle- and lower-class mobilization. They also had the support of the militant young intellectuals who had returned from universities abroad. The PPP, because of its radical approach, subsequently became a formidable threat to the interests of the local elite and British colonial hegemony in the country than any other nationalist movements in the English-speaking Caribbean. Burnham wasted no time in duplicating Jagan's political strategy with the GIWU and was elected president of the BGLU in 1952, still the largest and most powerful black union in the country. He was as popular among the black working class in the urban centers as was Jagan among his East Indian supporters in the rural areas of the country.

From the outset, the PPP advocated an end to colonialism, a demand for self-government, and a higher standard of living for the masses in Guyana. On the basis of ideology, the PPP, through its April 1, 1951, constitution, advanced a socialist ideology as its principal policy to economic and political development in Guyana. The party had no serious opposition as a nationalist movement. Its only opponents were a few independent Guyanese politicians, most of whom were mouthpieces of the British Empire, and the National Democratic Party (NDP) which, like the PPP, employed a strategy of balance in that it was headed by Lionel Luckoo, an East Indian lawyer, and John Carter, a black lawyer. Unlike the Marxist PPP, the NDP was conservative in nature and depended mostly on urban middle-class support. Thus, for the first time in the history of Guyana, there existed a nationalist movement in the PPP that provided the momentum for political change. That change came in 1953 when the party scored an impressive victory in the first national elections held under universal suffrage in Guyana. As the data in table 5.3 reveal, the PPP had won eighteen of the twenty-four available seats in the National Assembly with 51 percent of the popular vote. Jagan became the premier and Forbes Burnham the minister of education[14] The PPP success came mainly from the predominantly lower-class constituencies in the urban and rural areas of the country; many of them were new wage earners interested in bread-and-butter issues. The lower classes were undoubtedly attracted to the militancy of the radical trade union and political leadership of Burnham and Jagan who promised them a better economic future if only the economic interests of the ruling elite were expropriated.[15]

Table 5.3
Guyana Election Results 1953-1964
% of Votes Cast (Number of Legislative Seats)

Party	1953 % (Seats)	1957 % (Seats)	1961 % (Seats)	1964 % (Seats)
PPP	51.8 (18)	46.5 (9)	42.6 (20)	45.8 (24)
PPP (Burnham)	–	25.5 (3)	–	–
NDP	13 (2)	–	–	–
UDP	–	8.4 (1)	–	–
NFL	–	9.4 (1)	–	–
PNC	–	–	41 (11)	40.5 (22)
UF	–	–	16.3 (4)	12.4 (7)

Sources: Burnham 1970; Jagan 1966; Despres 1967; Spinner 1984.

The election of the first Marxist PPP government to office in the British Empire was sudden and proved dangerous both to metropolitan economic interests in the country and to the local elite who benefited the most from the very status quo that they had supported and was under such vehement attack by the PPP leadership. There is no doubt that the British government had hoped and expected the local moderate middle class would achieve political power under a representative government in Guyana. As it turned out, this was not the case. The British experiment with representative government in Guyana backfired because a radical group of political leaders employed a socialist ideology similar to that of the British Labour Party and straddled the racial divisions of the country and won the election. The rapid emergence with which the radical leftists came to power in Guyana was catastrophic to British colonial officials. It allowed them little or no time for the gradual transfer of power to a regime sympathetic to the interests of the British and the local elite. There was absolutely no guarantee that the PPP government, based on its anticolonial and anti-imperialist rhetoric, was prepared to protect the political and economic interests of the ruling class or those of the metropolitan powers in the country, even though their power was limited by the constitution.

The PPP in Power

Upon taking office, the PPP government pressed its constitutional powers to the limit to push through its radical domestic program that, among other issues, included land and welfare state reforms, trade union legislation, and the removal of church control of the schools.[16] Among the pieces of legislation passed by the Jagan government were the Rice Farmers Security of Tenure Bill and the Labor Relations Act. These legislation were very contentious and threatened not only the economic interests of the local propertied, professional, and administrative middle class, but those of the metropolitan interests as well. The Rice Farmers Security of Tenure Bill had a very controversial provision that protected East Indian farmers from rent increases by unscrupulous landlords and empowered the government to confiscate land from landlords who failed to meet their obligations of good estate management. In particular, the Labor Relations Bill, which directly precipitated the suspension of the constitution, was drafted by Cheddi Jagan. Its legal structure provided for fair election for trade union representation which had heavily favored the PPP-affiliated sugar workers union, the GIWU, over the conservative MPCA as the principal union on the sugar estates.[17]

Although these reforms significantly increased and strengthened Jagan and the PPP support among the East Indians, their quick passage under the Emergency Measures Act on October 8, 1953, proved to be too drastic for the governor and the local conservative middle and upper classes in the country. These groups had earlier established a strong alliance with the colonial elite and made much use of the communist threat of an alleged PPP conspiracy to turn Guyana into a communist state and seized all foreign assets. The governor, acting partly on these charges, was able to convince Prime Minister Churchill and the Colonial Secretary to suspend the country's constitution and expelled the PPP government after being in office for only 133 days.[18] The removal of the duly elected PPP government from office was difficult to justify in the eyes of the masses in Guyana and to the rest of the world. It was an extremely unwise decision by the British government, which had been strongly condemned as immoral and unjustifiable by a substantial number of members of the British House of Commons, as did much of the British Press, and Afro-Asian Commonwealth and other world leaders. Despite the constitutional guarantees of representative government and the supposed devolution of power to the local leaders, the ultimate political authority in Guyana had rested with the colonial office and the governor. Therefore, any legislation, even though passed by the Legislative Assembly, could not be enacted by the PPP government without the consent of the State Council (Upper House) and the governor.

There is little doubt that the suspension of the constitution and the expulsion of the PPP government were motivated by attacks on the interests and privileges of the local upper classes in a very class-polarized society, and the reaction of foreign political leaders both in London and in Washington to communist subversion. Equally, there is also little doubt that the PPP regime was not attempting to subvert the democratic process in the country. Be that as it may, in the heat of the Cold War, the Marxist faction within the PPP and Jagan's contacts with Russia and several communist states in Eastern Europe were enough to convince the British to take drastic action against newly elected PPP government. The decision by the British government to suspend Guyana's constitution was justified by the Secretary of State for the Colonies:

> What emerges from British Guiana is a coherent picture of ministers largely dominated by communist ideas, who are . . . threatening the order of the colony, threatening the livelihood of its inhabitants and undermining not only its present economic stability but also chances of building it up. . . . they are unfortunately all part of the design to turn British Guiana into a totalitarian state dominated by communist ideas.[19]

The power of the colonial office was well known, but became even more blatant when the British installed an interim government in Guyana and curtailed the movements of leading PPP politicians, including the Jagans and Burnham. The Jagans and a number of radicals followed the party directive and violated the curfew and were imprisoned. Burnham and some of the moderate leaders complied with the emergency orders rather than risk being arrested and detained. While the Jagans were in prison, Burnham attempted to gain control of the PPP by denouncing the anti-imperialist and Marxist rhetoric of Cheddi and Janet Jagan and the more radical leaders of the PPP and adopted an ideological position compatible with the metropolitan and the local middle and upper classes' interests in the country. His actions not only led to a split within the party in 1955, but also made him the most favored leader by British colonial officials to assume the mantle of power in a post-colonial Guyana.

Racial Mobilization in Guyana

The suspension of the constitution polarized the ideological cleavage within the PPP and intensified pluralist pressures in Guyana. From early in their political careers, both Jagan and Burnham had differed on the question of ideology. As a product and representative of the black middle class, Burnham had rejected the radical Marxist ideology of the PPP and sought political solutions to Guyana's problems. He believed that the solutions to Guyana's problems had to be found at home and not in the ideals of international communist alliances. Burnham wanted Jagan to put Guyanese nationalism above his communist posturing and to strive for the attainment of political independence for Guyana. To this end, he favored a bargained solution to Jagan's strategy of mass protest and confrontational politics with the British. Burnham also supported Britain's proposal for independence within the general framework of a West Indian federation and an electoral system based on proportional representation for Guyana.

By contrast, Jagan rejected the idea of a West Indies federation and Britain's economic and political domination of Guyana. He saw economic exploitation as the fundamental problem to Guyana's economic development and his solution to it was nothing less than state nationalization of private foreign enterprises. In international politics, Burnham favored a neutral non-aligned approach and was opposed to the anti-American and anti-imperialist position of Jagan and the other radical members of the PPP. Jagan, on the other hand, had preferred alignment with the socialist bloc of Eastern Europe, a position that antagonized Britain and the United States and proved dangerous to Western interests during the height of the Cold War. These factors figured heavily in Burnham's strategy for gaining control of the colonial state while they drastically reduced Jagan's chances to head a government in the postcolonial period.

The ideological and policy differences were the basis for the split in the PPP in 1955, and the subsequent development of racial politics in Guyana, and here, interpretation of the events remains very controversial. Jagan's view is that the split was largely the work of British and American imperialist forces and his claim is based solidly on the fact that as early as 1951, U. S. trade unions did work to undermine the GIWU in Guyana. Also, there is enough evidence to show that the British governor formed an alliance with the local middle and upper classes to oppose the PPP, and that the British Labour Party encouraged Burnham to split with Jagan.[20] Burnham, on the other hand, not only blamed Jagan and his Marxist forces for the split, but points to the suspension of the constitution by the British as the root cause of the division of the nationalist movement in the country on racial lines. Whatever the interpretations are, Burnham can hardly be blamed for the fracture of the PPP, given the racial balance in Guyana (table 5.2), he had much to lose from such a division. The causes of the division and the events that led to it are well documented. Suffice to say that the split between Jagan and Burnham resulted in two political factions within the PPP, one led by Forbes Burnham, and the other remaining under the leadership of Jagan.

For almost five years (1953-1957), British Guiana was under a somewhat confused state of affairs, first, with the suspension of the constitution and second, with the division within the PPP, which ultimately led to the development of racial politics in the country. It is important to note that initially the split did not lead to racial politics, because most of the black radicals remained with Jagan while the moderate East Indians departed with Burnham. The emergence of racial politics can be directly linked to Jagan's speech to the PPP congress in 1956 in which he appealed to the East Indian business community to support the PPP on the basis of ethnicity. This led to the resignation of the black radicals from the party.[21] The resignations were a serious blow to Jagan because they represented a further erosion of his claim that the party was a multiracial nationalist organization.

The division of the PPP was ideally suited to the British who introduced a new constitution of limited self-rule that reduced political representation in Guyana's parliament from twenty-four to fourteen seats. The British also encouraged the formation of other political parties, including the United Democratic Party (UDP) and the National Labour Front (NLF). These moves by the British were intended to weaken the political base of the PPP and prevent Jagan from gaining power. The suspension of the constitution could have been sustained only as a temporary measure. International opinion in favor of political self-determination and the removal of the British Labour Party from power in Britain intensified the pressure on the British government to grant new elections.

Bowing to pressure from within the British Parliament and from the Commonwealth of Nations, the British government granted new elections to Guyana under a limited constitution of self-government that was less representative than the suspended constitution of 1953. The election was held in August 1957 and was contested by the Jagan and Burnham factions of the PPP, the UDP, and the NLF. The UDP was an outgrowth of the NDP that comprised the militant anticommunist, middle-class Catholics, some black radicals, and the more conservative Portuguese, Chinese, and near-white middle and upper classes. The UDP was an uneasy alliance whose intent was to capitalize from the split between Jagan and Burnham. It was led by John Carter, one of the coleaders of the former NDP. Similarly, the NLF was formed by Lionel Luckoo (the former coleader of the NDP) with the goal to corral all the East Indians who disliked Jagan's radicalism.[22]

The explicit use of the racial Hindu slogan "*Apan Jhaat*" (vote for your own race) in the 1957 elections and Jagan's appeal to East Indian laborers, peasants, and frustrated youths, some of them with high school diplomas and no jobs, contributed to an impressive win of nine of the fourteen seats for his faction of the PPP with 47.5 percent of the popular vote. Burnham's appeal to voters for support on the basis of his beliefs and not his ancestry earned his group three seats and 25.5 percent of the vote. The UDP and the NLF won one seat each (table 5.3). Jagan's triumph at the polls can partly be attributed to the PPP's appeal to "apan jhaat" politics which had acquired wide currency in the East Indian communities throughout the country.

Reelection of the PPP

With the PPP in power for the second time, Jagan did not learn from his earlier mistakes. He immediately advanced the interests of the East Indian business community by liberalizing Guyana's trade policy as part of his campaign promise. Tariffs were removed on some imported items used predominantly by East Indians while those used by blacks were increased. Furthermore, the PPP threat to "Indianize" the urban areas fed fears among the urban black population who are the primary city dwellers. This was particularly true for the civil service and other public service employees since they were vulnerable to the overt attempt by the Jagan government to recruit East Indians into the public and para-public sectors. The party made equally aggressive efforts to place East Indians in the police force and military establishments. Jagan also instituted educational reforms that gave the PPP government direct control and management of the country's fifty-one denominational schools. The PPP also built a number of schools in the rural areas of the country where there were large concentrations of East Indians and recruited teachers of East Indian origin only to teach in those schools.[23] The policies of the 1957-61 Jagan government disproportionately benefited the East Indian masses as they heavily favored agriculture over urban development, and helped small and medium business at the expense of large business. The problem was these policies were interpreted by the urban black population as part of Jagan's strategy to consolidate East Indian support with the aim of promoting "apan jhaat" politics in the country. Their objective effect was to feed African fears and racial antagonism and also to force Burnham into racial mobilization. Most black intellectuals, however, had become acutely aware of Jagan's racist policies and were sensitive to his threat of Indian domination. Their anxiety generated anti-Indian sentiment which took precedence over their ideological views and cemented the unification of black politics in Guyana under the leadership of Forbes Burnham.

In 1957, Burnham's faction of the PPP merged with the UDP and created the People's National Congress (PNC) as an alternative to the PPP. The UDP was overwhelmingly supported by the black and colored middle classes who had strongly opposed the PPP Marxist philosophy. The merger was made possible by Burnham's political shift from a class appeal to a racial appeal that mobilized the black and colored middle classes in support of the PNC, which was also ideologically to the left. Racial mobilization also assured Burnham of the continued support of the black lower classes who were locked in through racial politics. The PNC leadership sole commitment was to end the East Indian and the PPP domination of the political system in Guyana. Consequently, Burnham set himself the dual task of winning political power for the PNC and independence for the country. These feats were achieved in 1964 with changes in the electoral system that led to the formation of the PNC-UF coalition government and political independence for Guyana in 1966.

The political polarization of the two largest ethnic groups in Guyana into a Marxist-Leninist directed East Indian faction and a socialist-led African and colored alliance left the more conservative Portuguese, Chinese, and near white populations without ideological or racial representation. Support from the leadership of the NLF, which was dissolved in 1959, paved the way for a group of businessmen and professionals under the leadership of a prominent Portuguese industrialist named Peter D'Aguiar to form the United Force (UF) in 1960. The UF was a right wing party that represented the interests of the whites and local capitalist class and was organized to defend the status quo. It was firmly supported by the local Catholic church, foreign multinational corporations, and by some Western governments. This brief but complicated description of the development of political parties in Guyana during the 1950s is illustrated in figure 5.1.

The formation of political parties along racial lines in Guyana could have resulted in the consolidation and sustenance of a genuinely mass-based, national-oriented political culture. Politics thereafter became identified with the pursuit of narrow and sectional interests as racial groups became aligned with specific political parties. Political scholar Leo Despres has convincingly argued that the political leaders of the three main parties in Guyana "have become symbols of a racial expression in Guyanese politics which is representative of the plural society in its most vicious form. That is to say, parties and leaders are no longer seen as national coalitions but as exclusive ethnic groupings fostering a kind of ethnic chauvinism."[24] This was the political situation when the British government introduced an advanced constitution of internal self-government for the 1961 elections. The new constitution added fuel to the already racially charged political atmosphere in the country by promising to discuss the terms of its political independence after the elections.

The PPP Struggle to Control the State

After a racially charged election in which the PPP won twenty of the thirty-five seats and 43 percent of the popular vote, the PNC gained 31 percent but only eleven seats, and the UF, a meagre four seats with 16.3 percent of the vote. Jagan was now confronted with a situation in which the majority of the votes had gone against the PPP. Once again the voting had conformed to racial patterns and a considerable amount of racial bitterness had, as a result, been engendered in the country. British Guiana had become a microcosm of the world's most aggravating problems that had to be solved by Britain. They include economic poverty, racial animosity, an East-West ideological conflict, class warfare, and even religious prejudice. The situation had its irony too in that the East Indian population, religiously committed to the Hindu and Muslim faiths, was to a large extent the landed and property owning class, yet they supported a communist-led party. Blacks and other minority racial groups who were mainly wage earners and the unemployed in the urban areas supported the liberal left and right of center parties. The situation was an explosive one, and it was not long before that explosion occurred.

The PPP victory came in the wake of the Cuban revolution of which the U.S. was very wary of, and was determined not to let the Marxist Jagan lead Guyana into independence despite international pressure on Britain from many Global South countries, who used the United Nations as a forum to push for decolonization. Jagan's reputation as a Marxist, his proclamation of Castro as one of the world's greatest liberators, and his widened trade relations with Cuba and the Eastern bloc states stirred fears in the Kennedy administration. On the other hand, Forbes Burnham's impressive visit to

Figure 5.1
Development of Political Parties in Guyana

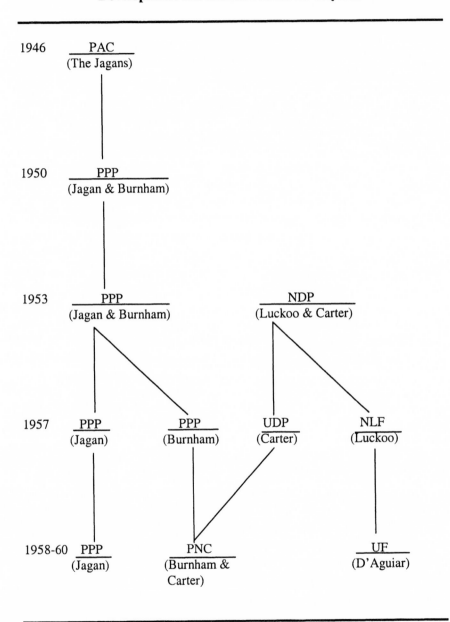

Washington, D.C., in May 1962, and the failure of the Bay of Pigs invasion which was still fresh in the mind of the Kennedy administration, heightened tension between Cuba and the United States. At the time, the U.S. had orchestrated an economic embargo against Cuba and was in the process of isolating the Castro regime diplomatically. Jagan's actions seemed to be in open defiance of U.S. policy and heightened fears in Washington that an independent Guyana under the PPP might follow the path of Cuba. As a consequence, the situation in Guyana came directly under U.S. scrutiny. Arthur Schlesinger, Jr., a senior advisor to President Kennedy, assessed the political situation in Guyana:

> An independent British Guiana under Burnham (if Burnham can commit himself to a multilateral policy) would cause us many fewer problems than an independent British Guiana under Jagan. And the way was open to bring it about because Jagan's parliamentary strength was larger than his popular strength. He had won 57% of the seats on the basis of 42.3% of the vote. An obvious solution was to establish a system of Proportion Representation. This, after prolonged discussion, the British finally did in October, 1963.[25]

It was this assessment that motivated the United States to assume a more activist role in Guyanese affairs. With Britain's encouragement, the Kennedy administration intervened in the country's internal affairs indirectly through the U.S. trade union link, and, directly, through the CIA. American intervention in Guyana also took the form of intense pressure on the British government to change Guyana's electoral system to proportional representation (PR). Given the racial composition of the country and the racial voting pattern, a change to PR seemed plausible to the United States to be the most obvious way of removing the Marxist PPP government from office. In the 1961 elections, the PPP won 57 percent of the seats in the legislature with 42.6 percent of the popular vote while the PNC obtained 41 percent but received only 31.4 percent of the seats. It was obvious that proportion representation would produce a much more accurate reflection of seats in the elected house than the first-past-the-post electoral system. Once the British government had agreed to the Kennedy administration proposal to introduce proportion representation in the country, the fate of the PPP government was sealed.

On January 31, 1962, the Jagan government introduced a budget in the National Assembly later to be described by the trade unions as a scheme to tax the poor. Three unions representing most of the government employees declared a strike against the government. Almost immediately the strikers were joined by housewives and children, but most importantly, by Burnham and D'Aguiar in a march of over 60,000 persons through the streets of the capital city. Riot, arson, and looting of several East Indian owned businesses ensued as the police and paramilitary units comprised mostly of blacks and sympathetic to and supportive of the PNC looked on idly.[26] This lack of support and loyalty to the state by the security forces forced the PPP to rely upon the intervention of British troops to restore order. Though these events outwardly appeared to be spontaneous, they were, in fact, carefully planned by Burnham and the PNC hierarchy.[27] This was the beginning of the end of the Jagan government and, retrospectively, Guyanese democracy for the two-and-a-half decades that followed.

This state of disorder continued for the next two years with the high point being an eighty-day general strike that was covertly supported and financed by the CIA and the AFL-CIO.[28] The strike was a catastrophe for the PPP regime in that it exposed Jagan's inability to govern the country with any semblance of order. Over the entire period anti-PPP demonstrations cost the country over 300 lives in interracial warfare and some G$30 million in revenue. The strike has left a legacy of racial hatred that has permanently scarred the national psyche of the Guyanese people. Although the strike did not remove the PPP government from office, it, however, was used as the bargaining chip to force Jagan and the PPP leadership to accept the constitutional change in the electoral system from first-past-the-post (winner-take-all) to proportional representation (PR)—a solution that was highly favored by the PNC and UF leadership and by Washington. For all it's worth, PR was bitterly opposed by Jagan and PPP supporters throughout the country. The December 7, 1964, election in Guyana was held under the new constitution after which a conference was convened in London to set the date for political independence. This was decided by the British Colonial Secretary Duncan Sandys at the October 1963 Constitution Conference in London. It was at this conference that Jagan made the biggest blunder of his political career when he, along with Burnham and D'Aguiar, signed a letter authorizing Sandys to settle the electoral crisis in Guyana.

Like the 1957 and 1961 elections, "apan jhaat" politics dominated the 1964 election. It was the unofficial election campaign slogan of the PPP and of East Indians all across the country. The voting in the 1964 election followed the same racial pattern as in previous elections in which the PPP polled 45.8 percent of the popular votes, the PNC 40.5 percent, and the UF 12.4 percent (table 5.3). However, under the PR system, there was no anomaly between the popular vote and representation in Parliament. The number of seats obtained by each party differed significantly from those of previous elections held under the first-past-the-post system. The PPP proportion of the vote gave the party twenty-four seats, the PNC received twenty-two seats, and the UF obtained the remaining seven seats.[29]

It was at this critical period that Burnham sublimated the socialist beliefs which he had hitherto professed before his split with Jagan and the PPP and entered into a coalition government with the relatively small conservative and capitalist-oriented UF. The PNC-UF coalition government fulfilled the twin objectives of keeping the PPP out of power while assuring the PNC the dominant partner in the government. By joining with the UF, Burnham assured his foreign power brokers and the local capitalist elite that they had made the right choice and that parliamentary democracy and free enterprise were safe under his political stewardship. This shift in ideology by the PNC was also prudent because Burnham did not want any obstacle placed in the path to Guyana's independence. At best, the PNC/UF coalition was an uneasy alliance of political convenience. It was, in fact, more of a defensive coalition against the PPP, and, as a result, was incapable of resolving the real political issue of who or which party should control the newly independent country. In the end, it took an alliance of U.S., British, foreign, and local business, and the Guyanese upper, middle, and the black urban lower classes to remove the Marxist PPP government from power. Buoyed by their political success, the PNC-UF coalition government took office on December 15, 1964.

The Road to Cooperative Socialism

With Burnham as prime minister and D'Aguiar, the conservative leader of the UF holding the most powerful and important portfolio of minister of finance, Guyana finally achieved its political independence from Britain on May 26, 1966, under the PNC-UF coalition government. During its term in office, the coalition government made considerable efforts to placate the East Indian majority by offering them jobs in the public sector. The extent to which the Indians were placated was reflected in their pleas for the partition of Guyana, an idea advocated by Sydney King (Eusi Kwayana) in 1961.[30] This idea gained momentum among East Indians after the defeat of the PPP in 1964, and again with the PNC victories in the 1968 and 1973 elections.

But Burnham was not pleased with the compromises the PNC leadership had to make to head a coalition government with the UF in order to keep the PPP out of office. Apart from handing the finance portfolio over to the UF, the PNC had to agree not to increase tariffs on imports or taxes on the capitalist class who overwhelmingly supported the UF in the 1964 election. The PNC also had to limit the amount of jobs to qualified overseas Guyanese because the UF had preferred expatriate skills to fill local positions. Furthermore, the D'Aguiar budget did not allocate resources to alleviate poverty among the poor or provide low cost housing to the urban lower classes who had supported the PNC in the election. To free the PNC of these constraints, the government, through judicious use of patronage, solicited and got the support of opposition members of parliament to acquire a parliamentary majority and dispose of the coalition government six months before the 1968 elections. The patronage resources of the state were also used to establish clientelistic alliances with powerful and influential leaders who would have otherwise supported the PPP and opposed the PNC on racial, class, or ideological grounds.[31] This brought political freedom to the PNC leadership who, for the first time, had acquired exclusive control of all branches of the government and sole access to the state coercive apparatus to be used against potential political opponents.

With election required every four to five years by the constitution, there was no guarantee that the PNC could maintain its exclusive control of the government, given the fact that its black and colored supporters did not constitute a large enough group to provide the party with the majority needed for an electoral victory. It could not depend on the leaders it had co-opted from the opposition to deliver the requisite votes mainly because these leaders' decision to join the PNC had alienated their former supporters. The PNC leaders knew that they were short of the votes needed to win an election. To remain in power, the PNC regime took control of the election machinery. The Election Commission was restructured to allow Guyanese nationals living overseas to vote in elections supervised by its embassy staff, most of whom were PNC supporters. It also staffed the polling booths with its own supporters who had easy access to ballot boxes and who tabulated the votes. These developments led to massive electoral fraud which enabled the PNC to win a landslide victory in the 1968 elections with 55.8 percent of the popular vote and thirty of the fifty-three seats in Parliament and, as indicated in table 5.4, all subsequent elections prior to 1992 were rigged in favor of the PNC regime.

The PNC electoral victory ushered in an era of controversial elections, a scourge that plagued the nation and haunted Guyana's electoral process for nearly a quarter of a century. The dysfunction of the electoral system became increasingly blatant in later elections to facilitate the emergence of a one-party authoritarian political culture in Guyana during the PNC reign which ended in 1992. Until his death in August 1985, Burnham dominated the

PNC party, which he founded in 1957. To party members, supporters, and government officials, Burnham was known as the "Comrade Leader." In reference to the personality cult that had developed around the PNC leader, Walter Rodney asserted, "They have seriously promoted him as the ultimate in wisdom, all-knowing, all powerful, next to God."[32] During this period all strands of power led to Burnham.

The PNC regime won landslide electoral victories in the 1973, 1980, and the 1985 elections (table 5.4). Six parties contested the December 17, 1985, elections against the PNC. Apart from the PPP, and the UF, there were the People's Democratic Movement (PDM), the Democratic Labour Movement (DLM), the National Democratic Front (NDF), and the Working People's Alliance (WPA) (see table 5.4). The voting pattern was the same and the election was conducted in the same manner to previous ones won by the PNC. Percy Hintzen has explicitly argued that after the 1968 electoral victory, the PNC regime was able to assure itself of absolute domination of the state through racial mobilization, control of the machinery of elections, support of a loyal state bureaucracy, and control of highly politicized police and armed forces.[33] Thus, coercion, control, patronage, and racial mobilization became the four main pillars upon which the PNC regime power rested from 1968 to 1992.

Shortly after the election, the leaders of the PNC resumed their socialist posture as they advocated cooperative socialism as a new brand of socialism unlike that which existed in the West or in the East. Unshackled from what was perceived by the PNC hierarchy as a constraining political alliance with the UF, Burnham shrewdly and effectively expropriated the mantle of leftist radicalism from his principal political opponent, Cheddi Jagan, his erstwhile copartner whom he labelled "a communist stooge" in 1955.[34] As Burnham put it:

> The People's National Congress is a socialist party. Socialist, not in terms of any European or North American definition which others may seek to thrust upon us, but in terms of our own social needs and wants in creating a just society for the people of Guyana. . . . A just society cannot be achieved unless the majority of people, the masses, the little men, have a full share in the ownership and control of the economy, a share which corresponds realistically with their political power.[35]

To underscore the importance of the cooperative sector, the PNC has named Guyana a Cooperative Socialist Republic. It has argued that "cooperatism, conceived in both its organizational and psychological forms, is rooted in the psyche of our people and can best fulfil our developmental goals."[36] It involved the development of a number of socialist strategies designed to restructure the political economy of Guyana and thus significantly reduce its heavy dependence on the core capitalist countries. The manner in which this was to be achieved is the subject of the next section.

The Declaration of Cooperative Socialism in Guyana

On February 23, 1970, four years after its attainment of independence, Guyana was officially declared a Cooperative Socialist Republic by the PNC government. A number of economic and political factors contributed to this particular development. First, during the mid-1960s, the dominant structural relations of Guyana's economy, and the social form through which they were systematically reproduced, delineated many of the classic features associated with underdevelopment and dependency relations. Second, most of the country's productive assets, including sugar and bauxite, were owned and controlled by foreign multinational corporations. Third, Guyana's economy was heavily dependent on foreign corporate investment, foreign technology, and external trade, particularly from the United States and Britain, the two countries from which most of the foreign owners and controllers of the country's productive assets, foreign economic decision making, and control of the world's financial institutions originated. Fourth, the country's extensive reliance was on imported foodstuffs (despite its agricultural economy), and intermediate goods, such as oil, fertilizers, and capital equipment to develop its economy. Fifth, in addition to its small size, the economy could not provide enough jobs for the workforce, which at the time was estimated to be as high as 21 percent, while approximately 35 percent of the unemployed were underemployed due to seasonal work in the agriculture sector.[37]

In seeking to overcome these pressing socioeconomic problems, the PNC regime pursued various development strategies such as industrialization by invitation and import substitution industrialization. These development strategies produced several negative features in the country. Most of the industries that were created were branch plants of foreign corporations which assembled only semi-finished products and employed highly capital-intensive technology. Profits were extremely high and because of free capital mobility, most of it was siphoned to the home countries of the MNCs. The external drain of foreign exchange was so substantial that it led to a severe shortage of foreign currency in the country. Regional economic integration within the institutional framework of CARIFTA and CARICOM was

Table 5.4
Guyana Election Results 1968-1985
% of Votes Cast (Number of Legislative Seats)

Party	1968 % (Seats)	1973 % (Seats)	1980 % (Seats)	1985 % (Seats)
PPP	36.5 (19)	25.5 (14)	19.0 (10)	16.0 (8)
PNC	55.8 (30)	70.2 (37)	78.0 (41)	78.0 (42)
UF	7.4 (4)	0.5 (0)	3.0 (2)	3.0 (2)
LP[1]	–	3.0 (2)	–	–
WPA	–	–	–	2.0 (1)
PDM	–	–	–	0.1 (0)
DLM	–	–	–	–
NDF	–	–	–	
IND	–	–	–	2.0 (2)

Sources: Spinner 1984; Guyana Electoral Commission 1980.

[1]The Liberator Party (LP) was formed in 1972 as a result of a split within the UF. Its leader was Fielden Singh, who in 1972 was suspended as leader of the UF. The LF had ceased to exist when its leader retired from politics in 1984. IND is the abbreviation for independent candidates.

introduced as a means to enhance intra-Caribbean trade and reduce the region's dependence on the core capitalist states. This, too, did not produce a halt to the country's collapsing economy or significantly increased intra-regional trade because most Caribbean countries were in dire need of hard currency and therefore continue to trade more with the U.S. than with each other.

And last but not least, the government attempted to establish an agri-business industry by merging the agricultural and manufacturing sectors.

With this strategy, the use of local agriculture products for raw materials was expected to increase domestic manufacturing with the aim of reducing Guyana's traditional dependence on foreign exchange to finance imports. It was also intended to advance the production of local food and other products in the country. To say the least, this experiment floundered apparently because of an inadequately trained labor staff, poor organization and mismanagement, and backward agricultural methods. What is perhaps not so self-evident and what should be made clear is that the country's production structures which were internationalized after the sixteenth century to bolster the capitalist mode of production remained essentially dependent even after a decade of independence. In light of the above, the economy displayed widespread signs of very high unemployment, severe poverty, backward communications and electrical facilities, underdeveloped medical services, and an inadequate educational system. School, sanitation, hospital, and housing facilities, while substantially better than in a number of Third World countries, were inadequate for a significant portion of the population.

Politically, the development of cooperative socialism in Guyana was, to an appreciable extent, due to the fact that there existed at the time a very militant population in the country that was influenced by the Marxist-Leninist philosophy promoted by the PPP leadership in the 1950s and 1960s as a means to challenge the country's colonial status. This militancy resulted in part from the brutal and harsh conditions of plantation labor and enclave mining suffered by the East Indians and Africans and from the early maturity and formation of relatively highly developed trade union organizations in the country. The PPP, which is the first Marxist-Leninist party to win fair and free elections in the British Empire, and its associated trade union, GIWU, the largest in the country, began to politically mobilize the lower working classes since the early 1950s. Economist Clive Thomas succinctly explains that it was in the interest of the Burnham regime to adopt a popular socialist strategy comparable to the main political opposition, the Marxist PPP, and acceptable to the masses in order to gain their support and maintain its grip on power.[38] This strategy was consistent with the willingness of the PNC leadership to implement policies and adopt ideological positions favorable to the interests of the most powerful strategic domestic and international actors. Thus, in order to remain in power, the PNC ideological position had to reflect and cater to the interests of the members of the state bureaucracy and the trade union movement. These two groups emerged from the political crisis of the early 1960s as the most powerful and formidable political forces in Guyana in the postindependence period. The PNC success was largely due to the unwavering support of these two groups that forced the PPP government to withdraw its budget in 1962.

As a Fabian socialist, Burnham began his political career by joining with a group of radical Marxists and formed the PPP which, in 1950, seemed to offer the best political chance of gaining control of the state. This was the case in 1953 when the PPP leadership successfully appealed to the working classes and won the elections that year. With the suspension of Guyana's constitution in 1953, Burnham disassociated himself from the more radical rhetoric of Cheddi Jagan and other leaders of the PPP. He adopted a more moderate position and complied with the orders from the colonial office that curtailed the political activity and movement of PPP leaders. Burnham was also aware that metropolitan political and economic interests and those of the local elite had to be protected if the transfer of political power was to take place. At the time, it was the colonial office and the economic elite who had a virtual monopoly over decisions determining the future political direction of the country. This was true for all colonies. The PNC acquiescence to these interests reflected its ideological flexibility during critical periods when its attempts to form the government and its efforts to maintain its hold on power were in danger. It was the only possible way to ensure that Burnham and the PNC leadership would head a postindependent state in Guyana.

Once independence was attained, however, conditions for assuming and maintaining control of the state were no longer dictated by the colonial office or metropolitan interests. The PNC leaders were now free to change their pro-business, pro-imperialist ideological position they had adopted during a coalition government with the conservative pro-business UF to prevent the Marxist PPP from taking power. These ideological shifts were consistent with the power interests of the PNC and of the socialist policies it embarked upon in the post-independence period.

The socialist development strategy adopted by the PNC government in Guyana advocated, among other things, the expansion of state control of the economy. This approach was consistent with the interests of the bureaucratic elite and the trade union movement in that it provided state employees with unlimited opportunities to fill the high paying and prestigious positions left vacant by private-sector workers. The expansion of welfare programs and state services had also required an expanded state bureaucracy which, in turn, had generated more jobs in the public sector. Trade unions were also the principal supporters and beneficiaries of the socialist programs because of their commitment to social welfare services and their strong advocacy of the paramountcy of workers' rights. The Civil Service Association, the Guyana Teachers Union, the Transport Union, and the Postal and Telecommunications Workers Union were among the trade unions that directly benefited from the PNC's state expansion program. The pursuit of a state-controlled economy in Guyana was a conscious strategy by the PNC regime to reduce the influence of the foreign and local capitalist class in the broader sociopolitical environment of the country. The objective was for the state to encounter the minimum amount of opposition from these groups as the regime solidified its grip on power. This, in effect, signalled an end to MNCs branch plant domination of the country's economy and productive structures. The proof of the PNC socialist intent and state intervention in the economy was enshrined in the national policy initiatives of cooperative socialism.

Policy Initiatives of Cooperative Socialism

In Guyana the concept of cooperative socialism was a novel ideology. The domestic label placed on this development strategy showed that the state was pursuing its own independent and indigenous path to development. The objective was to rid the economy from the effects of dependent capitalist development and eliminate the classical features of underdevelopment and dependency that have for centuries been the hallmark of the country's dependent economic structures. But as we shall observe, a decade after the establishment of cooperative socialism in Guyana, most of these structures remained essentially the same while many others have actually deteriorated and, in some cases, collapsed altogether.

Cooperative socialism was conceived with the primary goal of allowing the Guyanese people a greater role in the operation of the country's economy. It was supposed to be the means by which the small man would become a real man, and to change in a revolutionary fashion the social and economic relationships to which the population has been heir as part of its monarchical legacy.[39] Indeed, arguably, the socialist policies advocated and practiced by the PNC regime were by no means doctrinaire. The regime was committed to state ownership and control of the natural resources and management of the economy in the interests of the Guyanese people in order for them to have some control of the economic structure as they have politically. This was the goal sought by Burnham who said: "Constitutionally the people's representatives run the country; economically they do not. We must shift the emphasis in the economy. We must put economic power where it belongs."[40]

The concept of cooperative socialism also had a local and international element. It was developed as a local alternative to the rival international systems of capitalism spearheaded by the United States and other Western developed nations, and communism as practiced by the former Soviet Union, China, and Cuba, among others. It was as a third path to development that was based on the particular historical and psychological makeup of the Guyanese people. Again as Forbes Burnham put it:

> Because of the history of our people, we have decided that we will use the instrument of the cooperative. There again we do not approach it dogmatically. We do not join with those who say no good things come from the West nor do we join with those who say no good things come from the East. We recognise that in the Western world, the cooperative is an appendage to the given capitalist system. We recognise that in the East the cooperative is an appendage to a given system of state monopoly. We are not prepared to sell ourselves short. We feel that we are capable of using the cooperative as the main institution in our economic progress and in our attempt, desire and irreversible goal to make the small man a real man.[41]

Cooperative socialism was developed with the twin objectives to rid the Guyanese society of some of the exploitative and dependency features of the capitalist world order and to strengthen Burnham's hold on power. It was comprised of nine national policy initiatives of the state. The first of these was the expansion of state property over the commanding heights[42] of the economy through a program of nationalization.

Historically, the economy of Guyana has been based on the production and sale in the world market of three primary products: sugar, bauxite, and rice. Sugar and bauxite together accounted for approximately 90 percent of the export earnings and 70 percent of GDP, and continue to be as they have been during the twentieth century and even now the primary source of foreign exchange and the largest employers of wage labor in the country. In the mid-1960s, bauxite replaced sugar as the primary source of foreign capital and constituted between 40 and 50 percent of Guyana's total exports, sugar, roughly 30 to 35 percent, and rice, between 7 and 10 percent.[43] Both the sugar and bauxite industries were owned and controlled by foreign companies. About 90 percent of the sugar facilities in Guyana were owned by Bookers Sugar Estates—a subsidiary of Booker McConnell Limited of London. The remaining 10 percent of the industry's assets were under the control of another British firm, Jessel's Securities of London. The bauxite industry was also owned by two TNCs. Prior to the nationalization in 1971, the bulk of the bauxite production was owned by the Demerara Bauxite Company (DEMBA), a subsidiary of the Aluminum Company of Canada

(ALCAN). The other bauxite company was controlled by Reynolds Metals of the U. S. Rice, the basic domestic staple of the nation, is grown primarily by East Indian peasants on small family farms. Rice cultivation is second only to the sugar industry as the largest source of employment in Guyana. Like sugar, rice is a seasonal crop.

Nationalization of the Bauxite Industry

It should be emphasized that the nationalization of DEMBA was not the original plan of the PNC regime. At first, the government sought to acquire 51 percent equity of the company's assets, presumably in the belief that a mutuality of corporate and national interest could exist. The main thrust of the government's argument for meaningful participation in the activities of the bauxite industry was centered on the difficulty of assuring fair prices to Guyana for bauxite when much of the country's output was transferred into the multinational corporate system. The government had little information on the company's annual income or profits or the actual amount of bauxite extracted from the country annually. It had to rely on figures posted by the company. When negotiations between the government and DEMBA for joint ownership failed in 1971, the regime nationalized the entire operation of DEMBA and declared that this was the first step in the building of co-operative socialism in the country. There was a very strong possibility that had there been a favorable response to the government proposals regarding joint ownership of the bauxite company, the PNC's approach to socialism could have been different.

Bauxite exploration and the purchase of bauxite lands in Guyana began in the early 1900s by the Aluminum Company of America, which at the time owned ALCAN. The British colonial government had very little concern for the long-term welfare of Guyanese residents and, as a result, sold most of the main bauxite lands to ALCOA. While accurate data are hard to come by, it is fair to say that the land was sold at very low prices. In 1916 DEMBA was a local affiliate of ALCOA, and in 1928, it became a subsidiary of the independent ALCAN. Based on agreements with the Crown government, DEMBA was allowed to purchase bauxite it mined on Crown lands for only 5 cents per ton while it paid absolutely no royalties on bauxite it mined on its own lands.[44]

At the time of nationalization in 1971, DEMBA operated bauxite mines, a bauxite processing plant, an aluminum plant, and related engineering and maintenance facilities valued at over 130 million Canadian dollars. In spite of these assets, most of the 3.4 million tons of bauxite produced annually in Guyana were shipped to ALCAN plants in Canada, processed, and sold to the abrasive and refractory industries in North America and Western Europe.[45] The company did not invest in infrastructure beyond the extraction and production of raw bauxite. As an ALCAN official stated, "the subsidiary in Guyana represented a raw material foundation on which most of ALCAN's international aluminum superstructure is erected."[46]

Acquiring the assets of the bauxite industry was perhaps the single most decisive event that determined Guyana's future economic policy and the PNC socialist strategy. It was decisive, not because it heralded a fundamental break with the past. Much more important was the positive economic benefits that accrued to middle-class supporters of the PNC from which the company's new managerial staff was selected. Consequently, there emerged a strong support among the black middle class for the PNC government to take similar action against other multinationals in the country. This enabled the PNC government to successfully push through its program of massive state takeover of the private sector as the basis for a socialist transformation of the country's economy. Without the patronage benefits of the state, such a radical policy would certainly have met with considerable opposition from the black middle class traditionally hostile to socialist policies. But for this strategic group, nationalization was synonymous with socialism if it meant more jobs for them.

Nonetheless, the PNC regime did not embark on a full-scale program of nationalization until 1974. By that time it had acquired a two-thirds majority in Parliament by means of widespread electoral fraud. In the two years that followed, the PNC government took control of all the major corporations in the country. In addition to DEMBA, the PNC, in 1975, nationalized Reynolds Guyana Mines, a subsidiary of the U.S.-owned company, Reynolds Metals.

Nationalization of the Sugar Industry

Having brought the bauxite industry under state control, the regime turned to the sugar industry. In May 1975, it nationalized the smaller of the two sugar companies, the British-owned Jessel Securities Limited.[47] The largest move toward state control of foreign enterprises in Guyana was formalized to mark the nation's tenth independence anniversary. In May 1966 the PNC regime took control of the enormous assets of Booker McConnell after it agreed to pay close to G$500 million in compensation out of future profits. The company's local assets of twenty-two subsidiaries had directly employed 23,500 persons of which over 80 percent were Guyanese. Booker McConnell was the country's largest sugar producer in that it provided 40 percent of Guyana's exports and 35 percent of its gross domestic product.[48] So extensive were its operations that, in the colonial era, it was often said that in reality British Guiana was Bookers' Guiana. The nationalization of Bookers was supported by the PPP since Jagan had always advocated an end to foreign domination of the sugar industry. The PPP domestic policy of critical support to the PNC regime resulted in several defectors of some of its staunchest activists and right-wing supporters, including an amalgam of East Indian religious leaders and professionals. The defections not only stunned the PPP leaders and lent credibility to the PNC claim to being a true socialist party, but to Jagan's surprise, the defectors were also courted by the Burnham regime to join the PNC.

The government nationalization policy was further extended to include retail distribution outlets, drug manufacture, alcohol production, shipping, public transport, communications, banking, and trade through the formation of an official External Trade Bureau. The expansion of the state into the private sector was so extensive that by the end of 1976, it had owned and controlled almost 80 percent of the economy.[49] The state had twenty-nine public corporations and companies, four banks, three bauxite enterprises, and the vast sugar corporation with assets valued at over G$1.5 billion and 65,000 employees under its control (see figure 5.2). Parallel to this was the fact that government ministries increased from twelve in 1968 to twenty-one in 1977.

Education

This extraordinary corporate expansion of the state into the private sector was matched by similar expansion in the public welfare sector, particularly in education, which is the second policy initiative of co-operative socialism. The government made education the centerpiece of its socialist program. Burnham was critical of the state of the country's educational system which obscured the general truth that the historical development of the Guyansese society has been shaped by colonialism, slavery, and indentured labor. These factors made it difficult for the masses to build up the inborn sense of their natural ability that is so essential to self-confidence. He asserted that the country's reliance on textbooks mostly from England have socialized the population into accepting British culture, values, and quality of life to be superior than their own. The PNC intention to change the educational system was most clearly pronounced by the creation of the Caribbean Examinations Council which replaced the general certificate of education, a standardized examination administered by the University of London.

The Burnham regime had recognized that the successful development of a modern and prosperous Guyana depends on a well-trained and well-educated population not only in academia but also in technical skills. The PNC goal was to make education, which was a privilege to the rich instead of a right for all during the colonial period, available to all Guyanese, irrespective of ethnicity or political affiliation. As Burnham put it: "For us, education is the cornerstone of equality and one of the chief instruments for the abolition of snobbery, the removal of discrimination, the development of creative beings and the production of a race of men who will never surrender to mediocrity or dictatorship of any kind."[50] To achieve this lofty goal, the PNC regime launched a vicious assault on the colonial educational system which it dubbed as irrelevant to the history, culture, and values of the Guyanese society and instituted a new educational program relevant to the needs of the country. Its aim was to reduce the high level of illiteracy and make the masses more self-reliant and productive so that they can participate fully, political or otherwise in the affairs of the country.

Under the new education program, the government, in September 1976, took control of all private schools and instituted a policy of free education from nursery to university. By 1978, there were over 400 government-owned nursery schools, some of which were established after 1976. In the period from 1974 to 1977, government-owned primary schools increased from 395 to 445, government secondary schools increased from thirty-one to forty-five, and four new technical and vocational schools were built, thus bringing the total to five in that category. Two additional schools were introduced for teaching home economics and domestic crafts, and a new Teacher's Training College was established to increase the amount of trained elementary and secondary school teachers in the country. The existing Agricultural College was expanded in addition to a new one which was built to accommodate more students, especially from the rural areas of the country since agriculture was central to the PNC socialist development plan.[51]

The government also introduced the President's College as a school of excellence and the Cooperative College to train supervisors and managers for cooperative enterprises. For many, including the opposition, the underlying goal of the PNC educational policy was to indoctrinate the population to its dominant socialist ideology. This was evident with the creation of the Kuru-Kuru and the Cuffy Ideological Institutes where party activists, workers, and military personnel were trained to inculcate the cooperative ethos and make an ideological commitment to the party's socialist philosophy. Advancement in the state-controlled economy was

Figure 5.2
List of Government Corporations in Guyana 1972-1990

Public Utilities and Service Corporations
  Guyana Electricity Corporation
  National Insurance Scheme
  Guyana Housing Corporation[1]
  Guyana Transport Services[2]
  Guyana Water Works Corporation

Trading Corporations
  External Trade Bureau
  Guyana National Trading Corporation[2]
  Guyana Gajraj Limited[1]
  Guyana Wrefords Limited[1]
  Guyana Stores Limited[1]
  Guyana National Lithographic Co. Ltd.[1]
  Guyana National Pharmaceutical Corporation[1]
  Guyana National Shipping Corporation[1]

Information and Communication Corporations
  Guyana Tele Communications Corporation[3]
  Guyana Broadcasting Services
  Guyana Cable and Wireless Corporation
  Guyana National Newspapers Limited[1]

Agricultural and Food Processing Corporations
  Guyana Agricultural Producers Corporation[2]
  Guyana Marketing Corporation
  Guyana Marine Foods Limited[1]
  Guyana Food Processors Limited[1]

Industrial Corporations
  Small Industries Corporation[2]
  Guyana Timbers Limited[1]
  Guyana Forest Industries Corporation[2]
  Guyana Rice Marketing Corporation[2]
  Guyana National Engineering Corporation[1]
  Guyana Post Office Corporation
  Guyana Construction Company[1]

Figure 5.2 (continued)

Guyana Oil Company Limited[1]

Banks
Guyana National Co-operative Bank[2]
Guyana National Co-operative Bank Trust Company[2]
Guyana Agricultural Co-operative Development Bank[2]
Guyana Cooperative Mortgage and Finance Bank[2]

Bauxite Corporations
Guyana Bauxite Company[1]
Berbice Mining Enterprises[1]
The Bauxite Industrial Development Company[2]

Sugar Corporation
Guyana Sugar Corporation[1]

Source: *Guyana Information Service*, Georgetown, 1978.
(1) Acquired since 1970; (2) Created in 1971; (3) Guyana Telecommunication Corporation is now owned by AT&T.

contingent on the successful completion of theoretical and practical courses at these institutions.

Feed, Clothe, and House the Nation
The third initiative of cooperative socialism was an undertaking by the Guyana government to feed, clothe, and house (FCH) the nation by 1976. Its aim was to substitute the private profit motive with the social goal of making "the small man a real man." By means of this five-year program, the Burnham regime had hoped to make Guyana self-sufficient, particularly in regard to food, clothing, and housing. It substantially de-emphasized the role of private foreign capital, imports of food and clothing, and was devoted to the development of agriculture which would create a considerable number of employment opportunities through backward and forward linkages and expand the economy. Under this plan Guyana would become self-reliant, producing the basic requirement of the people who would determine the pace and direction of the country's social and economic development.[52] One of the goals of the five-year program was to catapult blacks into agriculture,

fishing, and small and mid-size industries, which were dominated by the East Indians.

The government's intention was to utilize some of the profits derived from the nationalized industries to finance the project and fulfil its social goal of making the small man the real man. The government established the Cooperative Finance Bank to provide long-term credit for the construction of low cost housing units through self-help schemes. At the party level, attempts were made to expand the PNC base of support by recruiting East Indians into the program and then enticing them to become members of the party. These efforts failed because the East Indians were not interested in joining the PNC government which was seen as being very corrupt and dictatorial. The triple development plan of feeding, clothing, and housing the nation was aimed at utilizing 25,000 acres of land for agriculture, to create 11,000 new jobs, build 65,000 housing units, put some G$50 million into circulation within the country, and export agricultural surpluses to the Caribbean and other countries by 1976.[53] The plan met with very little success and had to be abandoned because it was plagued with administrative mismanagement, lack of finance, and massive corruption.

Development of a Trisector Economy

The fourth initiative of the PNC socialist policies was the development and promotion of the cooperative sector as the dominant part of Guyana's trisector economic structure of private, state, and cooperative. This plan was consistent with the PNC strategy that the socialist foundations of the society were to be laid through cooperative ownership and control of the economy of Guyana. The cooperative was to be the principal institution by which the masses would pool their material and physical resources in order to gain control of the economy and uplift themselves. The PNC model of the cooperatives bore a strong resemblance to that practiced by Julius Nyerere as a form of kinship communalism in the ujamaa villages in Tanzania during the 1960s. The PNC claimed that the institution of the cooperative was the little man's vehicle for eliminating the country's economic dependence on the core countries.

> The small man will, through the cooperative, be able to own large and substantial business enterprises and make decisions which will materially effect the direction which the economy takes and where the economy goes. In the Cooperative Republic we will be no longer drawers of water and hewers of wood. . . . if there is to be economic upliftment in this country it can only come about through the cooperative. . . . the cooperative

movement in Guyana is not any longer a social welfare exercise. It has
gone into building, into manufacture [and] into logging.[54]

To achieve these objectives, the government created the Ministry of Cooperatives and National Mobilization and a number of cooperative banks
(figure 5.2), schools, and social and cultural institutions.[55] Despite these
developments, the cooperative sector in Guyana remained a very small part
of the nation's economy. Most of the institutions created by the state and
designated as cooperatives, such as the Guyana National Cooperative Bank,
operated under ordinary commercial principles with profit making as their
primary goal. Those formed through private initiatives also operated along
capitalist lines. Thus, the cooperative sector like the private sector employed
and exploited wage labor. Moreover, many private enterprises frequently
established themselves into cooperatives to take advantage of tax shelters or
carry out limited objectives, such as acquiring a plot of arable land and then
dissolving the cooperative once it had served its purpose.[56] Apart from its
rhetoric, the regime did not establish any cooperative rules or principles
under which these institutions were to operate.

Foreign Policy
    The fifth national initiative of cooperative socialism was the regime's
shift towards a bold and radical foreign policy position of non-alignment in a
tight bipolar world and a Cold War environment of superpower rivalry. This
shift was accompanied by a decidedly Marxist-Leninist orientation that was
anti-imperialist. The government self-proclaimed foreign policy initiatives
included a vigorous and vocal opposition to the racist apartheid policies in
South Africa; support for Castro's communist regime, the Movimento
Popular de Libertacao de Angola (MPLA) in Angola and other liberation
movements in Africa, Asia, and Central America; for the Arab cause, as well
as the respect for the concept of sovereign equality. On the international
realm, Burnham was determined to defy the policies of the powerful United
States. His declaration that Guyana would be "a pawn of neither East nor
West"[57] proved his commitment to the non-alignment movement and his
pursuit of an independent foreign policy. Despite strong opposition from the
United States government, the PNC regime established diplomatic relations
with the Soviet Union, China, and Cuba in 1972. The government also
developed political and economic relations with a number of former socialist
states in Eastern Europe and East Asia. It did not support the U.S. resolution
at the United Nations that condemned the former USSR for shooting down
an American passenger airline that strayed into Russian airspace in 1982.

The government was actively involved in the formation of an International Bauxite Cartel with Jamaica and Surinam and in the Third World's demand for a new international economic order based on equity and morality[58] (see chapter 4).

However, a careful examination of the PNC regime radical foreign policy positions revealed that there was more rhetoric than substance. For instance, the government had initially supported the anti-Marxist and the CIA-backed group UNITA (the National Union for the Total Independence of Angola) and only gave its support to the MPLA during the final stages of the war. The regime's recognition of Cuba was part of a Caribbean wide policy to unite governments of different outlooks and ideology in the interest of establishing an independent and separate identity for the region.[59] In light of these radical moves by the government, Guyana's relations with the U.S. cooled, despite the fact that it was Washington that had supported Burnham to head a postcolonial government in the country.

Party Paramountcy

The sixth initiative of cooperative socialism was the introduction of a doctrine known as the "paramountcy of the party" which made the ruling PNC party supreme over all other political parties, institutions, and state agencies. It was a sophisticated variant of the Marxist-Leninist doctrine that recognized the vanguard party as the leading force in society. In Guyana, the doctrine of party paramountcy was enunciated in 1974 to mark the tenth anniversary of the PNC government at a Special Congress where Burnham declared that "the Party should assume unapologetically its paramountcy over the government which is merely one of its executive arms and that the country should be given practical and theoretical leadership at all levels—political, economic, social and cultural—by the PNC which had become the major national institution."[60] This declaration bestowed on the PNC the hegemonic role that socialist parties in the former USSR and Eastern Europe enjoyed prior to the collapse of communism in 1990. The policy of party paramountcy was formalized with the merger of the Office of the General Secretary of the PNC into the newly created government department, the Ministry of National Development, headed by Hamilton Greene, then the deputy prime minister of Guyana. The new ministry became one of the most strategic and important agencies of the government. Significantly, it was given the responsibility to coordinate the day-to-day activities of the state and to monitor the progress of every government department and state-owned corporations. This single act of party paramountcy made the PNC the vanguard party and thus placed it at the apex of institutional authority in the

Guyanese society. It also signalled the end of liberal democracy in the country that was entrenched in the constitution.

The merger of the PNC office into a department of state accomplished a number of things for the regime. First, as the principal state agency, the PNC, unlike the PPP, the UF, and other political parties in the country, was financed by public funds. Second, by making the PNC the supreme organ of the state freed the political leadership from the need to consult with the legislative branches of government and with other representative bodies in the making and implementation of policy. Third, the merger enabled state bureaucrats and the political executive to have direct control of the party's resources and its organization. Finally, the merger also created the machinery for the transfer of state resources to the PNC, which were used as patronage to mobilize support for the party executive. As it turned out, between 1975 and 1980, the sum of G$54.3 million was allocated to the new department, but only G$1.4 million was accounted for by the regime.[61] This suggests that the paramountcy principle had freed the government accountability to any but the PNC.

The fact that the PNC did not gain power either on the basis of free and fair elections, or as a result of a popular socialist strategy, made the idea of party paramountcy no more than an ultimate rationalization of the PNC authoritarian rule. It was the doctrinal guise under which the party extended its supremacy over the crucial institutions in the country. The ideological goal of party paramountcy in Guyana was the legitimization of the PNC by identifying its leader Forbes Burnham as the embodiment of the party, the PNC as representative of the state, and the state as being identical with the country as a whole, or with society at large. In this regard, the PNC flag was flown on all state buildings, and all anti-PNC or anti-Burnham criticism or activity was therefore viewed by the PNC leadership as antistate or anti-national and was considered unpatriotic and even subversive.

Intimidation and Expansion of the Armed Forces

Intimidation of certain sections of the population was the seventh policy initiative of cooperative socialism. This was made possible with the creation and expansion of the military and paramilitary forces in Guyana. From the beginning of his career as a politician, Forbes Burnham was adept at using situations to his own advantage. The secessionist outbreak by a small group of Amerindians (native Indians) in the vicinity of Guyana's borders with Venezuela in 1969, the forcible seizure of Guyana's territory by Venezuela in 1970, and the need to repel Suriname's armed forces from Guyana's Eastern border also in 1970, provided opportunities for the regime to expand

and politicize the armed forces.[62] These incidents made it extremely difficult for the opposition to seriously oppose the progressive strengthening of the military and security forces by the PNC regime in the 1970s.

During this period, the PNC embarked on a program of conscious militarization of the society with the creation of a number of paramilitary forces and informal armed groups as institutional supports to the more traditional police and military forces. In addition to the police force and the Guyana Defence Force (GDF), the regime created seven different military and paramilitary organizations: the People's Militia, the Guyana National Service, the Guyana Youth Corps, the National Guard, the Revolutionary Guard, the Pioneers, and the Youth Arm of the Young Socialist Movement.[63] While the buildup of the armed forces was partly motivated by the border disputes with Venezuela and Suriname, and they were used by Burnham as a justification for it, its main purpose was domestic intimidation. Estimates have shown that the top ranks of the armed forces were overwhelmingly black, and more than 95 percent of the recruits were blacks mainly from the rural and urban lower classes.[64] The East Indian youths were not motivated to enter the security forces. Most were rural dwellers who were interested in the sugar and rice industries. The middle- and upper-class colored, Chinese, and white population showed little interest toward a career in the armed services, or, for that matter, in the state bureaucracy.

These developments subsequently increased the organizational strength of the country's armed forces tenfold between 1964 and 1977 from 2,135 to 21,751. This means that during this period there was one military personnel for every thirty-seven citizens in 1977 compared with one for every 284 in 1964.[65] This increased the country's military and paramilitary expenditure from 3.2 percent of its GDP in 1971 to 13.7 percent by 1980, and to a substantial 16.4 percent by 1986. In that year alone, the number of military personnel rose to over 25,000. With the exception of Nicaragua, which was involved in a protracted armed struggle with the "contra" rebels, Guyana's military expenditure in proportion to its GDP was much higher than those of the Caribbean and Latin American states.[66] The government had insisted that the functions of the other armed forces have been political education, hinterland development, agricultural production, and small-scale industrial and cooperative activities.[67]

The rapid growth of the armed services was accompanied by aggressive efforts to make the members act and think in a partisan manner in favor of the PNC party. Associated with this political process were rituals, including the simultaneous daily raising of the national and PNC flags in places such as the National Service and the Youth Corps camps, the singing of the party solidarity song at public functions immediately after the national anthem, the compulsory attendance of PNC rallies by members of the armed forces and their pledge to defend the PNC party. In addition, some members of the Youth Corps, the National Service, and the People's Militia were given ideological orientation training for up to six months about the significance and importance of the Marxist-Leninist philosophy at Cuffy's Ideological Institute, which was founded by the PNC. Others attended the President's College that was established as some sort of intellectual farm. These regular seminars and teach-ins at the various institutions were aimed at educating and raising the consciousness of the members of the armed forces in order to help them function in the emergent socialist state.[68] These educational exercises scared the daylights out of many parents, especially mothers, who viewed the training as an attempt to indoctrinate their children whose ages at the time ranged between fourteen and seventeen years. In order to have direct control of the military and paramilitary forces, the PNC government, in 1979, consolidated the armed services under one central administration, the Defence Board of which Burnham appointed himself as chairman.[69]

As head of the Defense Board, Burnham had exclusive power to appoint and to dismiss the heads of all the branches of the armed forces.[70] This was most evident in 1979 when the army's two top officers, the chief of staff and the brigadier general (the official head of the army), were removed from their positions partly because of their disagreement over some party policies. They were replaced by a police officer highly loyal to the regime and with close personal ties to Burnham who changed the entire structure of command in the armed forces. The new chief of staff was responsible for the police, the Guyana Defence Force, the militia, and the other paramilitary forces in what constituted the consolidation of leadership and control of the armed forces in the country.[71] The PNC regime's next logical step was to formally make Burnham the supreme leader of the country.

Supreme Leader of Guyana

The promulgation of a new Constitution and the installation of Burnham as the supreme leader of Guyana in 1980 was the eighth policy initiative of the PNC regime. This was achieved under extraordinary circumstances. Shortly after the 1973 elections, Burnham declared the constitution to be "out of step with modern trends, and our own ideas and ideologies; a Constitution which reflects for the most part the beliefs and ideology of our former imperialist masters."[72] Before 1978, all constitutional changes had to be approved by a national referendum and by a two-thirds majority in Parliament. To solve this problem, the PNC introduced the Constitutional

(Amendment) Bill in 1978 in which it proposed a referendum to ask the citizens to waive their right to be consulted in future constitutional changes. A referendum was held on July 10, 1978, of which the regime or anyone else had no doubt the PNC would win. The certainty of electoral fraud caused all opposition parties and antigovernment groups to urge their supporters to stay away from the polls. Although opposition and independent sources claimed that boycott was successful with voter turnout estimated between 12 and 15 percent of the electorate, the PNC regime, through intervention by the army and massive electoral fraud, maintained that the official voter turnout was 71.45 percent with 97.4 percent voter approval of a new Constitution.[73]

With the plebiscite abolished and with a two-thirds majority in Parliament, the PNC regime passed a new constitution into law in October 1980 which installed Forbes Burnham as the executive president of Guyana for life. It increased the number of members in parliament from fifty-three to sixty-five. The twelve additional seats comprised of one member selected from each of the newly created ten regional councils and the two from the National Congress of Local Democratic Organs.[74] The new constitution placed all powers in the person of Forbes Burnham and exempted him from all legal proceedings during and after his term of office. Under the new constitution, Burnham assumed the position of commander in chief of the armed forces. He was also the supreme leader over Parliament, the people, and all organs of the state. This supreme authority gave the PNC leader the right to veto legislation, proclaim laws in the interest of national security, and to summon, suspend, or dissolve Parliament based on his discretion.[75] According to Sam Silkin, a former British attorney general, the constitution gave the president "virtually imperial powers."[76] With the title of executive president and supreme leader, Burnham finally crowned himself.

Subordination of the Judiciary

Autocratic domination of the judiciary was the ninth and final initiative of the PNC regime's socialist policy. In 1978, the judiciary came under the control of the PNC regime with the passage of the Administrative of Justice Bill and the Criminal Law Bill against intense pressure from the Guyana Bar Association (GBA) and the Organization of Commonwealth Caribbean Bar Associations (OCCBA). The law rescinded, in the majority of cases, the right of citizens to choose trial by jury and permitted the courts to enter into a guilty verdict even though the accused was acquitted by a jury. More importantly, the law preempted the use of the courts to mount legal and constitutional challenges against the actions of the PNC government and its decisions.[77] In addition, it gave the president the power to appoint the chief justice and the chancellor of the judiciary (the official head of the Court of Appeal), which was the task of the political executive. The appointment of judges and magistrates also became the exclusive responsibility of the president based on the advise of the Judicial Service Commission, comprised of the chancellor, the chief justice and the chairman of the Public Service Commission, who like the judges and magistrates, were also presidential appointees.

To further emphasize the dominance of the regime over the judiciary, the PNC flag was flown over the Court of Appeal.[78] This act undermined public confidence in the judicial system since it suggested that the courts were subservient to the party. With government control of the courts, the judiciary became part of the coercive apparatus of the state to intimidate and punish political opponents arrested on trumped-up charges by the PNC regime. The Guyana Human Rights Association (GHRA) has observed that "The courts have been used as an instrument of political harassment on a widespread scale. This has been made possible by the subordination of the judiciary to the political executive in a number of ways."[79]

These national policy initiatives of the government were supposed to be the guiding ideological basis for the development of Guyana's political economy and the reduction of its economic dependence on the developed countries. Instead, they have produced a personalistic, authoritarian bent for power and survival in the plural environment of Guyana by the PNC regime. This led to the existence of a monolithic radical political system that was, in part, accompanied by antidemocratic measures in four major areas: rigged elections; the denial of basic human and trade union rights; the suspension of the rule of law; and the subordination of the judiciary and state agencies to the PNC.

Assessment of Cooperative Socialism

Forbes Burnham and the PNC leaders' initial articulation of socialism was premised on the cooperative as the dominant sector of the internal economic organization and development process of foreign enterprises in the country, and a cautious strategy of nationalization. In terms of its practical significance, the nationalization of foreign assets was a major success up to the mid-1970s. In 1974, the bauxite companies enjoyed record sales, which were boosted by increased production of calcined ore bauxite, the price of which skyrocketed on the international market, and by a greater demand for alumina on the world market.[80] Also, in this period, the world market price for sugar increased substantially to the point where it produced enormous profits for the local sugar industries.

The performance of these two industries and the huge profits generated by the increase in prices for sugar and bauxite on the world market resulted in a period of general economic prosperity in Guyana. The country's foreign reserves increased from G$41 million at the end of 1973 to approximately G$110 million by 1974. Its growth in GDP also increased by 37 percent.[81] In 1975, Guyana's economic growth continued as its foreign exchange reserves rose to an unprecedented high of over G$250 million and its GDP to 22 percent, the highest in the Caribbean at the time.[82] These increases, which were largely due to the favorable conditions for sugar and bauxite on the world market, improved Guyana's economy and reduced its dependence on foreign borrowing. Thus, the nationalization of foreign assets seemed, at the time, to be a successful and viable economic strategy for the country's development.

State ownership and control of the economy in Guyana allowed the PNC regime to dispense patronage benefits to the politically strategic bureaucratic black and colored middle class. These groups, which were instrumental in ousting the Marxist PPP government of Cheddi Jagan from office in 1964, received an enormous increase in salary, a substantial reduction in income tax, generous subsidies on major consumer items, easy access to foreign currency, opportunities to travel abroad, lavish housing and car allowances, and guaranteed low interest rates for mortgages and loans. These groups were also given preferential access to job opportunities, which eventually led to quick and easy promotions to managerial or higher level positions, and transfers to more desirable agencies of the state, such as the Presidential Secretariat, Foreign Affairs, or Finance. The government also expanded urban services, facilities, and infrastructure to satisfy the needs of its middle-class supporters. As a result of these and other actions taken by the government, most of the state employees supported the PNC regime and its socialist policies, as they would be for any party and any policy—socialist or capitalist—that served their interests as an administrative group. Patronage benefits to this strategic bureaucratic middle-class group were more important to the regime than at maintaining mass support of the lower class which was secured through racial mobilization or electoral fraud.

The use of the country's economic surpluses in the early part of the 1970s to provide huge patronage benefits to the bureaucratic middle class and to expand the military forces and the coercive and surveillance branches of the government were to maintain and strengthen the PNC hold on power. This pattern of spending and patronage came at the expense of the country's agricultural and industrial expansion as well as the development of its natural resources. The regime's initial dependence upon racial support for its survival precluded the choice of policies that was best suited to the development of a viable economic strategy geared towards self-sustained growth and the reduction of Guyana's dependence on the developed countries. Such a strategy could have involved the use of fiscal surpluses to finance a program of agricultural expansion and industrial development utilizing domestic resources, appropriate technology, and catered to domestic and regional needs.

The PNC preoccupation with political control of the state and the people contributed to a serious deterioration of the country's economy to the point where it was incapable of meeting food, health, education, and the welfare needs of the population. In 1980 real per capita income was less than it had been in 1970. Production in the three dominant sectors of sugar, bauxite, and rice declined steadily, despite the availability of these products on the world market. This resulted from the inefficient and administrative mismanagement of the state-owned industries which have been run for the private benefit of a ruling clique. The collapse of the economy in the mid-1970s led to the defection of the PNC strategic black and colored middle-class supporters to the Working People's Alliance, a small multiracial party built around the leadership of Walter Rodney. These developments served as explanations for the regime's dictatorial policies that followed.

The Economy under Cooperative Socialism

In Guyana, state ownership and control of the country's resources had not produced the sustained economic development anticipated by the government to overcome or significantly reduce Guyana's dependence on imports and foreign capital. In addition to utilizing the country's economic surpluses for the political survival of the government, the leaders of the PNC quickly realized that the prices for the country's products were ultimately dependent upon conditions operative in the international market. As a consequence, they had absolutely no control over the costs of production in the state-run enterprises since these were highly responsive to the costs of inputs imported from the United States and other developed countries.

The separation of the state-owned industries from vertically and horizontally integrated international corporate structures meant that losses or the decline in profits could not be offset by gains in other subsidiaries located in different countries. Moreover, the huge surpluses generated during the mid-1970s on the international market for the country's sugar, bauxite, and rice were insufficient to sustain the economy and stem the losses occurred during the latter part of the decade. By early 1980 the cost to service the debt was so large that the government was forced to refinance 80 percent of its debt payments that were due in 1980 and 1981.[83]

After record increases in prices for Guyana's principal products in 1974 and 1975, the price of sugar fell so low that in 1978 local costs of production per ton was G$301 above the price paid on the world market.[84] While the bulk of the country's sugar continued to be marketed under the EEC-ACP Lomé preferential agreements to Europe and the United States, the premium prices obtained were not enough to prevent losses in the industry. At the same time, low demand from the international steel industry, the major consumer of calcined ore bauxite, caused a decline in markets for Guyana's bauxite. The situation was the same for rice, the country's third traditional primary commodity. The annual output of rice in 1980 was 166,000 tons, whereas the capacity of the industry was rated at 250,000 tons, with its highest output of 212,000 tons being achieved in 1977. Sugar production in 1980 was 270,000 tons while the annual output capacity of the industry was 450,000 tons. The peak output level of 374,000 tons of sugar was achieved in 1971. Dried bauxite production in 1980 was 1.1 million tons compared with nearly 2.3 million tons in 1970. Calcined bauxite produced in 1980 was 600,000 tons compared with 699,000 tons in 1970. Aluminum production in 1980 was 215,000 tons while 312,000 tons were produced in 1970 (see table 5.5). It should be noted that in the 1960s and early 1970s, Guyana enjoyed a virtual monopoly in world sales of high-grade calcined ore bauxite which at the time accounted for 90 percent of the world market. By the early 1980s, the industry could only supply between 40 and 50 percent of the world demand. As shown in table 5.6, the decline in Guyana's productive structure has negatively influenced economic growth in the country between 1975 and 1986.

The poor performance of Guyana's traditional production sectors— sugar, bauxite, and rice—with little or no noticeable diversification of the country's economy was accompanied by a decline in the quality of social services available, a deterioration of the services of the various public utilities, and migration of a number of persons from the country. Public utilities such as electricity, fresh water supply, public transport, telephones, postal services, and sanitation had deteriorated to the point where they were incapable of providing adequate services to the population. Almost everything, even the ornate colonial buildings in Georgetown were in a state of decay. Electrical outages occurred frequently for several hours a day in the main production and residential areas of the country. Public transport was so poor that it took workers an average of four hours per day to commute to and from work. Fresh water, which was available for a few hours per day in Georgetown and the suburbs, was contaminated and unfit for human consumption. The contaminated water was partly the cause for the frequent cases of gastroenteritis in the country. In the rural areas fresh water was a scarce commodity due to broken wells in almost every village. For the most part, rainwater was the primary source of consumption for the rural population. Worse still, there was only one workable fire truck for the city of Georgetown and the suburbs with a total population of almost 250,000. Sanitation was also a major problem in Guyana, especially in the urban areas where garbage was piled high on the street corners. With only one garbage truck and an inoperable incinerator, garbage in the city was collected only once a month and burnt in open fields. The health risks during this period were magnified by intermittent availability of soap and detergent. Today, a fetid swampiness still hangs over the city of Georgetown which is built below sea level and drained by canals and streams that continued to be choked with weeds and garbage.[85]

Health, Education, and Housing Sectors

In the health sector, almost all of the hospitals are government owned and operated and all remain in poor physical condition. Space and beds are inadequate, and there is a chronic shortage of medical personnel and drugs. In 1970, the population per physician was 4,250, while in 1979, it had risen to 9,270.[86] Foreign medical personnel mainly from Cuba, India, and the Philippines accounted for 75 percent of the doctors in the country. Less than 10 percent of health personnel are engaged in preventative medicine. In the sphere of education, most of the primary and secondary schoolteachers were not paid on time, while there were shortages of pens, pencils, and books, and many schools were in disrepair. The result was that truancy and illiteracy had increased sharply, and students were performing poorly in the traditional examinations at both the primary and secondary levels. The University of Guyana was similarly affected. Its undergraduate programs in the arts and sciences and a limited number of advanced degrees had suffered from an exodus of qualified staff and from a shortage of funds. Libraries, including the one at the University of Guyana, were stacked with textbooks that were

Table 5.5
Guyana: Physical Output—Major Sectors 1970-1986

Year	Output (measured in thousands of tons)				
	Sugar	Rice	Dried Bauxite	Calcined Bauxite	Aluminum
1970	311	142	2,290	699	312
1971	374	120	2,108	700	305
1972	315	94	1,652	690	257
1973	266	110	1,665	637	234
1974	341	153	1,383	726	311
1975	300	175	1,350	778	294
1976	333	110	969	729	265
1977	242	212	879	709	273
1978	325	182	1,021	590	276
1979	298	142	1,059	589	171
1980	270	166	1,105	601	215
1981	301	163	982	513	170
1982	287	182	958	392	73
1983	252	149	761	315	00
1984	238	181	823	517	00
1985	243	154	1,096	478	00
1986	245	180	1,036	441	00

Source: Government of Guyana, Department of Statistics, Georgetown, 1970-1986.

Table 5.6
Real Growth of GDP in Guyana (Compound % per annum)

Year	1970-1975	1975-1980	1981	1982	1983	1984	1985	1986
Total GDP	3.9	-0.7	-0.3	-10.4	-9.6	2.5	1.0	0.3
Sugar	0.9	-1.3	10.9	-3.8	-12.6	-3.6	–	–
Rice	2.4	0.9	-2.2	15.6	-19.2	23.8	–	–
Mining	-2.3	-5.3	-11.4	-31.5	-22.4	47.0	–	–
Government	10.5	1.9	1.0	-7.7	-1.9	0.0	–	–

Source: Clive Thomas, *The Poor and the Powerless* (New York: Monthly Review Press, 1988), 257.

published in the 1950s and 1960s.[87] In housing, only 6,000 units were built out of the government's targeted production of 65,000 for the development plan period 1972-76.[88]

Food Production

There has also been a drastic decline in food production. By early 1978 the supply of milk fell by 56 percent and had become almost nonexistent by 1983. In the same period, beef production had tumbled by some 30 percent. Poultry production was reduced by 64 percent in the two years between 1981 and 1983 and the availability of pork fell by almost 20 percent. In an effort to conserve foreign exchange, the government banned or restricted the import of over 100 items. Incredibly, the ban included many essential food items such as milk, wheat flour, split peas, sardines, potatoes, butter, salt, onions, and pharmaceutical products, all staple foods and goods of the poor.[89] Food items that were available were distributed by PNC-controlled outlets in a discriminatory manner. The waiting lines for food items in this period were interminable, and in some cases were formed overnight. People absent themselves from work in order to be in the food lines. The food shortage in Guyana produced a nutritional crisis for the country's population. In June 1983, estimates from the Ministry of Health revealed that between 49 and 60 percent of the children below five years suffered from moderate to severe malnutrition. The infant mortality rate in 1981 was 42.7 per 1,000 live births.[90] The country's main hospital in Georgetown reported that deaths from malnutrition had increased 335 percent over the period 1981-83. In the population of pregnant women, 74.9 percent had inadequate dietary intake while there were dramatic increases in dietary related and infective and parasitic diseases that resulted from poor and deficient diets.[91]

By 1980 the production crisis together with the rise in import prices created a serious balance of payments and foreign debt crisis. The data in table 5.7 show that the public debt which stood at G$267 million in 1970, rose to G$673 million in 1974, and to G$1.33 billion in 1976. At the end of 1981, the debt was over G$3 billion of which G$1.8 billion was internal and G$1.2 billion was external. The country's net foreign reserves also fell from G$198 million in 1975 to minus G$99.8 million in 1977 and to minus G$482.7 at the end of 1981.

The dismal economic performance forced the government to make drastic cutbacks in capital expenditure which resulted in massive layoffs of state employees and in the removal of subsidies on food and other essential consumer items. Imports were curtailed in order to reduce deficits in balance of payments. This created grave shortages of spare parts and intermediate goods needed for production and the maintenance of public utilities. The government was also forced to raise revenue from direct taxes on incomes, custom duties, sales tax, and a special airport exit tax it implemented in the early 1980s.

The production crisis, combined with the decline in social services and widespread shortages of imported commodities, led to a reduction in the standard of living, a fall in real wages which, in 1978, was estimated at 44 percent, and a devaluation of Guyana's currency by 18 percent against the U.S. dollar in 1981.[92] They also produced an unemployment rate of over 30 percent of the labor force of approximately of 352,000.[93] As table 5.8 of consumer price indices shows, the cost of living skyrocketed after 1974, with the greatest increases occurring over the six-year period between 1977 and 1983. In general, conditions of life in Guyana were so horrible in the early 1980s that Guyanese from all walks of life began a migration pattern never experienced before in the country or the region as a whole. Out of a natural population increase of about 100,000 persons between 1976 and 1981, close to 70 percent or 70,000 migrated from Guyana, principally to the United States, Canada, Britain, and the Caribbean.[94]

The impact of these policies was severely felt among the regime's strategic black and colored middle class supporters who abandoned the PNC

Table 5.7
Guyana: Monetary Indicators 1970-1986

Year	Net Foreign Reserves (G$ million)	National Debt			Balance of Payments Current Account (G$ million)	Government Finances (G$ million)			Money Supply (G$ million)
		External (G$ million)	Internal (G$ million)	Total (G$ million)		Total Revenue	Total Expenditure	Surplus + Deficit -	
1970	54.6	160.0	107.2	267.2	-46.6	NA	NA	NA	165.0
1971	67.3	291.6	144.6	436.2	-13.2	NA	NA	NA	192.5
1972	89.7	316.2	189.4	499.6	-22.6	NA	NA	NA	231.7
1973	41.8	348.6	289.0	637.6	-123.4	NA	NA	NA	274.1
1974	105.4	403.6	269.1	672.7	-17.0	468.2	619.4	-151.2	317.9
1975	197.7	533.4	399.2	932.6	-35.2	497.7	638.8	-141.1	449.4
1976	-29.2	662.5	657.9	1330.4	-350.8	389.9	803.0	-413.0	491.5
1977	-99.8	689.8	837.1	1526.9	-251.1	355.1	543.6	-188.5	603.6
1978	-50.6	744.0	1000.1	1744.1	-72.3	365.8	542.2	-176.4	667.2
1979	-181.6	811.7	1271.2	2082.9	-208.1	410.2	690.7	-278.5	713.3
1980	-396.4	911.3	1637.0	2548.3	-300.4	455.1	935.2	-480.1	850.4
1981	-482.7	1261.4	1779.2	3040.6	-475.8	578.9	1205.7	-626.8	997.1
1982	-628.8	681.3	2775.7	3457.0	-426.0	550.6	1570.9	-1020.3	1269.3
1983	-919.7	692.6	3820.8	4513.4	-468.0	568.2	1291.0	-722.8	1533.7
1984	-1104.5	682.5	4544.0	5226.5	-434.0	651.4	1830.2	-1178.8	1814.9
1985	-873.4	691.0	5425.7	6116.7	-426.0	1200.2	1562.8	-362.6	2169.7
1986	-922.3	707.0	5399.3	6106.3	-497.0	1618.1	2858.4	-1240.3	2691.7

Source: Government of Guyana 1970-1986, Department of Statistics, Georgetown, Guyana.

for the Working People's Alliance party. Almost immediately, the WPA gained the support from most of the major politicized segments of the Guyanese society, including the PPP, the country's moderate and conservative political parties, trade unions, the radical intellectual community, the Guyana Council of Churches, the Guyana Bar Association, and the Compass Group, which was an alliance of professionals and top executives in the state and private sector. By 1979, it was estimated that three-fourths of the population had supported the WPA against the Burnham regime. [95] Led by Walter Rodney, the WPA conducted a scathing campaign against the PNC regime. This was buttressed by a series of industrial strikes and other forms of social unrest that culminated in a near insurrection against the government in 1979.

Stunned by the huge number of WPA supporters, and the threat to wrestle power away from the PNC, Burnham warned his opponents that the state would not "sit idly by and permit reactionary and political zealots to ruin the economy and jeopardise the well being of the workers and the nation. We shall match steel with more highly-tempered steel. What is at stake is the revolution itself."[96] As the WPA attacks against the regime grew sharper, Burnham and the PNC leadership turned to the armed forces to maintain political stability in the country. In this context, the PNC regime's commitment to make the small man a real man and to reduce Guyana's economic dependence on the developed countries fell to dictatorial policies. In other words, a dictatorship emerged as the crisis of production became generalized into a social and political crisis.

As the economic situation worsened, the government turned everything into ideology. It demanded and got a pledge of loyalty to the PNC from members of the armed forces, including the police and firemen. It also took control of the country's only daily newspaper, the *Chronicle*, and both of the radio stations and used them to promote its ideology, impose administrative restraints, and to restrict publication of opposing or independent views. At the time, Guyana did not have television. Newsprints were denied to the PNC's main opponents, the PPP's weekly newspaper, the *Mirror*, the *Day Clean*, a biweekly newspaper published by the WPA, and the *Catholic Standard*, a Roman Catholic tabloid. Opposition views were not aired on the two state-owned radio stations, and all foreign newspapers and magazines were banned from the country by the PNC regime. Overseas correspondence deemed unacceptable to the totalitarian policies of the PNC regime was destroyed. Moreover, troops in full combat were deployed to protect all government buildings and state-owned corporations throughout the country. Military exercises aimed at deterring civil unrest were common practices in

Table 5.8
Guyana: Consumer Price Indices (1970 = 100)

Year	Composite Index
1970	100.0
1971	101.0
1972	106.0
1973	114.0
1974	134.0
1975	144.0
1976	157.6
1977	170.7
1978	196.5
1979	231.4
1980	264.0
1981	322.7
1982	390.2
1983	448.7

Source: The World Bank, *Guyana: A Framework for Economic Recovery*, Washington, D.C., 146.

the urban areas of the country during the early 1980s.[97] The regime also curtailed the power of the trade unions. Strikes were deemed political and, as such, were considered subversive activities by the government. Workers who indulged in strikes were either fired, demoted, or transferred to the remote areas of the country. Others were imprisoned on charges fabricated by the regime.[98]

Having gained control of the judiciary and the state coercive apparatus, the PNC regime, despite the rapid deterioration of the economy, intensified its campaign against its opponents, particularly the leaders of the WPA, which included physical harassment and even assassination. By this time the regime coercive apparatus extended beyond the armed branches of the state. Some of the most brutal acts of violence were carried out by members of the House of Israel, a private black religious cult, headed by Rabbi Washington, a black American fugitive who had settled in Guyana. Washington, whose real name is David Hill, fled to Guyana while on bail for a series of crimes including blackmail, larceny, and tax evasion in the United States. The cult, which boasted a membership of 8,000, had developed very close ties with the PNC regime and became part of its coercive apparatus against political opponents and any form of antigovernment dissent. The House of Israel acquired a reputation for ruthlessness after its violent attacks against anti-government demonstrators, strikers, and protesting high school students. It was linked to several political assassinations, including Father Bernard Drake, a photographer for the *Catholic Standard,* a tabloid that had become extremely critical of the regime. Under considerable international pressure, the Hoyte administration finally charged Washington and key associates with the murder of Father Drake in July 1986. Washington pleaded guilty to the lesser charge of manslaughter and was sentenced to fifteen years in prison.

The victimization of the PNC was cloaked in a bogus legal framework made possible by the political control of the courts and legislature by the regime. In July 1979, arson charges were laid against eight WPA officials, including Walter Rodney and Rupert Roopernarine, Odle and Omawale of the University of Guyana by the state. Before the trial began, Rodney was killed on June 13, 1980, by a bomb concealed in a two-way radio given to him by Gregory Smith, a member of the Guyana Defence Force. Rodney's gruesome murder evoked enormous sympathy locally and internationally, especially by Caribbean heads of state who condemned the assassination. A few months later, Drs. Odle, Roopernarine, and Omawale were acquitted of the arson charges due to lack of evidence by the state. Walter Rodney was Burnham's principal tormentor. He taunted Burnham in a fashion no other politician had been able to or dared to do. The PNC leader who had loved the African name "Kabaka" or King was dubbed King Kong by Rodney. The comical significance of the name was amplified by the fact that the official residence of the president was next to the zoo in Georgetown.

With further erosion of the economy, the PNC regime used the media principally to promote an image of legitimacy for the government and to attribute responsibility for the country's economic crisis to high prices for imported oil, arsonists, and to the destabilization policies of the U. S., the IMF, and MNCs. This ignored completely the problems created by poor internal management, extensive corruption, and lack of capital and skills, among others. In addition, most of the initiatives of cooperative socialism were not implemented due to the preponderant interests of the PNC to maintain its hold on power. Party paramountcy, the expansion of the armed forces, and the enactment of a new constitution that conferred supreme authority on Burnham prolonged the PNC regime's stay in office. These developments proved that the initiatives of cooperative socialism were not in sync with policies that could have led to the development of the political economy of Guyana and reduce its dependency on external decisions.

However, the assumption by the state of the dominant role in the economy was not without exorbitant costs to the government, and ultimately to the masses. The state by the mid-1970s proved incapable of effectively carrying out its principal functions. Several explanations accounted for this. One was that the PNC regime was preoccupied with maintaining political power, which was the principal instrument for the creation of economic wealth and to provide patronage benefits to the PNC strategic middle-class supporters. Thus, the traditional capitalist sequence of economic power leading to political power was reversed by the regime. This is crucial for understanding the ideological and structural roles of the state in Guyana. Second, the rapid nationalization of more than 80 percent of foreign assets in Guyana between 1970 and 1976 resulted in a severe shortage of foreign currency needed to sustain the process. Third, Guyana's ideological position and its resultant socialist strategies were at diametric variance to those of the World Bank, the IMF, and other international financial institutions, where it sought financial assistance to ease the burden of its external debt. The government nationalization policy, socialism, and anti-Western rhetoric had already scared private foreign investors away from the country. Fourth, the nationalization of foreign assets in Guyana aided the expansion of the state in three major dimensions: military, bureaucracy, and ideology, which in turn increased the capacity of the PNC regime to assert its various forms of authoritarian control over the population.

During the period of cooperative socialism, Guyana was characterized by a political process which, in practical terms, evolved certain norms and behavior inconsistent with the economic development and the inherited constitutional system of the Westminster model of parliamentary democracy.

The political system in Guyana manifested in certain authoritarian tendencies that contributed to the emergence of a one-party-dominant system in the PNC, even as a pluralistic political process appeared to exist on the surface. The restriction of freedom and the rigging of elections that accompanied the nationalization process were not conducive to the reduction of dependency, which was the primary goal of cooperative socialism. Rather, it was to maintain the PNC stay in power and to reverse the racial practices of the PPP government of Cheddi Jagan that catered preponderantly to the interests of the East Indians during the 1950s and early 1960s. It was Burnham's belief that the only hope for blacks in Guyana was for the PNC to control the political process and to prosecute their interests in light of Cheddi Jagan's approach to governance. Thus, the national policy initiatives of cooperative socialism could not have significantly improved the economy of Guyana, let alone overcome or reduce its dependence on the core capitalist states and Western financial institutions.

Guyana in the 1990s

Guyana since the PPP came to power in 1992 is a more relaxed country. Elections are no longer rigged and police violence has decreased. Opposition parties have been permitted to operate more freely and there is more freedom for the media. Between 1987 and 1992, Burnham's successor, Desmond Hoyte, sought rapprochement with the United States and the IMF and has adopted an open door policy to foreign investors and tourists. This approach has since been the policy of Jagan and his successor Bharat Jagdeo. Both the PNC and the ruling PPP have abandoned their anti-imperialist rhetoric and have adopted a pro-Western position, which is a radical shift from their Marxist-socialist ideology. Hoyte also reversed some of Burnham's most hated policies, including the ban on food items. But while food is in some-what better supply, the economic crisis seems to be getting worse under the PPP regime. For most of the population, only gifts of foodstuffs, clothes, and foreign currency from relatives abroad permit a standard of living above the most crude subsistence. Despite increased bilateral aid mainly from Canada and the United States, and a flood of multilateral assistance from the World Bank, as well as improvement in investor confidence in the last ten tears, the promise of an economic takeoff has failed to materialize. Guyana's external debt continued to increase and its bauxite and rice production have dropped steadily due to the high costs of fuel needed to run those industries. More-over, the PPP government has been unable to attract foreign investors. These factors coupled with the exodus of talent from Guyana has become perhaps the most serious obstacle of all to economic development of the country.

Notes

1. The polity was known until independence on May 26, 1966, as British Guiana. However, the name Guyana is generally used in the text whether with regard to the preindependence or the postindependence period.

2. Tom Barry, Beth Wood, and Deb Preusch, *The Other Side of Paradise: Foreign Control in the Caribbean* (New York: Grove Press, 1984), 322; Leo A. Despres, *Cultural Pluralism and Nationalist Politics in British Guiana* (Chicago: Rand McNally Press, 1967).

3. Harold A. Lutchman, *From Colonialism to Cooperative Republic: Aspects of Political Development in Guyana* (Puerto Rico: Institute of Caribbean Studies, University of Puerto Rico, 1974), 2; Robert H. Manley, *Guyana Emergent: The Post-Independence Struggle for Nondependent Development* (Boston: Schenkman, 1979), 2.

4. Lutchman, *From Colonialism to Cooperative Republic;* Despres, *Cultural Pluralism.*

5. Raymond T. Smith, *British Guiana* (London: Oxford University Press, 1962), 42-44; Dwarka Nath, *A History of Indians in Guyana* (London: Butler and Tanner, 1970), 179-80.

6. Primary sources dealing with slavery in Guyana are widely scattered and difficult to find. There is also very little information on the subject in secondary sources, but what there is suggests that slavery in Guyana was not much different from that which existed in the West Indies as a whole. One important source is Eric Williams, *Capitalism and Slavery* (Chapel Hill: University of North Carolina Press, 1944).

7. Dietrich Rueschemeyer, Evelyn H. Stephens, and John D. Stephens, *Capitalist Development and Democracy* (Chicago: University of Chicago Press, 1992), 252.

8. Percy Hintzen, *The Costs of Regime Survival: Racial Mobilization, Elite Domination and Control of the State in Guyana and Trinidad* (Cambridge: Cambridge University Press, 1989), 21. Also see Hintzen for a general discussion on racial mobilization in Guyana. Leo Despres (1967) explains the persistence of racial politics in Guyana that began in 1955. Premdas (1978, 1980) shows how racial politics in Guyana have impeded efforts at political and racial integration.

9. Vere T. Daly, *A Short History of the Guyanese People* (London: Macmillan, 1975), 293-94; *West Indian Royal Commission Report: Statement of Action on the Recommendations* (London: Her Majesty's Stationery Office, Cmd 6656, 1939).

10. Lutchman, *From Colonialism to Cooperative Republic,* 22-27.

11. Janet Jagan is the niece of Ethel and Julius Rosenberg of Chicago who were convicted and executed by the U.S. government on communist spy charges in the 1950s. After the death of her husband Cheddi Jagan in March 1997, Janet became the president of Guyana. She is the first naturalized or non-born Guyanese and the first female to hold that position.

12. Cheddi B. Jagan, *The West on Trial: The Fight for Guyana's Freedom* (Berlin: Seven Seas Publishers, 1966), 94; Thomas J. Spinner, *Political and Social History of Guyana* (Boulder, Colo.: Westview Press, 1984), 25.

13. Hintzen, *The Costs of Regime Survival*, 33.

14. Forbes Burnham, *A Destiny to Mould* (Jamaica: Longman Caribbean Limited, 1970), xviii; Jagan, *The West on Trial*, 148; Spinner, *Political and Social History of Guyana*, 36.

15. Hintzen, *The Costs of Regime Survival*, 36; Ralph R. Premdas, "The Rise of the First Mass-based Multi-racial Party in Guyana," *Caribbean Quarterly* 20, nos. 3 and 4 (January 1975): 5-20.

16. Despres, *Cultural Pluralism*, 204; Spinner, *Political and Social History of Guyana*, 45-58. For contrasting accounts of these events, see Spinner, 33-58, and Despres, 172-220.

17. Daly, *A Short History of the Guyanese People*, 306-307; Despres, *Cultural Pluralism*, 207; Jagan, *The West on Trial*, 142-43.

18. Jagan, *The West on Trial*, 145; Burnham, *A Destiny to Mould*, xviii.

19. Cited in Burnham, *A Destiny to Mould*, xix.

20. Jagan, *The West on Trial*, 194-96. Despres, *Cultural Pluralism*, 199; Spinner, *Political and Social History of Guyana*, 31, 58, 70, 92-93.

21. Burnham, *A Destiny to Mould*; Rueschemeyer et al., *Capitalist Development and Democracy,* 255; Gordon K. Lewis, *The Growth of the Modern West Indies* (New York: New York Monthly Review Press, 1968), 274.

22. Smith, *British Guiana*, 180-81.

23. Despres, *Cultural Pluralism*, 236; Spinner, *Political and Social History of Guyana*, 74; Hintzen, *The Costs of Regime Survival*, 49-50.

24. Despres, *Cultural Pluralism*, 178.

25. Arthur Schlesinger, Jr., *A Thousand Days: John F. Kennedy in the White House* (New York: Houghton Mifflin, 1965), 779.

26. Manley, *Guyana Emergent,* 7; Despres, *Cultural Pluralism*, 264; Jagan, *The West on Trial*, 255-65.

27. Spinner, *Political and Social History of Guyana*, 101.

28. Rueschemeyer et al., *Capitalist Development and Democracy,* 256.

29. Despres, *Cultural Pluralism*, 266; Jagan, *The West on Trial*, 371; Burnham, *A Destiny to Mould*, xxviii.

30. *Daily Chronicle*, July 23, 1961; Ernst Halperin, "Racism and Communism in British Guiana," *Journal of Inter-American Studies* 7 (January 1965): 130; Eusi Kwayana is Swahili for "Black man of Guyana," the African name adopted by Sydney King who decided to cast off his European slave name in 1970. Kwayana headed the Association for Social and Cultural Relations with Independent Africa (ASCRIA). He is also the cofounder of the Working People's Alliance party with Dr. Clive Thomas, Dr. Ramsammy, and the late Walter Rodney in 1974. Between 1950 and 1957, King was the assistant general secretary of the PPP, and was general secretary of the PNC and editor of the *New Nation*, the party's newspaper, between 1957 and 1961. In July 1961, the PPP racist policies prompted King to

advocate the partition of Guyana into three zones: one for blacks, one for East Indians, and the third for those who wanted to live together. Burnham immediately condemned the partition proposal, disassociated himself from King, and suspended him from the PNC, but he was reinstated as a member of the party in the late 1960s.

31. Hintzen, *The Costs of Regime Survival*, 55.

32. Walter Rodney, *The Struggle Goes On!* (Georgetown, Guyana: Working People's Alliance, 1979), 8.

33. Hintzen, *The Costs of Regime Survival*, 56.

34. R. A. Glasgow, *Guyana: Race and Politics among Africans and East Indians* (The Hague: Martinus Nijhoff, 1970), 110.

35. Forbes Burnham, "A Vision of the Cooperative Republic," in *Cooperative Republic Guyana: A Study of Aspects of Our Way of Life*, ed. Lloyd Searwar (Georgetown, Guyana: Guyana Printers Ltd., 1970), 10.

36. People's National Congress, *Policy Paper: Cooperatism* (Georgetown: Guyana National Lithographic Co. Ltd., 1974), 13.

37. Clive Thomas, "The Rise and Fall of Cooperative Socialism," in *Dependency under Challenge: The Political Economy of the Commonwealth Caribbean*, ed. Anthony Payne and Paul Sutton (Manchester: University of Manchester Press, 1984), 77-78.

38. Clive Thomas, *The Poor and the Powerless: Economic Policy and Change in the Caribbean* (New York: Monthly Review Press, 1988), 252.

39. Burnham, *A Destiny to Mould*, 70.

40. Forbes Burnham, *Towards the Socialist Revolution* (Georgetown: Guyana Printers Ltd., 1975), 11; Forbes Burnham, *Economic Liberation through Socialism* (Georgetown: Guyana Printers Ltd., 1977).

41. Burnham, *A Destiny to Mould*, 74.

42. The phrase *commanding heights* of the economy describes those sections of a country's economy which are of strategic significance. It is used here to say that the *commanding heights* of the postcolonial economies of Guyana, Jamaica, and Grenada, and the Caribbean as a whole were largely owned and controlled by multinational corporations prior to their attempts to gain control over their own economies during the 1970s and early 1980s. The include public utilities, the banking system, the sugar and bauxite industries as well as the tourist industry. The phrase was believed to be first used by the French economist Aneurin Bevan.

43. *Guyana Statistical Bureau* (Georgetown: Government of Guyana, 1985), 3-6.

44. Thakoor Persaud, *Conflicts between Multinational Corporations and Less Developed Countries* (Austin: University of Texas Press, 1980), 56.

45. C. H. Grant, "Political Sequel to Alcan Nationalization in Guyana: The International Aspects," *Social and Economic Studies* 22 (1973): 251.

46. Persaud, *Conflicts*, 108.

47. Anthony Payne, *The International Crisis, in the Caribbean* (London: Croom Helm, 1984), 12.

48. Payne, *The International Crisis*, 12; Hintzen, *The Costs of Regime Survival*, 154.

49. Payne, *The International Crisis*, 12, Thomas, "The Rise and Fall of Co-operative Socialism," 90.

50. Burnham, *A Destiny to Mould,* 10.

51. *Guyana Information Service* (Georgetown, Guyana, 1978), 34-43.

52. Manley, *Guyana Emergent,* 74.

53. Forbes Burnham, *Breakthrough* (Georgetown: Guyana Printers, 1973), 9.

54. Burnham, *A Destiny to Mould,* 159.

55. Payne, *The International Crisis,* 12.

56. Thomas, *The Poor and the Powerless,* 253.

57. Burnham, *A Destiny to Mould,* 113.

58. Payne, *The International Crisis,* 13.

59. Thomas, *The Poor and the Powerless,* 254.

60. Forbes Burnham, *Declaration of Sophia* (Georgetown: Guyana Printers Ltd., 1974), 11.

61. *Guyana Human Rights Association, Human Rights Report January 1980-June 1981* (Georgetown: Guyana Human Rights Association, 1981), 8.

62. *Guyana Information Service* (Georgetown, Guyana, 1977), 63-64.

63. G. K. Danns, "Militarization and Development: An Experiment in Nation Building in Guyana," *Transition* 1, no. 1 (1978): 28-36.

64. G. K. Danns, *Domination and Power in Guyana* (New Brunswick, N.J.: Transaction Books, 1984), 121, 161; Spinner, *Political and Social History of Guyana,* 162.

65. James A. Sackey, "Dependence, Underdevelopment, and Socialist-oriented Transformation in Guyana," *Inter-American Economic Affairs* 33, no. 1 (1979): 46; Danns, "Militarization and Development," 23-44.

66. Tyrone Ferguson, *Structural Adjustment and Good Governance: The Case of Guyana* (Georgetown: Public Affairs Consulting Enterprise, 1995), 28-35. Some of the major countries in Latin America, Argentina, Brazil, and Venezuela, devoted 3.7, 1.2, and 2.1 percent respectively, of their GDP to military spending in 1986 while Jamaica spent 0.9 and Trinidad and Tobago 2.7 percent.

67. *Guyana Information Service* (Georgetown, Guyana, 1977), 67.

68. *Guyana Review* (Georgetown: Guyana Printers Ltd., 1993), 20; Burnham, *Economic Liberation through Socialism,* 10.

69. *Caribbean Contact*, October 1979, 7.

70. Cynthia Enloe, "Civilian Control of the Military: Implications in the Plural Societies in Guyana and Malaysia," in *Civilian Control of the Military*, ed. Claude Welch (Albany: State University of New York Press, 1976).

71. *Caribbean Contact*, October 1979, 12.

72. Burnham, *Declaration of Sophia,* 19.

73. *Caribbean Contact*, July 1980, 13; Spinner, *Political and Social History of Guyana,* 166.

74. *Constitution of the Cooperative Republic of Guyana* (Georgetown: Guyana National Lithographic Co. Ltd., 1980), 30-34.

75. Ibid., 88-123.

76. *Nation*, November 15, 1983, 510; Hintzen, *The Costs of Regime Survival*, 97.

77. Hintzen, *The Costs of Regime Survival*, 182; Clive Thomas, "State Capitalism in Guyana: An Assessment of Burnham's Cooperative Socialist Republic," in *Crisis in the Caribbean*, ed. Fitzroy Ambursely and Robin Cohen (London: The Chaucer Press Ltd., 1983), 40.

78. Mahu Matuda, "Power Galore for Guyana's Ruling Party," *Caribbean Contact*, January 1977, 17.

79. *Guyana Human Rights Association, Human Rights Report January 1980-June 1981* (Georgetown: Guyana Human Rights Association, 1981), 21.

80. Ministry of Economic Development, *Annual Statistical Abstract*, Government of Guyana, Georgetown (1974).

81. *Guyana Information Service* (Georgetown, Guyana 1975), 7-8.

82. *Guyana Chronicle*, December 21, 1976; *Guyana Information Service* (Georgetown, Guyana, 1976), 33-34.

83. Hintzen, *The Costs of Regime Survival*, 185.

84. *Guyana Chronicle*, June 21, 1978, 14.

85. *Catholic Standard*, March 13, 1984; Terrence K. Millington, "Guyana: Grudging Concessions but No Solutions," *Caribbean Contact*, January-February 1984, 11.

86. The World Bank, *World Tables* (Baltimore: Johns Hopkins University Press, 1983), 39.

87. *Catholic Standard*, March 13, 1984.

88. Thomas, "State Capitalism in Guyana," 35.

89. *Guyana Update*, Georgetown, Guyana, January-February 1984.

90. The World Bank, *World Tables*, 39.

91. *Catholic Standard*, October 16, 1983, 17.

92. *Catholic Standard*, November 15, 1981.

93. Thomas, "State Capitalism in Guyana," 35.

94. Ibid.

95. Spinner, *Political and Social History of Guyana*, 165.

96. *Caribbean Contact*, December 1979, 1.

97. Spinner, *Political and Social History of Guyana*, 172-73.

98. Thomas, "State Capitalism in Guyana," 38-39.

Chapter 6

Jamaica: The Declaration of Democratic Socialism

Jamaica, the largest of the English-speaking Caribbean islands and the third largest island in the Caribbean Sea after Cuba and Hispaniola (comprised of Haiti and the Dominican Republic), is situated ninety miles to the southwest of the southernmost tip of Cuba. A former British colony, Jamaica has a population of about 2.3 million people. Like other plantation economies in the Caribbean and elsewhere, Jamaica has suffered from underdevelopment and dependency, which have led to discontent and unrest. The most famous demonstration of this discontent in recent times was the labor rebellion of 1938, which was fuelled by economic deprivation and the lack of political power. The rebellion not only contributed to improved economic conditions for the masses, but also set in place a competitive political system with fair and free elections.

After more than 400 years of colonialism and slavery, Jamaica achieve its political independence from Britain on August 6, 1962. A decade later, it attracted international attention with the election of the socialist People's National Party (PNP) under the charismatic leadership of Michael Manley, son of Norman Manley and founder of the PNP. As a Fabian socialist, Prime Minister Manley in 1974 adopted the ideological concept of "democratic socialism" as a means of transferring the Jamaican economy, society, and external relations from many of the classic features of underdevelopment and dependency. The novel concept of democratic socialism was never free from profound ambiguities. It was a combination of capitalist and socialist socio-economic principles with parliamentary democracy as the mainstay of the political process in the country.

The PNP came to power during the height of the 1970s global economic recession and the dramatic rise in the price of oil. After a decade of political independence and a rapid economic growth rate of 5 percent per annum, Jamaica's economy clearly demonstrated some of the negative effects of dependent development. It bore all the marks of a truly underdeveloped nation: the growth of dependence on the developed countries; uncontrolled exploitation of its resources; high levels of poverty; double digit inflation; and unemployment which increased from 13 percent in 1962 to 24 percent in 1972.[1] Between 1972 and 1974, imports of food, vegetables, and other necessities rose by almost 71 percent, while the energy bill increased by 360 percent, from J$50 million to J$180 million. Foreign investment on which the economy depended declined sharply as the trade deficit grew to J$153 million, a full 35 percent of the value of imports. This, combined with a huge debt service, was dismal for the Jamaican economy. Affluence and poverty grew in visible sight of one another as the rich built mansions in the hills around Kingston while the poor lived in the slums below. During this period, the poorest 60 percent of the population received 19 percent of the national income while 31 percent of it went to the wealthiest 5 percent.[2] Among the beneficiaries were the local capitalist class and foreign investors whose excessive profiteering stifled the island's socioeconomic development. This pattern of economic activity did not benefit only the foreign investors and the local capitalists, but also the middle class who benefited at the expense of the subordinate classes.

The economic disparities not only created tensions between and within the social classes, but also led Manley and the PNP leadership to embrace the influential dependency theory and abandon neoclassical economics, which they increasingly blamed for Jamaica's economic problems. The PNP leadership concluded that Jamaica's socioeconomic and political salvation lay in breaking the bonds of its excessive dependence on the metropolitan powers and the international capitalist system which they dominate. The economic disparities advanced the promotion of economic nationalism, self-reliance, and ultimately, democratic socialism in Jamaica. Critical of the way in which foreign capital had inhibited economic growth and development in Jamaica during the 1960s, Manley said: "Jamaica has fallen into the same trap as many other developing countries by thinking that the indiscriminate granting of tax incentives to foreign capital—regardless of the contribution which the particular capital can make to development, or of the posture of that capital in the society—will necessary contribute to progress."[3]

The economic situation grew worse with the closure of migration outlets, especially to Britain, which, since the mid-1960s, had restricted West Indian immigration into the country. This resulted in a substantial increase in the country's crime rates and political tensions in the urban areas, which escalated into violence between opposing factions of Jamaica's two main political parties, the PNP and the JLP. These developments not only forced the conservative government of Prime Minister Hugh Shearer to declare a state of emergency in the capital city of Kingston during the early 1970s, but they also contributed to the massive defeat of the JLP and the landslide victory of the PNP in the 1972 general elections.

The PNP regime held power for eight years between 1972 and 1980. It was elected with the support of Jamaica's underprivileged and downtrodden classes who supported its wide-ranging program of social and economic reforms aimed to provide opportunities and improve their plight. Ironically, the PNP lost power precisely because of the consequences of those very socioeconomic reforms, as well as its mismanagement of the economy, indecisiveness, and by a series of economic and political destabilization measures spearheaded by the United States.

Overview of Jamaica

Like other Caribbean countries, Jamaica was first settled by natives and later by Europeans following Columbus's initial contact with the island in 1494. The Spanish who were the first to gain control of the island did little other than eliminate the indigenous Amerindian population. After more than 150 years of Spanish rule (1494-1655), the British gained possession of Jamaica in 1655 and ruled it until its independence in 1962. During the 1700s, the prosperity of the sugar industry ranked Jamaica as the most important colony in the West Indies and it remained so until the abolition of slavery in 1838, following a slave rebellion earlier that year by Sam Sharpe, a Baptist deacon from the parish of St. Thomas. In the postslavery era, the farmers tried to coerce the freed black slaves to continue to work on the plantations, but many of them chose to plant their own farms, while others moved to the urban areas in search of work. As a result, East Indians were imported from India as indentured laborers to work on the sugar plantations, though in far fewer numbers than in Guyana and Trinidad and Tobago. While the East Indians populated the rural areas of the country, Jews, Chinese, Portuguese, Syrians, and white Europeans established small businesses in the urban centers.[4] These groups, together with the mulattos or brown descendants of master and slave, constituted the urban middle to upper classes in Kingston and in Montego Bay, the second largest city in Jamaica.

While emancipation brought social change for the black lower classes in Jamaica, it did not change their economic and political status. The former slaves had no political rights and could not adequately sustain themselves from the small plots of farmland which they cultivated and from the meagre wages earned from their labor. Moreover, they were abused in the judicial system and they and their children were denied access to educational and other social institutions. These conditions as well as conflicts between the white planter class and some of the former slaves touched off a peasant revolt in 1865 known as the Morant Bay Rebellion in which fifteen whites were killed. Led by Paul Bogle, also a Baptist deacon in the parish of St. Thomas, the rebellion generated a hysterical reaction from the white ruling class. The participants as well as potential leaders and sympathizers throughout the island were arrested, given summary military trials, and were hanged. In all, 439 blacks were executed, 600 were flogged in public, and more than 1,000 houses owned by blacks were burned by the white population.[5]

The Morant Bay rebellion drove so much fear among the white upper classes that Jamaica was made a Crown colony, governed entirely by Britain. In this form of government, all power was with the British governor and a legislative council appointed by him. Elected members were later added to the council to help govern the island in which less than 6 percent of the population who owned property were eligible to vote. As such, only the interests of the elite and the propertied class were represented.

Today, all of Jamaica's fourteen parishes are the home to approximately two-and-a-half million people of which more than 90 percent have African or mixed African and European ancestry. Over 80 percent of Jamaicans are Christians and about 20 percent have no religious affiliation. Respectable middle and upper class denominations such as Anglicans, Roman Catholics, Presbyterians, and Methodists accounted for 50 percent of churchgoers in Jamaica. The other 50 percent are members of less respectable religious groups that include the native Baptists, Church of God, Ethiopian Orthodox, and other religious sects.[6] Whether through mainstream Christian churches or Afro-Jamaican cults, religion has played a dominant role in the politics of Jamaica. This role, which spanned history and the class structure, continued to be responsible for promoting and maintaining democratic principles and egalitarian attitudes at the levels of doctrine and practice on the island.[7] These democratic values were developed and practiced by early Methodist and Baptist missionaries on the island who delegated a significant portion of pastoral duties to local church members. The widespread practice of religion in Jamaica led to the development of a tradition of leaders that resulted in a proliferation of independent black churches on the island.[8]

The missionaries also encouraged the spread of democratic principles by their own participation in local politics. For instance, during colonialism and slavery, the missionaries supported the causes that promoted enfranchisement of the masses and the undermining of the ruling elite and the planter class. They also encouraged workers to demand higher wages and to support political candidates who favored peasant interests.[9] As Mary Turner wisely put it: "Missionaries of all denominations were both essential to the rebel cause and ancillary to it; leadership lay with the slaves they inspired and trained."[10] This basic ideal was at the core of local religious expressions which, to some extent, was the language of political theory and practice. Religious expressions also helped to maintain the African culture. According to Robert Stewart, James Splaine, a Catholic missionary to Jamaica, has observed that in the late 1800s various attempts by the ruling class to repress Afro-Jamaican culture failed, inasmuch as they could not control religion, which was its core and that local forms of religion "continued to develop as a vigorous alternative to mission Christianity and as a source of Afro-Jamaican identity and resistance at a time when European political and cultural hegemony was being asserted."[11]

Efforts to maintain an Afro-Jamaican culture and identity during British rule resulted in a protracted struggle between the European dominant class and the black masses. The struggle led to the development of a number of prominent local radical race conscious and religious-based groups such as Bedwardism, named after Alexander Bedward, a self-appointed messiah, Garveyism, named after Marcus Garvey, a prominent black leader who founded the United Negro Improvement Association (UNIA) in 1914, and the Rastafarian Movement, which derived its name from Haile Selassie, born Ras (Chief) Tafari, crowned emperor of Ethiopia in 1930.[12] These groups emerged out of the socioeconomic and political need and oppression of the masses and gained prominence mostly among the poor in the ghettos and in the slums in Jamaica.

The groups' principal goals were to preserve the Afro-Jamaican culture and identity through politics and religion, to oppose the racist policies and laws that oppressed blacks, and to seek equality and justice for blacks in Jamaica. They also promoted black nationalism and black capitalism in the country.[13] Bedward, in particular, advanced a comprehensive approach to social organization that included community life, land reform, political freedom, social welfare, education for children, self-reliance, and economic self-sufficiency for blacks in Jamaica. Bedwardism was a fusion of religious teachings and politics. The former were primarily based on the observance of the commandments, baptism as a form of soul cleansing, and the belief in black superiority.[14] Politically, he supported rebellions against the European planter class, the commercial elite, and the colonial administration. He was opposed to the white establishment and foreign domination of Jamaica.

Garvey advocated a more rational and reformist approach than Bedward that included social rehabilitation, black economic nationalism, and the political rights for blacks in Jamaica. In 1928, Garvey founded the People's Political Party, which became the forerunner of formal party politics in Jamaica. Its enlightened agenda stressed land reform, peasant housing, social welfare, the establishment of a Jamaican university, a minimum wage, and the expropriation of land for public use without compensation.[15] The message was for blacks to acquire power through self-reliance, education, science, industry, and politics. Its support for black capitalism was in direct opposition to the radical ideas then being propagated by the communists, with their focus on class rather than race.

The Rastafarian movement emerged in the early 1930s in response to Marcus Garvey's promotion of black nationalism and a black, redemptive God, which interfaced with the prevailing Afro-Christian orientations on the island. Rastafarians believed that the emperor of Ethiopia, Haile Selassie, was literally the God Incarnate, the black messiah of the Promised Land. Like other Afro-Christian movements in Jamaica, Rastafarians embraced a variety of biblical symbols, and created a cosmogony in which blacks were seen as the lost tribe of Zion of the diaspora, the true children of God, while the white rulers and the brown bourgeoisie are Babylon. This interpretation of a black God tells the story:

> If the white man has the idea of a white God, let him worship his God as he desires. If the yellow man's God is of his own race let him worship his God as he sees fit. We as Negroes have found a new ideal. . . . We Negroes believe in the God of Ethiopia, the everlasting God—God the Father, God the Son, and God the Holy Ghost, the one God of all ages. That is the God in whom we believe, but we shall worship Him through the spectacles of Ethiopia.[16]

The group's new identity and sense of dignity and power were expressed in personal appearance and lifestyle. Apart from wearing their hair in dread-locks of the Nayabingi warriors of Ethiopia, Rastafarians refused to work for whites, preferred instead to eke out a living through farming, crafts, and other nonwage labor. They were feared and reviled by the ruling elite in almost every society mainly because of their militant racial ideology, fierce biblical language, and radical political message. Their antiestablishment sentiments and their status as social outcasts made them the subject of constant harassment first by the colonial government and then by Jamaican governments in the postindependence period. Despite their status as social outcasts, the movement instilled in their members a sense of personal power, pride, and confidence, which has enhanced their potential for social reform and leadership. Its nonhierarchical organizations asserted an egalitarian and democratic ethos founded on their ability to reason and to contribute to the re-creation of a culture based on a common world view.[17] Rastafarians also advocated an end to the destitute and subordinate position of blacks in Jamaican society.

In a sense, the movement defies definition, as its various groups exhibit different ideologies and political orientations. By the late 1960s the Rastafarians had shed some of their outcast image and had begun to carve out a place for themselves in Jamaica's sociopolitical life. The group's focus on revivalism, with its unique stress on personal salvation, humanism, and an African identity, attracted new followers from Kingston and across the country. While the emphasis on African identity was strong, there was also clear recognition that brotherhood was deeper than one's skin color—a concept that opened the door for Jamaican whites and Chinese to join the movement. Rastafarianism also evolved as a philosophy of life, and a way to reconnect with nature and to live in love and peace.[18]

Together, these groups brought into the open, in an organized manner, many of the unexpressed views of the black subordinate classes for radical change in Jamaican society. Their quest for equality between the races and economic classes contributed to the rapid growth of a kind of grassroots egalitarianism in Jamaica. Some of the fundamental principles espoused by the groups were incorporated into the manifesto of the two nationalist parties. Messianic claims aside, the groups' demand for land reform and for a new society to replace the paternalistic and oppressive socioeconomic and political structures in Jamaica became the central theme of modern politics in Jamaica. Their pursuit of social justice, freedom, and salvation for the black race was similar to what was for Norman and Michael Manley a humanistic quest.

As Fabian socialists, both Norman and Michael Manley advocated better housing and living conditions for the underprivileged class in Jamaica as a means to an end. They also shared the conviction that education, which was denied to blacks during slavery, provided the strongest impetus for the rapid development of the masses. Moreover, Garvey's consistent message that the white race did not have a monopoly on the laudable achievements of civilization was echoed in the elder Manley's recurrent extortion to Jamaicans that "man stands tallest when he rules himself"[19] and the younger Manley's rebuke to the imperialist forces that "Jamaica and Jamaicans are not for sale."[20]

In the midst of these linkages, there was, of course, a major discontinuity between these movements and the modern political leadership who did not make race an issue in Jamaican politics. For Bustamante, the causes were probably rooted in pragmatism while Norman Manley's reasons were located in ideology, which reinforced the claim that race relations were considered divisive and antithetical to the goal of uniting all Jamaicans under the banner of the common good. The common good is a theory of political obligation compelling a citizenry to obedience. The theory sustains its legitimacy from a process of historical interpretation that argued for the use of certain phenomena for achieving goals in the general interest. These phenomena maximally influenced legislation and the formation of policies, included race, social class, and community, among others.

In Jamaica, there were two versions of the common good. The first was the pre-1938 version, which was premised on racial superiority. This version of the common good claims that the ex-slaves were the burden of the white man who were born wiser than blacks and had the ability to set the agenda for Jamaica's economic development. The other was Norman Manley's version of the common good, which embraced egalitarian principle—a belief in human equality with respect to social, political, and economic rights and privileges. Equity in this sense required not just better wages for workers and peasants, but the ownership of fertile and viable agricultural land and new opportunities for economic growth. It was a political philosophy that was tied to an agenda for reshaping the economic and political structures in Jamaica, including land reform, the nationalization of public utilities and sugar companies, and the establishment of a national banking system. Manley's version of the common good was meant to foster self-reliance and undercut traditional patterns of inferiority and dependence, which had important insights for events of the 1970s. At the founding of the PNP on September 18, 1938, Norman Manley said:

> As I see it today there is one straight choice before Jamaica. Either make up our minds to go back to crown colony government and have nothing to do with our government at all, either be shepherded people, benevolently shepherded in the interest of everybody, with as its highest ideal the contentment of the country; or have your voice and face the hard road of political organisation, facing the hard road of discipline, developing your own capacities, your own powers and leadership and your own people to the stage where they are capable of administering their own affairs.[21]

The general notions of the common good embraced by Manley, while not problem free, were progressive and comprehensive in that they sought to effect change at the very core of the people's concept of their own humanity. They eventually contributed to the demise of plantations and their replacement by a class of independent peasants and small farmers. The principle of the common good was an essential part of the PNP agenda of postrebellion economic reconstruction in Jamaica. Until the 1930s, the Jamaican economy was dominated almost exclusively by British economic interests and economic ideology. The imperial agenda was that the colony should continue to produce agricultural commodities to the exclusion of manufacture and industry. The only exceptions were the manufacturing of pottery, cement, and brick making. On the political front, the colonial government maintained steadfast allegiance to the fact that Britain would not grant power to local politicians who would jeopardize the interests of the metropolitan powers. This, however, changed after the 1938 Caribbean-wide rebellion. The call for self-government and industrialization in Jamaica was accompanied by a restructuring of the agricultural sector.

The 1938 Labor Rebellion

In Jamaica, the system of Crown colony rule which resulted from the Morant Bay slave uprising in 1865 limited the number and powers of the Legislative Council. The domination of political power in Jamaica by the colonial office created considerable frustration among the elected and aspiring local politicians who remained marginalized to the exercise of political power and influence. This group, comprised mainly of the brown middle class (mulatto), demanded from the British constitutional changes toward more effective self-government for Jamaicans based on universal suffrage. The demand for self-government was initially articulated primarily by several professional associations, including the Jamaican Union of Teachers, founded in 1894, the Jamaican Agricultural Society, established in 1895, the People's Political Party, formed in 1927, and various religious groups.[22] The legalization of trade unions gave birth to the Longshoremen's Union and the Jamaican Federation of Union in 1932, and in 1935, the Jamaican Workers and Tradesmen Union, which became the base for Bustamante's rise to fame. However, these organizations did not have any major impact on political developments in Jamaica until the 1938 rebellion, which shocked the British government and local elites into an awareness of the urgent need for political change in the colony. It also contributed to the creation of the PNP as the first nationalist movement, and set in motion a process that resulted ultimately in political independence for Jamaica.

The 1938 rebellion was part of a Caribbean-wide phenomenon that grew out of the depressed economic conditions of the 1930s in which prices for the country's sugar fell by some 40 percent on the world market between 1927 and 1937. Real incomes per capita declined drastically, export earnings reduced, taxes increased, and unemployment was aggravated by the return to Jamaica of large numbers of workers who had lost their jobs in other countries also affected by the depression, particularly from Panama and Cuba. In this period between 25 and 33 percent of Jamaica's urban workforce, that is, wage earners in the nonagricultural sector, were unemployed.[23] In other words, the 1938 rebellion was largely a radical and violent response by West Indians to the harsh economic conditions caused by the worldwide depression. It was also the unleashing of pent-up aspirations against the British government for more political freedom and against the planter class and the commercial elite for better wages and working conditions in the region.

The crisis of the economy spilled over into politics and gave rise to strikes and widespread violence in the urban areas of Jamaica, but was quelled by British troops. After the riots, sentiments that had been previously articulated mainly by the brown middle class concerning greater measures of political freedom were supported by the black masses who, by this time, were galvanized into labor unions. Strikes and work stoppages by sugarcane workers or dock laborers were no longer illegal acts but quasi-legal means of obtaining better working conditions for the masses. The consensus among Caribbean scholars is that the 1938 labor rebellion stands as an important threshold in modern Jamaican history in that it marked the end of Crown colony rule, the beginning of modern politics, and the rise of nationalist political parties in Jamaica.

The Rise of Nationalist Parties

The 1938 rebellion as well as the recommendations by the Moyne Commission which investigated the crisis in the Caribbean gave rise to organize domestic politics in Jamaica controlled by an educated middle-class leadership. With official encouragement from the British government, the number and strength of labor unions increased and from this base the PNP was founded in 1938. Although the British consent to constitutional changes which granted more power and authority to local elected politicians on the island was primarily a response to the demands of the Jamaican nationalist movement, other forces and circumstances were also favorable to the process of constitutional changes not only in Jamaica but in the anglo-Caribbean as a whole. The United States, on whom Britain's war effort depended, was clearly bent on expanding its influence in the English-speaking Caribbean. This was due to the Second World War, which had severely weakened Britain's colonial hold in other areas of the world and, as a result, the British government was forced to accommodate U.S. interest in the region. By the early 1940s, Jamaican civic life featured political parties, trade unions, and adult suffrage.

The People's National Party

The idea of forming a nationalist party in Jamaica came in the wake of the labor rebellion and the colonial government's response to it, which revealed serious weaknesses in the political system in which the masses had no voice. This prompted Norman Manley, a Rhodes Scholar and eminent lawyer, and a group of disgruntled middle-class intellectuals to form the PNP in 1938. The PNP immediate priorities included political education, raising the standard of living of the poor in Jamaica, and the development of a national spirit to help prepare the country for self-government.[24] In 1940, the PNP adopted a Fabian-type socialist position that advocated, among other issues, public ownership and control of the means of production, social justice, equality, and self-government. As a socialist party, the PNP set itself the daunting task to supplant paternalistic authoritarianism with democratic self-rule and economic justice, in what effectively constituted Manley's version of the common good. Politically, the main focus of the PNP was on self-government and democratic institutions. On social and economic issues, the party stressed self-reliance and a shift away from the plantation system toward a more egalitarian distribution of land to the peasantry. The PNP was not only innovative and open to ideas, but was also determined to make the transition from colonialism to self-government.

In the beginning, the PNP had the support of the Jamaican Workers and Tradesmen Union (JWTU) of which Alexander Bustamante (nee Clarke) and cousin of Norman Manley was the treasurer, and later, the Bustamante Industrial Trade Union (BITU) founded by Bustamante. Both Manley and Bustamante united the middle and working classes into a progressive movement. The unity, however, was short-lived. Tensions between the two leaders emerged when Bustamante was expelled from the JWTU after having forced the union's president to resign and hand the presidency over to him. In January 1939, Bustamante formed the BITU and installed himself as president general of the union for life in its constitution.[25] As a trade union leader, he was imprisoned for inciting violence during the 1938 disturbances and again under the Defence Regulations Act of 1940 in which he was imprisoned for seventeen months. On both occasions Norman Manley effected the release of Bustamante from prison. Upon his second release from prison in February 1942, Bustamante (with prompting from the colonial office) broke off relations with Manley and the PNP and formed the JLP in 1943.[26]

The Jamaican Labor Party

Like the PNP, the JLP emerged from a pragmatic, narrowly defined labor union in the BITU but became a conservative party that favored the capitalist status quo. The JLP embraced a political philosophy that, on the one hand, defended the rights of workers and, on the other hand, protected the interests of the capitalist class against the socialist threat of the PNP. It advocated the introduction of laws to reduce the wide economic and social gap that had existed between the masses and the elite in Jamaica.[27] The message was quite clear, the JLP would be at one and the same time the defender of workers' rights and of the interests of the capitalist class. This was a right about-turn for the feisty and confrontational Bustamante who, as a trade union leader, had defended the rights of workers against the ruling elite and the planters and earned almost legendary respect among the Jamaican lower class. His political philosophy was grounded in the founding principles of the JLP:

> The party is pledged to keep within a certain moderate conservative policy in order not to reduce beyond reason, or destroy the wealth of capitalists to any extreme that will eventually hurt their economic inferiors, but to advocate for the introduction of such measures and laws that will shorten the terrible wide economic and social gulf that exists today, that almost inhuman disparity between the haves and the have-nots.[28]

The fact that the JLP agenda defended the status quo and fitted snugly into the imperial mold made it a capitalist party which attracted a number of wealthy conservative owners with various interests in agriculture and industry. By virtue of a quid pro quo, the capitalists provided financial support to the party and Bustamante in exchange for the party's support of their interests.[29] While the JLP responded to the demands of the subordinate classes, the PNP was deeply anchored in the self-serving and reformist aspirations of the middle class and intellectuals of various political persuasions, including Marxism. In this and other respects, the PNP was the opposite of the JLP.

The Struggle for Power

The ideological difference between the democratic socialist PNP and the conservative JLP resulted in an intensive struggle for power. In composition and appeal, the PNP represented primarily the brown urban middle class, the JLP predominated in the rural areas among the black lower classes and the reactionary sectors of the capitalist class, and the Jamaican Democratic Party (JDP), the white upper class. The JLP's image as the party of the black man, the uneducated, and the poor persisted into the 1970s, as did the PNP's image as the party of the better educated and brown middle-class urban groups. As the first truly representative party, the PNP had hoped to become the party of the people as it sought to span social classes and pledged to work for the betterment of the Jamaican people and for the furtherance of the interest of the country as a whole.[30]

Since its creation, the PNP nationalism was based on universal suffrage, nation-building, self-determination, democratic institutions, and a more equitable distribution of goods and services. In contrast, the JLP primary emphasis was to maintain the status quo and address the subordination and oppression of the working class. The major difference between the PNP and the JLP was on the issue of self-government, which Bustamante viewed as a formula for Jamaicans to work out their own destiny according to their wisdom and collective good of the greatest number of people.[31] In the 1944 elections, Bustamante campaigned on the slogan "self-government means slavery." The JLP did not present a program but rather based its appeal on loyalty to the leader who would take care of the interests of the working class. The PNP on the other hand dropped most of its socialist policies and placed emphasis on nation-building, self-rule, maximum production, and full employment.[32]

Despite Manley's appeal for self-government and independence, the BITU-JLP alliance straddled the class divisions in the country and won the 1944 elections, the first to be held under universal suffrage. As indicated in table 6.1, the JLP obtained 41.4 percent of the votes cast and twenty-two of the thirty-two available seats in Parliament, the PNP gained 23.5 percent of the votes but obtained only five seats. Together, the independent candidates received 35 percent of the vote but also gained only five seats. The JDP was completely routed in the elections. The JLP's resounding victory was seen by the masses, that it, rather than the PNP, had represented the militant tradition of 1938. Yet ironically, it was the socialist policies of the PNP that were viewed as the greater threat by the ruling class. The results of the election revealed the strength of the nationalist movement and the weakened position of the ruling oligarchy, as none of the JDP's nine candidates managed to win a seat. It also showed how difficult it was for the two major parties to politically mobilize the middle and lower classes as only 58.7 percent of 663,069 registered voters cast a vote.

In the 1949 election, the PNP, with support among the lower working classes through the Trades Union Council (TUC), won a slim majority of the popular vote, with 43.5 percent compared with 42.7 percent for the JLP. However, the JLP won seventeen seats compared with only thirteen for the PNP and two for the independents. The significance of this election was twofold: on the one hand, it firmly established the PNP and the JLP as the two major political parties in Jamaica, and on the other hand, it made the PNP's socialist election manifesto an issue and generated a strange alliance between the black lower class and sectors of the white upper class which regarded Bustamante's populist and personal appeal and politics as a lesser evil to Manley's socialist policies.

The defeat of the PNP led to internal party conflicts between the trade union leftist faction and right-wing party activists. The PNP's right-wing faction purged a group of left-wing radicals and leaders of the TUC for their anti-imperialist stance during the election. The purge weakened the PNP's working class base as union leaders took their unions and their supporters with them. It also lessened the ideological and sociological differences between the two main parties at all levels—mass, leadership, and elite. At the mass level, the PNP managed to make inroads in the labor movement, and at the leadership level, the JLP experienced an influx of brown middle-class professionals interested in political careers but unwilling to earn it through party work in the PNP, where there was a larger group of qualified candidates than in the JLP.

As tensions between the two groups increased, the PNP leadership, in 1952, broke relations with the TUC and formed a new union, the National Workers Union (NWU), which was affiliated to the United Steel Workers of America (USWA). Headed by Michael Manley, the NWU became the industrial arm as well as an important asset of the PNP. It had a formidable task in that it had to compete not only with the BITU, but also with the TUC which had grown very strong in the urban areas, particularly in Kingston. Undaunted by its defeat in the 1949 election, the PNP moved closer to the center. It consciously changed its agnostic image and made religion a regular feature of party politics. The party new manifesto, "Programme for Action Now" bore only a slight resemblance to its founding document which declared the PNP a socialist party with nationalization of public utilities and the sugar corporations as part of the common good.

The philosophy of the common good was not abandoned but was shifted to a more practical plane to attract votes in order to win the next election. The PNP addressed issues such as employment, the development of the country's resources, health care, and welfare reforms, and the creation of cooperative farms which Bustamante dubbed as the first step to communist style expropriation and elimination of private property. Manley had assured Jamaicans that the PNP had absolutely no intention to nationalize the large plantations and sugar corporations, only four public utilities, transportation, electricity, telephones, and broadcasting, which he cogently defended as a sound public policy.[33] In a real sense, the PNP abandoned its policy of land reform, that is, collective agriculture. Only poor and nonarable lands would be made available to the peasantry. This was incompatible with Norman Manley's socialist concept and principles of equality and the common good.

With support from the NWU, the PNP retreated from its socialist policies and adopted a more moderate position toward economic development. For instance, the PNP dropped the issue of nationalization from its platform and instead supported foreign private investment as the primary means for social and economic development. As Norman Manley put it, "The PNP's socialist program would be based on an orderly political development and genuine business sense."[34] Several of its position papers, pamphlets, and its *Plan for Progress* program promised to enact legislation to create a favorable climate and to give foreign investors security and protection in all proper ways.[35] The most noteworthy efforts were the establishment of the Industrial Incentives Act and the Export Incentives Act, both enacted in 1956, one year after the PNP took office. The former was directed toward the promotion of import substitution while the latter provided incentives to industries manufacturing exclusively for the export market. The centrist and pro-capitalist policies of the PNP not only succeeded in forcing Bustamante to abandon his opposition to self-government, but also rewarded Manley with clear victories of 50.5 percent and 55 percent respectively in the 1955 and 1959 national elections.

Despite the pronounced retreat of the PNP from its socialist policies, the JLP campaigned on the danger of socialism and Manley's plan to nationalize the major industries in the country. This tactic failed to achieve the desired result as some sectors of the capitalist class clearly embraced the PNP liberal policies and democratic ethos, which had taken root among the subordinate classes. In contrast, Bustamante's autocratic and iron grip rule on the JLP and his continuing resistance to the politics of self-government contributed to his defeat. In need of an issue around which to arouse emotions and rally support, Bustamante and the JLP focused its message primarily on the PNP's

Table 6.1
Jamaica Election Results: 1944-1980

Year	No. of Seats in House	PNP		JLP		IND	
		No. of Seats Won	% of Votes Won	No. of Seats Won	% of Votes Won	No. of Seats Won	% of Votes Won
1944	32	5	23.5	22	41.4	5	35
1949	32	13	43.5	17	42.7	2	14
1955	32	18	50.5	14	39.0	–	–
1959	45	29	55.0	16	44.0	–	1.0
1962	45	19	49.0	26	51.0	–	1.0
1967	53	20	49.0	33	51.0	–	–
1972	53	37	56.0	16	44.0	–	–
1976	60	47	57.0	13	43.0	–	–
1980	60	9	41.0	51	59.0	–	–

Source: Office of the Chief Electoral Officer and Director of Prisons (various years), Kingston, Jamaica.

unfulfilled promises and the danger that the Manley government was about to sell Jamaica's interests to the West Indies Federation. The PNP countered with emphasis on its economic achievement and the attainment of internal self-government, which increased the numbers and powers of elected politicians. This, along with the usual patronage to which the PNP government had gained access, gave the party another huge victory in the 1959 election.

Jamaica's Preindependence Economy

During the 1940s, the Jamaican economy was more complex and diverse than ever before in the country's history. The days of sugar mono-culture and foreign plantation owners were over and neomercantilism was on the increase. Initiatives were directed toward the consolidation of agriculture for domestic use rather than for export, and the establishment of an independent peasantry was discouraged by the colonial office. Although British policy supported agriculture and discouraged industrialization ostensibly because of limited natural resources, and that it would compete with British exports, impetus was in the direction of the latter. The preindependence economy, which consisted mainly of merchants and traders importing manufactured goods from the developed countries in exchange for the export of primary products, extended beyond sugar to include bananas, coffee, citrus and, most important, the production of bauxite-alumina, which began in 1952. The reorganization of the banana industry in the 1940s and 1950s favored local mid-sized and large growers. It was supported by legislation such as the Pioneer Industries Act of 1949, which helped to diversify foreign capital into manufacturing, a trend that would become more pronounced in the 1950s.

With some measure of internal self-rule, the PNP government in the 1950s turned its attention to the country's economic problems, which though not as serious as during the depression of the 1930s, were still in a state of crisis as it remained heavily dependent on trade. Per capita income was less than $125 while the gap in income distribution widened, and over 20 percent of the workforce were unemployed. In this period, the PNP pursued policies of industrialization that led to the development of import-substitution and export-oriented manufacturing industries, including the North American aluminum giants of Alcoa, Alcan, Kaiser, and Reynolds. As indicated in chapter one, these policies were heavily influenced by the writings of the West Indian economist Sir Arthur Lewis. They were followed by successive Jamaican governments in the 1950s and 1960s, whose role was limited to providing infrastructure and protection to local and foreign capital. Spurred on by generous incentives such as tax concessions, loan guarantees, factory space at moderate rental, and the elimination or reduction of duties, these companies invested millions of dollars in the exploitation of Jamaica's bauxite reserves, estimated to be the largest in the world. During the 1960s, Jamaica supplied 28 percent of the bauxite used in the market economies of the world. At the same time, the tourist industry was expanded and became a valuable provider of foreign currency. The underlying goal of the PNP policies was to reduce poverty, unemployment, foreign imports, and to transform the country's economy into a modern capitalist one, and ultimately reduce its economic dependence on the developed countries.[36]

The economic growth rate generated by the bauxite, tourism, and other industries was quite spectacular in the 1950s and 1960s (see tables 6.2 and 6.3). Not only did gross domestic product increase at an impressive annual rate of 7 percent in this period, but the economy also underwent a structural transformation. Foreign trade increased sevenfold as manufacture rose to 13 percent of GDP and 9 percent of merchandise exports, mining to 14 percent of GDP and 50 percent of merchandise exports, and per capital income grew by 700 percent. Also, in this period tourist arrivals in Jamaica increased five-fold and by the late 1960s the tourist industry accounted for approximately 10 percent of GDP and over 25 percent of gross foreign exchange earnings. In real terms, GDP growth averaged 5 to 6 percent per annum overall, while per capita GDP had grown at 3 to 4 percent per annum.[37]

The rapid economic growth experienced by Jamaica during the 1950s and early 1960s led to significant transformations of the country's economy and social structure. In the late 1940s the traditional exports of sugar, bananas, coffee, citrus, and other agricultural products accounted for 96 percent of merchandise export, but by 1968 their share had been reduced to 37 percent, and, as a proportion of the country's total export value it was only 22 percent. As shown in table 6.4, the displacement of agricultural products was effected by three main groups of new industries: bauxite-alumina, tourism, and manufactures, all of which fuelled the postwar Jamaican economy and provided most of the country's foreign exchange earnings.[38] Added to these is the illegal marijuana trade which continues to make a significant contribution to foreign exchange earnings and to employment in Jamaica. Although it is not easy to assess the marijuana trade because of little reliable data on it, and while no estimates exist for it during the late 1960s, the U.S. Drug Enforcement Administration (DEA) estimated that in the period 1979-1981, an average of 740-1,400 metric tons of marijuana were shipped from Jamaica to the United States. The exact amount of money that returned to the Jamaican economy is still unknown, but given the high increase in U.S. consumption patterns, several estimates placed the figure at approximately one billion dollars annually. This means that marijuana's contribution to foreign exchange earnings in Jamaica was probably comparable to bauxite during the same period.

The rate of growth in Jamaica as in the case of a number of Global South countries in this period was impressive by the historical standards of the growth patterns of the advanced capitalist states. But all that glittered was not gold. Despite this apparently credible achievement and, in particular, a net investment rate of over 15 percent of GDP for the period 1950 to 1967, the Jamaican economy did not achieve self-sustained economic growth and made very little improvement in the level of unemployment. Even though unemployment was reduced largely through emigration to England and, in the postindependence period, to the United States and Canada, Jamaica retained at the end of the 1960s a weak economy that was heavily dependent on foreign capital and imports, and a high unemployment rate of 24 percent with the rate for youth and women in excess of 30 percent.[39] The assertion of development theorists and economists during the 1950s that a rate of net investment of approximately 10 percent of national income was sufficient for developing countries to reach the point of takeoff proved to be wrong in this particular case.[40]

The expanding economy benefited the capitalists and the middle class, who experienced significant growth in purchasing power, and unionized workers, particularly those in the bauxite industry. Income distribution in Jamaica, which was already very unequal, grew worse. The share of personal income earned by the poorest 40 percent of the population declined from 7.2 percent in 1958 to 5.4 percent in 1968. In absolute terms, the annual income of the poorest 30 percent of the population fell from J$32 per capita in 1958 to J$25 in 1968, measured in constant 1958 dollars.[41] Illiteracy, poor health care and housing, poverty, and high unemployment, to name a few, were the lot of most Jamaicans as many of the industries established were capital-intensive rather than labor-intensive, which meant that few jobs were created. Furthermore, a substantial amount of Jamaica's sugar was processed abroad although it was technically and commercially feasible to refine the sugar locally. The island's bauxite was exported as ore despite the economic benefits to build a smelter to process bauxite on the island. In addition, most of the operations in the manufacturing sector relied heavily on imports of raw materials and partly finished products from the industrialized countries. The tourist sector was known for its foreign tastes that contributed to Jamaica's huge imports, which grew from 33 to 52 percent of GNP, while exports increased from 26 to 40 percent. The resulting deficit was financed primarily by capital inflows into bauxite, tourism, and manufacture, and by loans. Despite a vigorous economic growth rate, Jamaica's economy by the late 1960s was heavily dependent on imports of consumer goods, services, and even foodstuffs, particularly from the United States. Imports and the rise of unemployment were the two most striking visible features of Jamaica's pattern of dependent capitalist development, which profoundly have and continue to shape the structure of Jamaica's economy.

Table 6.2
Jamaica's GDP by Economic Sector, 1950, 1960, 1970

Sector	1950 J$M	1950 %	1960 J$M	1960 %	1970 J$M	1970 %
Agriculture	43.2	35.5	51.9	12.0	78.9	7.4
Mining*	–	–	41.6	9.6	146.7	13.7
Manufacturing	15.8	11.5	58.7	13.6	139.8	13.0
Construction and Installation	10.6	7.7	51.1	11.8	155.7	14.5
Electricity, Gas, and Water	1.5	1.1	4.5	1.0	11.8	1.1
Transportation and Communication	10.0	7.3	33.4	7.7	62.9	5.9
Distribution	21.2	15.5	77.8	18.0	179.5	16.7
Financial Institutions	2.8	2.0	16.2	3.8	43.6	4.1
Ownership of Dwellings	8.3	6.1	13.5	3.1	104.7	9.8
Public Administration	7.0	5.1	26.6	6.2	91.6	8.5
Miscellaneous Services•	16.6	12.1	56.3	13.0	57.1	5.3
Total	**137.0**	**100.0**	**431.6**	**100.0**	**1072.3**	**100.0**

Source: For 1950 and 1960 data see Owen Jefferson (1972, 42-43), and for 1970, see the Department of Statistics, Kingston, Jamaica (1973, 44-45).

*The mining sector in Jamaica was virtually nonexistent in the 1950s.

•Miscellaneous services are those not mentioned in table 6.2.

Table 6.3
Annual Rate of Growth of GDP by Industrial Sector, 1950-1970

Industry	1950-55	1955-60	1960-65	1965-70
Agriculture	4.9	–	2.4	1.6
Mining*	–	21.8	5.6	11.9
Manufacturing	9.9	7.3	7.1	6.0
Construction & Installation	16.0	10.0	2.6	1.6
Public Utilities	9.5	10.3	12.2	10.4
Transportation & Communication	5.2	9.4	9.3	3.4
Distribution	11.6	8.4	–	6.9
Financial Institutions	10.3	–	6.6	9.2
Ownership of Dwellings	4.1	-2.2	2.5	0.6
Public Administration	8.0	10.2	6.5	9.5
Miscellaneous Services	11.5	6.2	7.0	5.6

Source: Jefferson (1972, 46); Department of Statistics, Kingston, Jamaica (1973).

Much of the explanation for Jamaica's increased dependence on imports lay with the extent and nature of foreign domination to which the island's political economy was subject when the PNP came to power in 1972. Foreign ownership dominated the pillars of Jamaica's economy: bauxite, sugar, tourism, the financial institutions, and the public utilities. The island's largest sugar estates were owned and controlled by a British firm, whilst the bauxite industry was in the hands of three American and one Canadian corporations. Most of the island's hotels, banks, insurance companies, a large part of the communication network, and a number of basic public utilities, including telephone, electricity, and transportation, were also in foreign ownership. Only in the manufacturing and distribution sectors were some companies in majority local ownership, although it was not certain how much of the managerial decisions were made externally. What was certain, however, was that Jamaica's economic growth was largely dependent on private foreign capital transmitted to the island by way of investment of financial aid, but then lost to the local economy through profit repatriation and intra-company transfer pricing. Jefferson has argued that the amount of capital that flowed out of the Jamaican economy between 1959 and 1969 actually exceeded all incoming investments attracted by the generous incentive investment policies of the government.[42] By 1972, the bulk of the exchange of this capital was with American multinational corporations, which effectively inserted Jamaica into the domain of the U.S. economy.

Much of the local economy was owned and controlled by a tightly knit group comprised of twenty-one families, including five of the most prominent members, the Ashenheims, the Desnoes-Geddes, the Harts, the Henriques, and the Matalons. This group of wealthy capitalists accounted for

Table 6.4
Contribution of Major Sectors to Exports in Jamaica in 1968

Sector	%
Bauxite-Alumina	29
Agricultural Products	22
Tourism	19
Manufactures	8

Source: Norman Girvan, "Why We Need to Nationalize Bauxite and How," in *Readings in the Political Economy of the Caribbean*, ed. Norman Girvan and Owen Jefferson, New World Group, Trinidad and Tobago, 1971, 244.

125 of the 219 directorships in foreign enterprises registered in Jamaica, and approximately 70 percent of the chairpersons of the various corporate boards. While Chinese, Syrians, Jews, Lebanese, and white Jamaicans had control of some of the companies, not one of these firms was actually owned by blacks, who represented 80 percent of the population at the time. Of the 219 directorships, only six were held by blacks, and of these, two were government appointments through joint ownership. Jews, who numbered less than 0.025 percent of the Jamaican population, accounted for roughly 23 percent of the entrepreneurial elite.[43]

When the PNP assumed power in 1972, Jamaica had a dependent economy, particularly in trade in which it imported more than it exported, and both its imports and exports were heavily concentrated on a few partners and products, and in terms of ownership. As shown in table 6.5, foreign interests had owned 100 percent of the mining industries, especially bauxite, 75 percent of the manufacturing sector, more than half of the sugar industry, and much more than half of the tourist industry, financial institutions, and transportation. In spite of a well-established two-party democratic system, the Jamaican society was still firmly elitist and as mentioned earlier, those sections of the economy which were in local hands were controlled by a tight oligarchy. The state's capacity to promote and direct development in the interest of the masses was severely hampered because decision making in public corporations and agencies increasingly came under the influence of the private sector, which constrained the operation of the public sector and resulted in a high degree of inequality and unemployment in Jamaica.

The Road to Democratic Socialism

In Jamaica, the exhaustion of the growth phase of the economic development strategies in the early 1970s added to the country's problems and led to a serious change in direction in economic and social policy. From the moment he succeeded his father Norman Manley as leader of the PNP in 1969, Michael Manley demonstrated a clear understanding of the nature of the post-World War II political economy and its impact on Jamaica and the Caribbean as a whole. As a former trade union leader, Manley was fully aware that the social benefits of the economic growth of the 1950s and 1960s had barely trickled down to the poor in Jamaica. The PNP leader was also cognizant of the fact that the postwar development strategies had produced high levels of unemployment, double digit inflation, weak infrastructure, and poverty next to affluence, all of which aggravated class and race conflicts in the urban areas. These conflicts manifested themselves in labor unrest, political violence, violent crimes, and spontaneous riots directed against the JLP government.

Table 6.5
Foreign Ownership in Jamaica: 1970-1974

Economic Sector	%
Mining	100
Manufacturing	75
Financial Institutions	66
Transportation	66
Communications	> 50
Storage	> 50
Tourism	64
Sugar Industry	55

Source: (EPICA) Ecumenical Program for Interamerican and Communication Action Task Force, 1979, 52.

The first outbreak of large-scale violence occurred in Kingston between August and September of 1965 and was called the Chinese riots because most of the crimes and violence were directed against the Chinese business community. The Chinese were predominantly owners of medium and small business with a reputation for hard work. In his book, *Violence and Politics in Jamaica, 1960-1970*, Terry Lacey contends that the Chinese, more than any other ethnic group, were the envy of many poor and underprivileged blacks from the ghettos of Jamaica principally because of their economic success and business skills which, along with their highly visible minority status, made them easy targets for violence and crimes.[44] The disturbances which lasted for a week resulted from a dispute between an employee of a Chinese store and the owner.

This was followed by a series of demonstrations and riots with political overtones sparked by the deportation of Walter Rodney from Jamaica by the government of Hugh Shearer in October 1968. Rodney, a radical Guyanese intellectual who was a lecturer at the University of the West Indies at the Mona Campus, was not allowed to reenter Jamaica upon his return from Canada.[45] Rodney was deemed a communist instigator who had incurred the state's wrath and displeasure on various occasions in his discussion of race and organization of the lumpen proletariat for revolutionary purposes in the ghettos of Kingston. Known as the Rodney riots, the incident provoked a student demonstration in Kingston that was joined by faculty from the university and many members of the middle and subordinate classes. The demonstration escalated rapidly into mob action in which three people were killed and more than two million dollars in property destruction occurred. Immediately after the disturbances, the Shearer government banned marches and books, seized the passports of Jamaicans suspected of radical activity, and censored radio programs.

Unlike the Shearer government, which was probably the most repressive since the advent of universal suffrage, the PNP leadership addressed themselves to the rising discontent that had resulted from high unemployment, poverty, and the need for more political participation by the masses in the country. The social and economic deprivation and gross inequalities that had prevailed in Jamaica during the early 1970s were, according to Manley, "an affront to any notion of social justice, however loosely defined."[46] As leader of the PNP, Manley focused on the JLP government's high-handed approach towards political dissent and corrupt practices and won the 1972 elections. The PNP election victory was by far the largest majority ever gained by either party in Jamaican political history up to that time. It received 56 percent of the popular vote and thirty-seven of the fifty-three seats in the House (table 6.1). The victory reflected the broad range of support Manley and the PNP had received from the youth, the unemployed, large sections of the working class and peasantry, most of the professional middle class and intelligentsia, and even some of the new members of the capitalist class disaffected by the economic failures and abuses of the JLP government.[47]

During the election campaign, Manley appealed to the traditional Christian community, the Rastafarian movement, and the racial and cultural identity of the younger black generation by identifying issues and symbols associated with them. His allegiance to the Christian community in particular was expressed in such scriptural verses as: "And I saw a new heaven and a new earth, for the first heaven and the first earth were passed away." This type of biblical appeal cast him in the role of a prophetic figure for analyzing the social and economic injustices in Jamaica and earned him the title of Joshua. Manley skillfully adopted a political rhetoric that was unashamedly Rastafarian and contained distinct lower class cultural nuances.

In open-air rallies, the PNP leader displayed his "Rod of Correction" which was especially significant because it was a walking cane given to him by Haile Selassie during his visit to Ethiopia in 1969. As a result, PNP politics and Rastafarianism became even more closely joined. He skillfully deployed such popular Jamaican slogans as "Massa Day Done," "Betta Must Come," and "Power to the People." These slogans were widely used in reggae lyrics and had become the currency of PNP politics.[48] The slogans were rooted in a climate of change beyond the capacity of the JLP government and garnered much of their ideological and ethical content from Rastafarianism, black power, and socialist and other leftist expressions that energized local discontent. To some extent, the slogans courted a radicalism that was based on what was termed "Robin Hoodism" which is to take from the rich and give to the poor. Despite their improper spelling and random grammar, the slogans communicated a sense of social and political urgency in a way that reflected the trepidation of the subordinate classes. Moreover, they expressed the wishes, grief, and aspirations of the poor, and the hope that their economic plight would improve under the PNP government. The PNP also attacked the JLP government on the issues of corruption and abuse of power, such as gerrymandering, the dispensation of jobs and housing to party supporters, the disenfranchisement of voters, and the corrupt use of office for personal gain. Sensed that the popular mood was strongly behind the PNP, the JLP in a desperate attempt to turn the tide accused the PNP of anti-Christian blasphemy and dictatorial tendencies.[49]

As prime minister, Manley was relentless in his pursuit to change the economic and social structure of Jamaica. He criticized the local educational system which, according to him, "was imported lock, stock and barrel from England without a moment's thought about its relevance to Jamaica's needs and aspirations." Manley also claimed that social debilitation and economic malformations in the periphery resulted from the legacies of colonialism in which the African slave was torn from his family, transported across the ocean and was assiduously prevented from forming new family groups which could pass on the African culture. This cultural vacuum continued for three-and-a-half centuries under colonialism. As Manley put it: "All colonialism involves a process of cultured displacement [and] . . . that colonial economies were conceived in the context of dependence."[50] Manley was aware that Jamaica's economic dependence was deeply rooted in its colonial heritage and the international capitalist economy controlled by the

Western capitalist powers. It was this colonial legacy and the exploitation of Jamaica's resources by foreign capitalist powers that Manley sought to change under the ideological label of democratic socialism.

Jamaica: The Adoption of Democratic Socialism

In his quest to reform Jamaica's economy, Manley abandoned neoclassical economics, which he blamed for most of the island's economic dependence on the developed countries. The PNP leader repeatedly advanced the notion that Jamaica's socioeconomic salvation lay in reducing or eliminating its economic dependence on the metropolitan powers, particularly the United States. This was based on a combination of factors. First, as a nationalist, Manley was committed to the service of Jamaica and to assert its place in the international community. He was also committed to the achievement of a greater degree of economic independence for the country within the international capitalist system. Second, as a populist and a firm believer in social equality and individual liberty, Manley was hostile to race and class politics and was determined to bring the benefits of reform to all sectors of society. Third, Manley was a social democrat, educated in the Fabian tradition at the London School of Economics and was a strong admirer of the reformist policies of the British Labour government. Above all, he was determined to change the economic, political, and social direction of Jamaica and to eliminate its dependence on the industrialized nations.

It was clear that Manley's thinking and his vision for change in Jamaica disavowed, either explicitly or by implication, Marxist-Leninist notions of class struggle and proletarian dictatorship. Rather, democratic socialism was based on what Manley termed the "single touch tone of right and wrong" and his belief in the Christian ideal of equality of all of God's children. In other words, the Christian principles of brotherhood and equality, the ideals of equal opportunity and equal rights, and the prevention of exploitation of Jamaicans laid the foundations of democratic socialism in Jamaica.[51] This notion of equality reflected Manley's Fabian views of social organization which were the foundation of the PNP strategy of change for Jamaica in both its internal and external dimensions. As Manley himself explains:

> Social organisation exists to serve everybody or it has no moral foundation ... the fact that society cannot function effectively without differentials in rewards together with the fact that men are manifestly not equal in talent must not be allowed to obscure the central purpose of social organisation.

That is, and must always be, the promotion of the welfare of every member of the human race.[52]

Armed with this set of ideas and possessed of the power of the state, Manley embarked on a number of significant social reforms. The first was in the area of education, which was made free at both the secondary and post-secondary (university) levels by the PNP government in 1973. The expanded opportunities for secondary and university education were to give every Jamaican a chance to become educated and to improve their situation. These policies generated intense opposition from the middle and upper classes whose elitist attitudes resented any type of class or race mixing and free education for all. This group was also concerned about the expense of the PNP programs and Manley's determination to make Jamaica a classless society.

Second, in 1972, the PNP regime implemented an adult literacy program with the intention to eliminate illiteracy among the masses in Jamaica by 1976. To achieve this goal, the government established a National Literacy Board comprised of some 20,000 volunteers to teach the 500,000 illiterate Jamaicans to read and write.[53] Overall, this program was too ambitious for the Literacy Board to manage and to accomplish its set target. As a result, it was replaced by a Statutory Board for Adult Education, the Jamaican Adult Literacy and the set target of 500,000 people by 1976 was reduced to 100,000 per year.

Third, in March 1972, the government created the Special Employment Program (SEP) as a temporary measure to relieve the high unemployment in the country. One of the goals of the program was to provide employment primarily to PNP supporters who, because of their victimization by the JLP government, had been unemployed for almost ten years (1962-1972). The jobs created included such tasks as street cleaning, painting of schools and other public buildings, sidewalk improvement in the urban areas, and road work and afforestation in the rural areas. By August 1972, the program was made permanent, and even though it was a success, it was criticized by the JLP because it was beset by the perennial problem of patronage, lack of work effort, which was the practice of the previous JLP government.[54]

Fourth, the PNP government embarked on a comprehensive land-reform program under Project Land Lease. The goal was to increase the production of food in the country. Although the government was the largest landowner in the country in 1972, much of this land was unsuitable for farming. In order to accomplish its goal, the government forced the larger landholders to either utilize their idle lands for production or lease to someone who would.

Under Project Land Lease, privately held lands were leased by the government, which was then leased for a period of five years to small farmers as a supplement to their own holdings. The program had three phases. Phase one began with some 2,700 farmers who cultivated 4,300 acres of land in 1973, the first year of the operation of the program.

By 1974, another 3,500 acres were brought under cultivation, which were expected to produce about 10,000 tons of food worth over one million dollars. Under phase two, idle lands owned or acquired by the government were leased for a period of forty-nine years (with hereditary rights) to farmers who already had some land in the area. The goal was to increase the net yearly income of the farmers to J$1,500-2,000. Under phase three, full farms were leased to farmers under the same conditions as phase two. By the end of 1980, Project Land Lease had placed 37,661 farmers on 74,568 acres of previously idle lands. The success of the Land Lease program was twofold: on the one hand, it contributed to the increase of domestic food production and, on the other hand, it improved the wealth and living standards of the farmers. One of the main problems with Project Land Lease was that it was relatively expensive; its accumulated cost by 1980 was J$39.1 million of which J$13.7 were loans to be repaid. However, only J$2.8 million were repaid by the time the PNP government was defeated in the October 1980 election.[55]

Prime Minister Manley also reorganized most of the state agencies and institutions and placed them under the control of the capitalist class and some of the most prominent individuals of the PNP. For example, Aaron Matalon, one of the members of the twenty-one ruling class families, was made chairman of the Urban Development Corporation. Donald K. Duncan and Paul Miller, who had been the leading proponents of the black power movement in the Caribbean, were promoted to senior government positions by Manley.[56] This approach was entirely in keeping with the PNP multiclass electoral base and, in particular, Manley's Fabian principles of equality. Moreover, the Ministries of Defence and Home Affairs were combined into the Ministry of National Security in order to facilitate joint police–military anticrime operations. The government also established a Gun Court in 1973 to deal with crimes involving legal and illegal firearms after a wave of shootings earlier that year had killed seven prominent citizens and wounded dozens of others.[57]

The first two-and-a-half years of the PNP government reforms brought a number of social and political changes, but no fundamental break with the previous direction of Jamaica's economy or of the island's dependence on the developed countries. The PNP realized that in order for its domestic

reforms to be successful, the government had to renegotiate better terms for
Jamaica in all its dealings with the core capitalist states and to begin to
exercise local control over the development of the economy. Its efforts to
transform Jamaica's economy came on the heels of the sudden rise in the
price of oil and the generalized recession of the world economy that
followed. The inflationary spiral of 1973 and thereafter severely dislocated
the PNP's economic reform program. The drastic price increases in raw
materials and machinery, the erratic fluctuations in imported food and
manufactured goods, and the steep rise in interest rates charged by foreign
banks and financial institutions curtailed investment and increased the cost
of living and balance of payments in the country. The island's import bill for
oil climbed from J$65 million in 1973 to J$177 million one year later.[58] The
lack of resources to sustain the sudden expansion of the government social
reforms substantially increased state expenditure and the public debt.
Between 1972 and 1974, Jamaica's public sector debt rose by 56.6 percent
from J$332.6 million to J$520.8 million. In the same period, the foreign
component of the debt climbed even higher, from J$117.3 million to J$206.3
million, an increase of 75.9 percent.[59] The severe dislocation of Jamaica's
economy forced the Manley government to press ahead with more radical
reforms of the economy.

The first sign of change came in January 1974 when the government
sought to renegotiate the tax agreements signed with the American- and
Canadian-owned bauxite-alumina companies. These agreements, which were
signed during Crown rule in the early 1950s when the bauxite industry was
first established, produced only a token tax yield for the government. Under
the initial bauxite-mining agreements, Jamaica received only twelve cents
per ton for its bauxite.[60] Efforts by the PNP government to bring the bauxite
industry under national control and increase its economic contribution to the
country received widespread support from the national bourgeoisie, the
radical intelligentsia, government bureaucrats, and workers. The Jamaican
capitalist class also supported the decision mainly because their economic
well-being, which had depended on substantial imports of goods not only for
personal consumption, but also for their manufacturing industries, was being
threatened by a shortage of foreign exchange. This group had relied heavily
upon the state for investment capital, which the government had made
available to national lending institutions such as the Jamaican Development
Bank.[61]

However, Prime Minister Manley was faced with a major difficulty in
his effort to assert national control over the bauxite industry. The problem
was how to tax a product that was not sold in a competitive market. The

prices for Jamaica's bauxite were arranged between divisions of the same company, as was the case with Reynolds Jamaica Mines which sold its bauxite to Reynolds smelter of Louisiana. The price was intentionally kept low to avoid paying the full amount of taxes and royalties to the government of Jamaica. The Manley government solved this problem by imposing a bauxite levy on all bauxite produced in Jamaica and sold in the U.S.[62] In pursuit of its tax policy, the PNP government initiated talks with the bauxite companies aimed at increasing the country's revenue through higher taxes on bauxite produced in Jamaica to compensate for the double-digit inflation which had eroded the island's economic base and hopes for development. As Manley explains: "We intended to secure justice for our country through the bauxite levy which would permit us to share in the benefits of inflation while offering a measure of protection against its consequences."[63]

From the outset, the government knew that negotiations with the bauxite companies were going to be the most difficult Jamaica had ever undertaken. To avoid some form of reprisal from the United States and Canada, Manley assured Prime Minister Pierre Trudeau and U.S. Secretary of State Henry Kissinger that his government's decision to impose a tax on bauxite was purely economic in its implications and was not intended as any form of political hostility towards the United States or Canada. He specifically told Kissinger that he fully recognized the strategic importance of aluminum to the industrial and military interests of the United States and that his government would not prevent U.S. access to Jamaica's bauxite and other products and asked him to pass these assurances on to the president and the members of the National Security Council. Both Pierre Trudeau and Henry Kissinger expressed satisfaction with Manley's explanations. Trudeau, in particular, showed considerable sensitivity to Jamaica's economic predicament and the importance of the bauxite industry to its long-term development.[64]

After three months of unsuccessful negotiations, Prime Minister Manley, on May 15, 1974, annulled all previous agreements with the bauxite-alumina companies and unilaterally imposed a production levy on all bauxite mined or processed in Jamaica. This was a novel method of raising revenue in the sense that the levy was set at 7.5 percent of the selling price of alumina ingot, instead of the former method of a tax assessment based on an artificial profit level negotiated between the companies and the government. In other words, the tax was computed based on the final product rather than on the ore produced locally. The bauxite levy had often been described in terms that suggest that it was a draconian measure imposed without regard to the needs and interests of the companies.[65]

The government's unilateral decision to impose a bauxite levy surprised the aluminum companies which made a two-pronged counterattack. First, all the companies balked at paying the levy and filed suits against the government with the World Bank's International Center for the Settlement of Investment Disputes (ICSID). This led to a long, drawn-out legal battle which the government eventually won. The ICSID ruled that the Jamaican government had not expropriated the companies' assets by means of the bauxite levy. In this period, relations between the government and the aluminum companies were tense and at their lowest ebb ever. Second, the companies transferred bauxite and alumina production from Jamaica to other countries. The result was that Jamaica's share of the world bauxite market fell from 19 percent in 1973 to less than 14 percent in 1976, whilst that of other bauxite producing countries such as Australia and Guinea increased substantially.[66] In spite of these factors, the government's bauxite policy received overwhelming support from the local capitalists, not to mention the masses. In all, only 7 percent of the conservative capitalist oligarchy opposed the levy on the grounds that it violated the sanctity of contracts and warned of dire consequences.[67]

Although the policy led to some discomfiture of the capitalist interests, Jamaica was fortunate in that all the major North American bauxite and aluminum companies had large investments in the country. Its bauxite was highly valued because, unlike Guyana, it was abundant and was usually close to the surface of the earth and consequently inexpensive to mine. Also, bauxite was relatively scarce, as deposits in countries like Australia, Guinea, and Brazil were just being explored. Moreover, the operations of most of the aluminum industries in the United States were geared specifically to the composition of bauxite from Jamaica which, prior to the mid-1970s, was the world's largest producer (table 6.6). The Kaiser aluminum company, for example, was over 80 percent dependent on Jamaican bauxite for its operation. At the end of World War II, the average annual world output of bauxite stood at 755,000 tons, by 1973, production had increased tenfold to reach 75 million tons. Of the 87 percent of U.S. bauxite imports in 1974, 60 percent was supplied by Jamaica. Furthermore, in 1965, the country supplied 28 percent of the world's bauxite, the base mineral in the manufacture of aluminum, a metal that played a key role in postwar development of the world capitalist economy. The aluminum companies were so dependent on Jamaica's bauxite that it gave Prime Minister Manley the leverage to bring the industry under tighter national control. Caribbean economist Norman Girvan has contended that among the bauxite exporting countries, Jamaica had both the motivation to seek higher returns for its ore and the leverage to secure them, even over the opposition of the companies.[68]

The bauxite levy was indeed an effective and profitable venture for the government in that taxes from the bauxite industry increased from a meager J$22.71 million in 1972 to J$170.34 million in 1975 and to J$196 million

Table 6.6
Bauxite: World Market Shares (%)

Countries	1970	1975
Jamaica	27	17
Australia	14	24
Guyana	12	7
Guinea	2	23

Source: Anthony Maingot, 1979, 297.

in 1979.[69] The huge increase prompted the Manley administration to create the Capital Development Fund (CDF) to manage the additional revenue and to bolster the productive capacity of the economy. To reinforce its socialist image, the government used the CDF to provide funds for government investment in bauxite and alumina production; to finance agricultural projects, such as sugar cooperatives and collective farming; and to gain substantial ownership of some public utilities. In this context, the PNP industrial and agricultural policies were directly dependent on the success of the bauxite industry.

Income from the bauxite levy allowed the Manley government to relax restrictions on certain imports and set aside $40 million to build up cash reserves, finance new capital projects, and to expand the employment program.[70] In the period 1974-1976, government spending increased from J$596 million to J$751, and the import budget rose from J$600 to J$851 million.[71] Despite the success of the bauxite tax, Manley remained convinced that Jamaica could not conquer its socioeconomic problems and become a genuinely effective society with a bauxite strategy that begins and ends with taxation policies inside the country. What was required was increased national control of the bauxite industry and other foreign enterprises in order to achieve a more equitable distribution of the existing wealth. It was under these circumstances that the PNP regime embarked on democratic socialism.

The Declaration of Democratic Socialism

The bauxite levy initiated by the Manley regime in Jamaica set in motion a process of change which quickened as the 1970s unfolded. In September 1974, with the social violence and the general political discontent of the previous decade apparently contained, the Manley regime declared Jamaica a democratic socialist state. This declaration was made out of a sense of equality and justice typical of Manley's approach to reshape the economic and social structures in Jamaica. It deepened U.S. concerns not only on the island, but also in the entire Caribbean. Democratic socialism was conceived as a means of allowing the people of Jamaica to achieve greater control of the various foreign interests that for more than four centuries had dominated the island's economy. It was developed with the intent to mobilize the masses in Jamaica more actively behind the PNP strategy of change. As an ideology, the spirit of democratic socialism underlay the ambitions of a new indigenous development plan that, in part, was designed with the aim to overcome or significantly reduce Jamaica's economic dependence on the advanced developed countries. Democratic socialism was a shift in relative class power from the dominant capitalist classes to the subordinate classes by the state that was meant to create a local economy independent of foreign control and domination and responsive to the needs of the local population, as well as to reduce Jamaica's dependence.

The concept of democratic socialism adopted by Prime Minister Manley was meant to be a third path of development for Jamaica. The rationale for Manley's search for a third path of development was to pursue a different strategy from the neocolonial capitalist model of the Puerto Rican type and the Marxist-Leninist model of the Cuban type. For Manley, neither one of the traditional paths of development has led to the achievement of real economic growth and equity despite their universal espousal of such goals. In his own words: "The PNP won a landslide victory in the general elections of February 1972. Before our eyes were these two models—Puerto Rico and Cuba. Surely there was another path, a third path. . . . We were to spend the next eight and a half years in our periphery exploring that third path."[72]

According to Manley, Puerto Rico's Operation Bootstrap was similar to the industrialization by invitation development strategy pursued by Jamaica and several other Caribbean countries in the 1950s and 1960s. It emphasized economic growth and foreign investment but neglected social welfare and, as such did not lead to self-sustained development. Under this development strategy the degree of Jamaica's economic dependence increased rather than decreased. By contrast, the Cuban socialist model was one of revolution with impressive social achievements in such areas as health, education, and employment, but was based on the Marxist-Leninist view of democracy that did not allow political rights outside the concept of the dictatorship of the proletariat.[73] For these reasons, Manley condemned both development models for their respective dependence on the United States and the former Soviet Union and sought a new development model for Jamaica. As he himself put it:

> It is self-evident to us that we want to be pawns neither of East nor West, economically or politically. If [Jamaica] is to be free of dependence on any external source of power; democratic in the complete sense of pluralism and participation; and seek to provide both a material basis for prosperity and a system ensuring that it is equitably shared, it can only pursue this third path.[74]

Objectives of Democratic Socialism

Democratic socialism was comprised of five principal objectives, four of which focused on domestic economic and political reforms, and the fifth on Jamaica's foreign policy goals. The first objective was to reduce foreign domination and control over Jamaica's economy through a combination of three policies, namely selective nationalization of foreign enterprises, the imposition of taxes on the bauxite companies, and joint ownership of some private corporations. Selective nationalization was directed to the public utilities, those parts of the sugar industry that were foreign owned, some textile operations, the flour industry, some financial institutions, and hotels in the tourist sector. The government nationalized the Jamaican Telephone Company which was owned by the Continental Telephone Company of the U.S., the electric power company, the Kingston Transportation Service, and the Barclay's Bank of England, among others. The Water Commission, the Jamaican Railway Company, the Jamaica National Development Bank, and the Jamaican Mortgage Bank were already government owned.[75] These nationalizations reflected the PNP policy to extend state control over the commanding heights of the economy and to minimize economic and social dislocation. They were also aimed at increasing the state's influence over the pace and direction of the company's resource and capital and to reduce its dependence on foreign ownership. Manley asserts that the purpose of these reforms was to reduce dependence of the economy as a whole on foreign ownership, reduce the degree of control of the local oligarchy, widening the degree of social control over the economy through direct state activity and widening the participation of the people at large in beneficial economic activity.[76]

The Manley administration also set up joint ventures and state-sponsored agreements. To begin with, the government established a new relationship with the mining companies. Under the terms of the new agreements, the PNP purchased all bauxite-producing lands and in turn leased portions of the lands back to the companies to mine bauxite at 7 percent of the purchased price. The companies were guaranteed access to bauxite reserves for forty years. By purchasing the lands, the government achieved two objectives. First, it gained the use of the lands for agricultural purposes, and second, it gained control of the bauxite reserves. The government also purchased 51 percent of the local operations of the bauxite mining companies, Kaiser and Reynolds, and between 6 and 7 percent of Alcan and Alcoa, the two firms that were involved in bauxite mining and alumina processing. The terms of purchase were favorable to the companies and, as a result, they withdrew their lawsuits that were filed with the ICSID against the government.

The government also established the Jamaican Bauxite Institute (JBI) to monitor the operations of the bauxite industries. In 1977, the JBI revealed that Jamaica's high-grade bauxite reserves totaled two billion tons instead of the 600 million tons claimed by the major bauxite and aluminum companies.[77] The contradiction prompted Minister of Finance David Coore to acknowledge that "Jamaica had been at the mercy of the bauxite and aluminum companies because they knew the facts about their industry and we had only such knowledge as they saw fit to let us have."[78]

In the period between 1974 and 1977, the PNP government diversified bauxite-alumina sales to a number of countries in Eastern Europe, but by all accounts, the price was not compensatory. In like manner, the government's efforts to persuade its regional neighbors to pool their resources to build an aluminum smelter fell through partly because of Jamaica's actions (see chapter 3). Similarly, the inability of the IBA to assert its monopoly on the bauxite industry was a major disappointment for the government of Jamaica. As a developed capitalist country, Australia did not want to disrupt the international economy which was already affected by the Arab oil embargo. Moreover, three of the IBA members, Suriname, Sierra Leone, and Guinea, contrived to secure a comparative advantage by imposing a bauxite tax lower than that of Jamaica's. Whether this was due to pressures of a contracting bauxite market, or an attempt by those countries to increase their market share, or both, is still an open question.

The bauxite policies pursued by Prime Minister Manley must be seen in the light of the government's overall strategy of diversification, independent local development of the industry, and increased revenues. The repatriation of the lands from the bauxite conglomerates by the government, for instance, was not only aimed at bringing the land back into local ownership and putting the portions that were idle into food production, but was also tied to the control of bauxite reserves. Based on their rate of extraction, it was estimated that some mining companies had 150 years of ore reserves under their control. Together, the aluminum companies had control of more than one-and-a-half billion tons of bauxite but mined only twelve million tons annually.[79] This proved that the land ownership was related to the control of reserves and, in turn, to the rate of extraction, and therefore, revenue for the Jamaican government.

Despite claims by the aluminum companies that the bauxite levy of 7.5 percent was unjust, the combined net income of the four North American aluminum companies with operations in Jamaica, Alcoa, Alcan, Reynolds, and Kaiser, increased from U.S. $209 million in 1973, the last year before the levy, to U.S. $581.7 in 1974, the first year of the levy. Equally interesting was the fact that in 1973, Jamaica received U.S. $26.9 million for twelve-and-a-half tons of bauxite. In 1980, the Jamaican government earned U.S. $209 million from twelve million tons of bauxite.[80] From these figures it seemed that both the companies and the government were doing well after the levy, but this was not the case for the government because bauxite production was systematically reduced as an act of retaliation by the companies.

The second objective of democratic socialism was the creation of a mixed economy comprised of public, private, and cooperative sectors with public ownership as the dominant sector. It was based on a combination of capitalist and socialist policies evident in the PNP's policy of selective nationalization and joint ownership between the government and the private sector of some of the bauxite and sugar industries. The aim was for the state to take control of the economy. According to the Jamaican government, joint ownership was a technique that was particularly suited to the peculiar circumstances in Jamaica and the concept of democratic socialism.[81] It was a compromise solution through which the government acquired foreign assets on terms that fell somewhere between outright nationalization and expropriation. Under a mixed economy, foreign investment, the main engine of growth, was to be part of the development process. It also allowed foreign capital that was vital to the economy of Jamaica to flow into the country. Manley realized that a complete break with the multinational corporations for an indefinite period of time was not a feasible proposition given the vertical and horizontal integrated oligopolistic nature of the world's sugar and aluminum industries and commercial banks. Moreover, there was no way the PNP regime could have found substantial markets for the country's bauxite and sugar outside the Western industrialized nations. In stressing the importance of foreign capital to developing countries in general, and Jamaica in particular, Prime Minister Manley said:

> No developing country can hope to bridge the gap between performance and expectation without substantial injections of overseas investment. Egypt could not have built the Aswan Dam, nor could the Castro regime have survived without Russian capital and technology. Similarly, Jamaica could not have established her aluminum industry by herself.[82]

As part of its socialist development strategy to promote and maintain a mixed economy, the PNP government took complete control of the various public utilities but quickly acknowledged that "as a matter of common sense and reality, public ownership will have to work together with foreign and private capital for the foreseeable future in such areas as bauxite, sugar, banking and tourism."[83] The regime rejected the idea of nationalization of the entire private sector and insisted that both the private and public sectors were merely parts of the whole and were complementary to each other. Manley explains that once certain priorities have been overtaken in the field of human resources, infrastructure, and in certain strategic areas of the economy, private enterprise is the method best suited to the production of all the other goods and services which are necessary to the functioning of the economy. Manley summed up the PNP's socialist strategy:

> We were clear that we would never expropriate property, but would make acquisition in the public interest on a basis of fair compensation. We also had a firm and unwavering commitment to the preservation and development of a strong private sector. We did not believe in a pure free enterprise model of economic development and, consequently, saw the private sector as having a particular place and filling a particular role.[84]

At the core of the government agricultural policies was Project Land Lease, which was an extension of the 1972-1974 land reform program that was fashioned after Tanzania's communitarian model in which government and privately owned lands were leased to small farmers by the government for up to forty-nine years. Hereditary rights were attached to this form of tenure and compensation was to be paid to farmers for capital improvements. The land reform program was aimed at achieving a more equitable distribution of land, food self-sufficiency, and reduction in the size of the food import bill, which increased substantially during the early 1970s. This was a vexing problem for Prime Minister Manley who said:

> We have failed to meet the domestic food requirements of our people, and . . . most of our staple foods are not those produced by ourselves. It is interesting that in 1962, our imports of food amounted to $30.4 million . . . whilst the population increased by twelve percent during the period . . . our imports of food in 1971 amounted to $76.3 million, or an increase of 150 percent in the import food bill—an increase much greater than the population and price increase when we put them together.[85]

The land reform took two forms. The regime placed emphasis on individual small farms, cooperatives, and Community Enterprise Organizations (CEO), a community-owned, cooperatively operated enterprise. The plan was to have CEOs in agriculture, livestock, and manufacturing. The second plan focused on construction, with the main thrust on housing. This sector was to provide 7,500 new jobs at the cost of an additional $120 million to the government budget and $49 million to the foreign exchange budget. The first two phases of Project Land Lease were successful while the third phase was in total disarray. The first and second phases placed 23,886 farmers on 48,000 acres of land with an estimated crop value of $20 million. Before these reforms, 37 percent of these farmers had been forced to seek outside employment; with Project Land Lease only 17 percent did so and 67 percent hired part-time labor.[86] But by 1980, both phases fell short of projections due to crop failures, lack of government funds, diminished support, and IMF stringent policies. The third phase was the victim of patronage and, as such, became targets of vandalism.

Along with Project Land Lease was the Crop Lien program established under the Emergency Production Plan in 1977 to provide credits to small farmers quickly and on easier terms than commercial banks to purchase seed, manure, fertilizer, and other necessities. In the first year of the program, $20.7 million were made available to farmers, and by December 1980, the amount had increased to $37.5 million. On a similar but smaller scale was the Pioneer Farms program launched in 1978 to help unemployed youths in the rural areas of the country. The PNP agrarian programs which were aimed at promoting self-reliance in domestic agriculture met with some success, but again fell short of most of their targets. The goal was to bring an additional 36,500 acres of land into production and to settle an additional 10,000 farmers under Project Land Lease. The achievements of the programs were 7,700 farmers settled, 30,200 acres of land cultivated, and gross output increased from 58,000 to 86,000 short tons.[87] Elsewhere, the results were not so impressive as some of the programs were hampered by adverse weather conditions such as floods in 1979 and hurricane Allen in 1980, inexperience with designated crops, and poor irrigation facilities.[88]

The expansion of the state into the industrial sector began with the PNP government restrictions on imports in order to promote the development of local industries. This reflected the wish of the regime's expressed support for local small business with the hope to neutralize the entrenched influence and dominance of the wealthy capitalist class, especially the famous twenty-one families. Paul Chen-Young explains that the intention of the government was to allow existing big business to continue to operate but the thrust of government policy would be to develop small-and medium-scale enterprises, especially by providing financial assistance.[89]

The first substantial move by the government against the commercial establishment was the formation of the Jamaican Nutrition Holdings (JNH) in 1973. This state-owned agency was responsible for the business aspects of the government's nutrition program, such as the importation of foodstuffs for the country's public school lunch program. It became the sole importer of certain foods, such as wheat, soy, rice, and salt fish. It allowed the PNP government to diversify foreign trading relations and to exercise greater control over the economy, which effectively reduced the scope of private-sector commercial activities in the country. The private-sector monopoly on trade was further reduced when the JNH was replaced by the State Trading Corporation (STC) in 1977, and was granted exclusive license to import medical supplies, building materials, textiles, grains, and other basic staples. The STC created three subsidiaries—Jamaica Building Materials Ltd., Jamaica Pharmaceutical and Equipment Supplies Ltd., and Jamaica Textiles Imports Ltd., which together put an end to the merchant's monopoly on trade and the so-called 20/80 rule.

Initially, the STC had control of 20 percent of the total value of imports while the remaining 80 percent went to the traditional business enterprises. By the end of 1977, however, the STC was empowered to handle 80 percent of all imports other than oil and those for the bauxite-alumina industry.[90] The economic activities of the government were extended to the banking industry with the creation of the Bank of Jamaica, the Jamaican Mortgage Bank (JMB), the Workers Bank, and the Jamaican Development Bank (JDB). The

JDB was especially important because it had total control of the Capital Development Fund that was specifically earmarked to manage the funds from the bauxite levy.

In the area of communication, the state, in 1973, founded a newspaper, the *Jamaican Daily News,* to rival the conservative *Gleaner* which for the most part was critical of the PNP policies. The government also took control of Radio Jamaica, which had 79 percent of the total radio audience, and a television station, the Jamaican Broadcasting Corporation (JBC).[91] The Manley government also transformed the Jamaican Information Service (JIS) into the Agency for Public Information (API) as part of an effort to promote its concept of democratic socialism and to mold public opinion to support it.

Despite Manley's socialist rhetoric, there is evidence to suggest that the Jamaican Development Bank, the State Trading Corporation, and other state-owned enterprises functioned and operated under capitalist principles during the 1970s, the most effective period of democratic socialism. They included profit making and the exploitation of wage labor. This was particularly true of the JDB because most of its funds came from capitalist institutions such as the World Bank, the IMF, and the Inter-American Development Bank. Also, both the United States and Canada attached strict conditions to their loans to the JDB that reinforced capitalist principles as they requested 70 percent and 66 percent respectively to be in the form of goods and services from their economies. The Jamaican Industrial Development Corporation (JIDC) provided incentives to foreign capital and worked closely with the Small Business Development Agency, a new entity created in 1977 to maximize profits through expanded and more efficient production.

With the exception of the sugar industry, which was organized into co-operatives, most of the public enterprises operated under capitalist practices with profit taking as the main goal. Also, the joint ownership agreements in which the government purchased all the land and controlled 51 percent of the mining industries, the parent companies kept their refining plants and maintained control over technology, capital and the market. In the end, the state did not succeed in its drive to restructure the capitalist economy, which by the late 1970s was once again under the control of the capitalist class in Jamaica. In these circumstances the PNP's nationalization policy and control of the economy appeared rather more muted.

The third objective of democratic socialism was the development of a more egalitarian society not only in terms of providing opportunities to the masses, but also the promotion of a deeper sense of mutual respect and appreciation among Jamaicans. To achieve these objectives, the Manley government used the state to make sure that certain basic rights, particularly in social and cultural areas, were respected and enjoyed by all Jamaicans. The Labor Relations and Industrial Disputes Act of 1975 decreed a national minimum wage for all categories of workers, including domestic servants and agricultural workers, a forty-hour work week for industries, and work programs in the public sector to help the unemployed. The act established a social security program, which granted benefits such as unemployment insurance, severance pay, pensions, sickness and disability payments to workers, and maternity leave with pay to mothers both in the private and public sectors. It compelled employers to recognize unions democratically elected by workers, created a tribunal to settle work-related disputes, and provided for arbitration at the request of any parties involved in an industrial dispute. In addition, it gave the minister of labor the authority to declare illegal any strikes that were deemed to be gravely injurious to the national interest. It was the intention of the PNP government to protect the interests of both workers and unions and curb any excesses on either side.

In the area of education, the PNP government regarded the educational system inherited from Britain as outdated and implemented a program based on equality. Accordingly, the government reformed the school curricula which provided free education to every child from primary to secondary academic, secondary technical, and university. Education facilities previously narrow and elitist were expanded and opened to all Jamaicans irrespective of their social status. Inevitably, the removal of all educational costs from the private citizen established a system of merit in which wealth was no longer a guarantee of educational opportunity. The PNP made it clear that "all children must pass through similarly endowed institutions wherein they must mix, regardless of parental background, and from which they must proceed to higher levels on the basis of merit alone."[92] Jamaicans also benefited from a voluntary educational program in which some 12,000 volunteers taught in primary and secondary schools, vocational training centers, and the literacy program. By 1980, more than 200,000 Jamaicans graduated with literate and numerate skills.

The government also updated the teacher-training program and increased the age to seventeen years instead of fifteen required for a primary school education. The objective was to transform the method of teaching and the educational system to meet the national objectives of the government. In addressing this issue Prime Minister Manley said:

> Teachers must undergo a process of self-transformation: they must comprehend a new set of objectives; they must evolve a new set of techniques that can give effect to new targets. A teacher, literally, must

carry the whole brunt of the battle to create a new generation with a different value system. Theirs is the task to inspire future generations of children with positive attitudes towards work, social responsibility and cooperation . . . of devising the techniques which will make the young learn to experience production on the land. Education is the means by which we equip today's generation for tomorrow's possibilities. The education system must seek to produce skills which are a calculable part of our opportunities and the kinds of attitudes without which skills are sterile and the successful pursuit of objectives unlikely. The whole area is fundamental and is an indispensable key to development.[93]

With this in mind, the government also provided free books, free school uniforms, and free meals to elementary school children from low-income families. It also increased subsidies on education from J$6.7 million in 1969 to J$26 million in 1974 and to J$43.5 million by the end of 1976.[94] These reforms made education, which was a privilege for the rich and not a right for all, available to the poorest Jamaican.

In the health sector, the Manley regime embarked on a reform program of preventive medicine which provided free health care to all Jamaicans and established a number of clinics to facilitate access to medical drugs and increased the number of doctors and dentists in the country. It involved widespread inoculations, health and hygiene education programs, waste disposal, and water purification. Hospitals were upgraded and health clinics and a paramedical system were established in the rural areas of the country. The main focus of these efforts was on primary health care rather than the curative and to eradicate disease-carrying insects. The government had contended that sound hygienic practices and the cleaning up of sources and carriers of infection were a much sounder way to improve public health. An overall assessment of the success of the PNP government health program is difficult; it is probably fair to state that while the quality of health care did not appreciably improve, its availability did increase. On the negative side, drugs were always in short supply due to lack of foreign currency, and nurses, doctors, and other medical personnel remained underpaid for the most part of the PNP's tenure in office.

Other social programs included the expansion of day care centers, food subsidies, and the creation of the National Housing Trust (NHT) in March 1976. The NHT established a growing fund for housing construction through compulsory contributions based on a 3 percent payroll tax and 2 percent of gross earnings by workers and employers. It was designed to provide low cost housing to the working class and freed some of the finance from the budget earmarked for housing construction. Distribution of houses under this program was by lottery rather than patronage, which put an end to the practice established by previous governments. In the three years leading up to 1980, the NHT built 17,381 units and created thousands of jobs.[95] These social reform programs represented the PNP government's commitment to the use of public funds to increase the level of egalitarianism for the poor and the impoverished population in Jamaica. They were also the bedrock principles upon which democratic socialism was constructed.

The fourth objective of the PNP program was political. From the outset, the PNP leader was critical of the remoteness of traditional multiparty democracy in Jamaica which, apart from everything else, is reduced to the act of choosing a party to form a government once every four or five years. To enhance this historical political process, Prime Minister Michael Manley advocated a more popular form of democracy known as the politics of participation. The politics of participation involved worker participation, group cooperation, even among elementary and high school students, and the establishment of institutions and organizations to plan and link the process at every level of society. This was a conscious attempt by the government to create institutions through which the masses must be continuously involved in the political decision-making process. It was more than periodic national and local elections; rather it was meant to democratize the Jamaican society or as Manley eloquently explained: "We believe that Parliament is the foundation of democracy but recognize that parliamentary democracy is only a beginning to the democratic process. To democratize a society you have to experiment in forms and institutions which bring decision-making to the broad mass of people."[96]

Accordingly, the Manley regime reorganized the political process within the local government and established a number of regional and community councils throughout the country's fourteen parishes. The regional councils provided political direction at the parish level and mobilized the masses to participate in community affairs. Comprised of representatives of all the mass organizations in a particular parish, and under the direction of senior party members, the councils were responsible for initiating, developing, and implementing programs for their respective communities. They also planned and coordinated mass rallies in support of the PNP's programs and to ensure that all organizations within each parish were fully involved in them. More importantly, the PNP was deployed as an instrument to disseminate public information and provide a forum for mass political education both at the local and national levels. These symbolic gestures were important steps towards political inclusion of the masses psychologically in the building of a stronger national consciousness and identity.

Obviously, social inclusion and national identity as well as policies such as the Status of Children Act, which gave full legal status to children born out of wedlock, have helped to give the black masses of Jamaica the feeling that they were full members of the Jamaican society and first class citizens for the first time. This "bottom-up" policy approach not only scaled down the elitist character of decision making and political inequality, but also increased the social and economic power of the lower class both directly in their dealings with employers and providers of services, and indirectly through political participation and mobilization. At the very least, these policies intensified the level of popular political support for the PNP leadership and deepened the democratic process, which was the underlying principle of democratic socialism. As Manley indicated: "The democratic was to be given equal emphasis with the socialist, because we were committed to the maintenance of Jamaica's traditional and constitutional plural democracy; and more importantly, because we intended to do everything in our power to deepen and broaden the democratic process of our party and in the society at large."[97] By 1978, the process was overwhelmed by the contradictory and often conflicting interests of the masses, most of whom were frustrated by political habit and distrusted the changes of the PNP.

The fifth objective of democratic socialism was the PNP articulation and adoption of a radical foreign policy, the contours of which have been discussed in chapter 4 and are well known to social scientists. So here we will focus on the main thrust of the PNP foreign policy and how it relates to the overall national objectives of the Manley regime. The PNP pursued an open foreign policy as distinct from the closed policy of the JLP, which only envisaged relationship with the West. Its primary objectives were rooted in political non-alignment and the development of relations with noncapitalist countries while maintaining strong economic and political ties with the West. It also signaled a commitment to the right to self-determination for Jamaica and other Global South countries. Manley was fully aware of the problems faced by small developing countries in their dealings with the metropolitan powers and, as a result, was opposed to imperialism and the international economic system created and dominated by the Global North countries.

Prime Minister Manley's prescription for a sensible Jamaican foreign policy involved a positive commitment to Caribbean economic regionalism, support for Third World solidarity, and a common Third World strategy of development designed to reduce Jamaica's dependence on the capitalist system. It also involved broad support for the United Nations which created an international forum through which the voices of the smaller countries could be heard; and a commitment to international morality separate from bold assessments of self-interest. Prime Minister Manley had become increasingly discontented with the fractures and dislocations within the international capitalist system, which he linked to Jamaica's dependence and underdevelopment. Manley asserts that "Jamaica is a part of the West geographically, historically, economically, by political tradition and by cultural penetration . . . being part of the West . . . primarily implies dependence and the occupying of a minor, peripheral status in the total Western system."[98] It was Manley's belief that the world economy continued to work in favor of the industrial powers and against the interests of the newly independent developing countries.

These considerations were the primary reasons that led the PNP regime to establish full diplomatic relations with Cuba and the People's Republic of China during its first years in office. The PNP pursued economic and political cooperation with several other states beyond Jamaica's traditional partners, including Russia, and the former socialist states in Eastern Europe, as well as in the Middle East and East Asia. It actively supported measures to overthrow the apartheid regime of Peter Botha in South Africa, the Smith regime in Rhodesia, and the Portuguese tyranny in Angola and Mozambique. In his quest to promote Third World cooperation, Manley boldly stated that "I intend to lay the foundations from now for this idea of cooperation among the underdeveloped nations because I believe if we in the underdeveloped parts of the world had only the diplomatic vision to see that we could forge links of steel around the world that would give us for the first time an opportunity to throw the begging pans away."[99]

On the economic front, efforts were made by the government to diversify trade away from Canada, Britain, and the United States, which together in the early 1970s, accounted for 90 percent of Jamaica's trade. To this end, the PNP signed trade agreements with Cuba, Russia, and a number of Eastern European states, Japan, Iraq, and Latin America and Caribbean countries. Manley was also extremely vocal in his support for the NIEO, the NAM, the G-77, and the IBA. These organizations were intimately linked to the PNP goals of reducing Jamaica's economic dependence on, and vulnerability to, market fluctuations and political relations with the core capitalist countries. The trade agreements and offers of assistance from Russia and Eastern Europe, however, did not reduce the island's dependence on the West. One reason was that Jamaica's economy remains heavily dependent on imports, and the goods that were exchanged in the barter trade arrangements with the socialist bloc were not always in line with the country's economic needs.

Second, loans from nontraditional sources came in the form of soft currency, which resulted in the regime's perpetual struggle to service its foreign debts that required hard currency. And in spite of the PNP trade diversification policy, the U.S. and Britain dominated Jamaica's share of exports and imports (tables 6.7 and 6.8).This remains true today for Jamaica as for other Caribbean countries despite the creation of CARICOM.

The PNP's most radical foreign policy shift was its development of closer economic and political ties with the Castro regime in Cuba, Jamaica's closest neighbor. This particular relationship began when Prime Minister Manley accompanied Castro in his jet to the Non-aligned conference in Algiers in 1973. The relationship intensified in 1975 with the formation of the Jamaica-Cuba Joint Commission on Economic, Technical, and Cultural Cooperation. Under this joint agreement, the Castro regime provided technical assistance to Jamaica in a variety of areas, such as in agriculture, fishing, education, and science and technology.[100] During the 1970s, Cuba trained over 1,400 Jamaican youths in construction technology and several Jamaican police officers in methods of security provision for diplomats, government officials, and in secret service operations. Cubans were brought to Jamaica to build, at the Cuban government's expense, several schools, dams, and residential housing. Cuban doctors also came to Jamaica to work in public hospitals and in medical clinics in the rural areas of the country.[101]

In July 1975, Manley visited Cuba where he made several speeches about the Jamaican-Cuban relationship and solidarity, which did not sit well with the U.S. government. While in Cuba, Manley was awarded the José Martí Medal, the highest Cuban order.[102] Manley's trip to Cuba was just the first of a number of visits to the island by other PNP ministers, party leaders, advisors, and activists. Two years later, Castro visited Jamaica and praised Manley and the Jamaican people for their stance against imperialism. The close relationship between Jamaica and Cuba, coupled with Manley's anti-imperialist and anti-American rhetoric, disturbed the U.S. Washington was particularly concerned about Manley's position in the Socialist International, his support of Angola and Cuba's efforts to defend it, the formation of the IBA, and the diplomatic support which the PNP government gave to Cuba on various issues in international forums. These events not only soured the relationship between the U.S. and the Jamaican government, but also resulted in strong U.S. actions, which undermined and destabilized the Manley regime and the economy of Jamaica.

Table 6.7
Jamaica's Share of Exports to Major Trading Partners, 1970-1980

Countries	1970	1971	1972	1973	1974	1975	1976	1977	1978	1979	1980
U. S.	51.9	45.0	42.4	41.2	47.1	40.3	48.0	47.4	43.2	44.9	37.1
Britain	15.6	19.6	21.7	22.8	16.8	22.3	15.7	18.5	22.2	19.1	19.3
Canada	8.2	8.3	7.1	5.5	5.6	3.3	5.0	8.0	7.7	6.0	3.9
CARICOM Countries	3.4	4.8	5.8	6.3	5.3	4.5	6.9	6.7	7.3	7.6	5.9
EEC	1.3	0.7	0.9	3.2	1.1	0.6	1.1	1.1	1.2	1.0	0.9
Latin America	1.1	1.1	0.9	1.4	1.8	1.0	3.5	1.9	2.8	2.7	1.6
Norway	7.9	8.7	11.5	10.4	11.5	9.5	10.1	9.5	6.4	5.1	10.8
Other	10.9	11.8	9.8	9.2	10.8	18.4	9.2	6.9	9.2	13.7	20.6
Total	**100**	**100**	**100**	**100**	**100**	**100**	**100**	**100**	**100**	**100**	**100**

Source: Bank of Jamaica; Department of Statistics, Kingston, Jamaica, 1982.

The Demise of Democratic Socialism

Shortly before the 1976 elections, Jamaica was in dire economic straits. The PNP's nationalization policies did not insulate the country's economy from the inflationary spiral that dragged on after the 1973 oil price increases. The drastic increases in the price of raw materials, spare parts for machinery and other imported supplies, and the sharp rise in interest rates charged by foreign banks ruptured Jamaica's economy. These developments, together with capital flight, the increase in foreign investment income repatriated abroad, and the shortfalls in receipts from tourism and foreign exchange earnings contributed to the deterioration of the balance of payments situation and negative growth in real GDP. Despite extensive foreign borrowing by the PNP government, Jamaica's foreign exchange reserves reached a crisis

Table 6.8
Jamaica's Share of Imports from Major Trading Partners,
1970-1980

Country	1970	1971	1972	1973	1974	1975	1976	1977	1978	1979	1980
U. S.	43.0	39.6	37.3	37.9	35.2	37.4	37.2	36.0	36.8	31.8	31.4
Britain	19.1	19.8	19.3	16.4	12.4	13.1	10.9	9.7	10.4	9.8	6.7
Canada	9.0	7.5	7.3	6.7	5.4	4.9	5.9	5.6	5.6	4.9	6.0
CARICOM Countries	1.7	2.4	5.4	5.3	7.6	8.4	7.0	5.7	5.5	5.7	7.2
Latin America	6.0	6.6	7.4	9.4	17.6	16.1	16.3	18.3	18.5	19.3	17.0
EEC	8.1	9.1	8.7	9.8	8.3	6.8	6.3	5.9	6.1	6.7	4.6
Other	13.1	15.0	14.6	14.5	13.5	13.3	16.4	18.8	17.1	21.9	27.1
Total	**100**	**100**	**100**	**100**	**100**	**100**	**100**	**100**	**100**	**100**	**100**

Source: Bank of Jamaica; Department of Statistics, 1982, Kingston, Jamaica.

point in mid-1976 when it fell from J$137 million in June 1975 to minus J$74 million in December 1975 to minus J$238 million in 1976.[103]

Prime Minister Manley's attempt to solve Jamaica's economic problems through democratic socialism met with stiff opposition from the capitalist class, both internal and external. This group was strongly opposed to the bauxite tax and the government's socialist strategy. These difficulties were compounded with the expansion of the state into the private sector, which had not produced the type of development needed to sustain the country's economy and reduce its economic dependence on foreign private capital. In articulating and implementing its socialist policies, the PNP underestimated the importance of foreign capital and trade, which were required to support the government's social reforms and reduce its foreign debt. Even before the nationalization and joint-ownership programs were completed the country's economy was in a state of severe crisis. The demise of the economy was largely due to the PNP's uncoordinated, ad hoc expansion of state property, inefficient planning and gross mismanagement of the country's resources, as well as a combination of U.S.-led destabilization policies. Not only were nationalizations paid for promptly and in full, but to minimize social and economic dislocation, the PNP government purchased enterprises that were in danger of economic collapse. This was the case with the sugar companies which mirrored the inefficiencies and uncoordinated expansion of the state into the private sector. In spite of these problems, the PNP won a landslide victory in the December 1976 elections. The party captured 56.8 percent of the popular vote and forty-seven of the sixty seats in Parliament as opposed to 43.2 percent and thirteen seats for the opposition JLP (table 6.1).

The decline of Jamaica's foreign exchange reserves was accompanied by a negative growth in GDP, mainly because of a decline in production in the mining sector. This resulted from the decline in world demand for bauxite and alumina, the transfer of bauxite production in other countries by the aluminum companies, labor unrest at the country's aluminum plants, and low level investments in new plants and equipment. Underlying the foreign exchange crisis was the predicted shortfall of J$120 million in earnings from bauxite and sugar in 1976, which forced the government to further restrict imports. The flight of capital out of the country continued, and this prompted the formation of a special detection unit in the security services to monitor the amount of money leaving Jamaica. For example, capital inflows into Jamaica had averaged U.S. $254 million in 1973 but fell to U.S. $115 million in 1975 and became negative by 1976. The rapid expansion of imports, particularly oil, which Jamaica was 97 percent dependent on rose from J$63 million in 1973 to J$178 million in 1976. External debt payments also rose from J$49 million in 1974 to J$100 million in 1976, as the external debt increased from U.S. $195 million in 1973 to U.S. $489 million in 1976. Also in this period, the government's budget increased from J$67 million to J$278 million.[104]

To generate new revenue to make up for the shortfall in foreign reserves and budget deficits, the regime instituted a new tax program that increased the price of liquor, beer, and cigarettes. It also imposed a 10 percent increase on incomes over J$10,000 per year; 2.5 percent on property tax; 15 percent on capital goods; 10 percent on consumer goods; 25 percent on pleasure boats; and 50 percent on jewelry. These tax measures no doubt hurt the capitalist class who responded with more production cutbacks and layoffs and the repatriation abroad of foreign investment income. The government also regulated trade, limit business travel allowances to U.S. $50 per person per year, and intensified its borrowing efforts. Externally, it borrowed $70 million from the CARICOM countries and $32 million from Canada with a $59 million Canadian line of credit. Internally, the government relied on transfers from the Capital Development Fund and the printing of money by the Bank of Jamaica.[105]

The foreign exchange crisis and the near collapse of Jamaica's economy prior to the 1976 elections eventually forced Manley's government to seek financial assistance from the IMF and laid the basis for its eventual removal from office. Only Manley, Finance Minister David Coore, and the leading civil servants responsible for the management of the economy were aware of the depth of the impending economic crisis, the seriousness of the foreign exchange situation, and the PNP discussion with the IMF. The IMF credit was conditional on the implementation by the PNP government of a program of anti-working-class measures, including a wage freeze, a reduction in public spending, layoffs of some 11,000 government employees, and a 40 percent devaluation in the Jamaican dollar.

However, the left-wing faction of the party became aware of the IMF proposals and warned the PNP leadership that IMF programs which were supposed to cure ailing economies in underdeveloped countries had resulted in massive pressure on the poor, collapse of civilian governments, riots, and a general history of mayhem. The group argued that there is not a single case where IMF prescriptions benefited a Third World economy. They pointed out that IMF policies would push Jamaica deeper into the very position of dependence from which the PNP had pledged to extricate it. The decision to devalue the dollar was rejected by Prime Minister Manley:

> The International Monetary Fund, which is the central lending agency for the international capitalist system, has a history of laying down conditions for countries seeking loans . . . this government, on behalf of the people, will not accept anyone anywhere in the world telling us what to do in our country. We are the masters in our own house and in our house there shall be no other masters but ourselves. Above all, we are not for sale. . . . We reject any foreign imposed solution to the present crisis we face.[106]

As the economic crisis deepened, Manley retreated from his hard-line policies and resumed negotiations with the IMF. After extensive discussions with the IMF, an Extended Fund Facility was obtained in May 1978 and lasted until December 1979. The agreement included a freeze on civil servant wages, a reduction in public expenditure, an immediate devaluation of 15 percent of the Jamaican dollar, and a further reduction of 15 percent a year later. The result was that the Jamaican dollar which was slightly higher than the U.S. dollar during most of the 1970s was devalued to J$1.76 to U.S.

$1.00. This was meant to reduce the demand for imports by making them more expensive, while stimulating exports by making them comparatively competitive. The government also lowered the bauxite levy tax from 7.5 percent to 7 percent in an attempt to encourage the aluminum companies to increase production and expand their investment. The 1978 IMF agreement was expected to generate a growth rate in real GDP of 1.5 percent in 1978, 3 percent in 1979, and 4 percent in 1980. However, none of these measures made any decisive impact on Jamaica's economy as its GDP declined by 1.7 percent in 1978 and unemployment rose from 23 percent in April to 26 percent in October of that year.

The IMF policies did not generate additional inflows of foreign capital or stop the flight of local capital. In fact, various estimates have shown that hundreds of millions of dollars had left Jamaica illegally between 1976 and 1977.[107] Furthermore, the government's decision to seek financial help from the IMF not only demoralized and alienated the PNP's popular support among the masses, but also resulted in the split between the left-wing and moderate factions of the PNP and the resignation of two cabinet ministers, including the minister of finance. The consensus among Caribbean scholars and economists was that the IMF policies could not have worked in a structurally dependent economy like Jamaica's that lacked adequate productive capacity. As revealed in table 6.9, there were major policy differences between the PNP government and the IMF.

In view of these difficulties for which the Manley government could not be held responsible, Jamaica failed the net international test which the IMF had set the limit at minus U.S. $380 million. Its real position was minus U.S. $475-500 million.[108] After prolonged negotiations failed to get the IMF to waive the international test, Prime Minister Manley, in March 1980, broke off all relations with the institution and implemented an alternative "Self Reliant Economic Program" to rescue Jamaica's ailing economy and to regain the support of the masses. But with national elections due in less than a year, it was a little too late for the PNP to recapture its political support.

By the end of the PNP rule in 1980, there had been no real improvement in Jamaica's economy. Trade as a ratio of GDP increased from 72 percent in 1970 to 107 percent in 1980 and the external debt climbed from U.S. $370 million in 1972 to U.S. $1,700 million in 1980. The debt-service ratio in 1979 was 17 percent of exports of goods and services, net foreign reserves stood at minus J$900 million, a decrease of 1,014 percent, and real investment fell by some 65 percent. The bauxite, sugar, tourist, and construction industries were all in a state of such crisis that between 1972 and 1980 real income fell by 25 percent and unemployment rose to 29 percent. Also in this period, Jamaica's GDP decreased by 18.3 percent while inflation reached an all-time high of 320 percent. By October 1980, the country's factories were operating at only 30 percent of capacity.[109]

Despite massive borrowing from Canada and from CARICOM states, and the incessant printing of money by the Bank of Jamaica, the country's economy collapsed to the point where it was incapable of meeting the basic necessities of the population. Shortages of basic food items, medicine, hygiene products, and foreign currency were common throughout the country. The situation was compounded by the fact that all public utilities were in a state of disrepair and required huge investments to upgrade their capacity and the quality of their services. The major social services such as education, health, welfare, and housing had also drastically deteriorated. As the economy continued its downward slide, some of the most qualified Jamaicans emigrated in large numbers, legally and illegally, to just about any country they could. Few will disagree that instead of reducing Jamaica's economic dependence, democratic socialism plunged its economy into a severe crisis and, in the process, increased significantly its dependence on foreign investment and trade. The collapse of Jamaica's economy eroded Manley's political support base and caused the PNP to lose the October 1980 election to the conservative Edward Seaga and the JLP.

During the eight-and-a-half years of the Manley government and six years of democratic socialism, Jamaica emerged in the 1970s as a leading country in the Third World. The government's bauxite policy received wide support from a majority of Jamaicans, support that seemed to stretch across most if not all classes. Only the capitalist elite was outraged by the bauxite tax. Prime Minister Manley's fight with the bauxite companies and the U.S. government, and his role in the formation of the IBA, brought Jamaica high praise from many other Global South countries similarly subject to foreign economic domination, uneven terms of trade, and economic dependence.

Politically, as a Third World country, Jamaica charted a new course with the institution of democratic socialism as an ideology aimed at reducing its economic dependence on the developed countries. It represented the hopes of many developing countries wanting to pursue a new development path without resorting to socialist revolutions and a complete break with the capitalist world order.

While the policies of democratic socialism led to some success for a brief period in education, health and welfare, and in foreign affairs, they did not reduce the powerful influence of the capitalist class, improve Jamaica's economy, or reduce its economic dependence. The PNP's embrace of

Table 6.9
Policy Differences between the IMF and the PNP Government

Issue	Manley Government	IMF
Type of Economy	Mixed	Dependent Capitalist
Dominant Sector	State	Capitalist
Ownership of the means of production	State/cooperatives/ capitalist	Capitalist
Allocation of resources	Planning/Market	Market
Openness	Reduced	Complete
Accumulation and distribution	State-directed capitalist cooperatives	Laissez-faire capitalist
Investment	State/cooperatives/ capitalist. State to invest in production, distribution, and infra- structure	Capitalist investment in production and distribu- tion. State confined to infrastructure investment
Savings	Private and public	Emphasis on capitalist savings out of profit
Foreign capital	Aid, loans, and regulated foreign investment	Direct foreign investment
Income distribution	Increase the share of labor	Increasing the share of accruing capital
Economic management	Increased state intervention and planning	Laissez-faire, emphasis on monetary policy
Monetary policy	One of many policy instruments	The most important policy instrument
Fiscal	Expansion	Contraction
Exchange rate	Dual exchange rate	Devaluation

Table 6.9 continued

Issue	Manley Government	IMF
Exchange controls	Yes, to effect foreign exchange budgeting	Elimination of controls
Trade	Import restrictions and licensing	Removal of import restrictions and licensing
Prices	Control and subsidies	Removal of controls and elimination of subsidies
Wages/Incomes	Increased: pegged to cost of living	Decrease in real terms

Source: R. Bernal, "The IMF and Class Structure in Jamaica 1977-1980," *Latin American Perspectives* 11, no. 3 (Summer 1984).

democratic socialism not only instilled fears among the capitalist class, but also produced an unfavorable investment climate in the country. This along with his zigzag and middle-of-the-road politics led the PNP government to a dead end. On the one hand, Manley was critical of the Western capitalist system while on the other, his regime sought loans from the IMF and the commercial banks to prop up Jamaica's ailing economy. These policies were incompatible with the PNP's economic strategy, which was based on a combination of joint-economic ventures between the PNP government and private corporations and selective nationalization of foreign assets. This generated widespread dissatisfaction among the capitalists and supporters of the JLP. Caught between the demands of the upper and lower classes, the PNP government could not represent the interests of either group. In fact, the PNP policies alienated the professionals and foreign investors and failed to establish an alternative base of economic support with the masses, most of whom had resented the decline in their living standards brought on by democratic socialism.

However, it was Manley's foreign policy, in particular, his position in the Socialist International, his close friendship with Castro, and Jamaica's support of Cuba's involvement in Angola that perturbed the United States. The PNP had no need to lose the support of either the local capitalist class or the U.S. government, yet Manley sacrificed both and found that without the former he could not run the country effectively, and without the latter, he could not manage the external environment in the way the PNP strategy of change required. His view of the world underestimated the reality of the international capitalist system and of Jamaica's strategic location in the American sphere of interests. The hostility of these two powerful interests contributed to the collapse of Jamaica's economy and the demise of democratic socialism, and thus ended Manley's political will to improve the living standard of the masses in Jamaica and overcome or reduce the country's economic dependence on the core capitalist countries.

Notes

1. Clive Thomas, *The Poor and the Powerless: Economic Policy and Change in the Caribbean* (New York: Monthly Review Press, 1988), 211; Norman Girvan, *Foreign Capital and Economic Underdevelopment in Jamaica* (Mona, Jamaica: Institute for Social and Economic Research (ISER), University of the West Indies, 1971), 226-27.

2. Nelson W. Keith and Novella Z. Keith, *The Social Origins of Democratic Socialism in Jamaica* (Philadelphia: Temple University Press, 1992), 5-6.

3. Michael Manley, "Overcoming Insularity in Jamaica," *Foreign Affairs Quarterly* 49, no. 1 (October 1970): 105.

4. The brief discussion in chapter 5 of slavery and race relations in Guyana was similar throughout the English-speaking Caribbean. For a good discussion on the development of the Jamaican race and class structure, see George Beckford and M. Witter, *Small Garden; Bitter Weed: Struggle and Change in Jamaica* (Jamaica: Maroon Publishing Company, 1980).

5. Evelyn Huber Stephens and John D. Stephens, *Democratic Socialism in Jamaica: The Political Movement and Social Transformation in Dependent Capitalism* (Princeton, N.J.: Princeton University Press, 1986), 12.

6. Keith and Keith, *The Social Origins,* 63.

7. Fernando Henriques, *Family and Color in Jamaica* (London: MacGibbon and Kee, 1968); Noel Leo Erskine, *Decolonizing Theory: A Caribbean Perspective* (New York: Orbis Press, 1981); Mary Turner, *Slaves and Missionaries: The Disintegration of Jamaican Slave Society, 1787-1834* (Urbana: University of Illinois Press, 1982).

8. Turner, *Slaves and Missionaries,* 147-50.

9. Samuel Hurwitz and Edith Hurwitz, *Jamaica: A Historical Portrait* (New York: Praeger, 1971), 130.

10. Turner, *Slaves and Missionaries,* 153.

11. Robert Stewart, "The 1872 Diary of James Splaine; Catholic Missionary in Jamaica: A Documentary Note," *Caribbean Quarterly* 30, nos. 3-4 (September-December 1984): 99-109.

12. Keith and Keith, *The Social Origins,* 64.

13. Robert Napier, "The First Arrest of Bedward," *Jamaica Historical Review Bulletin* 2, no. 1 (March 1957): 14.

14. Paul Bradley, "Mass Parties in Jamaica: Structure and Organization," *Social and Economic Studies* 9, no. 4 (1960): 394.

15. Theodore G. Vincent, *Black Power and the Garvey Movement* (Palo Alto, Calif.: Ramparts, 1976), 173.

16. Amy Jacques Garvey, *Philosophy and Opinions of Marcus Garvey*, 2 vols. (New York: Atheneum Press, 1967), vol. 1, 44.

17. Keith and Keith, *The Social Origins,* 160-61; Horace Campbell, *Rasta and Resistance: From Marcus Garvey to Walter Rodney* (Trenton, N.J.: Africa World, 1988).

18. For a detailed discussion on Bedwardism, Garveyism, and Rastafarianism, see Keith and Keith, *The Social Origins,* 63-78.

19. Rex Nettleford, ed., *Manley and the New Jamaica* (London: Longman Caribbean Ltd., 1971), 18.

20. Michael Manley, *Jamaica: Struggle in the Periphery* (London: London University Press, 1982).

21. Nettleford, *Manley,* 16.

22. Trevor Munroe, *The Politics of Constitutional Decolonization: Jamaica 1944-1962* (Mona, Jamaica: ISER, UWI, 1972), 16.

23. Ken Post, *Arise Ye Starvelings: The Jamaican Labor Rebellion and Its Aftermath* (The Hague: Martinus Nijhoff, 1978), 88-89, 134.

24. Nettleford, *Manley,* 11-22.

25. Post, *Arise Ye Starvelings*, 35, 69, 72.

26. There is much speculation about the reasons for the split between Manley and Bustamante. The interpretations range from personality rivalry, the less-educated Bustamante tried to outdo his brilliant cousin (Post 253), to suspicion that the PNP leadership was trying to reduce Bustamante's prominence in the party.

27. Keith and Keith, *The Social Origins,* 54.

28. *Daily Gleaner,* August 12, 1943, 5.

29. John C. Gannon, "The Origins and Development of Jamaica's Two Party System, 1930-1975," doctoral dissertation, Washington University, St. Louis, Mo., 1976, 167-78.

30. Trevor Munroe, "The People's National Party: A View of the Early Nationalist Movement in Jamaica," Master's thesis, University of the West Indies, 1966, 23-24.

31. Gannon, "The Origins," 31.

32. Munroe, *The Politics of Constitutional Decolonization,* 37-42.

33. People's National Party, *Plan for Progress* (Kingston, Jamaica, 1954), 9.

34. People's National Party, *Report of the Second Annual Conference* (Kingston, Jamaica, 1949), 15.

35. Ibid., 11.

36. Stephens and Stephens, *Democratic Socialism,* 22-26.

37. Owen Jefferson, *The Post-War Economic Development in Jamaica* (Mona, Jamaica: ISER, UWI, 1972), 285; Stephens and Stephens, *Democratic Socialism in Jamaica,* 22. For a complete understanding of economic development in Jamaica,

see Girvan, *Foreign Capital*; R.W. Palmer, *The Jamaican Economy* (New York: Praeger, 1968).

38. Thomas, *The Poor and the Powerless,* 211; Stephens and Stephens, *Democratic Socialism in Jamaica,* 26.

39. Jefferson, *The Post-War Economic Development,* 285; Manley, *Jamaica,* 33.

40. Girvan, *Foreign Capital,* 226-27.

41. Thomas, *The Poor and the Powerless*, 211-12; N. Girvan, R. Bernal, and W. Hughes, "The IMF and the Third World: The Case of Jamaica," *Development Dialog* 2 (1980): 115.

42. Jefferson, *The Post-War Economic Development,* 285.

43. Stanley Reid, "An Introductory Approach to the Concentration of Power in the Jamaican Corporate Economy and Notes on Its Origin," in *Essays on Power and Change in Jamaica,* ed. Carl Stone and A. Brown (Kingston: Jamaica Publishing House, 1977); also see Fitzroy Ambursley, "Jamaica: The Demise of Democratic Socialism," *New Left Review* no. 128 (July-August 1981): 76-87; Beckford and Witter, *Small Garden*; Thomas, *The Poor and the Powerless*, 212; Keith and Keith, *The Social Origins*, 136-37.

44. Terry Lacey, *Violence and Politics in Jamaica, 1960-1970* (Manchester: Manchester University Press, 1977), 86.

45. For a good description of events surrounding the Rodney riots in Jamaica, see Lacey, *Violence and Politics in Jamaica,* 94-99.

46. Michael Manley, *The Politics of Change: A Jamaican Testament* (Washington, D.C.: Howard University Press, 1975), 27.

47. Carl Stone, *Electoral Behavior and Public Opinion in Jamaica* (Mona: ISER, UWI, 1974), 31-63.

48. Keith and Keith, *The Social Origins,* 163-64.

49. Keith and Keith, *The Social Origins,* 67; Stone, *Electoral Behavior,* 19.

50. Manley, *The Politics of Change,* 20-22.

51. Manley, *The Politics of Change,* 17; Keith and Keith, *The Social Origins,* 23-24.

52. Manley, *The Politics of Change,* 17.

53. *Gleaner,* 1 June 1972, 7.

54. *Gleaner*, 30 May 1972.

55. Government of Jamaica, *National Planning Agency Bulletin*, 1979; Stephens and Stephens, *Democratic Socialism in Jamaica,* 73-74.

56. Lacey, *Violence and Politics,* 29.

57. Stephens and Stephens, *Democratic Socialism,* 75.

58. Government of Jamaica, *National Planning Agency,* Economic and Social Survey, 1979.

59. C. D. Kirton, "A Preliminary Analysis of Imperialist Penetration and Control via the Foreign Debt: A Study of Jamaica," in *Essays on Power and Change,* ed. Stone and Brown, 80-81.

60. Thakoor Persaud, *Conflicts between Multinational Corporations and Less Developed Countries* (Austin: University of Texas Press, 1980), 57.

61. *North American Congress on Latin America* (NACLA) (May-June 1978): 19-22.

62. Tom Barry, Beth Wood, and Deb Preusch, *The Other Side of Paradise: Foreign Control in the Caribbean* (New York: Grove Press, 1984), 103.

63. Manley, *Jamaica,* 99.

64. Manley, *Jamaica,* 99-100; Michael Manley, *Up the Down Escalator, Development and the International Economy: A Jamaican Case Study* (Washington, D.C.: Howard University Press, 1987), 47.

65. Manley, *Jamaica,* 103; Stephens and Stephens, *Democratic Socialism,* 79.

66. S. Keith and R. Girling, "Caribbean Conflict: Jamaica and the U.S," *NACLA* 12, no. 3 (1978): 24.

67. Manley, *Jamaica,* 102; *Gleaner,* 16 May 1974.

68. Keith and Keith, *The Social Origins,* 10; Norman Girvan, "Caribbean Mineral Economy," in *Caribbean Economy,* ed. George Beckford (Mona: ISER, UWI, 1978). For more on the bauxite industry in Jamaica, see Manley 1987, chapters 1, 2.

69. Thomas, *The Poor and the Powerless,* 215.

70. *Gleaner,* 17 May 1974.

71. Government of Jamaica, *National Planning Agency Bulletin,* 1976, 38.

72. Manley, *Jamaica,* 38.

73. Ibid., 36-37.

74. Ibid., 221.

75. Stephens and Stephens, *Democratic Socialism,* 76; Manley, *Jamaica,* 42.

76. Manley, *Jamaica,* 43.

77. The main sources for these agreements are press releases: Consulate of Jamaica, New York and Washington, D.C.; Government of Jamaica, December 20, 1974; *New York Times,* 21 November 1974; *Daily Gleaner,* 21 December 1974, *Wall Street Journal,* 11 April 1975.

78. *The New Internationalist,* no. 94 (December 1980): 15.

79. Stephens and Stephens, *Democratic Socialism,* 77-78.

80. Manley, *Jamaica,* 102-103; Manley, *Up the Down Escalator,* 60.

81. Manley, *The Politics of Change,* 105-108.

82. Ibid., 106.

83. Ibid.

84. Manley, *Jamaica,* 43; Manley, *The Politics of Change,* 215.

85. John Hearne, *A Search for Solutions: Selection from the Speeches and Writings of Michael Manley* (Ottawa, Canada: Maple House Publishers, 1976), 117.

86. Keith and Keith, *The Social Origins,* 256-59.

87. *National Planning Agency Bulletin,* 1977, 99; 1978, 115.

88. Stephens and Stephens, *Democratic Socialism,* 277-79.

89. Paul Chen-Young, "Commentary," *Economic Report, Jamaica* 2, no. 11 (January 1977): 1-11.

90. Keith and Keith, *The Social Origins*, 242-44; Stephens and Stephens, *Democratic Socialism*, 176-77.

91. *Gleaner,* 12 November 1977.

92. Manley, *The Politics of Change*, 39.

93. Ibid., 181.

94. Keith and Keith, *The Social Origins*, 229.

95. Manley, *Jamaica,* 76.

96. *Daily Gleaner,* 5 October 1975, 8.

97. Manley, *Jamaica,* 123.

98. Manley, *The Politics of Change*, 145.

99. Hearne, *A Search for Solutions,* 180.

100. *Daily Gleaner,* 9 May 1975.

101. Stephens and Stephens, *Democratic Socialism*, 108.

102. José Martí was a Cuban patriot, author, and journalist who founded the Cuban Revolutionary Party in 1892. He led the struggle for Cuba's independence against Spain and was captured and imprisoned by the Spanish government.

103. Girvan, Bernal, and Hughes, "The IMF and the Third World," 138.

104. Thomas, *The Poor and the Powerless*, 221-22.

105. Stephens and Stephens, *Democratic Socialism*, 129-31.

106. Quoted in M. Henry, "Getting into the IMF" (unpublished paper, Department of Government, Mona, Jamaica, UWI, 1980), 40.

107. Manley, *Jamaica,* 151.

108. Stephens and Stephens, *Democratic Socialism*, 203.

109. Thomas, *The Poor and the Powerless*, 221-22; F. Ambursley, "Jamaica: From Michael Manley to Edward Seaga," in *Crisis in the Caribbean*, ed. F. Ambursley and R. Cohen (New York: Monthly Review Press, 1983), 84-86.

Chapter 7

Revolutionary Socialism: Grenada's Experience

In the Caribbean, the challenge to the traditional order in the 1970s achieved a temporary success in Grenada where, on 13 March 1979, some 200 ill-armed members of the so-called People's Revolutionary Army (PRA) over-threw the government of Prime Minister Eric Gairy. The Grenadian coup d'etat briefly captured international attention and was the first successful revolution in the history of the English-speaking territories of the Caribbean. It marked the beginning of revolutionary socialism on the island and a challenge to the legacy of dependency in all its many forms. During this period, the other reform movements in the region had fallen by the wayside. Cooperative socialism in Guyana had become nothing more than a strategy for control of the state coercive apparatus to maintain the PNC in power, and democratic socialism of Michael Manley in Jamaica had collapsed due to the intransigence of the IMF with which the PNP government had cumulatively become entangled, and by the U.S.-led destabilization policies.

By contrast and for a short period, revolutionary socialism in Grenada appeared to be much more substantive. Sustained by a firm understanding of the problem of underdevelopment and dependency, staffed by committed party activists, and led by Prime Minister Maurice Bishop, Grenada was the only Caribbean country where in the early 1980s serious socioeconomic and political change was actively pursued. This tiny island-nation shattered the conventional wisdom that had prevailed in the region since the mid-1960s that smallness of itself was a powerful independent constraint upon the development potential of a state. By its determination to achieve economic independence, the People's Revolutionary Government (PRG) reversed for all the territories of the region the vision of a permanent dependency which was a large part of the English-speaking Caribbean's psyche.

Grenada attained its independence in 1974 under Gairy, a flamboyant and mystical figure who dominated the country's politics for nearly three decades. Prior to the coup, Gairy governed Grenada with such a mixture of brutality, inefficiency, and corruption that it gained notoriety beyond the Caribbean region. The only effective and lasting opposition to the Gairy government during the 1970s was the New Jewel Movement (NJM), led by Maurice Bishop and Bernard Coard. This group had to contend with Gairy's despotic rule which included widespread corruption of public funds, control of the public service, organized manipulation of the electoral process, and savage physical assault on NJM leaders and supporters by the police and Gairy's personal security groups known to Grenadians as the Night Ambush Squad and the Mongoose Men.[1]

Soon after the coup, the PRG declared Grenada a revolutionary socialist state which, in just over four-and-a-half years, generated its own internal conflicts that led to the murder of Prime Minister Bishop and five members of the cabinet in October 1983. The consequence of these dramatic events was that during the last two weeks of October 1983, Grenada acquired a prominence in international affairs that was totally out of proportion to its small size and population. The questions that were uppermost in the minds of the people were: Why was Maurice Bishop, a seemingly popular leader, executed in such a cold-blooded manner? Why did the United States, the world's greatest superpower, invade such a tiny island, just 133 square miles in area, with a mere population of 110,000 people, and whose best known export is nutmeg? The short-term answers to these questions could be traced to the internal power struggle that developed within the NJM between the Coard faction and Bishop supporters. In a wider context, the answers are to be found in the long and bitter experience of colonialism and dependency in Grenada which the Bishop regime sought to eradicate through revolutionary socialism.

For over three centuries (1650-1983) the tiny island of Grenada had been plagued with several conflicts, either between local groups or classes or between rival imperial powers and cultures or between ideologies. In almost all of the cases the conflicts were settled violently, with one group gaining control over the other. Briefly, the first conflict occurred in the early fifteenth century between the relatively peaceful Arawaks and the hostile and warlike Carib Indians. By the time of Columbus's arrival in 1498, Grenada was under the control of the Caribs. The second conflict was between the French settlers and the Caribs. This conflict began in 1651 and ended in 1654 with the massive destruction of the Carib population and way of life by the French. The third conflict took the form of a struggle between the British and the French settlers, which ended with the former gaining control of the island in the latter part of 1763. The fourth conflict was essentially one of class that erupted in 1839 between the former slaves and the dominant mulattos and white Creoles. The latter two groups at the time had owned most of the land, estates, and commercial enterprises on the island. They also had control of Grenada's finances and the political, social, and economic systems. At the core of this conflict was the low wages paid to black workers by the mulattos and white Creoles for extremely long hours of work. The class conflict dragged on for more than a century before it finally exploded into violence and riots in 1951 during a general strike by plantation workers on the island. The strike was led by Eric Gairy who, later that year, was elected chief minister of Grenada, and for the next twenty-eight years, but especially between 1967 and 1979, ruled the island with an iron fist. In this period, Gairy not only violated the very principles he fought for as a trade unionist, but also exploited the very masses whom he defended against the planter class and the commercial elite earlier. The fifth conflict took place on 13 March 1979 that led to the overthrow of the Gairy regime and the establishment of the first socialist government in Grenada. The sixth and perhaps the most brutal conflict in Grenada's modern history was initiated by a power struggle within the NJM that resulted in the brutal slaying of more than one hundred Grenadians, and the summary executions of Prime Minister Bishop and several other NJM officials in October 1983. This fratricidal act spurred the seventh and final conflict which also took place in October 1983 when U.S. military forces invaded Grenada and installed an interim government charged with restoring democracy on the island. Within sixty days of the invasion, all U.S. combat units had departed, leaving the responsibility of law and order in the hands of the local police and para-military forces.

Grenada's attempted abandonment of capitalist principles was a direct challenge to the impersonal forces that control the international political economy and more importantly to the power of the United States whose opposition from the very beginning was both persistent and virulent. This occurred at the time when U.S. hegemony in the hemisphere was being threatened more seriously than ever before. Because of the PRG's defiant attitude towards U.S. domination of the Caribbean region, Grenada was the target of a counterrevolutionary offensive mounted by the U.S. government.

The Genesis of Colonial Rule in Grenada

Grenada is an island nation in the Caribbean that comprised of Grenada proper and two smaller islands, Carriacou and Petit Martinique. It is about

90 miles north of Trinidad and Tobago and is the most densely populated of the Lesser Antilles. In part, Grenada's beauty lies in its lush jungle-covered mountains, sparkling waterfalls, an abundance of flowers, and exquisite beaches. Its capital, St. George's, is the Caribbean's most picturesque port city, where rows of two-story wooden homes are located on both sides of the calm harbor. It is also where cruise liners unload passengers twice a week to shop and dine in the cafes and restaurants overlooking the port. Known as the Isle of Spice, Grenada became famous for its nutmeg which it exports along with cocoa, cinnamon, mace, rum, bananas, and a variety of other agricultural products. Recently, tourism has boosted Grenada's economy and has become one of the major sources of foreign exchange for the island.

Like its many conflicts, Grenada had also been known by many names throughout its recorded history. Originally called Camerhogue by the Caribs, the island was renamed Conception by Columbus on 15 August 1498. Two years later, it was called Mayo by Amerigo Vespucci, and Granada by the Spanish in 1523. In 1650, French settlers captured the island and renamed it La Grenade but in 1783 the British defeated the French and gained control of the island once again and immediately changed its name from La Grenade to Grenada, which is still its official name.[2] Despite more than two centuries of British domination, French rule has left a permanent implant upon the island. Nearly half of the towns and villages in Grenada still bear the French names of Gougave, La Sagesse, Parcalete, Lance-aux-Epines, and Sauteurs, to name a few. Today, most Grenadians are Roman Catholics and many of them in the rural areas of the country speak patois, a mixture of French and African languages.[3]

In the seventeenth century, more than 12,000 black slaves were brought from Africa by the British to work on the sugar plantations in Grenada. In this period, Grenada became the second most valuable British possession in the West Indies after Jamaica.[4] However, during the American revolution of 1770, France recaptured Grenada from the British through subversion and insurrection, but after a protracted struggle, Britain regained control of the island with the 1783 Treaty of Versailles. To avoid future insurrections, the British government enacted laws which prevented non-British subjects on the island from taking part in the political process. The British also forced the French Catholics on the island to pledge allegiance to the Church of England and confiscated all lands and buildings owned by the Roman Catholic churches in Grenada. All births, baptisms, marriages, and deaths among French Catholics had to be registered with the Anglican Church before they were considered legal by the British. The aim was to destroy the religious institutions of the French Catholics and force them to convert to Anglicanism.

These acts relegated the French Catholics and blacks to second-class status and created hostility between the Anglo-Saxon and Francophone populations in Grenada. This hostility climaxed into a rebellion in 1795 led by Julien Fedon, a French colored planter. Although the rebellion was put down by British soldiers in 1796, popular resistance even though sporadic, continued long after emancipation on the island. In 1848, wage reductions due to sharp decreases in the price for sugar in London resulted in riots on the island, as did unemployment and poverty. The situation grew worse during the interwar years by the Great Depression, particularly for returning soldiers, who in 1920 attempted to burn down the capital of St. George's.[5]

The abolition of slavery in Grenada was followed by Crown rule in which all powers were with the governor who established a legislature and appointed an executive council with members from Grenada's elite. This group had virtually no power and, as a result, could not in any way overrule the governor. The establishment of Crown rule in Grenada denied the 25,000 former black slaves who represented 85 percent of the island's population a voice in the legislature. The Grenadian elites were strongly opposed to Crown rule, but nevertheless, supported it, since they too did not want blacks to have a say in the government.

These developments helped to create a politically conscious population, whose demands for self-determination and better living conditions for blacks were pioneered by Theophilus Albert Marryshow and Tubal Uriah Butler, two immensely popular Grenadian leaders at the time. In 1914, Marryshow, a journalist and essayist, founded the Representative Government Association which advocated limited self-government for the island. The middle-class Marryshow also founded the Grenada Workingmen's Association and the Grenada Labor Party and campaigned vigorously against the subjugation of the black masses by both the commercial and bureaucratic elites. Butler, who came from a working-class background, had migrated to Trinidad in search of work but was imprisoned for encouraging oil field workers to riot during the Caribbean-wide disturbances. A war veteran, Butler organized the Grenada Union of Returned Soldiers and the Grenada Representative Government Movement and staged marches and strikes aimed at reforming the island's social and economic structures. He also demanded universal suffrage and the enfranchisement of blacks in Grenada.[6] Both Marryshow and Butler were opposed to the deep-rooted dependency that went far beyond the island's subservience to London. Although the dependency was Caribbean-wide and was built around the profitable export of sugar to Europe, they campaigned against it.

While the political demands of Marryshow, Butler, and their followers contributed to a new constitution for Grenada in 1925 and the election of five local members, including Marryshow to the sixteen-seat legislature, it was not until 1951 that the island achieved self-rule based on universal adult suffrage. The granting of self-rule, however, was due more to a greater sense of tact and enlightenment on the part of British officials who recognized the dominant social position of the Grenadian middle classes in this period than demands made by the masses and their leaders.

In the meantime, the subjugation of the masses by the commercial and bureaucratic elites continued. The workers remained largely nonunionized under very poor working conditions set forth by the capitalists. The reason was most of the local leaders were co-opted by the capitalist and commercial elite whose primary goal was to maintain the status quo. This was in sharp contrast to the other eastern Caribbean islands where dynamic leaders such as Ebenezer Joshua of St. Vincent, Vere Bird of Antigua, and Robert Bradshaw of St. Kitts had emerged to press for better working conditions for workers in their respective countries. The neglect of the Grenadian working class by its leaders left a political vacuum into which Eric Matthew Gairy stepped, in 1950.

Political Change in Grenada

Grenada's political transition from British colony to an independent state was associated closely with one man, Eric Gairy, who reaped the benefit of the constitutional reforms Marryshow and others had fought for. Like many Grenadians of his generation, Gairy, a former schoolteacher, had emigrated to Trinidad in search of work during the Second World War and to the U.S. oil refineries on the Dutch island of Aruba. Expelled from Aruba in 1949 for his involvement in union activities, Gairy returned to Grenada and formed the Grenada Mental and Manual Workers Union (GMMWU). The estate owners who had managed to hold wages down to 82 cents per day for men and 68 cents for women until 1950 had refused to recognize Gairy's union as a legal bargaining entity for the workers.[7] Gairy responded with sporadic strikes on selected estates which finally culminated in a general strike in February 1951 that lasted for over a month, which by this time had involved workers in both the agriculture and the public works department. The strike did not only vent the frustrations of the masses, but also led to violence, the declaration of a state of emergency, and the detention of Eric Gairy by the colonial office.[8] The strike was highly successful in that for the first time in the history of Grenada the planter class was forced to concede substantial increases in wages to the island's workers. This represented a fundamental change in Grenadian politics in that it ended the colonial domination of the plantocracy over the black masses in the country. Anthropologist Rottenberg has observed that the crisis had deeper consequences than a mere industrial dispute between the planter class and the workers. He stated that:

> Violence is done to the planter class values if workers lay claim to equality in the bargaining process, if workers share in the making of economic decisions, and if their bargaining representatives are, like themselves, black and of lower-class origin. . . . The violent, personal tones in which planters refer to the union leaders indicates that they are concerned with something a good deal more fundamental than wage demands.[9]

Indeed, the strike advanced permanently the politicization of the masses and the labor movement as well as the emergence of universal suffrage in Grenada. It also elevated Gairy to the status of a savior who, according to the masses, had returned to Grenada to liberate them from the domination of white rule. Gairy was revered by the masses and was rewarded with the paternal title of Uncle Eric, but as was expected, he was very much disliked by the middle and upper classes in Grenada.[10] In 1951, Gairy followed the footsteps of other Caribbean leaders and established the Grenada People's Party (GPP), later renamed the Grenada United Labor Party (GULP). He once again dramatically demonstrated the power of the black rural masses when he won a landslide victory in the October 1951 election, Grenada's first national election under universal suffrage. His party, GULP, received 60 percent of the popular vote and five of the eight seats in Parliament. As shown in table 7.1, Gairy for the most part dominated the electoral process in Grenada, winning six of the eight elections held in the country between 1951 and 1976.

Gairy's political success stemmed from his efforts to defend the rights of the working class against the business and bureaucratic elites whose attitudes were highly offensive to the independent-minded black peasants, agricultural workers, and to the masses in Grenada. Their grievances went far beyond wages to matters such as greater access to cultivate lands and to acquire credit. It also stemmed from his charismatic and flamboyant leadership style, and his belief in mysticism which, in a predominantly Christian society, was taken seriously by a large number of Grenadians. For instance, in February

1951, Gairy, in his address to a group of agricultural workers, asked God to send him a sign that he (God) favored a strike. As M. G. Smith observed: "That night there was a downpour, heavy even by Grenadian standards. The road between St. George's and Guoyave was blocked by fallen rock, which many regarded as a sign of divine support. The Public Works Department tackled the road block . . . but took a fortnight to remove it."[11] Believing that the rain was a sign from God, Gairy called a general strike on the following day that was supported by nearly all the workers on the island. His ability to mesmerize and channel the emotions of the masses for short but intensely emotional periods of time caused political scientist A. Singham to describe him as a hero of the crowd.[12]

Table 7.1
Grenada Election Results 1951-1976
% of Votes Cast (No. of Seats Won in the Legislature)

Party	1951 % (seats)	1954 % (seats)	1957 % (seats)	1961 % (seats)	1962 % (seats)	1967 % (seats)	1972 % (seats)	1976 % (seats)
GULP	60 (5)	46 (5)	40 (2)	54.9(8)	49.4(5)	54.5(7)	58.9(13)	51.8(9)
Independents	40 (3)	53.9(3)	14.6 (2)	4.5 (0)	--	--	--	--
GNP	--	--	24 (2)	27.5(2)	50.4(5)	45.5(3)	41.1(2)	--
PDM*	--	--	19.6 (2)	--	--	--	--	--
GFLP*	--	--	1.0 (0)	--	--	--	--	--
PPM*	--	--	--	15.9 (0)	--	--	--	--
People's Alliance	--	--	--	--	--	--	--	48.2 (6)

Source: Grenada Electoral Results Report, 1951-1976, St. George's.
*The People's Democratic Movement (PDM), the Grenada's Federated Labour Party (GFLP), and the People's Progressive Movement (PPM) were founded in 1957 by a number of union leaders.

But it was not long before Gairy changed course. As chief minister, he aligned himself with the colonial elites and ignored the cause of the working class who had supported him in the 1951 election. Gairy's attempts to gain the social recognition for which he craved from the elite gradually eroded his power base among the rural proletariat. He narrowly won the 1954 election but his hold on power was challenged by the founding of the Grenadian National Party (GNP) in 1956. Led by Herbert Blaize, a lawyer, the GNP formed an alliance with other opposition groups and won the 1957 election. Holding on to power, however, proved troublesome for the GNP government which represented the interest of the urban middle and upper classes. Blaize and the other leaders of the GNP ignored the interests of the working class and supported those of the plantocracy and the business elite. Gairy skillfully exploited the lackluster leadership of Blaize and the GNP's lack of direction in dealing with unemployment which, by 1960, was over 40 percent of the Grenadian workforce.[13] Disappointed with the GNP, the Grenadian voters reelected Gairy to office in 1961. However, in 1962, the British government suspended the island's constitution and removed the Gairy government from office on charges of corruption and gross mismanagement of public funds as well as the intimidation of civil servants.[14] With the aid of the British, the GNP won the 1962 elections, but its complete lack of response to working-class demands and expectations resulted in a resounding victory for Gairy in the 1967 election.

The return of Gairy to power in 1967 coincided with Grenada's new status of Associated Statehood, which meant full internal self-rule, with defense and foreign affairs under British control. This new constitutional arrangement allowed Gairy to manipulate Grenada's parliamentary system, imposed his personal rule on the country, and used his personal bodyguards to physically assault those who disagreed or spoke out against him or his government. Soon after the election, Gairy distanced himself socially and politically from his erstwhile supporters and aligned with the middle class who basically provided him with lip service support in order to gain access to lucrative government contracts, tax concessions, and the like. Gairy's widespread powers of patronage enabled him to promote his cronies and punished those who opposed him. The unfair treatment dished out to Grenadians by the Gairy administration sowed the seeds for the revolution of March 1979.

The Seeds of the Grenadian Revolution

The most direct cause that gave rise to the March 13, 1979, coup d'etat in Grenada was linked to Gairy's personal rule, known to many in Grenada and the Caribbean as Gairyism. It was the most despotic form of oligarchic rule to have emerged in the English-speaking Caribbean between 1967 and 1979. Gairyism had some striking physical similarities to Burnham's rule in Guyana. Both the Burnham and the Gairy regimes, for example, used force to silence their opponents, and both circumvented the electoral process to maintain their hold on power. Gairyism also meant the promotion of Gairy as a messianic indispensable force with mystic powers appointed by God to rule the people of Grenada.[15]

During this period, extensive corrupt practices and abuse of power by Gairy as well as gross inefficiency and chronic mismanagement robbed Grenada of badly needed human and capital resources needed to develop the island's already fragile economy. The basic feature of the economy was its heavy dependence upon three agricultural products—cocoa, nutmeg, and bananas—for the bulk of its export earnings. But as Ambursely noted, these earnings were insufficient to cover the growing costs of imports such as food, manufactured goods, raw materials, and fuel. This led to a persistent and growing balance of trade deficit which was partially reduced by inflows from the tourist industry and remittances from Grenadians resident abroad. Added to this was the fact that the level of corruption was so high that the Caribbean Development Bank (CDB) and other financial institutions refused to grant loans and aid to the Gairy government.[16]

The appalling economic situation manifested in high levels of unemployment, increased poverty, and a drastic deterioration in the social services, especially in education and health care. The educational system in Grenada during the 1960s and 1970s was a disaster at all levels. The vast majority of the island's eighty-two public schools were in disrepair and many had to be abandoned. The result was that most of the classrooms that were designed for thirty-five students had to accommodate twice that number. Moreover, only 7 percent of Grenada's 400 secondary school teachers and 36 percent of the 900 primary school teachers were professionally trained. School books became nonexistent and functional illiteracy rose to nearly 40 percent.[17]

The health system was also in a deplorable state. The island's hospitals and medical clinics lacked basic equipment, medicines, beds, doctors, and even linen. No sheets, pillow cases, blankets, or even aspirins were to be found in the hospitals. Quite often, the sick were not attended to and a good number of women died in the process of childbirth. As a result, the infant mortality rate in the country climbed to 29.5 per 1,000 live births. It was for this particular reason that the General Hospital at St. George's was referred to derisively by Grenadians as La Qua—the name of the largest funeral home on the island.[18] In addition, the country's basic infrastructure in such areas as roads, water and electricity supply, telephones, and housing were in a state of severe crisis.[19]

These developments increased Grenada's dependence on imports, foreign aid, and loans from the developed countries and reduced Gairy's support among the masses which, in turn, threatened his hold on power. To consolidate his position, Gairy, in 1968, introduced the Firearms Act, which rescinded all licensed firearms, particularly from his political opponents. The act was an attempt by Gairy to control the island's population by ensuring that the government and its supporters and not the opposition controlled the means of violence in the country. Gairy also distributed farmlands to his loyal supporters and personalized the public service and other government agencies by making all government employees accountable to him. Those who had opposed him or the government or showed any strong leanings toward the opposition were either transferred, suspended, or fired from their jobs. Such widespread victimization practices were intended to make public servants and their families economically dependent upon the government in order for Gairy to control them. Gairy's manipulation of the public service not only demoralized the public servants, but also stripped the agency of all autonomy in decision making and thus made it an impotent body.[20] George Brizan explained: "Hiring and firing of persons in the Public Service was decided by Cabinet and in Cabinet, Gairy was boss. The Public Service Commission was, therefore, reduced to a mere rubber stamp."[21]

In order to control the agricultural sector and reduce the influence of the planter class over the economy, Gairy brought the three main agricultural marketing organizations—the Grenada Cooperative Nutmeg Association, the Grenada Cooperative Banana Association, and the Grenada Cocoa Industry Association—under government control. These were statutory bodies that had exclusive powers to buy and market the entire crops they represented, deduct an operating cost, and pay producers according to their output. The participation of the peasantry in these associations was minimal. Moreover, the associations made very little contribution to the development of export agriculture and instead served to buttress the economic and political interests of the planter class who dominated them. As a result, they were perceived by Gairy to be a threat to his regime. Government reorganization of these organizations enabled Gairy to have control of the decision-making process of Grenada's primary products, nutmeg, cocoa, and banana, and the political control of some 10,000 producers and their families of these products.[22] At about the same time, Gairy invoked the further wrath of the big landowners with his land reform program. Under this plan, the government purchased and, in some cases, confiscated the estates of a number of real or imagined enemies of Gairy and parceled them out into smaller plots to his supporters. The objective was to reduce drastically the influence and confidence of estate owners in agricultural production.

In 1970, Gairy's hold on power was further threatened by the emergence of the black power movement in Grenada. Led by Maurice Bishop and a group of young intellectuals, most of whom had graduated from universities in Britain and North America, and radicalized by such issues as the Vietnam War, Marxism, and the rise of the black power movement in the U.S. This group appealed to the rural and urban poor and the unemployed youth, most of whom were casualties of the decay and disintegration of the Grenadian economy under the Gairy administration. Gairy denounced the leaders of the black power movement as communists, "irresponsible malcontents," and "disgruntled political frustrates."[23] What Gairy did not know at the time was that the new leaders were articulating policies that fit the needs and demands of the very people who had once given him their allegiance.

Shortly after the black power solidarity demonstration in St. George's, Grenada, on May 10, 1970, Gairy invoked the Emergency Powers Act to buttress his grip on power. The act restricted the movements of Grenadians and authorized police to search without a warrant their premises for guns, ammunition, or subversive literature.[24] The Emergency Act, combined with massive government corruption and Gairy's personal rule, became a serious disincentive to the Grenadian capitalist class, the effect of which was felt by a prolonged recession of the economy. Political opposition, significantly composed of large numbers among the middle and upper classes in Grenada, grew in the months preceding the country's political independence in 1974 and culminated in a powerful opposition party—the New Jewel Movement (NJM).

The New Jewel Movement

In Grenada, the New Jewel Movement was not conceived as a political party in the traditional Commonwealth Caribbean mold in which most of the political parties grew out of trade union movements. The NJM grew out of various ad hoc groups that were formed in the wake of the black power disturbances in St. George's. Among the groups were FORUM, founded by

Maurice Bishop and a group of radical professionals to advance the causes of the poor in Grenada. In 1972, FORUM was replaced by the Movement for the Advancement of Community Effort (MACE), which focused on political research and education of Grenadians to the functions of governments and elections, and to the ways and means of making the Gairy regime responsive to their needs. Also in that year, a former GNP candidate, Unison Whiteman, established the Joint Endeavor for the Welfare, Education, and Liberation of the People (JEWEL) in the rural parish of St. David to mobilize farmers to work for social and political change.[25] Similarly, some younger members of the commercial establishment created the Committee for Concerned Citizens (CCC) which merged with MACE to form the Movement for the Assemblies of the People (MAP) in the latter part of 1972. As a political organization, MAP's objective was to get rid of the Gairy regime and abolish the two-party system of the Westminster type of parliamentary democracy in favor of "participatory democracy of people's assemblies." Modeled on the *ujamaa* villages of Tanzania, participatory democracy was meant to permit mass participation in the decision-making process in the villages, parishes, and in the workplace. As its leader Maurice Bishop put it: "We envisage a system which would have village assemblies and workers' assemblies. In other words, politics where you live and politics where you work . . . elections in the sense of the elections we now know would be replaced by Assemblies at different levels. Grenada is small enough for this type of mass participation."[26]

Finally, in March 1973, MAP and JEWEL joined forces and organized a mass protest in St. David's Parish against the action of Lord Brownlow, a British landowner who had blocked public access to a beach through his La Sagesse estate. Gairy's refusal to intervene on behalf of Grenadians sparked off a demonstration against Brownlow. Led by Bishop and Whiteman, the demonstrators tore down the fence constructed by Brownlow and marched triumphantly to the beach where they denounced Eric Gairy as a traitor for ignoring their cause. Soon after the incident, JEWEL and MAP merged into a political group—the New Jewel Movement—which emerged as the most powerful opposition to Gairyism.[27] This rather complicated development of opposition forces against the Gairy government is shown in figure 7.1.

Led by Maurice Bishop and a group of radical professionals, the NJM rose to prominence by attacking Gairy on all fronts. It also addressed itself to the discontent of the masses, particularly the poor and the unemployed youths. Its principal objectives were to rid Grenada of Gairy's dictatorial and corrupt rule, develop the country's economy, and reduce its economic and political dependence on the outside world. To achieve these goals, the NJM leaders adopted a noncapitalist or socialist trend in ideas and policies that was in many ways similar to the Marxist-Leninist ideology and principles. Among other things, the NJM advocated an end to party politics in Grenada that was based on the Westminster system and the institution of People's Assemblies as well as the permanent involvement of Grenadians in decision making. At its core was a Political Bureau and a Central Committee, both of which placed particular emphasis on the formation of principled positions on a wide range of issues. Domestically, it includes economic independence for the people of Grenada, a higher standard of living for all Grenadians, agricultural and land reforms, free secondary education, a national health

Figure 7.1
The Development of Opposition Movements to the
Gairy Regime in Grenada in the 1970s

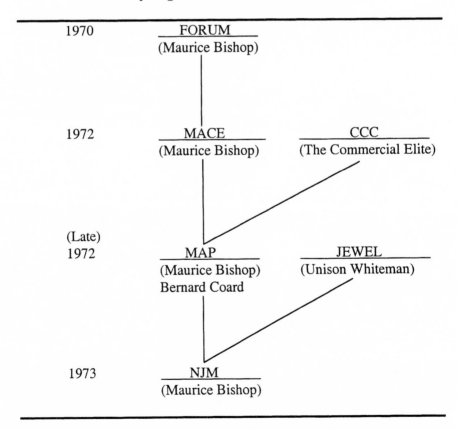

insurance scheme and a preventive medicine program. Internationally, the PRG advanced a foreign policy based on non-alignment and an end to foreign control and domination of the island's economy.[28] Within a short span of time, the NJM succeeded in supplanting the GNP as the vanguard party for the youth, the working class, the poor, and the anti-Gairy forces on the island. It also laid the foundation for the development of revolutionary socialism in Grenada, the murder of its leader, and the U.S. invasion in October 1983.

The Roots of Revolutionary Socialism

In Grenada, the roots of revolutionary socialism emerged from the radical politics of the NJM leadership, which was based on the principal themes of economic independence, self-reliance, anti-Gairyism, and anti-imperialism. Its manifesto urged Grenadians to take their destiny into their own hands and to start to define their national identity. The NJM adopted the slogan "We'll be free in 73" and its leaders bluntly warned Gairy that no government can continue to function in the face of the organized opposition and mobilization of the people. They claimed that when a government ceases to serve the people and instead steals and exploits them at every turn, the people are entitled to dissolve and replace it by any means necessary.[29]

Political Independence
    The first major clash between the Gairy regime and the NJM was on the issue of political independence for Grenada. The NJM was not opposed to political independence for the island, but was critical of an independence full of pomp and ceremonious settings and did not address the economic and social problems of the country. The NJM leadership argued for a genuine independence based on the sound development of economic projects and not the changing of flags or the singing of national anthems. They contend that the granting of independence to Grenada by Britain must be accompanied by some of the wealth extracted from the country by the British during more than two centuries of colonialism. They also argued that while independence would promote national identity, Grenada's economy was too dependent on foreign capital and far too fragile to support real independence. As outlined in the NJM Manifesto: "Independence must mean better housing for our people, better clothing, better food, better health, better education, better roads and bus service, more jobs, higher wages—in short a higher standard of living for workers and their children."[30]

Contrary to the NJM's viewpoint, Gairy insisted that independence was a right for Grenada, and would not be an economic burden to Grenadians. In fact, it would result in more international financial and economic aid for the country. Gairy insisted that independence will support Grenada, and the people of Grenada do not have to support independence. As he explained, "it is only when we attain full independence that our independent brothers and sisters, numbering over 150 prosperous, progressive countries, can come directly to our aid."[31] Ignoring all opposition forces, Gairy departed in early May for a second round of discussions on an independence constitution in London where he was opposed by GNP leader Blaize and Bernard Coard of the NJM. Meanwhile, on May 6, the NJM leadership organized a "People's Convention on Independence" near Grenville, Grenada's second largest city. The leaders unequivocally declared to a crowd of thousands that the people of Grenada would not accept independence decided upon by Gairy and the British government, nor would they be bound by a constitution that they had not helped to frame. By mid-1973, opposition to independence under Gairy came in the form of widespread strikes and violence, most of which were neutralized by Gairy's police squads. Among the strikers were dockworkers, utility workers, students, teachers, and merchants who closed their shops to protest Gairy's dictatorial and corrupt policies.

Concerned with the plight of the poor, unemployed youths, the economic viability of an independent Grenada, and Gairy's corrupt and brutal rule, the NJM leadership, on Sunday, November 4, 1973, convened what was labeled the "People's Congress" which, despite police harassment, was attended by approximately 10,000 people. This was in marked contrast to the mere 2,000 GULP supporters who attended a similar rally sponsored by Gairy on the same day. The People's Congress unanimously passed a resolution indicting the Gairy government on twenty-seven charges against the people, including murder and corruption. The indictment called for the resignation of Gairy no later than November 18, 1973, or face a general strike. Gairy responded with fifty-four charges against the NJM leaders, including treason and sedition.

Knowing Gairy, he did not wait for the NJM leaders to strike the first blow. On the scheduled day of the strike, six members of the NJM, including Maurice Bishop, were arrested and brutally beaten by Gairy's police squads in what came to be known in Grenada as "Bloody Sunday." This single act was, in many ways, the catalyst for a nationwide repudiation of the Gairy regime. It galvanized his opponents into a militant unity that the NJM could not have achieved by itself. In fact, the beatings precipitated the very strike they were intended to prevent as all the major trade unions, except Gairy's GMMWU, all the major churches, and a number of organizations joined the strike. These groups came together and formed a "Committee of Twenty-Two" that presented a list of demands to the government, some of which were accepted by Gairy. The strikes crippled Grenada's economy mainly because the seamen's union shut down the port of St. George's and made the independence day celebrations a dismal failure. Gairy managed to ride out the storm as the striking businesses and unions ordered their workers to return to work out of financial necessity.

As support for the NJM increased, the brutality of the Gairy regime intensified and reached its climax with the murder of Rupert Bishop (father of Maurice) on January 21, 1974, by Gairy's notorious police squads. Several other NJM supporters suffered the same fate. Together, these dastardly acts weakened Gairy politically as his actions were viewed by Grenadians as the epitome of brutality and by other Commonwealth Caribbean governments as an embarrassment to the region who realized that such callous behavior unavoidably brought the whole area into disrepute. Amidst the turmoil and near anarchy, Grenada achieved political independence from Britain on 7 February 1974 against the wishes of the masses and with several members of the opposition NJM, including Bishop, imprisoned.[32]

After independence, Gairy showed every intention of remaining in power indefinitely. His repressive measures against his opponents continued with the proclamation of the Public Order Act of 1974 that prohibited the use of loudspeakers by opposition groups at public gatherings. This was followed by the Newspaper Amendment Act of 1975, which increased the deposit from EC$900 to EC$20,000 for the right to publish a newspaper in Grenada. This act was intended to prevent the publication of the NJM's newspaper, the *New Jewel*, which at the time had over 10,000 subscribers.[33] Opposition groups were prevented from using the island's only radio station, which was government owned—a monopolistic practice that continued under the Bishop regime. The government also denied eleven categories of workers their right to join unions. By late 1978, less than 30 percent of the Grenadian workforce was unionized, causing employers to exploit their workers.

Despite these repressive acts, the 1976 elections, although allegedly rigged by the Gairy regime, catapulted Bishop into the position as leader of the opposition in a People's Alliance comprised of the NJM, the GNP, and the United People's Party (UPP), founded by Leslie Pierre. The People's Alliance obtained 48.5 percent of the votes cast and won six of the fifteen seats in the Grenadian Legislature. Of the six seats, the NJM obtained three, the GNP two, and the UPP one.[34] But Gairy's conviction and belief in mystic powers that he was appointed by God to lead the people of Grenada resulted in his domination of the country's Parliament which, prior to the March 1979 coup, became a one-man, one-party affair for his government in the face of six opposition members. As the NJM assumed the role of opposition, Gairy stressed its alleged Marxist ideology as further justification for repression in the name of anticommunism. With threats of violence looming, Gairy's Mongoose gangs under the command of Willie Bishop (cousin to Maurice) stepped up their persecutions against NJM members and supporters, some of whom occasionally and mysteriously disappeared.

The political struggle between the Gairy regime and the NJM severely affected Grenada's economy, already dangerously weakened by several years of mismanagement, corruption, strikes, and work stoppages. Political unrest and civil disturbances which accompanied independence, combined with the global economic recession in 1974, had a devastating effect on the island's tourist industry, which remained stagnated for the rest of the decade. By mid-1978, the picture of the island's workforce was very bleak: 50 percent or more than 16,000 male workers were unemployed. This official rate of unemployment disguised a 69 percent rate for female and a devastating 80 percent for youths under twenty years of age. The island's GDP declined in real terms as the number of tourists fell by more than 50 percent.[35] In this period, the government's finances dried up as foreign capital investment and foreign aid ceased to pour into the country. Grenada's trade deficit increased from EC$10 million to over EC$50 million due to a huge import bill, and the national debt rose to EC$60 million. Per capita income fell by almost 20 percent between 1974 and 1979 while the price of basic food items rose by 200 percent, clothing by 164 percent, and housing by 135 percent.[36] Because of its failure to pay its institutional dues, Grenada was on the verge of losing its vote and participation at the UN, UNESCO, WHO, and at the University of the West Indies.[37]

In February 1979, the inevitable end of the Gairy regime was in sight as the Mongoose gangs physically assaulted a number of striking employees of Barclays Bank in St. George's. This brutal act led Bishop and other NJM leaders to conclude that force and not parliamentary elections in a deeply corrupt political system was the only means to get rid of the Gairy regime. Trained in revolutionary socialism in Cuba during the mid-1970s, and armed with weapons smuggled in from the United States in oil drums, the PRA, a clandestine military wing of the NJM, in a dawn attack upon the army head-quarters at True Blue on March 13, 1979, overthrew the Gairy regime. The coup d'etat occurred just one day after Gairy, whose belief in the mystical powers was so great, departed Grenada confidently to New York to persuade

UN Secretary-General Kurt Waldheim to establish a UN agency to study UFOs and other cosmic phenomena.[38] Gairy had been aware that the leaders of the NJM were planning a coup which he was trying to forestall, so he gave orders on his departure for their indefinite imprisonment. As to why Gairy chose that moment to get rid of the opposition, given the fact that since the 1976 elections Maurice Bishop had been the official leader of the opposition and a prominent figure in national and regional politics, is still not known. In his first radio address to the nation as the people's leader, Bishop promised to restore all democratic freedoms, including freedom of elections, religions, and political opinion. He also told his listeners that "the revolution is for work, for food, for decent housing and health services, and for a bright future for the children and grandchildren of Grenadians."[39] Three days later the People's Revolutionary Government (PRG) was formed with a nine-man cabinet with Bishop as prime minister and Bernard Coard as minister of finance. This was supposed to be the team to lead Grenada to economic independence via revolutionary socialism.

Revolutionary Socialism in Grenada

Following the overthrow of the Gairy government, the Bishop regime was preoccupied with security as it faced opposition from other Caribbean states, notably Barbados, Dominica, and St. Lucia, as well as the threat of a counter-attack by Gairy. The NJM leaders were fully aware that gaining international recognition for their government even from its neighbors in the Caribbean would be a difficult and delicate matter which could well undermine its very survival. At an emergency foreign ministers' meeting of CARICOM nations on March 14, 1979, Barbados, St. Lucia, and Dominica condemned the PRG while Guyana and Jamaica supported it. Antigua, St. Vincent, and Trinidad and Tobago did not attend. The government of Trinidad and Tobago adopted a policy to ignore the PRG. The issue of elections was the source of the problem. Grenada's Caribbean neighbors as well as its traditional allies, the United States, Canada, and Britain, had all made it clear that their relations with the PRG would depend heavily on its legitimacy in fair and free elections.

In their search for help and recognition, PRG officials first sought assistance from Britain, Canada, and the United States.[40] These countries not only denied military aid to Grenada, but refused to recognize the legitimacy of the PRG because of the fact that it overthrew the island's legitimate government. Faced with desperation and a counterattack by Gairy, the PRG sought and received military and economic assistance from Cuba. Within a month of the coup, the Bishop regime established diplomatic relations with Cuba and declared Grenada a revolutionary socialist state. The establishment of diplomatic ties with the Castro regime was not exceptional for CARICOM states since Grenada had been preceded in this matter by Guyana, Jamaica, Barbados, and Trinidad and Tobago as far back as 1972. But it was clear that relations between the U.S. and the Bishop regime were predicated on Grenada's relationship with Cuba. Despite earlier assurances from Bishop that his government would respect all democratic freedoms and the personal safety and property of individuals, and all foreign residents, the U.S. was firm in its demand that Grenada sever all ties with the Castro regime. Both Britain and Canada pledged not to intervene in Grenada and warned the United States government that any sanctions at this early stage against Grenada could be counterproductive and would serve only to strengthen the PRG ties with Cuba. Frank Ortiz, then U.S. ambassador to Barbados and the eastern Caribbean countries, also counseled Washington to have patience over a situation that was still unfolding. As Karen De Young explains:

> Strong U.S. diplomatic action . . . may succeed only in pushing Grenada further to the left. While the Cubans were responsive and helpful to the revolution, United States only expressed concern and displeasure and regret over budgetary procedures. Moreover, public opinion on the island had turned against the United States, viewing it as a bully and a stingy one to boot.[41]

Accordingly, on March 22, the U.S. government announced its intention to continue friendly and peaceful relations with Grenada as it had done since the island's independence in 1974. But the situation changed quickly within a few days in a direction that further alarmed the United States. On March 25, Bishop promulgated a series of what the PRG called "People's Laws" which, among other things, suspended the constitution, legalized the PRG, vested the PRA with full police powers, and provided for the preventive detention of persons deemed likely to endanger the public safety. Regarding elections, Bishop refused to fix a date, claiming that Gairy had left the electoral system in a mess and that elections would be held only after a new constitution. This was the complete opposite to Bishop's earlier pledge to guarantee and maintain all democratic freedoms. But the very nature of the regime and its ideology put the NJM leaders at odds with parliamentary democracies and led them to align themselves with countries such as Cuba and the Soviet Union that were inclined to support and defend dictatorships. They had no intention of holding elections, because if they were to lose such an election, they could have been tried for treason. On the other hand, if they were to win (as they might well have done in 1979), their socialist regime and its policies would have been subject to challenge at the polls and in the courts. Moreover, to submit to a vote under the existing constitution would have been to recognize the supremacy of the old imperialist institutions. Put bluntly, these were not alternatives for the socialist PRG.

The declaration of revolutionary socialism was outlined in an extremely detailed program of social, economic, and political reconstruction of the island, the mobilization of the masses for national development and self-determination, and support for the regime. Conceived as an indigenous model of development, revolutionary socialism placed greater emphasis on self-reliance and the appropriate use of Grenada's human and material resources. On the economic front, it stressed the rapid development of the tourist, agricultural, and fisheries sectors and insisted on local ownership and management of these industries. The PRG also denounced the way in which the Grenadian economy was inserted into the international capitalist system and vowed to change the country's economic direction and relations.

Politically, from its inception, the PRG rejected the Westminster model of government bequeathed to Grenada by Britain in 1974 on the grounds that it critically undermined any program of meaningful development of the island's social, political, and cultural systems for and by Grenadians. The PRG also claimed that the system was open to abuse as was evident during Gairy's rule and that it was impractical for a small population coexisting in a limited area.[42] According to the PRG, these factors, combined with the incompetence and corruption of the Gairy government, were the underlying reasons for Grenada's poverty, high inflation and unemployment rates, lack of educational facilities, and deficiencies in the health care service and the transportation system. Revolutionary socialism was a call for action and a blueprint for change aimed at breaking the bonds of imperialism and the elimination of Grenada's economic dependence on the core capitalist states.

In part, revolutionary socialism was linked to the NJM leadership's deep admiration for Castro and the Cuban revolution, the socialist experiment in Tanzania under Julius Nyerere, and the refusal of the United States to aid the regime during the early days of the revolution. It involved public displays such as revolutionary slogans, gestures of bravery, principled positions, hard manners, the wearing of beards and military outfits, and the fear of the NJM leadership to appear as petit-bourgeois reformists to the masses. Devotion to duty and to the revolution had to be absolute. These were not merely well-rehearsed exercises in public but important symbols to mobilize support for the regime and the revolution. This radical approach led some members of the NJM to become zealots who were unreasonable in their demands, plans, and decisions and, at times, irresponsible and elated with the Marxist-Leninist ideology and all that it stood for.

Noncapitalist Development

The development of revolutionary socialism was in the guise of the theory of the noncapitalist path of development or the path of socialist orientation as constructed by Soviet theoreticians.[43] Marxism had been lost to the region with the voluntary exile of C. L. R. James and Richard Hart, while Soviet theorists in Cuba were isolated by the division imposed by colonialism and U.S. diplomatic and economic sanctions. In the Caribbean, the theory's most prominent exponents were Trevor Munroe, Clive Thomas, Ralph Gonsalves, the NJM leadership, and Michael Manley. In essence, the theory of noncapitalist development sought to justify and map out a path for Third World political leaders who wanted to disengage their economies from the international capitalist system could do so by bypassing the capitalist stage on the road to socialism. The theory advocated an incremental approach to revolutionary transformation, to take into account the numerical weakness of the proletariat in international capitalist-dominated economies. Central to this process was the necessity to establish a national democratic regime soon after the attainment of political independence to provide firm and popular leadership to weaken the bonds of capitalist dependency and to develop nationally controlled economic and political institutions, while retaining public support. The key requirement was a period of socialist orientation following independence, a multiclass alliance comprised of the proletariat, the masses, peasants, and committed socialist leaders who would seek aid from the socialist world.[44] It claimed that a gradualist approach toward socialism—the hallmark of the theory—was only sustainable if there was popular mobilization, political education, and public awareness in support of the revolution.

The theory was an important guide to the development of revolutionary socialism in Grenada, although the revolution was in a number of ways more radical than the theory allowed for. Although socialist, the NJM leaders did not intend to promote socialism from the start, but to lay the groundwork for it. This was evident with the scant nationalization policy of Gairy's assets and of the public utilities, land reform, and virtually no attempt at collective ownership of property, which for Grenadians in general stood in sharp contrast to the collectivist heritage of Africa for which the theory of noncapitalist development was originally designed. Socialist orientation only became manifested in the PRG's foreign policy, especially its close ties with Cuba and the Soviet Union. In other areas, gradualism was supplanted by overzealousness and extremism that led to the internal power struggle and the ultimate collapse of the regime.

From the moment he was installed as prime minister of Grenada, Bishop set himself the daunting task to change the island's economic and political direction. He condemned the dependency relationship that existed between Grenada and the developed capitalist countries, which he claimed was the main source of the island's imports and the primary market for its exports. He claimed that it is this dependent relationship and not the small size of the island that is the primary cause for its underdevelopment and exploitation by the imperialist forces. As Bishop explains:

> We contend, comrades, that the real problem is not the question of smallness per se, but [that] of imperialism. The real problem that small countries like ours face is that on a day-by-day basis we come up against an international system that is organized and geared towards ensuring the continuing exploitation, domination and rape of our economies, our countries, and our peoples. That, to us, is the fundamental problem.[45]

Politically, the most startling and original proposal of the Bishop regime was its radical rejection of the Westminster system as divisive and undemocratic in nature. The vast majority of Grenadians had hoped and expected that once the revolution had been consolidated, the PRG would incorporate the legal principles of the Westminster model, namely a commitment to constitutional elections, judicial rights, and the rule of law into the system of participatory democracy. This had not been the case. Instead, the PRG expressed its deep commitment to rid Grenada of the elitist Westminster type of parliamentary democracy and its constituent myths and presumptions, which it claimed have divided the population.

> Firstly, parties divide the people into warring camps. Secondly, the system places power in the hands of a small ruling clique. That clique victimizes and terrorizes members of the other party. Thirdly, the ruling party seizes control of all avenues of public information, for example, the radio station, and uses them for its own ends. Finally, and most importantly, it fails to involve the people except for a few seconds once in every five years when they make an "X" on a ballot paper.[46]

Accordingly, the Westminster model was replaced by an elaborate system of People's Assemblies at the village, parish, and national levels and a national government based on collective leadership. This provoked hostile reaction from a number of Caribbean leaders who claimed that elections and not coup d'etats were the acceptable means of changing governments in the region. In rebuking the NJM leadership, Eric Williams said, "There is more to the Westminster model than just elections: there are the rule of law, the multi-party system, the separation of Church and state, the traditional civil liberties and so on. To reject all of them, on the ground that the model is inapplicable to Third World conditions, is to throw out the baby with the bath water."[47] By the indefinite suspension of the constitution of Grenada, the Bishop regime signaled to the world that the coup d'etat of 13 March 1979 was not only intended to replace a corrupt and brutal dictator, but rather a revolution designed to chart a new direction for Grenada under the ideological concept of revolutionary socialism.

Goals of Revolutionary Socialism

In Grenada the proclamation of revolutionary socialism embraced the kind of social welfare goals and certain foreign policy principles similar to the policies of the Manley and Burnham governments in Jamaica and Guyana respectively. It constituted six major policy goals, the first of which was the introduction of a new political culture called participatory democracy. It involved the creation of the Ministry of National Mobilization to oversee and encourage popular participation through a number of mass organizations such as the National Women's Organization, the National Students Council, the National Youth Organization for youths between the ages of fourteen and twenty-two, the Young Pioneers Movement for the five to thirteen year olds, trade unions, the People's Militia, Community Work Brigades, and several other groups. The PRG also established Parish and Zonal Councils in the island's six parishes and a Coordinating Bureau in each village with the sole purpose to involve everyone in the struggle. The Parish Coordinating Bodies were at the center of the mobilization process. Composed of representatives of the mass organizations in a particular parish under the direction of senior party members, the Coordinating Bodies were responsible for coordinating all political and mobilization activities within the parish. They provided political direction to the village and zonal councils where citizens convened to discuss local and national issues such as adult education, primary health care, housing, the budget, and the government's annual financial assessment of all sectors that made up the national economy. As one commentary has it:

> Today in Grenada, Parliament has moved out of town into the communities. Government has escaped . . . and spread into community centers, school buildings, street corners, market places, factories, farms, and workplaces around the country. Political power has been taken out of the hands of a few privileged people and turned over to thousands of men, women and youth . . . in every nook and cranny of Grenada, Carriacou, and Petit Martinique.[48]

The aim of participatory democracy was to end the deep divisions and victimization of the masses by the two-party system. The development of the Parish and zonal councils and mass organizations was based on the PRG's popular concept of "People's Power" which it claimed was a prerequisite of the construction of a new Grenada, free of foreign domination and control of its resources. They were the vehicles for maintaining the party's link to the masses as well as the political indoctrination of the youth and women. The Parish and zonal councils were to change the deep-rooted prejudices and values inculcated upon the people of Grenada through the experience of colonialism and imperialism. People's Power legitimized the Bishop regime which was not an elected body. For the PRG, People's Power was nothing less than the creation of a new sense of national identity, patriotism, and pride and every Grenadian was expected to identify with the revolution and be part of the decision-making process. As Bernard Coard put it:

> The New Jewel Movement was born . . . as a reaction to and repudiation of old-style . . . politics of bribery and corruption . . . a process that consciously sought to divide the people into two warring camps, the "ins" and the "outs." The Government can only mobilize half the people with the other half being by definition completely opposed to it. The New Jewel Movement . . . most fundamental [principle] is that whatever the task that confronts us, whether political . . . economic . . . or defence . . . the people must be involved.[49]

During the early part of PRG rule, the activities of the councils and the mass organizations enjoyed widespread support from the people who were encouraged to discuss policy with and question the PRG leadership and civil servants. Although the formation of the Ministry of National Mobilization, self-styled the "People's Ministry," encouraged and accelerated the decision-making process, by mid-1982, participatory democracy was a failure. This was due largely to the fact that party power and control manifested itself in the councils' operations in a number of ways. The councils had no power and no direct role in the decision-making system. The councils and the mass organizations were established for the explanation of policy, mobilization of political support for the PRG, political education, and the defense of the revolution. At no time could, or was, policy challenged, let alone changed by the delegates. In fact, the delegates were not allowed to debate priorities; they were only permitted to ask questions and to approve the decisions made by the Bishop regime. Furthermore, neither the delegates nor the members of the councils could have challenged the membership of the NJM Central Committee. As the vanguard party, the NJM ultimately expected to be obeyed, its rule was not open to challenge. This was contrary to the NJM manifesto which had promised a system of direct democracy, in which power would flow from the bottom up. Instead, the system established in 1979 was quite the opposite in that it became an instrument for controlling the people from the top down.

The ideological justification for this system was the backwardness of the Grenadian people, the low political consciousness of the masses, their lack of education and understanding of the Marxist-Leninist ideology, their long history of political and economic suppression, and their poverty and poor living conditions. Therefore, it was the task of the vanguard party to reverse these conditions and liberate the masses so that they could intelligently manage their own affairs. This was to be achieved through the dictatorship of the proletariat exercised by the party acting on behalf of the interest of the people. Thus, the PRG concept of participatory democracy emerged into a paternalistic brand of socialism headed by an authoritarian and undemocratic core, who dished out severe punishment to dissenters, as was the case with Bishop and several other government officials. The result was an almost total failure. The NJM not only lacked money, personnel, and expertise, but it was confounded by its ideology and its insistence on rule from the top, which lost the popular support of the people.

The second goal of revolutionary socialism was the development of a mixed economy whose cornerstone was the dominance of the state sector over the private and cooperative sectors. This was meant to reduce the role and influence of the private sector in the development process and provide the PRG with the mechanism to guide and regulate economic development through the imposition of taxes, the granting of credits and concessions, and the full use of all arms of the state apparatus. It was also part of a larger PRG economic strategy of building a national economy more responsive to local needs, more locally owned, and less dependent on foreign capital, especially from the West. The stated aim and purpose of the mixed economy was for the state to provide the material means by which the PRG social goals were to be achieved and to facilitate as quickly as possible the transition to the socialist-type command economy, rather than to continue with the market-oriented approach of the Gairy years. According to the PRG, it was highly inappropriate and risky for a country of Grenada's size and with a socialist philosophy to be dependent on foreign private resources over which it had no control.[50] However, despite its socialist rhetoric, the regime was very sensitive on the issue of private capital, which was justified as a benefit, not a threat, to Grenada's economic and political development.

Consequently, the radical proposals of the 1973 NJM manifesto which called for a complete nationalization of the tourist industry and banks, a radical restructuring of land tenure, and wage and price controls, among others, were postponed. Not only did the PRG fear provoking an international and domestic reaction against such unpopular and radical policies, it also simply did not have the resources and expertise to undertake such huge projects at once. The program as outlined by the PRG was a rational plan for reform through economic diversification and import substitution under strong government leadership. The regime's adoption of a mixed economic model of development reflected the existing dominance of private local and foreign capital in Grenada's economy and the need for the state to lead in the development process. In an address at the First International Solidarity Conference with Grenada in November 1981, Coard eloquently remarked:

> Our economy as a mixed economy will comprise the state sector, the private sector, and the cooperative sector. The dominant sector will be the state sector, which will lead in the development process . . . we intend to provide assistance to the private sector wherever possible, whether it be local or foreign, or in partnership with the state or with other private individuals so long as it is in keeping with the country's economic development.[51]

As head of the economic development program, Coard imposed very tight control over public spending. Government agencies had to submit monthly expenditure reports to the Ministry of Finance where they were checked as to whether they were in line with projected spending before being approved. No purchases were allowed to be made without a voucher countersigned by the Ministry of Finance. The government also imposed price controls and placed some restrictions on the big import-export firms that had traditionally conducted most of the country's foreign trade. Through its Marketing and National Importing Boards, the government monopolized the import of such commodities as drugs, hospital supplies, fertilizers, cement, rice, agricultural equipment, powdered milk, and other basic food items from Cuba as well as from other sources, notably the U.S., Britain, Canada, and the E.U. The PRG also imposed a licensing requirement on all imports and exports which allowed it to monitor prices and establish some profit ceilings. It was this tight fiscal management that allowed the PRG to increase social services and capital expenditures considerably and to bring inflation under control. The involvement of the PRG in commercial activities led to the relative decline of the private sector whose investment fell by over 25 percent in 1981.[52] The decline alarmed Coard who responded with tax reductions and concessions for those companies, both local and foreign owned that invested in areas of agriculture, tourism, and manufacturing. These and other government incentives resulted in a 10 percent increase in production in the private sector by 1982 and a corresponding increase in company tax revenue.[53]

As part of its economic program, the PRG adopted a strategy of selective nationalization which was directed to most of the public utilities, including the Electricity Corporation, the Telephone Company, and Public Transportation. The hotels and nightclubs owned by Gairy and his attorney general, Derek Knight, were confiscated by the government to be part of the state-owned Grenada Resorts Corporation, through which the government had hoped to influence and expand the tourist industry. The Holiday Inn, by far the largest hotel on the island, was also purchased by the government but only after it had been badly damaged by fire and its owners did not want to rebuild.

The government also moved aggressively into the banking industry. The Bishop regime inherited an agricultural bank, which became the Grenada Development Bank. To this it added the National Commercial Bank in the premises vacated by the Canadian Imperial Bank of Commerce which ceased its operations in 1979, and the Grenada Bank of Commerce as a successor to the Royal Bank of Canada, which also closed its operations on the island. Some private banks remained, among them Barclay's, the largest and most influential in the country. The main function of the state-owned banks was to finance the government's ambitious capital investment projects. The PRG doubled the $8 million budget for 1979 capital expenditures it inherited from Gairy to $16 million and increased it even more in subsequent years. These nationalizations reflected the wish of the government to keep certain monopolies in state hands so as to minimize economic and social dislocation and allow the public sector to compete with the private and cooperative sectors. By these means, it was argued that the inefficient monopolies which plagued many socialist countries would be avoided. Furthermore, as noted earlier, as a peripheral state, Grenada did not have the personnel and the expertise to manage all sectors of the economy—a point of view shared by Prime Minister Maurice Bishop:

> We are not in the least bit interested as a government in attempting to run all sectors of the economy. That would be an impossibility. The massive problems we already have with storage space, with qualified personnel, and that kind of thing in the few areas we have moved into, like the National Commercial Bank and the National Importing Board, shows very clearly to us that it would be a massive nightmare for us if, for example, we were to go and try to sell cloth or rice and saltfish or even operate a Coke factory.[54]

The PRG free-market approach to the manufacturing sector was equally apparent in the tourist industry. It abandoned its initial policy to nationalize all foreign-owned hotels. A number of factors contributed to this change. One was the tourism industry in Grenada and the fact that the rest of the Caribbean did not recover from the severe impact of the world recession in the 1970s and early 1980s. Another factor was the weakened U.S. dollar which at the time had induced American tourists to either stay at home or take their vacations in neighboring countries such as Canada, Puerto Rico, and Mexico. Added to these was the adverse publicity which Grenada attracted in the U.S. press, most of which was promoted by forces hostile to the Bishop regime and the development of revolutionary socialism in the country.

With respect to the cooperatives, which was the potential third sector of the economy, there were several notable developments. The PRG established the National Cooperative Development Agency (NACDA) in April 1980 under the Ministry of Agriculture to develop farming cooperatives in each parish, with the hope to reduce Grenada's chronic youth unemployment. It was also crucial to the transformation of the island's agriculture in that it provided land, buildings, equipment, loans, and training to Grenadians to set up cooperatives. Various government agencies and foreign donors were solicited for contributions to the program. The PRG also established fishing and handicraft cooperatives with the objective of bringing those industries under national management. Elaborating on the significance of the NACDA, Courd said:

> NACDA is changing the idea that the old colonial-style estate is the only model for agriculture, and showing our people how they can produce

together, sit down, organize, plant and reap their own harvests. In doing this, it has brought the youth back to the land in a significant way, sending down the average age of our agricultural worker from 62 to 51 years. . . . Comrades, our agriculture is becoming young again. And all that young muscle and brain power, working together, is what will cause real and solid economic construction.[55]

Cooperatives such as the NACDA was a new model of agricultural development in Grenada and the Caribbean as a whole. But novelty has its price and this was to account for the disappointing performance of the co-operative sector. Despite government efforts, the cooperative sector grew slowly and remained a very small part of the island's economy during the entire period of PRG rule. Two reasons accounted for this. One was the co-operative sector was poorly managed, and most young Grenadians had preferred to work directly with the state, particularly in the security forces, which expanded rapidly during the revolution. The other reason was the local peasantry was not deeply motivated by cooperatives mainly because of their traditional independence. This was most evident in the fishing industry where the preference of the vast majority of the island's fishermen was to use their own small boats to fish despite a fleet of eleven large Cuban fishing boats. Grenadians did not believe in collective ownership. The end result was that the PRG was forced to subsidize the fishing industry and the entire cooperative sector.

Agriculture was key to the PRG whole plan of restructuring Grenada's economy. It was the major sector of the national economy in that it employed some 30 percent of the workforce in a predominantly rural economy. It was also the major source of foreign exchange, contributing about 35 percent of GDP. Under the agriculture program, the PRG established a number of state-owned agro-industries to process Grenada's produce. The Grenada State Farms Corporation was established to manage, develop, and operate the estates and farms which the Bishop regime had inherited from the Gairy administration, improve rural feeder roads over which delicate crops had to be shipped, and manage the Agricultural Marketing Boards more efficiently.

The PRG also passed the Land Development and Utilization Act in 1981, one of the many People's Laws that allowed for the mandatory leasing of idle lands by the PRG. Idle lands, largely owned by Grenadians overseas, were taken over on short-term lease arrangements and allocated to the state farms of the Grenada Farms Corporation by the Land Reform Commission and to unemployed youths who wanted to become small farmers. It created a number of agricultural schools that provided basic training in bookkeeping, farm technology, and marketing techniques to young farmers. The focus on agriculture was aimed both at encouraging the more than 50 percent unemployed youths in the agricultural sector to join the existing 5,000 small farmers, and to reduce the country's food import bill. By late 1982, the distribution of hundreds of acres of land to some 2,000 farmers by the PRG, while another 1,500 found work in the new industries, public works, and construction, contributed to a considerable reduction in unemployment which had fallen to 14 percent, and was estimated to be 10 percent by late 1983. Women and youths were the main beneficiaries. It also led to a significant increase in food production on the island. Despite successive hurricane damages and periods of extensive flooding between 1979 and 1980, export earnings of fruit and vegetables rose dramatically, from EC$1.5 million in 1981 to EC$4.5 million in 1982, an increase of 314.5 percent. During this period, Trinidad and Tobago became second only to Britain as Grenada's chief food customer, accounting for 31 percent of the island's products while Britain took 36 percent.[56]

The success in agriculture during the first three years of PRG rule had very little impact on Grenada's food import bill, which fell by only 3 percent, from 30.6 percent to 27.5 percent between 1979 and 1982.[57] Thus, while land reforms and the nationalization of public utilities produced some significant changes in Grenada's economy, they did not reduce the island's economic dependence on the international capitalist system. In part, this was due to the damage created by the use of state control of the economy and a wide range of conventional economic problems experienced by Grenada and other Third World countries. They include inappropriate technology, lack of skilled labor, low domestic savings, limited resource endowment, natural disasters, and low prices for raw materials and high costs for manufactured goods. Furthermore, management and organizational skills were scarce, and foreign exchange was dangerously low. Many projects, especially those in the productive sectors, took considerable time to develop and implement, and in the medium term they turned out to be less productive than expected. In the face of these problems the PRG also had to overcome some important obstacles in legitimizing itself because of Grenada's colonial legacy. It was involved in a protracted struggle with sections of the local church leadership, fractions of the capitalist class, and owners of newspapers who were openly opposed to the revolution and to the regime. The seizure of power, the suspension of the constitution, the creation of a revolutionary government, and the commitment to socialism were actions resisted by those who were committed to and believed in freedom and democracy.

The third goal of revolutionary socialism was to improve the quality of life of Grenadians through a comprehensive program aimed at upgrading the educational and health systems and housing facilities and to ensure that the basic needs of the population were met.

Educational Program

From day one of the revolution, the government was determined to reform the educational system, which like every other facet of Grenadian society, was seen as a colonial relic designed to serve the interests of the colonial power. English nursery rhymes, poetry, kindergarten songs and events took precedence over local activities and issues. Prime Minister Bishop described the educational system inherited from Britain as perhaps the worst crime that colonialism has left in the island. According to Bishop, the system had been developed by the British to strip Grenadians of their own history, culture, and values, to stifle their creativity, and to perpetuate class struggle. It had divided the Grenadian society into an intellectual elite, an educated middle class, and an undereducated majority. The PRG was convinced that recurrent problems such as weak management, poor record-keeping and accounting practices, low worker productivity, and the constant use of primitive technology were products of the colonial educational system. To deal with these problems, the regime adopted an educational policy that constituted a bold and radical break with the traditions implanted by the British in Grenada and elsewhere in the Commonwealth Caribbean. Its aim was to liberate the masses from ignorance and a sense of cultural inferiority, and to make them more productive, self-reliant, and independent as individuals and as a people. As Bishop explains: "We must use the educational system and process as a means of preparing the new man for the new life in the new society we are trying to build."[58]

The PRG's educational policies were based on the cardinal principle that education involved everyone, both young and old, and must be a lifelong process. Minister of Education Jacqueline Creft, a former secondary school-teacher, highlighted some of the problems associated with the colonial education system:

> Comrades, ever since our party was founded in March 1973, high upon our list of priorities has been the transformation of this twisted education system that we inherited from colonialism and from Gairy . . . a system which so powerfully excluded the interests of the mass of our people, and which also wove webs of fear, alienation and irrelevance around our children's minds . . . we called for an education system which not only serviced all our people, secondary schools which would freely open the doors to all our people without the constraint of fees, but also a curriculum which would eliminate absurdity from our classrooms and focus our

children's minds upon their own island, their own wealth, soil and crops, their own solution to the problems that surround them. For too long we had been brainwashed to think that only Europe and America held the answer.[59]

At the core of the PRG new educational policy were five major programs: Continuous Education; National In-Service Teacher Education Programme (NISTEP); Education for All; New Content in Curriculum; and the Work-Study Education Approach. Under the Continuous Education program, the PRG established a number of Centers for Popular Education (CPE) in 1980 with the goal of eradicating illiteracy, which was still rampant in Grenada, especially among the rural population most clearly linked to the production process. The CPE was a new layer of educational system designed to help those left behind by the primary and secondary layers. Under the slogan "each one teach one," CPE mobilized volunteer tutors to teach illiterates in order to improve the country's adult literacy rate by 30 percent within six months, by February 1981. This goal was achieved with the creation of forty-eight CPE centers across the country in which a variety of skills were taught. It led to a substantial decline of the illiteracy rate, from 15 percent to 3 percent as 881 individuals were given CPE adult education certificates upon completion of the program.[60] The CPE was instrumental in removing the taboo and old prejudices about Grenadian Creole. In CPE classes it was taught as a second language in order to bring about normal relations between standard English and Grenadian Creole so that both could play their crucial roles in the communication process. This was integral to the literacy and the shaping of the new Grenadian culture sought by the PRG. Thus, in addition to the teaching of specific skills, the CPE was also a socializing agency. As Prime Minister Bishop put it: "The Center for Popular Education is not just reading and writing, it is also about consciousness, about developing a nation that for the first time will begin to put proper values on those things that are important."[61]

In spite of its success, the CPE did not escape the problems that plagued the PRG social and economic programs. Its organizational structure was geared towards the mass mobilization and registration by village and parish coordinators and party activists at almost every village center in the country. The PRG's ideology hampered the success of the program. Some students did not like the political messages that were placed in the educational materials and the tactics the regime used to recruit new registrants. Others were turned off by the arrogance displayed by some of the tutors. The CPE also experienced leadership and organizational problems and equipment failures. But above all, by mid-1982, a large number of Grenadians were either disappointed with the revolution in general or hostile to it. Support and enthusiasm for the CPE had remained low despite Minister of Education Jacqueline Creft's efforts to revive the program. In spite of its initial popularity and limited success, overall, the CPE was a failure.

Another educational program initiated by the PRG in November 1980 was the National In-Service Teacher Education Programme to upgrade the low education level of about six hundred primary school teachers, most of whom had completed only primary school, or, at the most, a secondary education. It was a three-year program designed to increase the number of teachers in the country as well as to improve their knowledge in language, mathematics, arts, educational methods, social studies, agricultural science, and health education.[62] Again, the need was real, NISTEP was to replace the Grenada Teachers' College, which typically trained an average of forty-five teachers every year, while each year about half that number of qualified teachers left the profession either to get married, emigrate, or to seek more lucrative jobs elsewhere. In-service program was not new to the Caribbean. What was new was the attempt by the PRG to train all teachers who needed training. It was a bold, imaginative, and extremely ambitious undertaking by the regime. Under the NISTEP program, teachers taught for four days a week under the guidance of NISTEP tutors and their fellow trained teachers and attended training sessions on the fifth day at the University of the West Indies School of Education.

Meanwhile, on the days their teachers were away at training, students participated in various types of work activities through the complementary Community-School Day Programme. Field trips were arranged for students to visit factories where they were exposed to various kinds of skills and taught by peasant farmers and factory workers. The idea was for children to acquire an interest in and respect for productive labor which would help their choices of career later in life. "Exposure to this range of skills at such an early age obviously facilitates the students' choices of careers later in life, as much as it also enables them to understand fully their own roles in nation building and the revolution."[63]

Innovative and popular as the program was, the country's overall lack of skills and resources led to organizational problems as well as the difficulty of finding interesting field trips to hold the students' attention on the day the teachers were in training. It also resulted in a high rate of truancy on the days when teachers visited the centers for instruction. Moreover, study time in the classroom was constantly disrupted for students to attend rallies, ideological training sessions, and militia drills.

The ideology inculcated through these sessions undermined discipline both at home and at school. Parents were appalled by children who rejected their authority and became revolutionaries. They were shocked to learn that children as young as ten were issued weapons and given military training by the PRG. Principals and teachers also had trouble maintaining some semblance of order in the classroom. The situation became so serious that the minister of education had to form a committee of principals and teachers to draw up a new code of school discipline. The politicization of education created additional problems. Teachers resented the radical views espoused by many NISTEP instructors and this contributed to a high number of dropouts from the program. Many teachers were harassed, transferred, and, in some cases, dismissed for their opposing political views. Furthermore, Grenadians were alarmed over the large number of Cubans and other leftists from the Caribbean employed in the country's educational system. NISTEP is difficult to evaluate because the regime was not in power long enough for the program to have a significant impact on the educational system.

The third program, labeled Education for All, provided free secondary education to students who passed the common entrance examination. Its goal was to enroll some 12,000 Grenadians in adult educational courses in English, mathematics, and basic sciences. The PRG expanded the number of school places by building two new secondary schools during its first year in office compared to only one built by the Gairy administration between 1967 and 1979. By 1983, 40 percent of all the students in the country were attending secondary schools compared to only 11 percent prior to the 1979 revolution. At the university level, the PRG expanded opportunities for students to study abroad. It provided over 300 university scholarships to qualified graduates of the secondary schools to study abroad compared to three in 1978. Some of these scholarships were tenable at universities in the West and others in socialist countries such as Cuba, the Soviet Union, and the Eastern European countries. The latter approach was a new departure for Grenada and the Eastern Caribbean. The government also paid off the huge outstanding debt to the University of the West Indies that accumulated under the Gairy administration so that Grenadians could once again attend the regional university.

The PRG also placed greater emphasis on a New Content in the Curriculum, which is the fourth educational program that was developed to focus students on the history, culture, and values of Grenada and the Caribbean as a whole. The aim was to change the colonial school curriculum that was regarded as irrelevant to the needs, culture, and understanding of the local society. The importance of a new curriculum was emphasized by Prime Minister Bishop:

> We need a curriculum to practically aid our liberation, not to keep us dependent on outside powers that will do nothing but exploit us. Remember comrades, that the origin of culture itself is the land, the soil, the way we produce and feed ourselves, the way we survive and grow. We need a school curriculum that points directly to those necessities, for if we do not start that process at school, our new generation will grow up ignorant and incapable of developing their greatest asset—the rich and fertile soil of our land.[64]

The new curriculum focused on local and regional events and traced the purpose and process of the revolution in Grenada. Religious instruction, which had a traditional place in the curriculum, was confined to morning assembly sessions. Until the latter part of 1982, there were still no common texts for primary school students in Grenada. Students were taught how to read from antiquated British and Canadian texts that, apart from Columbus and his voyages around the world, were focused on English adventures and contained illustrations of white children and their surroundings that bore no resemblance to Grenada's society. With assistance from Cuba, thousands of standardized texts were printed featuring T. A. Marryshow as Grenada's national hero and showing life in the rural setting. Marxist education was introduced as part of the civics course into the curriculum. The political content of the PRG education program was geared towards raising the ideological and cultural levels of the population. Teachers were expected to promote the ideas of Marxism among their students until they developed a deep class consciousness. With this in mind, the PRG transferred some eighteen principals and teachers whom the regime dubbed as "reactionary and redundant elements" out of the school system and replaced them with more progressive ones who were attuned to the NJM political ideology. The PRG also established a new "Principals Council" to make sure that the principals follow the guidelines of the school curriculum. In Bishop's view:

> [The school curriculum] is . . . going to have tremendous relevance to the success of building a deeper and greater sense of national unity, and raising the national consciousness . . . it will be much easier for them not to be misled . . . it will be much easier for them to understand Imperialism. It will be much easier for them to understand what we mean when we talk of destabilization, what we mean when we say that the Revolution is for the people, and that the people are the revolution.[65]

The fifth program was the Work-Study Approach which was based on work experience and was aimed not only to help students find satisfaction in manual skills and technical knowledge, but to acquire certain knowledge, values, and behavior patterns.[66] As part of the NISTEP program, Work-Study had two interrelated aims. The first was to develop closer community-school relations, and second, to introduce a work-study approach to students. Together, they stressed the importance of practical education in areas of agriculture, health, nutrition, arts, crafts, and sports. Under this program, a two-track approach was developed to help students acquire the skills needed for a bright and prosperous career. Because secondary education was under the PRG and was available only to students who passed the common entrance examination, the slower students were trained in agriculture, carpentry, and home economics, while the brighter students pursued more academic subjects. Most of the activities of the work-study program were carried out by the Community Educational Councils (CECs) which were in charge of school curricula, the supervision and maintenance of schools, and the transition of students from school life to society.[67] During its first year, the CEC repaired more than sixty primary schools, thus saving the PRG almost EC$2 million. But like other programs, administrative inefficiency and the PRG's overt political goals took its toll on the education programs. Indifference and opposition to the reforms, especially at the village level, where little or no tradition of community involvement had existed, under-mined their overall effectiveness.

The restructuring of the educational system by the government was clearly intended to advance working-class interests. It was to make education which was a privilege for the rich during colonialism and under the Gairy regime available to every Grenadian. Its principal slogan, "Forward Ever, Backward Never," was meant to inculcate new values, attitudes, habits, and pride on the population. Education was an integral part of the cultural and social revolution, which Prime Minister Bishop summarized as "the spreading of the socialist ideology, the wiping out of illiteracy, and the building of a new patriotic and revolutionary-democratic intelligentsia."[68] While some of the education policies had some success, it is difficult to assess their overall performance mainly because of the premature collapse of the regime. How successful these educational reforms would have been in the long-term is impossible to say. But they clearly amounted to the most comprehensive attack ever made on the country's colonial educational system.

Public Health Program

In the area of public health, the PRG policy was sound. It acknowledged that a healthy population would be better able to increase production and cope with the problems of building the country. Consequently, it embarked on a program of preventative medicine that provided free medical and dental care to all Grenadians. The PRG public health program had also involved widespread inoculations, health and hygiene educational programs, water purification and waste disposal, and efforts to eradicate disease-carrying insects and vermin. The government not only abandoned curative medicine which had prevailed under the Gairy administration, but argued that the prevention of disease by implementing sound hygienic policies and cleaning up obvious sources and carriers of infection was a more sensible way to improve public health in the country. This approach was considered more economical than curative medicine, which had required expensive medical equipment and scarce foreign exchange to import drugs of all kinds. The overall aim of the PRG program was to improve the basic health and well-being of all Grenadians and to shift resources away from the major hospitals into the rural communities in order to correct the imbalance in social benefits between the cities and the rural areas of the country.

To achieve this goal, the PRG established a number of health clinics throughout the country and recruited medical personnel from Cuba and other Caribbean countries, and from Grenadian nationals who had left in search of opportunities overseas to staff the health facilities. Resident interns were also recruited from St. George's University School of Medicine, an offshore U.S. medical school set up for American students who were unsuccessful in their attempts to enroll in medical schools in the U.S. mainland. Special emphasis was placed on the recruitment of dentists because there had been no government dental service in Grenada during the last twelve years of Gairy's rule. During this period, the island's private dental care system catered to the needs of those who could afford to pay for the services, mostly the middle and upper classes. In 1979, seven doctors, three dentists, and a radiographer were recruited from Cuba, but by 1981 the number of Cuban doctors in the country had doubled. The Cubans provided specialist services in pediatrics, ophthalmology, orthopedics, ear, nose, and throat, and internal medicine in Grenada proper and in the smaller island of Carriacou where three of them were stationed.[69]

True to its Manifesto, the NJM also regulated fees for medical services at the General Hospital in St. George's. Prior to the revolution, physicians were allowed to conduct private practice at the hospital and determine the medical fees for their services. Free medical service was available to everyone but doctors understandably provided more and better care to patients who could pay. Based on the reforms instituted by the PRG, physicians were forbidden to see private patients in the hospital, but they were permitted to do private practice at their private offices. All patients treated at the hospital were admitted by the administration rather than by doctors, and all were given free medical care and drugs. This system not only standardized the health care provided by the government, but also prevented discrimination against poor patients who could not afford to pay for medical services.

With emphasis on community participation, the Ministry of Health conducted a nationwide information campaign through the media and local party and organizations to encourage Grenadians to clean their surroundings, eliminate breeding grounds for mosquitoes, get immunized against infectious diseases, and take advantage of local public health facilities. The PRG also established a District Health Team in each of the six parishes, increased the number of health clinics and visiting stations, and repaired or rebuilt those that were old and defective. A Food and Nutrition Council was established under the Ministry of Agriculture to coordinate a school lunch program and the distribution of free milk to students donated by the EEC. By 1982, the general hospital in St. George's was modernized with the addition of an eye clinic section, an intensive care unit, a maternity clinic, new X-ray facilities, an operating theater, a new emergency lighting system in case of power outages, more beds, drugs, and other hospital supplies.[70] Training was also provided to health workers in areas of health education, nutrition, and family planning.

While it is difficult to assess the PRG's health program, it is probably fair to say that the quality of health care in the country did improve, and its availability increased. There were more doctors, and more local medical clinics were built, which was a permanent improvement. In spite of these achievements, drugs were always in short supply, although there were free shipments of some pharmaceuticals from Cuba and the Eastern European countries. Grenadian nurses, doctors, and other medical personnel remained underpaid and demoralized as they had been prior to the revolution, and conditions in the public hospitals were deplorable. Efforts to improve public nutrition were inefficient and partially effective. The public health program was plagued with chronic problems similar to all other government programs due to poor management and overambitious goals set by some government officials who insisted on managing areas in which they had no expertise. Its implementation was slow and costly. By 1983, it was estimated that over 15 percent of Grenada's operating budget was allocated to public health care.

In the area of housing, the PRG embarked on a campaign to repair dilapidated houses on the island. With funds from OPEC, the government provided loans of up to $1,000 per household at repayment terms of as low as $5 per month. Supplemented by the work of voluntary labor, over 2,000 houses were repaired during the four-and-a-half years of the revolution. But like all programs, political favoritism undermined the success of the housing program.

The fourth goal of revolutionary socialism was the construction of a new international airport at Point Salines in Grenada with modern navigational and communications apparatus and a long enough runway to accommodate large and wide-bodied aircraft. It was by far the boldest and most visible project embarked upon by the Bishop government and was enthusiastically supported by the people of Grenada. The building of a new airport in the southwestern corner of the island was inclined to boost tourism and its associated industries. It represented the cornerstone of a new tourist industry that was expected to provide a quick and steady flow of foreign exchange to help finance the rest of the PRG's economic program. It became a token of the regime's conviction and determination to achieve its economic goals against all odds. As Bishop explained, "the airport would be the gateway to our future . . . it is what alone can give us the potential for economic takeoff . . . it can help us to develop the tourist industry more . . . to develop our agro-industries more . . . to export our fresh fruits and vegetables better."[71]

The absence of an international airport with facilities to accommodate modern passenger jet aircraft had, for decades, severely affected the growth of Grenada's economy. The airport at Pearls was situated near the high mountains on the northeastern corner of the island and was exposed to dangerous crosswinds. Built by the British in 1943, Pearls airport was small and geographically remote and was a forty-five minute ride to St. George's on one of the worst roads anywhere in the Caribbean. Whereas Point Salines was near the major tourist area and only twelve minutes from the city. Pearls airport had no landing lights and had to be shut down in the evenings. In addition, its aged terminals and short runway of 5,280 feet were capable of handling only Avro 748 propeller-driven aircraft with up to forty-eight seats. There was hardly any room to expand the runway further at Pearls due to the surrounding topography on three sides and the sea on the fourth. Also, its limited width forced pilots to use a visual rather than an instrument for landing.

This meant that many tourists travelling to Grenada were forced to stay overnight in Barbados or Trinidad, where hotel prices were much higher than those in Grenada. Not only was this expensive for visitors, but they were further inconvenienced by making connecting flights, claiming and reclaiming baggage, and the long waiting period to clear immigration and customs in those countries. It was estimated that some 50 percent of visitors to Grenada annually spent overnight in other islands at approximately U.S. $85 per visitor which meant a loss of U.S.$1.3 million to the country.[72] On account of these and other difficulties experienced by the tourists, tour operators and travel agents found it very difficult to recommend Grenada as a tourist destination to their clients, thus threatening further the future of the island's tourist industry.

As far as the PRG was concerned the solution to these problems lay in the building of a new international airport. Prior to 1979, the NJM leadership had not favored the building of a new airport. But on assuming the reins of power, they changed their mind and decided to commence construction on what was by far the biggest project undertaken in Grenada's history. They were not alone. Long before the PRG committed itself to this project the idea of an airport situated in this part of the island was, in fact, first planned since 1926, and had been the subject of several feasibility studies in the 1950s and 1960s. One study conducted in 1976 by the World Bank identified Point Salines as the most appropriate site for the construction of the new airport. Given the island's mountainous terrain between Pearls and the tourist area, Point Salines was the only area flat enough on which a runway of 9,800 feet could be built at a reasonable cost to accommodate wide-bodied, long-haul jets of the B-747, L-1011, and DC-10 variety, and even this involved filling in some areas covered by the sea.

The new airport would have given Grenada the same direct access to the tourist markets of North America and Europe that Barbados, Antigua, and St. Lucia had. The PRG had repeatedly stated that the building of the new international airport was absolutely necessary to boost tourism and economic development. The importance of the new airport to the island's economy was reiterated at a cofinancing conference of the EEC Commission in Brussels in 1981 by Bernard Coard who said: "in many countries the critical factor at a particular historical moment is to identify the major bottleneck, the major fetter to further rapid economic development and growth of a particular country."[73] In the case of the United States, it was the railroads that created the big push forward; in Grenada's case, it was the construction of the Point Salines airport to bolster the island's economic development.

The project was estimated to cost U.S.$71 million to construct. With Cuba supplying the heavy equipment, steel, cement, fuel, and manpower at a total cost of approximately U.S.$40 million, work on the airport began in January 1980. The PRG was left to raise the remainder of the funds, mainly from the EEC and the radical Arab states. This was no easy task for a small Global South country like Grenada. United States pressure on potential aid donors, particularly the EEC, was so intense that it came close to preventing the cofinancing conference by the EEC to raise U.S.$30 million for the airport project.

Apart from the benefits to Cubans and Grenadians, outside interests also benefited enormously from the project. Contracts were awarded to Layne Dredging Company of Miami to fill the ponds and dredge the runway; Norwich Engineering of Fort Lauderdale to design the fuel storage system; Plessy Airport Company of Britain to supply and install the air traffic control apparatus, navigational and communications systems, and the electronic equipment for the terminal building; and Metex of Finland to supply and install the lighting equipment for the runway, parking lot, and other outdoor facilities.[74]

The PRG had projected that the completion of the airport would increase tourist arrivals on the island by almost 60 percent above the prevailing amount of 32,000 tourists annually, excluding passengers on cruise liners. It was assumed that Grenada's share of total Caribbean tourism would have risen from 0.4 percent in 1981 to 1.0 percent in 1990, which would require a total of 1,225 rooms at a cost of EC$149.9 million. The increased number of tourists was also expected to triple tourist expenditure in the country which, in turn, would stimulate development in related industries such as hotels and other services, domestic agriculture, food supplies, clothing, local crafts, and furniture.[75] The government's predictions were not realized as the number of tourists to Grenada declined by 25 percent, to an all-time low of about 24,864 annually between 1979 and 1982.[76] As a result, the six hotels nationalized by the government operated at a loss and had to be supported by public funds. The island's other privately owned twenty hotels and eight guest houses had to reduce their staff in order to minimize their loss. The decline in the tourist industry seriously affected Grenada's economy.

Although the Point Salines airport was the centerpiece of the revolution, it, no doubt, stretched Grenada's financial resources to their limit. Financial assistance from the EEC was less than what was expected by the PRG, as a consequence of U.S. and British opposition. Libya and Iraq did not provide the extra U.S.$4 million as promised. France, Mexico, and Canada provided regular aid to Grenada. Thus, the PRG was left to find a lot of money from its own resources. It had to allocate EC$15.6 million from its 1983 budget of EC$50.6 million for airport expenditure.[77] The situation generated severe cash flow problems for the government and necessitated stricter expenditure control which incurred the wrath of the private sector. The PRG was forced to raise taxes and introduced a drastic law, which made it mandatory for all commercial banks to deposit 20 percent of their funds with the government. These initiatives did not ease the cash flow problem; in fact, it led to major layoffs in the public sector except the airport project. The PRG made a desperate plea to the Soviets for EC$15 million but the request was denied. Despite the poor shape of the economy, the PRG diverted money and supplies from every possible source in order to complete the airport in time for the fifth anniversary of the revolution in March 1984. As a last resort to rescue the airport project the PRG sought financial assistance from the IMF in August 1983 against its wishes. This move, in itself, was a serious threat to the survival and viability of the revolution since the country's economic policies would in effect be dictated by the IMF. The PRG knew this too well. The experience of the Manley government of Jamaica with the IMF in 1980 was still fresh in the minds of PRG officials. But apparently they had no real alternative. The airport project was unfinished in October 1983 when the regime collapsed.

The fifth goal of revolutionary socialism was to diversify overseas trade and sources of investment—aid, loans, and grants—with a particular view of establishing links with the socialist bloc through the Socialist International. This approach was consistent with the PRG socialist policies of expanding Grenada's trade and obtaining financial assistance from countries outside of its traditional allies. The objective was to steer a new economic course for Grenada and to reduce its dependence on a few Western countries. It was also intended to cushion the impact of U.S. economic sanctions against the island. The PRG diversification strategy is explained by Bernard Coard:

> For us the most important aspect in building an economically independent country (which is the only way that you can truly say that you are politically independent) is the method of diversification—in all ways and in all respects. First, diversification of agricultural production, secondly, diversification of the markets that we sell these products to, thirdly diversification of the sources of our tourism, the variety of countries from which our tourists come. The maximum of diversification, the minimum of reliance upon one country or a handful of countries means the greater your independence, the less able certain people are able to squeeze you, pressurize you and blackmail you. [78]

Based on this perspective, the PRG expanded the island's trade to a number of socialist countries, including China and the former USSR (see table 7.2).

Between 1979 and 1983, the Bishop government successfully obtained loans and grants from several socialist and capitalist countries and international organizations. This accomplishment is charted in table 7.3 in which Cuba provided over 30 percent of the total economic and military assistance to the island. The Soviet Union contributed much more military aid than economic assistance, which was merely a trickle. The Soviets were slow and cautious in establishing ties with the PRG. Several reasons accounted for their cautious approach. One was they wanted to avoid a confrontation with the United States over a small and distant island so close to its shores. While they tried to give Grenada every support possible, they did not want their assistance to be seen as provocative to the United States government and the international community. Another reason was the Soviets were content to let Cuba provide most of the aid, especially since the Castro regime had more experience in dealing with other Caribbean nations. Third, they have been burned quite often in the past by giving support to governments which have either squandered that support, or have turned around and become agents of imperialism or lost power as was the case of Egypt, Somalia, Ghana, and Peru. The PRG leaders' perception of the Soviets' cautious approach was that they were still trying to understand them.

Despite the Soviets' cautious approach, relations between Grenada and the USSR intensified by 1983 as aid and trade from the latter increased significantly. The Soviet Union helped the PRG sign trade accords with Bulgaria, Czechoslovakia, East Germany, Hungary, Poland, Romania, and Yugoslavia. The Soviets provided Grenada with construction materials, cars, buses, tractors, generators, a light airplane, arms, communication equipment, and a number of scholarships for academic, technical, military, and security training. The East Germans provided military trucks, equipment for security forces, a printing machine, and technicians to upgrade Grenada's dilapidated telephone system. Bulgaria built an ice-making plant in exchange for spices. Several other countries, including Libya, Algeria, Syria, Iraq, and China, provided technical assistance to build the airport. Algeria in particular pledged to supply all the oil and gas used by machines on the airport project. Aid from the West was quite small and, in most cases, was tied to the purchase of goods and equipment. U.S. aid in particular came primarily through the Caribbean Development Bank and the IMF, both of which did not accede to U.S. requests to limit aid to Grenada.

However, aid from the socialist bloc came with certain costs to Grenada. Most of the military equipment Grenada received from the Soviet Union was outdated and could not be used on the island because of lack of spare parts. At times the PRG found itself in severe financial straits, as aid arrived later than expected. When aid arrived, it was in the form of tied grants or short-term trade credits and could not be used for balance of payment purposes.

Instead of improving Grenada's economy and reducing its dependence on its traditional partners, the PRG's diversification strategy generated hostile reaction from the U.S. and some CARICOM countries. It was an enormously costly burden for the revolution in its early development phase. As shown in table 7.2, there was no significant increase in Grenada's exports to the socialist countries during the PRG's tenure in office.

The sixth and final goal of revolutionary socialism concerned Grenada's foreign policy with ideology as its main tenet. It was designed to defend and advance the revolution both at home and abroad. Characterized by political, security, and economic issues, ideology led the PRG to look to Cuba and the Soviet bloc as the main source of support for the revolution. The PRG leadership was genuinely convinced that communist nations had a greater concern than the core capitalist countries for the plight of the peoples in the Global South. They also seemed to believe that once they had established their Marxist-Leninist credentials and played a greater role for the Soviets on the world stage, they could expect massive assistance from the Soviet Union and its allies to support their development program. This was under-stood from their observation of both Cuba and Nicaragua, which have been accorded a high ranking in Moscow's order of priorities in the Caribbean. As Richard Jacobs, then Grenada's ambassador to the USSR, observed:

> For Grenada to assume a position of increasingly greater importance [in the Soviets' eyes], we have to be seen influencing at least regional events. We have to establish ourselves as the authority on events in at least the English-speaking Caribbean, and be the sponsor of revolutionary activity and progressive developments in this region at least.[79]

One of the main objectives of the PRG foreign policy was "One Caribbean," specifically meant to promote the idea that Cuba should no longer be isolated from the rest of the region, but should be united within the Caribbean family of nations. The PRG was strongly opposed to U.S. policy in the region. It was in this context that the United States became the real focal point of PRG foreign policy when it came to power. It was based on the premise that its own foreign policy was by definition non-aligned and peaceful, but that the nature of U.S. imperialism made good relations between the two countries almost impossible to maintain. From the beginning, the PRG anticipated opposition from Washington and it continued to view every U.S. gesture in the light of this expectation. Negative press reports on the revolution in the U.S. were viewed by the Bishop regime as evidence of the U.S. government anti-PRG propaganda while positive media coverage was interpreted as the

Table 7.2
Grenada's Trade with Socialist Countries 1979-1983
(millions in EC dollars)

	1979	1980	1981	1982	1983
EXPORTS					
China	0.67	0.00	0.00	0.00	0.00
Cuba	0.00	0.22	0.19	0.11	0.42
Czechoslovakia	0.00	0.00	0.00	0.09	0.00
German Democratic Republic	0.00	0.00	0.00	0.02	0.00
Poland	1.07	0.48	0.00	0.00	0.00
USSR	0.00	0.00	0.00	1.73	2.49
Total	**1.74**	**0.70**	**0.19**	**1.95**	**2.91**
All Nations	**55.61**	**44.51**	**50.28**	**47.75**	**48.46**
IMPORTS					
Bulgaria	0.00	0.00	0.00	0.00	0.03
China	0.62	0.66	0.31	0.66	1.05
Cuba	1.39	2.74	2.74	33.67	24.02
Czechoslovakia	0.26	0.26	0.22	0.30	0.21
German Democratic Republic	0.10	0.10	0.27	0.40	15.75
Hungary	0.12	0.12	0.07	0.02	0.13
North Korea	0.00	0.00	0.00	0.00	0.10
Poland	0.20	0.12	0.12	0.12	0.09
Romania	0.00	0.00	0.00	0.00	0.02
USSR	0.08	0.26	4.16	0.30	0.18
Yugoslavia	0.00	0.00	0.00	0.00	0.02
Unspecified	0.07	0.11	0.10	0.09	0.00
Total	**2.73**	**4.37**	**7.99**	**35.56**	**41.60**
All Nations	**117.98**	**135.57**	**146.71**	**152.42**	**154.48**

Source: *Annual Digest of Trade Statistics 1982* (St. George's: Government of Grenada, Central Statistical Office), 1983.

Note: E.C. (Eastern Caribbean) Dollars, EC$2.70 = U.S.$1.00

Table 7.3
Major Grants and Loans to Grenada by Source 1979-1983
(millions in U.S. dollars)

Source	Economic Grant	Military Grant	Loans
Socialist Countries			
Cuba	36.60	3.1	
Czechoslovakia	0.00	0.7	
German Democratic Republic	1.50	0.1	2.1
North Korea	0.00	1.3	
USSR	2.60	10.4	
Radical Third World Nations			
Algeria	2.3		
Iraq	7.2		
Libya	0.3		10.4
Syria	2.4		
Other Nations			
Canada	2.9		
Finland (Metex)	0.00		7.3
Nigeria	0.10		
UK Government	0.40		
UK (Plessy Ltd.)	0.00		1.9
Venezuela	0.60		
International and Intergovernmental Agencies and Banks			
Caribbean Development Bank	1.10		7.40
Eastern Caribbean Currency Authority			1.90
European Development Fund	2.70		2.10
EEC Emergency Fund	0.30		
IMF			6.60
Organization of American States	0.40		
OPEC	0.00		2.00
Underdevelopment Program	0.40		
UNICEF/Food and Agriculture Organization	0.10		
Nonspecified	0.70		5.70
Total	62.60	15.6	47.40

Source: Frederick L. Pryor, *Revolutionary Grenada: A Study in Political Economy* (New York: Praeger, 1986).

Note: Data does not include commercial banks.

PRG's ability to strike back against the imperialist forces. The PRG leaders' predisposition to suspect a CIA plot behind every sinister event in Grenada, whether related to the U.S. or not, doomed any hope of establishing even a civic dialogue between the two governments. Strictly because of Grenada's small size and limited resources, the regime could not afford to alienate potential sources of aid by openly asserting its communist allegiance. This consideration, along with its pro-Soviet stance, but rhetorical non-alignment, and its constant and vehement condemnation of imperialism—a concept which it used strictly as a synonym for U.S. hegemony in the Caribbean and elsewhere—explains the paradoxical nature of the PRG's foreign policy.

Cuba was the chief supporter of the PRG soon after it came to power. Not only was Cuban influence profound, but it was the only communist regime in a position to provide real moral and material support for the PRG during its first few days in office. Cuba not only supported the coup itself, but within a month supplied the regime with weapons and advisors to repel an attack by Gairy or other counterrevolutionaries. In return, the Bishop regime became an unfailing loyal ally of the Cuban revolution. In a letter to the Cuban dictator, Bishop remarked: "In whatever ways and at whatever price, the heroic internationalist people of Cuba can always count on total solidarity, support, and cooperation of the Grenadian revolution."[80]

The close ties developed between the Grenadian government and the Castro regime resulted in a strident and absurd exchange between Grenada and the U.S. This was evident during the early days of the revolution when Bishop requested the extradition of Gairy, whom he claimed was planning an invasion of Grenada from his exile in the United States. Frank Ortiz, then U.S. ambassador to Barbados and the Eastern Caribbean, assured Bishop that Gairy was under FBI surveillance and that while on U.S. soil he would not be permitted to indulge in any activities aimed at toppling the PRG. Then an arrogant Ortiz warned Bishop about the consequences of seeking assistance from Cuba. He said: "Although my government recognizes your concerns over allegations of a counter-coup, it also believes that it would not be in Grenada's best interests to seek assistance from a country such as Cuba to forestall such an attack. We would view with displeasure any tendency on behalf of Grenada to develop closer ties with Cuba."[81] But the straw that broke the camel's back was when Ortiz lectured and threatened Coard and Bishop in their offices, and then gave the same lecture and the same threats to the head of security at the airport.

Ortiz's actions infuriated Bishop, who three days later on April 13, in a radio address to mark the NJM's first month in power, delivered the most famous speech of his life. His "Backyard" speech criticized alleged U.S.

efforts to dictate Grenada's foreign policy and became the basis for the wide-spread view that Grenada was pushed into the communist camp by the heavy-handed tactics of the United States government. The speech was a stinging rebuke of Ortiz's threats against the PRG leadership:

> From day one of the revolution we have always striven to have and develop the closest and friendliest relations with the United States, as well as Canada, Britain, and all our Caribbean neighbors. . . . But no one must misunderstand our friendliness as an excuse for rudeness and meddling in our internal affairs, and no one, no matter how mighty and powerful they are, will be permitted to dictate to the Government and people of Grenada who we can have friendly relations with and what kind of relations we must have with other countries. . . . . When Grenada requested aid, the United States, the wealthiest country in the world, offered $5,000. . . . If the government of Cuba is willing to offer us assistance we would be more than happy to receive it. . . . No country has the right to tell us what to do or how to run our country, or who to be friendly with. . . . We do not therefore recognize any right of the United States of America to instruct us on who we may develop relations with and who we may not. We are not in anybody's backyard and we are definitely not for sale. Anybody who thinks they can bully us or threaten us, clearly has no understanding, idea, or clue as to what material we are made of. . . . Though small and poor, we are proud and determined.[82]

Bishop's speech represented a turning point for Grenada and the revolution. It was a nationalist appeal aimed at mobilizing grassroots support for the PRG against U.S. aggression. His anti-imperialist stance allowed the PRG to gain access to international funding for its projects, not only from Cuba, but also from countries such as China, North Korea, a few Arab states, and the Soviet Union. There is little doubt that, in terms of these objectives, the approach was successful. For quite some time funds poured in from these and other countries to finance several projects, including the construction of the new airport. The speech was also an attempt for Bishop to exploit his encounters with Ortiz as justification for the secret arrival in Grenada of Cuban arms and advisors that the regime could no longer conceal from the public. Also, requests for military assistance from the West without any follow-up led many in Washington to believe that Bishop had deliberately staged the confrontation with the United States. Finally, the speech set the tone for the PRG to portray Grenada to the world as a small, poor but proud developing country struggling to develop its economy and rid itself from its dependence on the core countries, and trying desperately to better its lot, but was being bullied and pressured at every turn by imperialist America. In the words of Prime Minister Bishop:

> From the first days of coming to power, the United States pursued a policy which showed no respect for our national pride and aspirations, and sought constantly to bring the revolution to its knees . . . we conclude that such an attitude [by the U.S.] exists principally because Grenada has taken a very decisive and firm step on the road to genuine national independence, nonalignment, and self-determination.[83]

Many reporters and analysts of the events in Grenada agreed with the Bishop regime that the United States caused much of the tension in the relationship and argued that U.S. heavy-handed policy pushed Grenada to Cuba and to the socialist bloc. This was also the view of one church group: "Through its attempts to dictate policy to the Grenada government, the United States had provoked the very development it sought to avoid."[84] Similarly, in his study of Grenada, Hugh O'Shaughnessy stated that: "It is ironic that the Cuban-Grenadian relationship should have been fostered by Washington, whose constant harping on the supposed strategic threat from a tiny Eastern Caribbean island caused by the New Jewel Movement to militarize their society more than they might otherwise have done."[85]

Determined to set a new course for Grenada on the international scene, the PRG, in 1979, embarked on a militant foreign policy which supported the non-aligned movement, a New International Economic Order based on equity and fairness, and leftist regimes and movements in the Caribbean and beyond. It stressed, among other things, the right to self-determination of all peoples; respect for sovereignty, territorial integrity, and legal equality of all states; an end to all forms of destabilization measures in the Caribbean by the United States; the right for the Caribbean to exist as a zone of peace and for the U.S. to accept ideological pluralism as a basis for the coexistence of states with different social and political systems. The PRG's foreign policy goals were outlined in its manifesto.

> We fully support the Organization of non-Aligned Nations in their courageous attempts to prevent big-power domination of their economies and internal politics. . . . We condemn in the strongest possible terms the intervention of the U.S.A. in the internal affairs of the South East Asian countries and the genocidal practices being committed on their peoples. We support in particular the heroic struggle of the people of Vietnam and Cambodia. We reject the right of the U.S.A. or any other big power to control the economies and lives of any people anywhere. We support fully

the liberation struggles being waged by our African Brothers in South Africa, S. W. Africa, Rhodesia, Mozambique, Angola, and Guinea-Bissau for self-determination.[86]

The PRG also articulated policies in support of national liberation movements in Africa, Asia, and Latin America and called for an end to U.S. domination of Puerto Rico, economic sanctions against Cuba and Nicaragua, and the return of Guantanamo Bay to Cuba.[87] Part and parcel of this strategy was an insistence on the regime's sovereign right to establish relations with countries other than its traditional allies, and the right for its sovereignty to be respected by other states as it would be theirs. As Bishop put it: "Small as we are, and poor as we are, as a people and as a country we insist on the fundamental principles of legal equality, mutual respect for sovereignty, non-interference in our internal affairs and the right to build our own process free from outside interference, free from bullying, free from the use of threat of force."[88]

In the Commonwealth Caribbean, the PRG had cordial relations with the socialist regimes in Guyana and Jamaica as well as leftists in those countries who saw the NJM as essentially a left-wing social democratic party. Among its nonsocialist neighbors, the NJM maintained conventional diplomatic contacts with the governments of Antigua, Trinidad and Tobago, Barbados, Dominica, St. Vincent, St. Lucia, and St. Kitts-Nevis through its Ministry of Foreign Affairs. These were aimed at promoting the political and economic objectives of the government, gaining recognition and diplomatic support, influencing regional institutions, and obtaining a fair share of international aid. It also established close ties with leftist groups in the region and supported an integrated Caribbean that will weed out the powerful force of imperialism in the region. As the NJM manifesto declared: "We support completely the political and economic integration of the Caribbean. But . . . we believe in real and genuine integration of all the Caribbean for the benefit of all the people. . . . We stand firmly committed to a nationalist, anti-imperialist, anti-colonialist position."[89]

Despite U.S. opposition, the PRG established diplomatic and economic relations with Cuba, the Soviet Union, China, a number of socialist states in Eastern Europe, and the radical Arab countries of Algeria, Iraq, Libya, and Syria—countries with strong ties with the former USSR. In addition, the PRG joined the Socialist International and collaborated with some of its members to manipulate the organization into an overtly anti-American posture. The Bishop regime openly supported the Soviet Union at the United Nations on its invasion of Afghanistan in December 1979, and its shooting down of a South Korean passenger aircraft in 1983. At a Socialist International meeting in 1983, Grenada's Foreign Affairs Minister Unison Whiteman rejected the idea put forth by Venezuela on behalf of the United States to add the names of Cuba and the Soviet Union to a group of countries that were supplying arms to El Salvador. The PRG goal was to harness moral, political, and economic support from the socialist bloc so as to counter U.S. policy in the Caribbean and Central America and to stave off and combat its aggression and subversion of Grenada.

Perhaps the most striking thing about Grenada's foreign policy was the high price the PRG paid for its strong support for the Soviet Union and how little it got in return from the Soviets as opposed to Cuba and other foreign donors. The Soviet Union took almost four years to establish a fully manned embassy in Grenada, and provided very little economic aid but a substantial amount of military assistance to the regime. The PRG's foreign policy also contributed to a steady deterioration in relations between Grenada and the United States. The U.S. government attributed the tension in the relationship to the PRG's hostility and suspicion of the United States, which provoked the U.S. policy response. But Grenada had insisted that there were repeated attempts by the PRG to maintain diplomatic ties with the U.S. Charge met countercharge in an increasingly harsh and offensive exchange in which the PRG no doubt achieved a number of propaganda successes, although it must be stated that many were handed to it by the extraordinary awkwardness of U.S. policy.

What the PRG was not able to do, however, was to reduce the real impact of U.S. hostility which by 1983 had resulted in the squeeze of Grenada's economy and extensive military maneuvers just off the island. This led to a rapid increase in military spending and considerable neglect of the economy by the PRG as it became preoccupied with security issues. The result was a major increase in the budget deficit and a significant decline in social services. The situation grew worse with the regime's pro-socialist, anti-U.S. rhetoric, which discouraged tourism to the island and thereby undermined its economy. These factors, combined with Grenada's small size and limited resources, as well as its dependence on tourists mainly from the United States, made it difficult, if not impossible, for the PRG to achieve its militant foreign policy objectives. The year 1983 began with a war of words between Grenada and the United States and ended in a war—with the latter invading the former.

Evaluation of Revolutionary Socialism

Efforts by the PRG to rebuild Grenada's economy after the devastation caused by the Gairy government, to expand the social services, and its daring scheme to build a new international airport were all clearly reformist goals aimed at combating the country's economic dependence on external sources. This was accompanied by the legalization of the PRG, the suspension of the constitution, the judiciary, and other liberal institutions, and the adoption of a radical foreign policy which, together, separated the state from its liberal foundations. It was an attempt to create a patriotic, politically aware, and educated Grenada and state mobilization of the masses to support the goals of revolutionary socialism. Mass organizations and organs of People's Power were developed to promote the concept of participatory democracy and advanced the NJM as a Marxist-Leninist vanguard party. The development of these mass organizations was rationalized on the grounds that political democracy based on the Westminster model was imperialistic in nature. In this context, revolutionary socialism as espoused by the PRG was therefore opposed to the Western type of democracy and, as a result, the real historical experiences of Grenada and the Commonwealth Caribbean were ignored by the Bishop regime.

On the economic front, revolutionary socialism led to the development of a mixed economy that operated under capitalist principles and not on the socialist mode of production advocated by the Bishop regime. Despite this contradiction, Grenada's economic growth rate during the PRG's period in office increased from minus 3.2 percent in 1978 to 2.1 percent in 1979, and to 3 percent each for both 1980 and 1981, and to 5.5 percent in 1983. Per capita income rose from U.S.$450 in 1978 to U.S.$870 in 1983. Tax revenue which was nearly 10 percent higher than what was forecasted by the PRG grew from EC$67.6 million in 1981 to EC$74.1 million in 1983.[90] The rapid expansion of construction associated with the building of the new airport, feeder roads, housing, and community projects increased Grenada's GDP from 2.1, 3, 3.4, and 4 percent over the years between 1979 and 1982. Investment as a percentage of GDP rose sevenfold, from 5.2 percent in 1978 to 36.1 percent in 1982. Airport construction alone averaged 45 percent of total construction investments. The country's unemployment fell from 50 percent of the labor force in 1979 to 12 percent in 1983. Inflation, which averaged 20 percent in 1979, stood at an annual rate of 5 percent in April 1983, and was the lowest in all the Caribbean.[91]

With only 3.7 percent of export earnings or approximately 3 percent of production needed to service the national debt, Grenada had one of the lowest debt ratios not only in the Caribbean but in the entire world. Added to these impressive economic achievements was that by mid-1982 almost a quarter of all goods and services on the island were produced by the thirty-two state-owned enterprises created by the government. Most of Grenada's capital expenditure, which totaled EC$237 million (U.S.$88 million), was externally financed, mainly by Cuba, which in turn increased U.S. hostility against the regime. Henry Gill explains that "Cuba has become the PRG's saviour. This is why Grenada's friendship with Cuba is not negotiable."[92] The PRG also received soft loans and grants from multilateral sources such as the Caribbean Development Bank, the IMF, the European Development Fund, the United Nations Development Programme, OPEC, and several countries, notably Canada, Mexico, and Venezuela. Its continued dependence on foreign funding was a clear indication that attempts by the government to move the economy away from its inherited capitalist characteristics to a socialist-oriented economy was, by 1983, still only marginal.

Grenada's economic achievements under the PRG improved the island's status as a creditworthy nation. This was exemplified by the fact that despite strong U.S. pressure, the IMF agreed to a standby loan of U.S.$14.1 million to the PRG in August 1983, without the harsh conditions it imposed on other Caribbean governments, notably Jamaica and Guyana.[93] Another surprising testament to the Bishop regime's economic success was a glowing report and a favorable comment from the World Bank on the growth and impressive development of most sectors of the island's economy in August 1982. As a proud Bernard Coard stated:

> This massive amount of investment achieved in only four years stands on its own as a remarkable achievement, and it completely overshadows the tiny amounts spent on capital projects during all of Gairy's 25-year dictatorship. . . . [It] reflects the growing confidence which other governments and International Organizations now have in our people and Revolution, and in the ability of the Government to manage the economy.[94]

The government's economic achievements bolstered the island's GDP which between 1979 and 1982 grew by approximately 14 percent at a time when the international economy suffered its worst downturn since the depression of the 1930s.

In line with its socialist goals, the PRG utilized part of the increased revenue derived from the success of its economic programs to carry out its social reforms aimed at improving the living standard of the masses. Over 14 percent and 22 percent of the 1982-1983 budget were allocated to health care and education respectively, the highest amount anywhere in the region. In addition to providing free secondary education, school lunches, uniforms, books, pencils, and free health care and dental services to the population, the government exempted 30 percent of workers with low incomes from paying taxes and increased family allowances. It also granted financial support to parents with children studying abroad. These social programs were a clear indication of the PRG's commitment to improve the living standards of the working class.

However, there is evidence to suggest that beneath this favorable picture was an economy which, by early 1983, was plagued by numerous economic problems. The combined export earnings from Grenada's major agricultural exports—nutmeg, mace, bananas, and cocoa—fell from U.S.$19.3 million in 1979 to U.S.$11.3 million in 1983 (table 7.4). As illustrated by the figures in table 7.4, the volume of banana exports declined steadily after 1979, as its production fell 12.2 percent in 1982, from 11,384 tons to 9,996. In contrast, cocoa earnings peaked in 1981, but fell by 15 percent in 1982 due to a reduction in prices on the world market, but recovered slightly in 1983. Its volume of exports fell from 5.9 million pounds in 1981 to 4.62 million pounds in 1982 but rose to 4.92 million pounds in 1983. This is also true for nutmeg whose earnings declined sharply during the period.

As evident in table 7.5, these problems were compounded by negative growth rates in the livestock, forestry, fishing, and manufacturing industries. Government services, one of the major sectors within the economy, increased slightly in terms of its contributions to GDP, from U.S.$14.8 million in 1980 to U.S.$15 million in 1983, a rate of growth of only 0.3 percent over the four years. Other sectors that recorded negligible rates of growth in this period were transportation, communications, hotels and restaurants, and retail and wholesale trade. Only the government-owned utilities, electricity, water, and telephone, the Port Authority, and the Marketing and National Import Boards showed a profit. And this was not because of any improvement in their operations, but because the PRG steadily raised taxes, rates, and custom duties. Table 7.5 also revealed that the rate of growth of GDP in real terms increased by 8.7 percent in 1980-81 and 0.7 percent in 1981-82, but fell by 2.7 percent in 1982-83. Over the entire 1980-1983 period there was a growth rate of 1.7 percent. This was a reasonable performance by the economy, especially given the fact that both production and prices of these crops were affected by bad weather, outbreaks of disease, lower prices, and shrinking markets as a consequence of the worldwide recession of the early 1980s. At the same time, private sector investment fell from U.S.$5.8 million in 1980 to U.S. $3.5 million in 1983, while public sector investment grew from nearly 13 percent in 1979 to about 35 percent in 1982. Earnings from the tourist sector dropped sharply, from U.S.$19.5 million in 1979 to U.S.$14.7 million in 1983. Grenada's high reliance on imports bloated the trade deficit, which increased from U.S.$25.9 million in 1979 to U.S.$45.7 million in 1983.[95] Claremont Kirton, an economic advisor to the PRG, has examined its policy on private capital and concludes that:

> Despite the wide ranging attempts by the PRG to promote the confidence of private capital and to improve the investment climate, the dominant response of private capital was an unwillingness to operate beyond the performance of minimum tasks . . . the private sector remained uncertain and apprehensive about future PRG policies citing government's ideological posture and related implications as major deterrents.[96]

The decline in labor discipline, which the PRG's policies encouraged, and the state control of the import-export trade contributed to the collapse of business confidence and a sharp reduction of private investment as several businessmen fled the country. The decline in private sector investment was accompanied by a drastic reduction in foreign and domestic reserves, poor management, shortage of skilled personnel, and political cronyism in the public sector. The PRG also had a habit of placing supporters in influential positions for which they were not trained or qualified. The economy was further burdened by government extravagances, such as extra large security for NJM leaders, international meetings and tours of foreign countries by government officials for purely ideological purposes, and the subsidization of foreign advisors to the regime. These developments produced a government deficit that climbed from 16.1 percent of GDP in 1979 to 32.3 percent in 1982, and to crisis proportions by early 1983. This development prompted Finance Minister Coard to inform his colleagues that the government was in desperate financial straits and would face even harder times ahead. As he explains: "The present period reflects the worst period of financial squeeze since the revolution and that 1983-84 will be our hardest year."[97] As the financial crisis continued to dry up funds for capital improvement, the PRG restricted imports, froze salaries and wages in the public sector, reduced capital expenditure, and laid off a number of state employees. These actions caused the vast majority of Grenadians to lose confidence in the revolution and the government which, by 1983, had gained control of the media. As the regime's popularity declined amidst the rising influence of the church and

Table 7.4
Grenada's Major Exports, 1979-1983

Item	1979	1980	1981	1982	1983
BANANAS					
Value	3.74	4.11	3.71	3.39	3.24
Volume	31.03	27.46	22.41	21.17	19.53
Unit Value	0.12	0.15	0.17	0.16	0.17
COCOA					
Value	10.03	6.76	7.06	4.62	4.06
Volume	5.34	4.11	5.90	4.62	4.92
Unit Value	1.88	1.64	1.20	1.00	0.83
MACE					
Value	0.89	0.68	0.63	0.93	0.76
Volume	0.74	0.55	0.46	0.72	0.75
Unit Value	1.20	1.24	1.37	1.29	1.02
NUTMEG					
Value	4.60	3.16	3.02	3.02	3.25
Volume	5.07	3.35	3.79	4.50	5.34
Unit Value	0.91	0.94	0.80	0.67	0.61
FRESH FRUITS					
Value	0.36	0.28	0.49	1.67	4.14
Volume	1.43	0.85	1.73	5.69	15.17
Unit Value	0.25	0.33	0.28	0.29	0.27
CLOTHING					
Value	0.37	0.88	2.17	2.43	1.77
OTHER					
Value	0.64	0.98	1.54	1.76	1.21
TOTAL EXPORTS					
Value	**21.41**	**17.39**	**19.02**	**18.57**	**18.92**

Source: Government of Grenada, *National Economic Report, 1979-1983*, St. George's, Grenada.

Note: Value is in millions of U.S. dollars; volume in millions of pounds; unit value is in U.S. dollars per pound.

Chapter 7

Table 7.5
Grenada's Gross Domestic Product by Industry, 1980-1983

Item	1980	1981	1982	1983	Growth Rate (%)
Agriculture	14.8	16.5	14.5	16.2	2.3
Crops	12.5	15.2	12.8	14.5	3.8
Livestock, Forestry, and Fishing	2.3	1.3	1.6	1.7	-7.3
Manufacturing	2.0	2.1	2.4	1.9	-1.3
Quarrying	0.7	0.8	0.9	0.7	
Utilities	1.5	1.5	1.5	1.5	
Construction	3.7	6.6	9.7	7.7	20.0
Transportation and Communications	5.2	5.3	5.8	5.5	1.4
Hotels and Restaurants	3.1	3.1	3.0	3.1	
Retail and Wholesale Trade	12.8	12.5	13.3	12.8	
Housing & Financing	4.5	4.5	4.9	4.9	2.2
Government Services	14.8	14.9	15.0	15.0	0.3
GDP per Capita	74.5	83.2	82.5	79.8	1.7

Source: Government of Grenada, *National Economic Report, 1979-1983*, St. George's, Grenada.

other national groups, it seized the premises of the island's leading news paper and imprisoned hundreds of its opponents on trumped-up charges. The aim was to silence reaction and solidify the revolution.

By 1983, efforts to solve Grenada's economic problems were hampered by an internal power struggle between Prime Minister Bishop and Deputy Prime Minister Coard. But even without this incident, in all probability, the goals of revolutionary socialism could not have been successfully executed primarily because of the island's geopolitical position within the U.S. sphere of influence. Ralph Gonsalves has pointed out that "the pace at which the state disengages from imperialism and embraces socialism internationally depends on its geopolitical position. A Caribbean country is probably more circumscribed in its actions by its giant neighbor, the United States, than say a non-strategic state in Africa."[98] The seizure of power in March 1979, the suspension of liberal politics, and the adoption of revolutionary socialism were actions resisted by those committed to democracy and the free enterprise system. These actions initiated a period of conflict and heightened competition as Grenada became a bone of contention between the U.S. and the USSR. In a tight bipolar world dominated by the two superpowers, there was little space in the international system for miniscule countries such as Grenada to chart a new and radical course. Thus, after some impressive achievements in the economy and in social services in the first three years of the PRG, revolutionary socialism collapsed under its own weight.

In sum, the strenuous efforts of the PRG to transform Grenada's economy and erase the legacy of its dependency and underdevelopment met with little success. From the outset, the NJM leadership sought to construct a party organization on strict, disciplined Marxist-Leninist lines with the aim to create a socialist state based on equality and justice. Bernard Coard, the party's chief Marxist-Leninist theoretician was first and foremost a man of doctrinaire principle who believed that only radical social and economic transformation of the island's economy could eradicate its dependency. This, however, did not happen. For one reason, the achievements of the PRG in the economic and social spheres were essentially reformist in character. While it suspended the constitution and the judiciary, capitalism and other traditional institutions such as the church were not seriously challenged. Second, efforts to transform Grenada's economy had become intimately bound up with the practical problems posed by its miniscule size and limited resources, a factor the Bishop regime acknowledged but refused to accept as the real cause of the island's economic problems.

Although corruption had been expunged, widespread inefficiency at all levels within the government and personal shortcomings had taken their toll on the economy. By early 1983, the goals of revolutionary socialism had become tenuous as the economy over which Coard presided was at the point of collapse. Private capital from the West declined substantially. To make matters worse, the government did not receive the financial and economic assistance from the socialist countries as promised. And the diversification of trade to the socialist bloc did not reduce its economic dependence on the West. The greatest benefactor during this period was Cuba, but much of its assistance was in the form of manpower, goods, machinery, and services. At this point, Grenada's economy was overextended and overtaxed.

Between 1979 and 1983, the NJM attempted to build a Marxist-Leninist state in Grenada, but succeeded in erecting a radical populist dictatorship that allied politically and military with the Castro regime in Cuba, the Soviet

Union, and the Eastern bloc. By mid-1983, it was apparent that neither its connections abroad nor its resources at home were sufficient to meet even the minimum expectations the regime had raised. The PRG delivered far less than it promised, in part, because of its inability to attract significant international economic assistance, and possibly because the only thing it had to offer besides spices and beaches was its international allegiance to Cuba and the Soviet bloc in return for weapons and political advice.

At all cost, reasons had to be found for collective and individual failures, the difficulties encountered by the PRG in its attempt to establish a socialist state, and the downward slide of the economy in 1983. At first, the NJM leadership attributed most of the problems to loose and improper planning of the PRG, organizational mismanagement, and being overworked and fatigued. But Bishop's appeal to the Reagan administration for a détente in political relations in the summer of 1983 was seen as a sign of serious ideological backsliding which provoked Coard. He thought that Bishop had become too powerful and popular as an individual figure and that he had drifted away from Marxism-Leninism and toward social-democratic politics. He feared that Bishop would eventually discard the party and rely instead on popular support and elections to guarantee his power. He also felt that Bishop had bowed to international criticism about the PRG's brand of revolutionary socialism and the lack of democracy and in the process unwittingly allowed the country to be destabilized. As a result, allegations of lack of leadership was specifically directed at Bishop by a group of radicals within the NJM, who supported Coard's anti-imperialist stance. This resulted in a power struggle between the Coard faction and supporters of Bishop that ended in the house arrest and the subsequent murder of Bishop and five members of the cabinet.

The collapse of Grenada's economy and the Bishop regime in October 1983 should not in any way mask the achievements of the first three years of revolutionary socialism in the country. Among them were land reforms, improvements in social services such as health and education, construction of the new international airport, reduction of unemployment and inflation, and the diversification of the country's trade and diplomatic relations. While the policies of the PRG have, for a brief period, stimulated economic growth and brought social benefits to large sections of the population, they have not reduced the basis of foreign domination of the island. The PRG's initial goal to nationalize foreign-owned hotels, banks, and insurance companies was incompatible with its economic strategy of securing financial assistance from the capitalist countries and Western financial institutions.

In like manner, the regime's retreat from its policy to establish a state monopoly of foreign imports resulted from the more sober reality of the extent of capitalism in Grenada, which was embedded in the three main sectors of the island's economy—agriculture, tourism, and distribution. Its failure to make substantial inroads in the transformation of these sectors, and the elimination of the other structural weaknesses of the economy, notably dependence on imports, aid, and loans, has significantly increased Grenada's dependence. Thus revolutionary socialism which embraced the Soviet theory of noncapitalist development and the principles of Marxist-Leninist doctrine was not a practical solution to develop Grenada's fragile economy which continued to be sustained by foreign capital and North American tourists.

Notes

1. The mongoose is a small agile mammal that lives in most tropical countries. It is best known for its vicious attacks on its prey, mostly young chickens and small snakes.

2. George Brizan, *Grenada, Island of Conflict: From Amerindians to People's Revolution* (London: Zed Books, 1984), xvii.

3. Kai P. Schoenhals and Richard A. Melanson, *Revolution and Intervention in Grenada: The New Jewel Movement, the United States, and the Caribbean* (Boulder, Colo.: Westview Press, 1985), 2.

4. Eric Williams, *From Columbus to Castro: The History of the Caribbean, 1492-1969* (London: Andre Deutsch, 1970), 183-85.

5. Anthony Payne, Paul Sutton, and Tony Thorndike, *Grenada: Revolution and Invasion* (New York: St. Martin's Press, 1984), 1.

6. Payne et al., *Grenada,* 2-3; Gregory Sandford and Diane B. Bendahmane, *The New Jewel Movement: Grenada's Revolution, 1979-1983* (Washington, D.C.: Foreign Service Institute, Department of State, 1985), 2.

7. W. R. Jacobs and I. Jacobs, *Grenada: The Route to Revolution* (Havana: Casa de las Americas, 1980), 17.

8. Anthony Payne, *The International Crisis in the Caribbean* (London: Croom Helm, 1984), 5.

9. S. Rottenberg, "Labor Relations in an Underdeveloped Economy," *Caribbean Quarterly* 4, no. 1 (1977): 54.

10. Brizan, *Grenada, Island of Conflict,* 320.

11. M. G. Smith, *Plural Society in the British West Indies* (Kingston: University of the West Indies, 1965), 290.

12. A. W. Singham, *The Hero and the Crowd in a Colonial Polity* (New Haven, Conn.: Yale University Press, 1968), 10; Schoenhals and Melanson, *Revolution and Intervention in Grenada,* 14.

13. Jacobs and Jacobs, *Grenada,* 69.

14. For a summary of the charges brought against Gairy by the British Colonial Office, see the "Report of the Commission of Inquiry into the Control of Public Expenditure in Grenada During 1961 and Subsequently," CMMD 1735, London, HMSO; Government Publications, St. George's, Grenada.

15. Chris Searle, *Grenada: The Struggle against Destabilization* (London: Writers and Readers Publishing, 1983), 10.

16. Fitzroy Ambursley, "Grenada: The New Jewel Revolution," in *Crisis in the Caribbean,* ed. Fitzroy Ambursley and Robin Cohen (New York: Monthly Review Press, 1983), 192, 199.

17. Schoenhals and Melanson, *Revolution and Intervention in Grenada,* 19; Payne et al., *Grenada,* 14.

18. Schoenhals and Melanson, *Revolution and Intervention in Grenada,* 19, 181.

19. Payne et al., *Grenada,* 14.

20. Brizan, *Grenada, Island of Conflict,* 330.

21. Ibid., 332.

22. Ibid., 329-31.

23. Searle, *Grenada,* 15.

24. Jacobs and Jacobs, *Grenada,* 95; Payne et al., *Grenada,* 9.

25. Tony Thorndike, "Grenada: The New Jewel Revolution," in *Dependency under Challenge: The Political Economy of the Commonwealth Caribbean,* ed. Anthony Payne, Paul Sutton, and Tony Thorndike (Manchester: Manchester University Press, 1984), 110.

26. Searle, *Grenada,* 16; Payne et al., *Grenada,* 9; Sandford and Bendahmane, *The New Jewel Movement,* 10.

27. Sandford and Bendahmane, *The New Jewel Movement,* 12; Payne et al., *Grenada,* 10.

28. "The Manifesto of the New Jewel Movement," in *Independence for Grenada: Myth or Reality?* (St. Augustine, Trinidad: University of the West Indies, reproduced in Institute of International Relations, 1973), 154.

29. Ibid., 156.

30. Ibid., 11.

31. Bernard Coard, "The Meaning of Political Independence in the Commonwealth Caribbean," in *Independence for Grenada: Myth or Reality?* (St. Augustine, Trinidad: University of the West Indies, 1974), 70.

32. Payne et al., *Grenada,* 13; Searle, *Grenada,* 22.

33. Schoenhals and Melanson, *Revolution and Intervention in Grenada,* 30; Bruce Marcus and Michael Taber, *Maurice Bishop Speaks: The Grenada Revolution, 1979-1983* (New York: Path Finder Press, 1983), 8.

34. Schoenhals and Melanson, *Revolution and Intervention in Grenada,* 30.

35. Rita Joseph, "The Significance of the Grenada Revolution to Women in Grenada," *Bulletin of Eastern Caribbean Affairs* 7, no. 1 (1981): 16.

36. Jacobs and Jacobs, *Grenada,* 47.

37. Ambursley, "Grenada," 199.

38. Jacobs and Jacobs, *Grenada,* 117.

39. Sandford and Bendahmane, *The New Jewel Movement,* 40.

40. Ralph Gonsalves, "The Importance of the Grenada Revolution to the Eastern Caribbean," *Bulletin of Eastern Caribbean Affairs* (March-April 1979): 8; Thorndike, "Grenada," 112.

41. Karen De Young, "U.S. versus Cuba on Caribbean Isle of Grenada," *Washington Post,* 27 April 1979.

42. Payne et al., *Grenada,* 18.

43. R. A. Ulyanovsky, *Socialism and the Newly Independent Nations* (Moscow: Progress Publishers, 1974); I. Andreyev, *The Non-Capitalist Way* (Moscow: Progress Publishers, 1974); and V. G. Solodwonckov and V. Bogoslovsky, *Non-Capitalist Development: A Historical Outline* (Moscow: Progress Publishers, 1975).

44. Ralph Gonsalves, *The Non-Capitalist Path of Development: Africa and the Caribbean* (London: One Caribbean Publishers, 1981), 2-3.

45. Maurice Bishop, " Imperialism is the Real Problem," in *Selected Speeches, 1979-1981,* ed. Maurice Bishop (Havana: Casa de las Americas, 1982), 190.

46. New Jewel Manifesto, 143.

47. Jorge Heine and Leslie Manigat, *The Caribbean and World Politics: Cross Currents and Cleavages* (New York: Holmes and Meier, 1988), 184.

48. *Is Freedom We Making! The New Democracy in Grenada* (St. George's, Grenada: People's Revolutionary Government, 1982), 22; Thorndike, "Grenada," 107.

49. Bernard Coard, *To Construct from Morning: Making the People's Budget in Grenada* (St. George's: Fedon Publishers, 1982), 150.

50. Wallace Joefield-Napier, "Macroeconomic Growth under the People's Revolutionary Government," in *A Revolution Aborted: The Lessons of Grenada,* ed. Jorge Heine (Pittsburgh: University of Pittsburgh Press, 1991), 84-85.

51. Bernard Coard, *Report on the National Economy for 1981 and the Prospects for 1982* (St. George's: Grenada Government Printing Office, mimeo, 1982), 64.

52. Coard, *Report on the National Economy for 1981,* 9; Grenada Chamber of Commerce, *Annual Report for 1982* (St. George's: mimeo, 1982).

53. People's Revolutionary Government, *Report on the National Economy for 1982 and the Budget–Plan for 1983 and Beyond* (presented to the National Conference of Delegates of Mass Organizations, St. George's, Grenada, 24 February 1983), 31.

54. Heine, *A Revolution Aborted,* 19.

55. Courtney A. Smith, *Socialist Transformation in Peripheral Economies* (London: Avebury, 1995), 95.

56. Payne et al., *Grenada,* 23.

57. *Report on the National Economy for 1982,* 24-25.

58. Sandford and Bendahmane, *The New Jewel Movement,* 70.

59. *Grenada Is Not Alone,* Speeches by the People's Revolutionary Government (St. George's: Fedon Publishers, 1982), 51.

60. Schoenhals and Melanson, *Revolution and Intervention in Grenada,* 49; Sandford and Bendahmane, *The New Jewel Movement,* 71.

61. Chris Searle, *Words Unchained* (London: Zed Books, 1984), 44.

62. Schoenhals and Melanson, *Revolution and Intervention in Grenada,* 51.

63. Sandford and Bendahmane, *The New Jewel Movement,* 72; Gregory Sandford and Richard Vigilante, *Grenada: The Untold Story* (New York: Madison Books, 1984), 72.

64. Maurice Bishop, "Education Is a Must," in *Education Is a Must,* ed. Maurice Bishop and Chris Searle (London: Education Committee of the British Grenadian Friendship Society, 1980), 39.

65. Smith, *Socialist Transformation,* 110.

66. C. A. Glean, "Reaching beyond the Grasp: A Revolutionary Approach to Education," *Bulletin of Eastern Caribbean Affairs* 7, no. 1 (1981): 10.

67. Schoenhals and Melanson, *Revolution and Intervention in Grenada,* 53.

68. Paul Seabury and Walter A. Mc Dougall, eds., *The Grenada Papers* (San Francisco: Institute for Contemporary Studies, 1984), 77-78.

69. Sandford and Bendahmane, *The New Jewel Movement,* 67.

70. Gordon K. Lewis, *Grenada: The Jewel Despoiled* (Baltimore: Johns Hopkins University Press, 1987), 28.

71. Marcus and Taber, *Maurice Bishop Speaks,* 30.

72. Smith, *Socialist Transformation,* 135.

73. Payne et al., *Grenada,* 33.

74. Schoenhals and Melanson, *Revolution and Intervention in Grenada,* 56.

75. Clive Thomas, *The Poor and the Powerless: Economic Policy and Change in the Caribbean* (New York: Monthly Review Press, 1988), 240-41.

76. Payne et al., *Grenada,* 26.

77. *Report on the National Economy for 1982,* 156; Payne et al., *Grenada,* 34.

78. Chris Searle, "Grenada's Revolution: An Interview with Bernard Coard," *Race and Class* 21, no. 2 (1979): 179.

79. "Grenada's Relations with the USSR," report from Grenada's Ambassador to Moscow, Richard Jacobs, 11 July 1983, Government Document unnumbered, 5, 7.

80. Maurice Bishop, "Forward Ever! Against Imperialism and Towards Genuine National Independence and People's Power," in *Maurice Bishop Speaks,* ed. Marcus and Taber, 82.

81. Thorndike, "Grenada," 115.

82. Chris Searle, ed., *In Nobody's Backyard: Maurice Bishop's Speeches, 1979-1983* (London: Zed Books, 1984), 11, 14.

83. Ibid., 237.

84. Ecumenical Program for Inter-American Communication and Action, *Grenada: The Peaceful Revolution* (Washington, D.C., 1982), 61.

85. Hugh O'Shaughnessy, *Grenada: Revolution, Invasion, and Aftermath* (London: Sphere Books, 1984), 105.

86. "The Manifesto of the New Jewel Movement," in *Independence for Grenada,* 154.

87. *Grenada Is Not Alone,* 105-109; Anthony Payne, "The Foreign Policy of the People's Revolutionary Government," in *A Revolution Aborted,* 127-29.

88. Bishop, "Forward Ever!" 118.

89. "The Manifesto of the New Jewel Movement," in *Independence for Grenada,* 154.

90. *Report on the National Economy for 1982,* 16.

91. Thomas, *The Poor and the Powerless,* 247.

92. Henry Gill, "The Foreign Policy of the Grenada Revolution," *Bulletin of Eastern Caribbean Affairs* 7 (March-April 1981): 2.

93. Payne et al., 25.

94. *Report on the National Economy for 1982,* 16-17.

95. Napier, "Macroeconomic Growth," 94-95.

96. Claremont Kirton, "Public Policy and Private Capital in the Transition to Socialism: Grenada 1979-1983," mimeo (1985): 32.

97. *Report on the National Economy for 1983,* 7.

98. Gonsalves, *The Non-Capitalist Path of Development,* 9.

Chapter 8

U. S.-Led Destabilization of Guyana, Jamaica, and Grenada

Throughout most of the twentieth century, and especially during the period of the Cold War, the most formidable threat to progressive and independent governments in the Caribbean basin came principally not from the Soviet Union or the former European colonial powers, but from the United States, whose policies, goals, and interests in the area followed a long imperialist tradition. The United States policy in the Caribbean region is distinguished from its policy towards Latin America by its readiness, willingness, and ability to intervene both overtly and covertly in support of its interests. The most rabid imperialist policies of the U.S. in the Western Hemisphere were openly advanced by the Monroe Doctrine of 1823, Manifest Destiny conceptions of the 1840s and beyond, and the notorious Platt Amendment of 1901,which made Cuba a protectorate of the U.S.

The Monroe Doctrine, apart from warning the European powers to stay out of the Western Hemisphere, was a blend of national self-interest, a realistic recognition of the status quo, and a declaration of economic intent, later to become the sphere of influence politics of the twentieth century. This was so because the United States at the time was composed of only twenty-four states and was hardly in a position to take on the world and so it indicated its acceptance of the status quo. Yet beneath these political considerations lurked the ambition of a nation which already regarded itself as a trader and a world leader. This was buttressed by the Roosevelt Corollary of 1904 when the United States unilaterally established itself as an international police power in the region and parts of Asia, to the projection of Roosevelt's Good Neighbor Policy in 1934 as shown in table 8.1. The Good Neighbor Policy was intended to change the image of the United States from a bully to a friendly nation, especially among its Latin American neighbors.

Although the Monroe Doctrine accepted the status quo and indicated an intention not to interfere in the internal affairs of Latin America countries, the United States during the nineteenth and twentieth centuries emerged as the world's leading capitalist power and began to impose its will upon other nations with little regard for moral scruples or international law. To this must be added that its sheer distance from any other major power willing or able to threaten it had rendered it invulnerable from any serious military threat. America, in a word, stood at the top of the world, and the belligerent rhetoric of its leaders, especially since the Monroe Doctrine, reflected a new national mood in that those who control its destiny felt that they were entitled to dispense justice and leadership to other nations in the manner of the old colonial powers of a previous era. This new American empire has been built on a capitalist expansionist economic system.

Since capitalism, by its very nature, is inherently expansionist, and since imperialism, seen as the last stage of capitalism is even more so, means that the American empire, like all other empires before it, has been characterized, certainly, since the period of the Civil War of the 1860s, by a history of overseas economic penetration and overseas military interventionism mainly designed to protect and expand that penetration. The record is well known and has been frequently documented in chapter 4 and elsewhere. Suffice to say that there were countless occupations or interventions by U.S. troops in the affairs of a considerable number of Caribbean Basin countries, all of them designed to make the region the great American archipelago.[1]

The U.S. also encouraged and supported several Caribbean and Central American regimes deemed friendly to its interests, including Batista of Cuba, Duvalier of Haiti, and Trujillo of the Dominican Republic. Alongside all of this was the expansion of its military bases in the Caribbean, some imposed by treaty, as with Guantánamo Bay in Cuba, others through the exchange of destroyers for ninety-nine-year leases from Britain in territories of Antigua, the Bahamas, Guyana, Jamaica, St. Lucia, and Trinidad and Tobago (see table 8.2). This resulted from Britain's inability to defend adequately this portion of its empire, its commitment of its limited strategic resources to Europe and Asia, and the need to protect the Caribbean from invasion by Germany and the axis powers during the war. It was largely in this context that the U.S. assumed the role of leader in the region. It also meant, among other things, the Latin Americanization of the Monroe Doctrine, which initially was a defensive declaration against further European colonization of the region, became transmuted into an offensive principle for the active pursuit of U.S. interests.

U. S. Destabilization of the Caribbean

In the Caribbean, the practice of destabilization by the United States government began in the early 1960s, following the emergence of the Soviet Union as a rival to America's hegemony in the region. It emerged as a product of superpower rivalry during the Cold War hysteria that led to the spread of leftist movements in the Caribbean Basin and the development of an active foreign policy by various U.S. administrations to confront radical ideologies in the region. This policy dates back to the resolution adopted at the Tenth Inter-American Conference held in Caracas, Venezuela, in 1954 that affirmed the incompatibility of communism with the Inter-American capitalist system. It became the sound basis for an active American policy of intervention in and destabilization of the region.

In the Hispanic Caribbean and Central America this policy became the hallmark of a series of nefarious CIA operations directed against Guatemala in 1954 that led to the overthrow of the Arbenz government and the disastrous Bay of Pigs invasion of Cuba by U.S.-sponsored Cuban exiles in Miami in April 1961 aimed at toppling Fidel Castro and his socialist regime. It was the one defeat suffered by the United States in the Western Hemisphere by Cuba, which remains an irritant to U.S. policy and dominance of the region. Apart from its importance to the international struggle against imperialism, the Cuban revolution also gave the Caribbean region significance in Soviet ideological and national perceptions. From the Soviets point of view, Cuba was construed essentially as a satellite state and a development model which the developing countries in the Caribbean and elsewhere ought to follow.

This was climaxed by a more dramatic event, the military invasion of the Dominican Republic by some 20,000 U.S. marines in April 1965 to prevent the communist regime of Juan Bosch from taking power. The invasion was justified by President Lyndon Johnson's blunt remark that "the American nations, cannot, must not, and will not permit the establishment of another communist government in the Western Hemisphere."[2] As far as Johnson was concerned, this was a legitimate claim consistent with Cold War politics and the division of the world into competing U.S. and Soviet Union spheres of influence. In this global struggle, only the most resolute and unwavering resistance could hope to succeed. The challenge was a test of military might, nerve, and moral fiber of the superpowers. This rather narrow perspective completely dominated U.S. foreign policy in the region from the 1960s onwards and allowed no other considerations to affect the nature of the relationship of the United States with the Caribbean or any other subregion within the hemisphere.[3] From the Soviets' point of view, the Caribbean is strategically located in the U.S. backyard, and any weakening of its control in the region inevitably shifts the international struggle between imperialism and communism to the advantage of the latter.

Then came Chile and the Allende tragedy in 1973. This marked the start of a new twist to the concept of intervention and a new understanding of the meaning of destabilization in the region. In this fiasco, no U.S. military personnel ever landed in Chile as they had in the Dominican Republic less than a decade earlier. The removal of the progressive Allende regime in that country was not contrived at first through a military coup, but by the CIA, which established an effective espionage network in the country. With help from local vested interests, the CIA penetrated every fabric of Chilean life and brought the society to the brink of anarchy. By the time the CIA was finished with Chile, many citizens, particularly members of the middle and upper classes, were convinced that the Allende regime intended to destroy virtually everything of value in the country. Such terror and confusion set the stage for General Pinochet and the Chilean army to overthrow and murder Salvador Allende.

This technique was first practiced against Muhammad Mossadeq, the popularly elected and progressive prime minister of Iran in 1953. Respected by Iranians for his uncompromising nationalism, Mossadeq opened Iran to communist influence against the wishes of the U.S. and was destabilized and overthrown by the CIA. The pro-Western Pahlavi Shah, who had escaped to Paris, returned triumphant to the Peacock Throne. With the support of a powerful and oppressive American-trained security apparatus, the Shah maintained his tyrannical and absolute rule over the Iranian people until he was ousted on January 16, 1979, by the Ayatollah Khomeini.[4]

Further refinements in the techniques of intervention set a new pattern in the English-speaking Caribbean, where the rise of leftist revolutions was viewed as symptomatic of a sharp decline of U.S. hegemony in the area. This perception led U.S. policy makers to see any challenge to the political status quo in the region as a consequence of communist subversion. In particular, many in Washington interpreted the revolution in Grenada not as the victory of a frustrated group of people against a brutal and corrupt dictator, but as strong evidence of the growing influence of Cuba and the communist system within the region itself. This attitude derived from a general view of Cold War politics in the Caribbean but was given additional significance in the region by the socialist revolution in Cuba in 1959 and Castro's subsequent close alliance with the Soviet Union. To prevent future communist regimes from appearing all over the Caribbean, various U.S. administrations have responded in the traditional way of hegemonic powers by intervening in the internal affairs of radical and progressive governments in the region.

Although this show of military strength by the U.S. was linked to recent developments in the Caribbean basin, particularly in Cuba, Nicaragua, and Grenada, it is important to understand that the U.S. has a long-established tradition of using force in the region to pursue its geostrategic interests. As already indicated, prior to the Cuban revolution, the U.S. intervened several times against radical governments in Central America and the Caribbean, of which thirty-eight predated the Russian revolution. Thus the expansionist designs of the Monroe Doctrine and the Manifest Destiny conceptions were therefore not the result of the anticommunism rhetoric of the day.

Where designated, appropriate policies of destabilization were fashioned by the U.S. to bring about desired results, as in the case of British Guiana between 1962 and 1963 when American trade unions and CIA influence were used to foment dissent against the elected Marxist PPP government of Cheddi Jagan that subsequently led to its removal from office in December 1964. The U.S. involvement in the internal affairs of Guyana occurred again in the 1970s and early 1980s against the socialist regime of Forbes Burnham; Jamaica, during the 1970s; and Grenada from 1979 onwards. These interventions were part and parcel of a long tradition by the U.S. to intervene in the Caribbean whenever its national interests appeared or alleged to be threatened by leftist regimes opposed to the status quo. The legitimacy of such an interpretation of the Caribbean Basin derives from a perception of the region as vital to U.S. security and economic interests. With regard to security, the interest is derived from geographical proximity, which is based on the notion that the Caribbean Basin countries are in the backyard of the United States, and the region's role as a vital link to U.S. fleets in the North and South Atlantic. In terms of economic interests, since the 1940s, U.S. transnational corporations have invested heavily in virtually every sector of the Caribbean economy. Traditional interests in export agriculture such as bananas and sugar, and in mining, including petroleum and bauxite, have been supplemented by investments in banking, insurance, transportation, construction, tourism, and manufacturing.

The income derived from such huge investment is almost impossible to calculate, but evidence from selected countries shows it to be considerable. According to George Shultz, the former secretary of state in the Reagan administration, "from the U.S. point of view, the Caribbean Basin is vital to our security and to our social and economic well-being. It is indeed our third border. Economic, social, and political events in the Basin have a direct and significant impact in the United States."[5] Shultz was in fact repeating what President Reagan had said to the Organization of American States (OAS) in February 1982 in which he stated that the Caribbean Basin is a vital strategic and commercial artery for the U.S. and that nearly half of the U.S. trade, two-thirds of its imported oil, and over half of its imported strategic minerals pass through the region encompassing the Panama Canal and the Gulf of Mexico. Such statements, especially coming from the highest officials in the U.S. government, are a strong indication of the extension of the Monroe Doctrine and the Manifest Destiny type of imperialism of the past rather than a new way forward.

The rise of socialist regimes in Guyana, Jamaica, and Grenada during the 1970s produced a series of U.S.-led destabilization policies that contributed to the disruption of those countries' political economy. At the core of the destabilization policies was the belief by the U.S. government that the spread of socialist ideology in the Caribbean was a threat to its security. In the interest of that security, presumed or real, the Reagan administration not only undermined the legitimacy of the socialist regimes, but also invaded the tiny island of Grenada. Thus, the policies of the Reagan administration drew on, and added to, a century-old pattern of America's readiness and ability to intervene directly or indirectly in the Caribbean in support of its interests. The intended goal was to put pressure on radical Caribbean governments to change their anti-imperialist positions. It was a direct approach by the U.S. to impose its will on the smaller and weaker governments in the region in order to preserve its hegemonic status and to prevent the development and spread of Marxist ideology in the area.

Destabilization in all its various forms is akin to intervention but distinguished from it by its reliance on both internal and external forces to achieve its desired goals. In practice, it involved an internal campaign of political espionage, economic sabotage, propaganda, a dimension of sense-less violence and brutality, and a series of external economic and financial sanctions by the U.S. government, multinational corporations, and financial institutions. These policies were designed to curtail foreign aid and foreign investment capital to progressive regimes in the region with the intent of toppling them. While destabilization by violence and economic sanctions was obviously disturbing to the countries of the Caribbean, destabilization by propaganda which includes lies, threats, and slander was perceived as more damaging because the primary objective of a propaganda campaign is to create instability and make it unbearable for governments to rule. As Manley explains: "Destabilization describes a situation where some source

Table 8.1
U. S. Imperialist Policies in the Caribbean
(Western Hemisphere)

Year	Policy	President	Political Party	Objective
1823	Monroe Doctrine	James Monroe	Democratic Republican	Created U.S. sphere of influence – political imperialism
1845	Manifest Destiny	James Polk	Democratic	American expansionist view – social and cultural imperialism
1901	Platt Amendment	Theodore Roosevelt	Republican	U.S. imperialistic control of Cuba
1904	Roosevelt Corollary to the Monroe Doctrine	Theodore Roosevelt	Republican	U.S. hegemony in Western Hemisphere – Military Imperialism
1909	Dollar Diplomacy	William Taft	Republican	Protected U.S. economic interests in the Caribbean – economic imperialism
1932	Good Neighbor Policy	Franklin Roosevelt	Democratic	Promoted hemispheric defense – collective security – diplomatic imperialism
1962	Alliance for Progress	John Kennedy	Democratic	Struggle against communism in the Hemisphere – Ideological Imperialism
1982	Caribbean Basin	Ronald Reagan	Republican	Promoted U.S. economic and strategic interests in the Caribbean – Ideological, political, and economic imperialism

Table 8.2
U.S. Military Installations in the Caribbean

Location	Facility	Function	Personnel
Antigua	-Naval Base	-Ocean Research and Tracking	191
	-Air Force	-Tracking Site	70
Bahamas	-Atlantic Underwater and Evacuation Center	-Naval Test Site for Anti-Submarine Warfare Capabilities	45
	-Eastern Test Range	-Airforce Missile Tracking Station	18
Bermuda	-Tudor Hill Lab	-Naval Test Site	28
	-Naval Air Station	-Patrol Aircraft	1,904
	-Naval Base	-Open Research	175
Cuba	-Guantánamo Naval Station	-Operating Base	2,673
Panama	-Fort Amador	-193rd Infantry Brigade Headquarters	465
	-Fort Gulick	-Training School of the Americas	30
	-Quarry Heights Command Center	-Southern Command General Headquarters	278
	-Howard Air Base	-Air Force Tracking and Searching Site	110
	-Camp Santiago Training Site	-U.S. Army & National Guard Training	122
	-Fort Buchanan Army Base	-Naval Base	1,053
Puerto Rico	-Roosevelt Roads Naval Station	-Naval Communication Center	3,009
	-Sabana Seca Communication Site	-Naval Fleet Training	459
	-Vieques Naval Base	-Air National Guard Activities	32
	-Air Force Base		994
TOTAL			**11,658**

Source: U. S. Department of Defense, List of All Military Installations, Authorized Full-Time Personnel, Territories, and Foreign Areas, Washington, D.C., 1993.

either inside or outside a country—or perhaps sources working in concert, one outside and one inside—set out to create a situation of instability and panic by design."[6] In this context, destabilization is similar to the concept of the "fifth column," which is a group within a country that deliberately gives aid and support to the enemy country by engaging in espionage or by acts of sabotage within its own national borders.

During the 1970s, U.S. destabilization, although practiced elsewhere before, represented a new, subtle, and formidable threat to progressive and independent governments in the anglophone Caribbean than the blatant caricature of gunboats and military interventions of a previous era. It was the latest addition to the lexicon of radical leaders in the region who viewed as a means to further control and exploit the poor and weaker countries like those in the Caribbean. Prime Minister Maurice Bishop summarized the concept:

> Destabilization is the name given to the most recently developed method of controlling and exploiting the lives and resources of a country and its people by a bigger and more powerful country through bullying, intimidation, and violence. In the old days, such countries . . . sent in gunboats or marines to take over directly the country by sheer force. . . . Today, more and more the new weapon and the new menace is destabilization. This method was used against a number of Caribbean and Third World countries in the 1960s, and also against Jamaica and Guyana in the 1970s.[7]

Following its successful liquidation of the socialist government of President Salvador Allende of Chile in 1973, the Nixon-Ford administration embarked on an orchestrated campaign of economic and political destabilization of the socialist regimes of Forbes Burnham of Guyana and Michael Manley of Jamaica. It involved the drastic reduction of U.S. aid to and trade with those countries, and cutbacks in loans and grants from the U.S., the IMF, the World Bank, and other multilateral financial institutions. In addition, the United States, along with opposition groups and churches in both countries, launched a vicious propaganda campaign against the two regimes in which nothing was spared. Facts and truths were simply disregarded or replaced with lies and half-truths. The centerpiece of the propaganda campaign was a strident attack on the nationalization policies of Guyana and Jamaica and their close ties with the Castro regime that sowed the seeds of discord and suspicion among the capitalist class, both local and overseas.

These policies continued in a systematic manner during the Carter administration. The result was that by 1980 most if not all of the planned projects in Guyana and Jamaica were stalled, as both countries moved into a state of virtual bankruptcy. In Jamaica, this led to political and economic instability which, in turn, contributed to the defeat of the Manley regime at the polls in October 1980. In Guyana, the Burnham regime was forced to moderate its position and, as a result, retreated from its socialist strategies and hard-line rhetoric against the West, particularly the United States.

Soon after his inauguration in January 1981, President Reagan adopted a policy of hostility against all revolutionary governments in the Caribbean. Determined to get rid of all radical governments in the region, the Reagan administration provided military and economic assistance to a number of Caribbean and Central American countries that supported U.S. interests in the region. In marked contrast, it imposed harsh economic and political sanctions on the radical governments in Nicaragua, Guyana, and Grenada. In the case of Cuba, the Reagan administration policy was that insurgency in the Caribbean and Central America was the direct product of Cuban conspiracy, acting as a surrogate for the Soviets' in the region. It claimed that Cuban policies abroad were directly linked to its relationship to the Soviet Union and that its intervention on behalf of armed struggle in the Caribbean and Central America meant that Cuba had injected the East-West dimensions of the Cold War rivalry into regional conflicts.

Whether or not this was true, it was clear that establishing the truth about Cuba was not an essential part of the Reagan administration's policies, but punishing the Castro regime was. It was against this background that the administration used its power in a variety of ways to prevent loans to Cuba and to tighten the economic blockade on the island, which made it more difficult for the Castro regime to import goods and to sell its products, particularly sugar, on the world market. With some measure of success, the U.S. isolated the Castro regime diplomatically within its Caribbean and Central American neighbors by pressuring Colombia, Costa Rica, and Jamaica, following the defeat of the Manley regime in 1980, to break off relations with Cuba. In 1982 the Reagan administration stepped up its propaganda war on the Castro government with the establishment of Radio Marti, an anti-Castro radio station in the Florida Keys. The administration also conducted a large naval exercise in the Caribbean under the code name "Ocean Venture 82" that involved some 45,000 troops, 60 naval vessels, and 350 aircraft. Part of this strategy came from an influential right-wing think tank that had prepared a report on a "New Inter-American Policy for the Eighties" which stated that:

> Havana must be held to account for its policies of aggression against its sister states in the Americas. Among those steps will be the establishment

of a Radio Free Cuba, under open U. S. government sponsorship, which will beam objective information to the Cuban people that, among other things, details the costs of Havana's unholy alliance with Moscow. If propaganda fails, a war of national liberation against Castro must be launched.[8]

These measures were intended to force the Castro government to retreat from its interventionist policies in the Caribbean, Central America, and Africa, as well as to abandon its close alliance with the former Soviet Union.

In respect to Nicaragua, the Reagan administration suspended President Carter's policy of coexistence with the Nicaraguan government, which even included a small amount of economic assistance and instead mounted a ruthless campaign to destabilize the economy and government of that country. Central to this policy was a decision taken in November 1981 to provide covert military and financial support to anti-Sandinista forces known as the "contras" who were operating from bases in Honduras against the socialist regime of Daniel Ortega. The U.S. also suspended all aid to and trade with Nicaragua, and excluded it from the Caribbean Basin Initiative in 1982. These destabilization policies were consistent with Reagan's 1980 campaign theme of "Resurgent America" which was intended to reassert U.S. hegemony in the Caribbean and Central America where it was seemed to be most threatened by a number of radical governments. In defense of his policy, President Reagan said: "I say to you tonight there can be no question: the national security of all the Americas is at stake in Central America. If we cannot defend ourselves there, we cannot expect to prevail elsewhere. Our credibility would collapse, our alliances would crumble, and the safety of our homeland would be in jeopardy."[9]

U.S.-Led Destabilization of Guyana

During the 1970s, the pursuit of cooperative socialism in Guyana by the Burnham regime was accompanied by the nationalization of the various foreign assets which dominated the country's economy. The government's nationalization policy was so extensive that by 1976 the state had owned and controlled approximately 80 percent of the economy. This development not only alerted the U.S. government to the sort of policies being developed and pursued in Guyana, but also led to a massive boycott of the country's principal products: bauxite and sugar by U.S. multinational corporations; chief among them were the aluminum and sugar companies. At the time of the boycott, there was a dramatic decline in the prices of these items on the world market and a steep rise in the price of oil and manufactured goods. These factors contributed to a serious decline in Guyana's foreign reserves and a deterioration in the country's economy to the point where the state was unable to provide the basic necessities to the population. By early 1978, economic hardships were such that the Burnham regime had to make major cutbacks on capital projects and social services in order to stave off total bankruptcy.[10]

The government's economic problems were compounded by the drastic reduction of U. S. economic assistance to Guyana, the oil crisis of the 1970s, and the economic recession in the core capitalist states, all of which not only increased the country's balance-of-payment deficits but also reduced its imports. The result was that all of Guyana's foreign reserves had practically dried up by the late 1970s. As a consequence, the government turned to the IMF for financial assistance to ease its balance-of-payment problems. This yielded a one-year IMF standby loan of U.S. $15 million negotiated on harsh conditions which the government was unable to meet. The IMF/World Bank conditions included the usual package of deflationary policies: cuts in public expenditure and imports; wage freeze; increased prices and interest rates; elimination of price controls; and the reduction in subsidies on a wide range of items, many of which had been in existence since the colonial period, and the removal of indirect tax increases, e.g., customs duties, licences, and fees.[11]

In the meantime, the U.S. government continued to exert pressure on the Burnham regime as it strengthened economic and political ties with Cuba and the Soviet Union and, had on several occasions voted against U.S. resolutions at the United Nations. As a case in point, in 1979, Guyana voted against the U.S. cosponsored United Nations resolution that condemned the illegal seizure of power in Grenada by the Bishop regime. In response, the U.S. government, in 1980, vetoed a loan of U.S. $20 million earmarked for Guyana from the Inter-American Development Bank. It also jeopardized Guyana's relations with the IMF and the World Bank after it learned that Cuban aircraft en route to the Angolan civil war in Africa were allowed to refuel at Guyana's international airport,[12] recently renamed the Cheddi Jagan International Airport.

Guyana's relations with the IMF-World Bank group, which were already difficult, grew worse in 1980. In that year, Guyana entered into an agreement with the IMF which, over a period of three years, provided resources in the form of special drawing rights (SDR)[13] of G$150 million, in addition to a World Bank structural adjustment loan of U.S. $23.5 million. In exchange for the loans, the Guyana government had to privatize the bauxite industry and reduce the scope of the Guyana Rice Board; reduce public spending and state intervention in the economy; establish an investment code; devalue the country's currency by approximately 40 percent; eliminate price controls; reduce public sector wages and social services; and last, but by no means least, reduce the number of state employees.[14] This stricter austerity plan by the IMF was due to the fact that Guyana had failed to meet the economic growth target of a previous IMF arrangement. Despite the economic crisis, lack of foreign reserves, and Guyana's increasing indebtedness, the PNC government rejected the demands by the IMF. Frustrated by the process and by the policies of the IMF as a whole, Forbes Burnham said: "The only thing that they have not proposed is raising the price of air, and God knows they might have it up their sleeves."[15]

It is important to point out, however, that the treatment accorded to the Burnham regime by the IMF/World Bank and the Carter administration was in sharp contrast to that received by other socialist regimes in the Caribbean, namely the Manley government in Jamaica. Two explanations accounted for this. One was that the U.S. government's influence over the IMF and the World Bank was designed to destabilize Jamaica and topple the Manley regime and replace it with the conservative Edward Seaga and the JLP. The second explanation was that Guyana under Burnham was still imperialism's best bet since the main opposition came from the Working People's Alliance (WPA) and the Marxist PPP and its radical leader, Cheddi Jagan, who was critical of U.S. imperialism in the Caribbean and elsewhere. The fact that both opposition parties in the country were to the left of the ruling PNC partly explains the tolerance and support given to the Burnham government by the IMF/World Bank group and by President Carter in the latter days of his administration.

These factors, however, were ignored by the Reagan administration, whose policies were hostile to the Guyana government because of its close ties with Cuba, its support for the Popular Movement for the Liberation of Angola (MPLA) and Cuba's efforts to defend it, its visits to and contacts with China, the Soviet Union, and Eastern Europe, its role in the NAM, and in the formation of the IBA. The establishment of the bauxite cartel greatly disturbed the U.S. government, which at the time was fearful of the effects of Third World cartels on Western economic interests. OPEC, which spear-headed the oil price increases in the 1970s, is a classic example of what cartels can achieve and this was still fresh on the minds of U.S. policy makers. These developments, along with the Burnham regime's criticism of the Caribbean Basin Initiative (a mini Marshall Plan for the Caribbean), resulted in Guyana's exclusion from the CBI in early 1983. At the same time, the U.S. used its influence and blocked two International Development Bank loans earmarked for the expansion of the agricultural sector in Guyana. Later that year, the U.S. government closed its USAID office in George-town, suspended all U.S. aid to the country, and again blocked Guyana's applications for loans from the IMF, the World Bank, and U.S. commercial banks and financial institutions. Such actions by the Reagan administration were a direct response to the Guyana government's harsh criticism and condemnation of the U.S. invasion of Grenada in 1983, and the Guyana government's refusal to join other Global South countries in support of the U.S. resolution at the UN which condemned the Soviet Union's shooting down of the Korean passenger aircraft, also in 1983.[16]

The Reagan administration went so far as to block technical assistance to Guyana so as to punish the Burnham regime for its radical anti-American position. It also removed Guyana from the list of Caribbean countries that received preferential treatment in terms of aid and trade from the United States. Citing such factors as economic instability, lack of foreign reserves, human rights violations, and the constant rigging of national elections by the Burnham regime, the U.S. government decertified Guyana as a creditworthy nation. And on 15 May 1985, the IMF declared Guyana ineligible to use its financial resources.[17] Not only did the IMF refuse to provide loans to Guyana, but the government did not have access to international credit. The Burnham regime claimed that it was a victim of an orchestrated effort by the U.S. to destabilize its commitment to cooperative socialism aimed to develop the country's economy and eliminate or reduce its economic dependence on the developed countries. In order to keep its economy afloat, the Burnham government borrowed extensively from its Caribbean neighbors, namely Trinidad and Tobago and Barbados.

The Effects of U.S. Destabilization on Guyana

The U.S. destabilization measures, coupled with gross mismanagement of the economy and the public sector, extensive corruption practices, short-age of skills, poor industrial relations, and adverse weather conditions, in that order, brought Guyana's economy to a virtual state of collapse by 1985. The effects of the deflationary pressures were visible in almost every sector of the society. As seen from the data in table 8.3, Guyana's average annual GDP at factor cost declined from 3.9 percent in the 1970-1975 period to an annual average of 0.7 percent between 1976 and 1980. With the exception of a GDP growth of 2.5 percent in 1984 and 1.0 percent in 1985, Guyana experienced negative growth rates of 0.3 percent, 10.4 percent, and 9.6 percent in 1981, 1982, and 1983 respectively.[18]

The downward spiral of the economy was also evident in the productive sectors which tumbled from an average annual growth of 2 percent between 1970 and 1975 to an average rate of minus 1.6 percent during the 1975-1980 period and to negative growth rates of 0.4 percent in 1981, 12.1 percent in 1982, and 14.1 percent in 1983, before recovering to show an increase of 9.3 percent in 1984. In the three primary production sectors, sugar, rice, and mining, where bauxite predominated, the picture was just the same (see table 8.3). The physical output levels of the bauxite-alumina, sugar, and rice industries were approximately 20 percent below the capacity developed in them in 1970.

Accompanying the declines in real output in the traditional producing sectors was a virtual collapse of the various public utilities: electricity, pure water supply, public transport, postal services, telephones, and sanitation, deterioration in the major social services, education, health, social welfare, and housing, and a considerable flight of persons and foreign exchange from the country. The poor state of the economy was also reflected in the public sector finances. The public sector deficit which stood at approximately 13.3 percent of GDP in 1978, climbed dramatically to 60.2 percent by 1984 and, as indicated in the data in table 8.4, there was a significant decline every year since 1978. This pattern of deterioration was manifested in the areas of savings and investment. Gross national savings which were about 15 percent of the country's GDP in 1978 declined to 3.7 percent in 1984, while gross domestic investment shrank from nearly 33 percent of GDP in 1979 to 24 percent in 1984.[19]

Furthermore, as far as the external performance of the economy was concerned, the situation was no different. For instance, in the export sector, sugar and bauxite which accounted for about 75 percent of overall export earnings in 1984 were a mere 49 percent and 48 percent respectively of their 1980 performance.[20] The result was that Guyana's external debt grew to a burdensome 81 percent of GDP in 1976, and to a whopping 168.8 percent of GDP by mid-1985. The country's scheduled debt service charges of 11.2 percent and 7.4 percent of export earnings and GDP respectively, in 1976, rose to 70.8 percent and 38 percent of the respective measures by 1985.[21] Guyana's situation grew worse as financial inflows in the form of development assistance and aid from Western donor countries had virtually dried up.

In addition, none of the policies the government implemented seemed capable of moving the economy out of its deep depression or improved the country's financial picture. The printing of extra money by the government only added fuel to the economic crisis which worsened on the external front on account of the worldwide inflation. The restriction of imports led to severe shortages of food, spare parts, intermediate goods, and to a general reduction in the standard of living. Increased taxes contributed to the decline in real wages which, since 1976, had been of the order of 44 percent.[22] Unable to meet its debt obligations, Guyana, in 1985, became an uncreditworthy nation within the international community and was ranked number 103 of the 111 poorest countries in the world. Its credit rating was an extremely poor 18 on a scale of 0 to 100 in 1986.[23] All the leading sectors of the economy were in a tailspin, thousands of professional people had left the country, the external debt was unmanageable, the trade deficit was sky high, and unemployment had reached record level. The collapse of Guyana's economy forced the Burnham regime to change its political and economic

Table 8.3
Guyana: Real Growth of GDP by Sectors 1970-1984 (%)

	1970-1975	1975-1980	1981	1982	1983	1984
Productive Sectors	2.0	1.6	-0.4	-12.1	-14.1	9.3
Mining	-2.3	-5.3	-11.4	-31.5	-22.4	47.0
Sugar	0.9	-1.3	10.9	-3.8	-12.6	-3.6
Rice	2.4	0.9	-2.2	15.6	-19.2	23.8
GDP at Factor Cost	3.9	-0.7	-0.3	-10.4	-9.6	2.5

Source: *World Bank Report, 1970 to 1985*, Washington, D.C.

orientation.

With regard to economic policy, there was an disavowal of the state-led development strategy under the ideological concept of cooperative socialism. The regime's reversal of its economic policy entailed the reintroduction of the free-market ideology of development. Externally, this was reflected in the normalization of Guyana's relations with the international creditor community, bilateral donors, and the IMF-World Bank group. The regime also cooled its anti-Western and anti-American rhetoric and supported the

Table 8.4
Guyana: Public Sector Savings (as a % of GDP)

	1978	1979	1980	1981	1982	1983	1984
Current Account Balance	4.3	4.1	2.1	-18.4	-19.9	-26.7	-38.6
Central Government	-4.7	-7.7	-10.8	-15.5	-15.0	-22.7	-32.9
Public Corporations	9.0	11.8	12.9	-2.9	-4.8	-4.0	-5.7
Overall Deficit	-13.3	-16.8	-22.7	-46.7	-47.2	-51.9	-60.2

Source: *World Bank Report 1970 to 1985*, Washington, D.C.

United States at international forums, including the UN. Internally, the process involved the implementation of a structural adjustment program under the aegis of the IMF and the World Bank group, the introduction of a new investment code to guarantee against the nationalization of foreign-owned assets in the country, and for the PNC government to restructure the economy away from its public sector orientation. This new set of policies was intended to make the private sector, which was marginalized under cooperative socialism, the central agents of economic activity in the country and enable the government to obtain foreign credit badly needed to meet its balance of payment obligations. Particularly pleasing to the U.S. was the hiring of American consultants by the Guyana government to advise local and foreign business owners on the creation of a more effective private sector, and a prominent U.S. law firm to design a private investment code for the country. Another U.S. firm was contracted to evaluate the performance of the public corporations, and a British investment company to assess the external debt situation. Liberalization of the economy was paralleled by the opening up of the political process, which resulted in a more credible and genuinely competitive electoral system of parliamentary democracy in Guyana. The culmination of this process was the October 1992 national elections that resulted in the defeat of Burnham's PNC for the first time in almost three decades. Thus, U.S. destabilization succeeded in its goal to rid the Caribbean of socialist regimes.

U.S.-Led Destabilization of Jamaica

The declaration of democratic socialism in Jamaica in 1974 brought the Manley government in direct conflict with the powerful local and international economic and political interests. In order for this new ideology to survive, the government had to accommodate or neutralize these interests or adopt measures to insulate itself from pressures from the United States and other Western powers. Under democratic socialism, the Manley government imposed a bauxite production tax on the aluminum companies, raised taxes, and nationalized a number of foreign-owned enterprises against intense resistance from the multinational corporations, the local capitalist class, the U.S., and other Western governments. This was accompanied by a radical anti-Western foreign policy which, among other issues, supported Cuba's role in the Angolan civil war, Jamaica's involvement in the NAM, the G-77, the formation of the IBA, the creation of a NIEO, and the establishment of diplomatic relations and close ties with Cuba. From this point on, local and international forces opposed to the PNP and Manley's brand of democratic socialism came together and worked in tandem to get rid of the regime.

Manley's ideological rhetoric and foreign policy positions in a period of acute Cold War rivalry served to over-"ideologize" the regime's concept of democratic socialism and consequently exposed it to U.S. destabilization measures. Manley repeatedly tried to convince the U.S. government and the capitalist elite that democratic socialism was meant to reform the capitalist system, and not to dismantle it, and that such democratic socialist order existed in such European countries like West Germany. Carl Stone wisely observed that:

> Mr Manley's radical foreign policy clothed his relatively moderate domestic economic and social policies in an aura of leftist radicalism far removed from the reality of what he attempted to implement. But the image of a radical, Marxist orientation to domestic social policies was sharpened both by the leftist rhetoric of Mr Manley and his party spokesman and by self-serving interpretations of what was happening in Jamaica promoted by North American media and the Jamaican bourgeoisie.[24]

This viewpoint is also expressed by Barry et al., who said that: "For all the criticism levelled at it by the United States, the Manley government was never a radical government with a plan for a substantial restructuring of the economy. The PNP had not formulated an overall plan to mobilise domestic agriculture and industrial workers. Consequently, it fell helplessly victim to international and local pressures."[25] But the U.S., the JLP, and the media, in particular, used the rhetoric to mobilize opposition to the PNP government.

Manley's pronouncements panicked the local capitalists and the upper class who became convinced that the PNP government was moving Jamaica towards communism and that their businesses and properties would be confiscated. They also incurred the wrath of the U.S. whose response to the Manley regime's new posture was a sustained effort to destabilize Jamaica's economy. The destabilization methods involved a combination of economic and political pressures by the U.S. government, multinational corporations, the IMF-World Bank group, the local capitalist class, negative press reports, principally in Jamaica and in North America and, in all probability, covert funding of the JLP, which allied with the groups that were opposed to the PNP. They also included unprecedented levels of violence, organized public protest, and a propaganda campaign locally and overseas. The events were strikingly reminiscent of the period just prior to the military coup in Chile which toppled the Allende government.

Given Jamaica's domestic political configuration, the U.S. government, foreign and local investors, and the media all had an ally in Edward Seaga and the JLP and, as a result, were determined to dislodge Manley's socialist regime from power in the 1976 election. They all took issue with Manley's socialist philosophy and were in the forefront of the economic and political destabilization efforts aimed to disrupt the economy and topple the government. As Manley put it: "Clearly, the multinational corporation, the conservative elements of the Western press, the champions of the capitalist system, the U.S. establishment and those who defended the status quo generally, were lined up solidly behind the JLP."[26]

During the 1970s, the United States government portrayed Jamaica as a pawn of Cuba and the Soviet Union, just as it did with Grenada before the invasion, and vowed to get rid of the Manley socialist regime at any cost. Consequently, its destabilization measures were aimed at undercutting Manley and the PNP's popularity and forced the regime to either abandon its progressive rhetoric, its socialist policies, and its close relations with Castro or be pushed out of office. A statement attributed to Larry Burns of the Council of Hemispheric Affairs revealed that "In the closing days of the Ford Administration, Kissinger had become almost manic about getting rid of Manley."[27]

Soon after the imposition of the bauxite tax, the MNCs transferred some of their bauxite and aluminum production from Jamaica to Australia and Guinea. The move reduced bauxite imports from Jamaica by almost 30 percent for a net industry-wide decrease of 20 percent.[28] This was accompanied by a massive reduction of private foreign investments in the manufacturing and mining sectors by other multinational corporations. In fact, the flight of foreign investment from the country was probably the main destabilizing factor during the PNP tenure in office. The drying up of investment was not due to dwindling profits but because of political reasons. In Jamaica, profits on investment declined slightly from 31 percent in the period 1970-1973 to 30 percent in 1977.[29] Foreign capital inflow shrank from U.S. $254 in 1973 to U.S. $115 in 1975, and by 1976, new foreign investment capital had ceased completely, as Jamaica became a net exporter of investment capital instead of a recipient.[30] The lack of investment deprived the government of badly needed foreign exchange required to service its external debt. It also convinced many Jamaicans, particularly the upper classes, that Manley, despite his good intentions, was leading Jamaica to economic ruin. As a result, thousands of Jamaicans, mostly professionals and members of the middle and upper classes, migrated to the United States and Canada with whatever resources they could take. Those who stayed created a mood of panic in the private sector and in the country as a whole that slowly drained the economy.

Jamaica's economic crisis was made worse by illegal work stoppages and prolonged strikes in the private sector, and by a new wave of violence in the urban areas of the country in 1976 that had required periodic curfews in an effort to curb the violence. Although violence and gang warfare in the ghettoes of Kingston were common scenes in Jamaica, the type of violence that swept the island in 1976 was neither of the gang warfare nor partisan terrorization nor of the ordinary criminal activity, but rather destructive acts without an apparent motive which could only be interpreted as part of a campaign of destabilization. They involved the senseless slaying of innocent citizens, including women, children, seniors, and the disabled, firefighters and police officers, the random burning of public buildings and houses in poor neighborhoods, and a number of vicious attacks on the business establishment and on foreign diplomats, one of which led to the murder of the Peruvian ambassador to Jamaica in June 1976.

According to the PNP government, these and other bizarre incidents such as the oiling of steep and dangerous stretches of roads on the days when PNP rallies were scheduled were part of a CIA-directed covert action of the type that occurred in Chile and aimed to destabilize the country. Despite repeated denials from the Carter administration and especially from the secretary of state that the U.S. was not involved in the destabilization of Jamaica, Prime Minister Manley thought otherwise. He was convinced that the violence and deliberate acts of sabotage were covertly orchestrated by the CIA. As Manley recalled:

> Looking back at the events of 1976 . . . I have no doubt that the CIA was active in Jamaica that year and was working through its own agents to destabilize us. They deny it to this day, but I prefer the judgements of the heads of the Jamaican security forces at the time. Police, army and special branch concurred that the CIA was actively behind the events. My common-sense left me with no option but to agree. [31]

Manley's claim was substantiated by Philip Agee, a former CIA agent who was stationed at the U.S. embassy in Jamaica at the time.[32] The result was a significant drop in production in all sectors of the economy, which together with rising oil prices, the flight of capital, conservatively estimated at some U.S. $300 million in 1977, and a sharp decline in tourist receipts exerted considerable pressure on Jamaica's balance of payments. In this period the budget deficit ballooned causing a drastic reduction in social services. A subdued Manley described the situation: "The economy was in deep trouble. The balance of payments crisis had us by the throat and production was down every-where."[33]

Meanwhile, from outside Jamaica there appeared to emanate all the signs of increased U.S. pressures and methods of destabilization. There were a number of negative and inaccurate foreign press reports on Jamaica by many reputable newspapers and magazines in the United States calculated to discourage tourists from the country, thereby undermining the tourist industry and hence the economy. They included the *New York Times,* the *Wall Street Journal*, the *Washington Post*, the *Miami Herald*, *Daily Express,* the *Toronto Globe,* the *Christian Science Monitor*, *Newsweek*, and *Time*, to name a few.[34] On the domestic front, the *Daily Gleaner*, a conservative newspaper, carried out a barrage of attacks against the Manley regime's socialist policies. The paper had been the only source of popular reading for so long in Jamaica that it had become a part of the status quo. It was viewed by some as revealing the truth about the government and by others as the propaganda arm of the opposition JLP. It was, in fact, indistinguishable from the opposition. Through its headlines and articles, the *Daily Gleaner* not only criticized the government but also joined with opposition forces, included the JLP, and conducted an incessant communist smear campaign against the PNP. While it was attacking the PNP, it was showering praise on the JLP. The tactics used by the *Daily Gleaner* in the destabilization process in Jamaica were similar to those of the notorious *El Mercurio* in Chile prior to the overthrow of Allende. Prime Minister Manley's perceptive observation of the *Gleaner* at the time was:

> The *Daily Gleaner*, which was founded in 1834, had been for more than a century the bastion of conservatism, defender of the status quo and the leader of reaction to any attempts at change. Originally the voice of the plantocracy and their merchant allies, it has been, in turn, the staunchest champion of the empire, the monarchy, and now of western capitalism. . . . In the days of empire and particularly after 1865, its views were those of the mother country. Subsequent to World War II, its views were those of the Washington establishment with an occasional nostalgic nod in the direction of Whitehall.[35]

The newspapers and magazines highlighted the violence and crime that had beset Jamaica during Manley's rule. They pointed to the declaration of the State of Emergency in 1976 as a sign of political instability on the island and lack of political leadership on the part of the Manley government to manage the affairs of the country. Although the State of Emergency Act was meant to quell the violence, it signalled to the outside world that the country was in a serious crisis, which at the time was damaging to the tourist industry and investment prospects in the country. It also generally involved the tacit admission that the normal democratic process in Jamaica had failed. On the positive side, during the Emergency all crime on the island decreased by 17.9 percent. In the first six months there was a 32.2 percent drop in gun crimes, and in the month before the Emergency Act, forty-two people were killed compared to only eleven during the first month of the Emergency.[36] The government had to grapple with the negative effects of the Emergency Act as it tried its best to persuade investors and tourists to come to Jamaica. Meanwhile, most of the press reports in North America had labelled Jamaica a communist state and branded the regime a surrogate of Soviet and Cuban adventurism in the Caribbean.[37] The negative press reports, the violence and crimes, and the State of Emergency discouraged U.S. visitors who, at the time, accounted for 75 percent of the annual total number of tourists to Jamaica.[38]

The connection between negative and, in some cases, inaccurate press coverage about Jamaica in the U.S. and elsewhere, and the decline of tourists to the island were acknowledged by the government of Jamaica. According to the Jamaican Tourist Board, "One of the reasons for the decline in the number of visitors can be attributed to the unfavourable publicity which Jamaica received throughout 1976."[39] Saul Landau of the *Washington Post* was more critical and blunt in his assessment of the destabilization methods used against Jamaica. He said, "There can be no doubt that the internal attack on the Manley Government—a campaign of violence and lies, plus strikes—combined with the external attack from the U.S. press . . . add up to a destabilization campaign."[40]

Probably the most damaging of all the destabilization measures against the government was the credit squeeze to which Jamaica was subjected to during the 1970s. Citing Manley's anti-imperialist rhetoric and his close relationship with Castro, the U.S. Agency for International Development (USAID), in 1975, turned down Jamaica's request for a $2.5 million food grant and refused to lend additional funds to the Manley regime until it changed its radical stance. One year later, the American Export-Import Bank dropped Jamaica's credit rating from a top to a bottom category and, as a consequence, the commercial banks ceased all lending to Jamaica. This act cut off the PNP government from multilateral, bilateral, and commercial loans from Western financial institutions. Jamaica's economy was temporarily maintained by means of bilateral loans from friendly governments such as those from Canada and Trinidad and Tobago.

By 1977, Jamaica's balance-of-payments situation had reached alarming proportions as its economy was in a serious crisis. The PNP government responded to the crisis by raising taxes on the rich, reducing imports, and restricting foreign currency exchange. This was a major blow to the business and commercial elite who intensified their opposition against the regime. Politically, the local capitalist class denounced the socialist policies of the Manley government and publicly announced their support for Seaga and the JLP. Economically, they responded with major cutbacks in production, massive layoffs of workers in the mining and manufacturing sectors, and the illegal transfer of large sums of foreign currency to North American and European banks.[41] Prime Minister Manley admitted that these acts shook the very foundation upon which the economy was built and that Jamaica had become like a time bomb ready to explode. The various methods of destabilization on Jamaica were summarized by Manley:

> Suddenly you find an upsurge of industrial unrest, the most incredible and inexplicable strikes begin to take place and not even the trade unionist can understand what causes some of them; the upsurge of unexplained violence, organized letters to the press, internationally orchestrated articles for newspaper publication, economic squeezes, slowing down and entangling of aid wherever possible.[42]

The Effects of U.S. Destabilization on Jamaica

After eight years of PNP rule and six years of democratic socialism, Jamaica, by 1980, was in complete economic ruin and turmoil. This was exactly the situation which the JLP and the capitalist class had hoped would happen to the country under democratic socialism. Political violence had left over 750 people dead; shortages of basic commodities were widespread; labor unrest continued; foreign capital inflows had dried up; and unemployment was 28 percent of the labor force.[43] Much of this was due to U.S. destabilization measures which were directed at the PNP government in retaliation of its socialist policies. The effects of these measures, coupled with gross mismanagement of the economy and the public sector, corrupt practices, shortages of skills, political squabbles, and substantial oil price increases in the 1970s, were felt in every sector of the Jamaican society.

The first major impact of the destabilization measures was a drastic reduction of bauxite production by the aluminum companies during the 1970s that resulted in Jamaica losing its status to Australia as the number one bauxite producer in the world. As illustrated by the data shown in table 6.6, Jamaica's share of total world bauxite exports fell by some 10 percent between 1970 and 1975. Tourist receipts to Jamaica fell by 13 percent in 1975 and again by 10 percent in 1976, and to almost 40 percent by 1979, due to press reports of violence, political instability, and presumed Cuban influence on the island.[44] The decline in tourists had a detrimental effect on both hotel room occupancy rates and tourist expenditure in the country as many of the hotels experienced financial difficulties to the point of bankruptcy. By mid-1976, the government was virtually forced to take control of almost 3,300 hotel rooms which, at the time, constituted half of the total hotel rooms in the country that were built with government-guaranteed loans.[45] Most of the rooms were not occupied and therefore had to be subsidized by the government, which was already in severe financial crisis. This produced shortfalls in foreign exchange earnings which, together with capital flight from the country, and the increase in foreign investment income repatriated abroad, led to a massive deterioration of the balance-of-payments situation and negative growth in the country's real GDP.

The decline in tourist receipts and the flight of thousands of Jamaicans and capital worsened the economic and financial situation in the country. For example, between 1977 and 1980, an estimated 18,000 skilled personnel from Jamaica migrated to the United States, taking with them over U.S. $600 million,[46] in addition to the $300 million that left the country prior to 1977. The brain drain was felt among the Chinese population, most of whom were the owners of small and medium-size business in Jamaica. Between 1972 and 1980, over 50,000 of the 78,000 Chinese in Jamaica migrated to North America. Also in this period, more that half of the world's 4.4 million Jamaicans lived outside Jamaica, mainly in Britain, Canada, and the United States. These developments produced a severe foreign exchange crisis and a huge budget deficit which, in turn, led to a major decline in services in all public utilities and social welfare agencies. With Jamaica's economic and social programs in ruin, and its balance-of-payments situation in chaos, the Manley regime softened its rhetoric and accepted on draconian terms loans from the IMF to ease the financial burden.[47] Given Jamaica's poor credit rating and its ideological position, the IMF loan agreement with the government was hinged on the implementation of a program of anti-working-class measures that included a freeze on wages, a drastic reduction in public spending and public service employees, an end to state intervention in the economy, a higher tax on gasoline and other essential commodities, and a 40 percent devaluation of the Jamaican dollar.[48]

From the outset, Manley believed that the IMF monetary policies were designed by members of developed capitalist countries for the ailments of those economies and, as a result, could not solve the economic problems in Jamaica or the countries of the Global South. He was suspicious of the IMF and the capitalist system, which he claimed had prevented development in the South. However, faced with acute foreign currency problems, the Manley government, in June 1977, agreed to a Stand-by-Loan Agreement with the IMF, which was subsequently terminated in December 1977 after Jamaica's economy failed to perform to the level set by the institution. In May 1978, Manley managed to obtain an Extended Fund Facility from the IMF, but again, this was cancelled in December 1979 because the Bank of Jamaica exceeded the required ceiling of its international reserves established by the IMF. Manley's capitulation to the IMF had had major political consequences in that it alienated his popular support among the masses. With elections just around the corner, Manley broke off relations with the IMF in March 1980, but this was too little too late for him and the PNP to recapture their popular support. The dramatic decline in living standards caused an equally drastic erosion of the PNP's popular support, which demoralized the party activists and added to the internal tensions in the leadership.

The shortage of foreign exchange and the continued decline of economic activity in Jamaica contributed to a spectacular growth in the illegal trade of marijuana known as "ganja" to most Jamaicans, West Indians, and many North Americans. According to the U.S. Drug Enforcement Administration (DEA), illegal shipments of marijuana from Jamaica to the U.S., which had the implicit support and blessing of the Manley regime, the opposition JLP, and the business elite, increased from over the estimate of U.S. $146 million in 1974 to over U.S. $1 billion by the end of 1980.[49] Even the island's security forces paid scant attention to the illegal drug trade. An immediate explanation for this was that law and order had been broken down in the country and the security forces were preoccupied in preventing a civil war. The illegal marijuana trade provided much needed funds to help the two main political parties in their quest to outspend each other in the election campaigns of 1976 and 1980. As Alan Gabbidon has observed:

> Ganja [marijuana] had become the alternative to the IMF, and both the business establishment and the government saw the ganja trade as vital to their survival. . . . Both parties were relying more and more heavily on the ganja trade to provide election funds, foreign exchange to buy election equipment, and on illegal flights to bring that equipment into the island (guns included). One side was doing this to preserve socialism and the other to save the country from communism. The ganja men were doing it to get rich. It was ganja's finest hour.[50]

The destabilization of Jamaica's economy contributed to the demise of democratic socialism and the defeat of the Manley regime. Edward Seaga and the JLP victory ended a long and bitter campaign, both international and local, that undermined the progress of the Manley government and democratic socialism in Jamaica.

U.S.-Led Destabilization of Grenada

After it rid Grenada of its autocratic leader, the Bishop regime received the immediate and enthusiastic support of the vast majority of Grenadians. Government social programs and attempts to integrate Grenadians into the economic and political decision-making process strengthened that support. Even the senior citizens observed the progress of the regime, while many youths became directly involved in the militia, farming, and educational outreach programs. Not all Grenadians, however, stood behind the People's Revolutionary Government of Maurice Bishop. Some, who had initially supported the overthrow of the brutal and corrupt Gairy government, felt threatened by the PRG's socialist and dictatorial policies and were critical of its anti-U.S. and anti-imperialist rhetoric, and its close ties with Castro and his communist regime in Cuba. Others were deeply concerned about the militarization and politicization of all sectors of Grenadian society. Many among the upper and middle classes were of the opinion that the regime would eventually seize their property and businesses and curtail their freedom. Despite the fears of the PRG socialist polices and practices, the majority of Grenadians backed the New Jewel Movement for its economic reforms and social programs, its overwhelming concern for the poor, and its efforts to involve the people in mass organizations, and parish and regional councils.

Unfortunately for the Bishop regime, its seizure of power in Grenada in 1979 coincided with the shift of policies within the Carter administration away from limited change and towards those supportive of the status quo in the Caribbean. As a result, a negative rather than a positive reaction towards the revolution emerged and was followed by policies of destabilization.

During the four years of revolutionary socialism, Grenada, because of its close relationship with Cuba and its anti-American stance, was the target of some of the toughest destabilization measures instituted by the U.S. government, particularly the Reagan administration. Its first and immediate manifestation was in a CIA plan to destabilize Grenada. According to Prime Minister Bishop, from the beginning of the revolution, the CIA, acting on behalf of the U.S. government, had devised a plan in the shape of a pyramid to discredit the government of Grenada and to turn back the revolution. At the bottom of the pyramid was the strategy to destabilize the government and the economy through the use of violence and arson and by planting false reports about Grenada in newspapers and on radio and television stations, locally and overseas, and also encouraging prominent individuals and leaders of organizations and governments in the Caribbean to attack the revolution. These fears were spelled out in typical Bishop style:

> The first part of the plan was aimed at creating dissatisfaction and unrest among the people of Grenada and at wrecking our tourist industry and economy. A second level of the pyramid involved the use of violence and arson in the country. And if neither of these two methods of destabilizing the country worked, then the plan was to move to the stage of assassinating the leadership of the country. [51]

The destabilization of Grenada began immediately after the coup d'etat of 1979 as bilateral relations between the U.S. and Grenada grew distant with no attempt by either government to improve matters. Instead, the U.S. government pressured a number of countries in the Caribbean to cut off diplomatic relations with the Bishop regime. The diplomatic isolation of Grenada was highlighted by the Carter administration's refusal to recognize Dessima Williams, Grenada's designated ambassador to the U.S. at the time, because of evidence that she had been involved in illegal arms smuggling to Grenada, and on the grounds that she was too young and inexperienced for the position. The Bishop regime responded in kind. It delayed accepting the credentials of Sally Shelton, the new U.S. ambassador to Barbados and the Eastern Caribbean states, for nearly seven weeks to which the U.S. retaliated by excluding Grenada from a fact-finding tour of the Eastern Caribbean in August 1979 by its envoy Philip Habib.[52] Under massive Cuban influence, the Grenadian government voted with Cuba against several U.S. sponsored resolutions at the UN, including the Soviet Union invasion of Afghanistan in December 1979.[53]

The policy of diplomatic isolation was reinforced with maneuvers by the U.S. government to deny economic assistance to Grenada. The denial of aid to Grenada manifested itself in a number of ways during the period of PRG rule. It involved a U.S.-directed campaign to block multilateral and bilateral assistance to the country. This was exemplified by the fact that in January 1980 the Carter administration turned down Grenada's request for bilateral assistance to rebuild roads, bridges, and schools that had been damaged or destroyed by severe rainstorms. During the same year, the U.S. government refused to give disaster relief funds to Grenada in the wake of Hurricane Allen which destroyed the island's fruits, even though it provided such financial assistance to banana planters in St. Lucia, St. Vincent, and Dominica, who were also affected by the hurricane.[54] The decision to punish the farmers of Grenada was similar to the sanctions imposed on Cuba by various U.S. administrations since the revolution of 1959 to punish the Castro regime, but instead, the sanctions have affected the people of Cuba.

In the beginning, the Carter administration had contemplated a naval blockade of Grenada to prevent Cuban ships from entering its ports. While this policy was not implemented, it led directly to the creation of a Caribbean Joint Task Force Headquarters in Key West, Florida, and the decision to expand U.S. naval exercises in the region. The task force was comprised of a rapid deployment of troops capable of responding to any progressive or revolutionary development in the region. It was supplemented by significant increases in U.S. military aid to a number of countries in the Caribbean, except Grenada, which received military assistance from the U.S. only after the collapse of the Bishop regime in 1983 (see table 8.5). The expansion of U.S. forces in the Caribbean culminated in a series of military exercises under various code names between 1980 and 1984 (table 8.6). The first was code-named "Operation Solid Shield" which occurred in May 1980 and involved over 20,000 troops, forty-two naval vessels, and 350 aircraft.[55] This show of force was never seen in the region since the Cuban missile crisis of 1962 and the U.S. invasion of the Dominican Republic in 1965.

In 1981, President Reagan, in a significant shift away from the practice of the Carter administration, drew no distinction between the Caribbean and Central America. The differing social and economic traditions and the different patterns of development of the two subregions were not considered as significant compared to the common security problem they posed for the region and for the United States. As a result, the Reagan administration treated both regions as constituents of a new concept called the Caribbean Basin, which was elevated to the foremost concern of U.S. foreign policy in the region. The countries that made up the Caribbean Basin had little in common beyond their close proximity to the United States, but were forced together by the U.S. determination to reassert its hegemonic power and remove Cuban and Soviet influence in the area. Such a policy dovetailed nicely with his stark Cold War view of the world as a battle between the forces of good (the United States) and the forces of evil (the Soviet Union). In the context of the Caribbean Basin, this was reinforced by the conviction that the U.S. would not tolerate Cuban/Soviet conspiracy and would use force if necessary to maintain the status quo and prevent the spread of communism in the hemisphere. In part, this policy grew out of the traditional American hatred of communism. President Reagan's denunciation of the Soviet Union as an evil empire was a logical extension to foreign policy of Senator Joseph McCarthy's assault against all those Americans who were seen as being soft on communism in the 1950s. It was also a new version of the traditional American distrust of the Old World, this time seeing the Soviet Union as a sort of savage, slavic, and uncivilized society.

The policies of destabilization applied by Carter to Grenada intensified under Reagan and comprised of regional and local pressures, propaganda, and diplomatic isolation. President Reagan pursued a relentless policy to isolate Grenada both economically and politically from its neighbors in the region. The initial position of the U.S. was to not even communicate with the Bishop regime until it ceased all ties and communications with Cuba and restored democracy to the people of Grenada. On both the day President Reagan was elected and the day he was inaugurated, Prime Minister Bishop sent letters to him expressing a desire for friendly relations between the two countries. The first letter was formally acknowledged and the second was not answered at all, nor was a third letter sent in August that year. The Reagan administration refused to accredit any Grenadian ambassador to the U.S. and refused to seek such accreditation from Grenada for its ambassador to the Eastern Caribbean and Barbados. Milan Bish, the new U.S. ambassador, was not accredited to Grenada by the Reagan administration, and Sally Shelton, the outgoing U.S. ambassador, was not allowed to pay a courtesy farewell visit to Grenada in January 1981, despite an invitation extended to her by the PRG for talks aimed at restoring dialogue. It also intensified its efforts to stop its allies from assisting the Grenadian government. In March 1981, the U.S. succeeded in restricting the number of countries in the region which sent representatives to the second anniversary celebrations of the revolution to St. Lucia, Guyana, Suriname, Venezuela, and Belize. Such actions by the U.S. government were viewed by the Bishop regime as deliberate attempts to discredit Grenada and isolate it from its neighbors in the Caribbean.

The policy of deliberate isolation of Grenada was also pursued by the British conservative government of Margaret Thatcher in order to help the U.S. contain the political impact of the revolution on other Caribbean states. The British government cut off diplomatic ties with the Bishop regime and urged other countries in the Caribbean to do likewise. Britain also cancelled an agreement to sell two armored cars to the Grenadian government and, more importantly, cooperated with the U.S. to bolster the military capability of other Eastern Caribbean states hostile to the revolution, notably Barbados. In justifying Britain's policy, Nicholas Ridley, the minister of state at the Foreign Office at the time, said: "Grenada is in the process of establishing a kind of society of which the British Government disapproves, irrespective of whether the people of Grenada want it or not."[56] His successor, Richard Luce, on a goodwill tour of the Eastern Caribbean refused to visit Grenada, citing the unattractive record of the Bishop government over civil liberties and democratic rights.[57]

The Reagan administration was without a doubt uncompromising in its efforts to destabilize the island's economy. In April 1981, it successfully pressured the IMF to delay a loan of U.S. $19 million to Grenada despite earlier approval by the managing director of the institution. It also excluded Grenada from its share of a U.S. $4 million standby credit to the Caribbean Development Bank for the Eastern Caribbean States for construction of schools and the expansion of social welfare services.[58] Despite the political and ideological differences in the region, all the English-speaking Caribbean countries closed ranks and refused the loan on the principle that it was discriminatory. An ecstatic Bishop said: "Our friends in the region, different countries in CARICOM, stood up to this latest blatant attempt on the part of the U.S. administration to divide and rule the region and to attempt to subvert this Caribbean regional institution."[59] However, some CARICOM leaders were careful not to associate their support with any approval of the regime's ideological posture or its close ties with Cuba. Their primary reason was not to support any form of discrimination against Grenada or any other country in the region by the U.S. By 1982, the rhetoric of President Reagan began to match that of Prime Minister Bishop for much of the same reasons. Both alerted the world community to the evil intentions of the other. The exchanges, sharp as they were, served to confirm the worst suspicions each had of the other.

At the heart of U.S. economic destabilization measures against the PRG was the construction of Grenada's new international airport. U.S. pressure on potential donors, particularly the EEC's decision to raise U.S. $30 million needed to complete the airport project, was intense. Despite such pressure, the EEC, with the exception of Britain, declared the airport to be an essential infra-structure and provided a grant, not a loan, of U.S. $2.5 million to Grenada and pledged EC $6 million more in aid.[60] The U.S. government opposition to the construction of the airport was that its 9,800-foot runway was far too long for the modest air traffic in Grenada. It claimed that the airport was being built to accommodate Cuban and Russian Mig-23 and Mig-25 fighter jets. Determined to prove his point, President Reagan not only portrayed Grenada as a pawn of the Soviet Union and Cuba, but also showed aerial photographs of the airport and insisted that it was a potential Soviet/Cuban military base which could threaten the oil fields in Venezuela and Trinidad and the oil routes that passed through the deep sea water channel separating Grenada from Tobago.

The PRG's response was that a number of countries in the Caribbean including Antigua, Guyana, St. Lucia, and Trinidad and Tobago have airports with comparable runways. Other islands such as Barbados, Guadeloupe, and Curacao have runways in excess of 11,000 feet. It also reminded the U.S. government that no military facilities such as underground fuel tanks and bomb-proof shelters were being built, and that British, European, and American companies as well as Cuban workers were involved in the construction of the airport. This was confirmed by Plessey Electronic Systems, the British company that had been in charge of the overall management of the airport construction and to whom the British government extended credit guarantees for the contract. It is hard to believe that the Thatcher government would have done this had it had any real doubt as to the airport's primary purpose. Shortly after the invasion, Plessey confirmed that the airport lacked at least a dozen facilities for military use, including radar, fortified shelters for fuel and weapons, and anti-aircraft defenses. As it turned out, the airport was not used for Cuban or Soviet aircraft but to land the U.S. invasion force. Worse still, the Reagan administration, even after the invasion, could not produce any conclusive evidence to support its claims, although the pretext for the invasion has been well documented.

Perhaps the most blatant form of U.S. economic destabilization policy was the Reagan administration's consistent attempts to persuade the IMF, the World Bank, and other multilateral lending agencies not to fund technically viable and positive projects for the development of Grenada. Its unilateral decision to exclude Grenada, Nicaragua, and Cuba from the Caribbean Basin Initiative in 1982 was criticized by friendly countries as well as opponents. Canada, Mexico, and Venezuela distanced themselves from the CBI, which they claimed was linked to U.S. military and security interests in the region and that it was prompted by the East-West conflict. In announcing the CBI, President Reagan painted a black-and-white view of the Caribbean with a bright future for the friends of the United States and a dark future foreshadowed by the poverty and repression of Cuba, the totalitarian regimes in Grenada and Nicaragua, and the Soviet-backed regimes in Central America. In direct reference to Grenada, President Reagan declared: "El Salvador isn't the only country that's being threatened with Marxism . . . all of us are concerned with the overturn of Westminster parliamentary democracy in Grenada. That country now bears the Soviet and Cuban trade-mark, which means that it will attempt to spread its virus among its neighbors."[61]

The Bishop regime wasted no time in denouncing the CBI as a plan by the Reagan administration designed to divide and exploit the Caribbean nations. It was never intended to help promote development in the Caribbean but to advance U.S. security interests in the region and to integrate the Caribbean Basin states even more into the orbit of U.S. capitalism. In the words of Prime Minister Bishop:

> [The CBI] is meant only to deal with narrow military, security and strategic considerations of the U.S.A., and is not genuinely concerned with the economic and social development of the people of this region . . . the CBI plan reflects the chauvinism and ugly Americanism of Reagan, in the vulgar way in which he has completely ignored and discarded the views of Caribbean countries, as to what kind of plan they wished to see. The concern of his plan is with his warmongering national security interests . . . his Basin plan has turned out to be the con game of this century.[62]

The CBI was also criticized by Grenada's Deputy Prime Minister Bernard Coard as a cowboy scheme for the Caribbean and an attempt by the Reagan administration to maintain the structures of domination, exploitation, and oppression of the region by totally inadequate bribery.[63] The Reagan administration retaliated by cutting off all aid to and trade with Grenada and used its influence to block all IMF-World Bank loans to the island between 1982 and 1983.

As the revolution progressed, the power of every conceivable monopolist U.S. media was brought to bear on Grenada. Not only were some of the most reputable newspapers and magazines hostile to the Bishop regime, but the media of film and television also played an overt destabilizing role against Grenada. In January 1981 the American Council Foundation (ACF) and the Coalition for Peace through Strength showed a 25-minute documentary titled "Attack on the Americas," which criticized and denounced the Cuban, Nicaraguan, and Grenadian revolutions. A few weeks later, a CBS-TV series called "The Prisoner and the Police State" depicted Grenada as a communist state controlled by Cuba and the Soviet Union. This was followed by a CBS *Special Report* on Grenada, which alluded to the fraternal bond between the Castro regime and members of the PRG, particularly Prime Minister Bishop. It highlighted the conflict between the PRG and the Catholic Church, the newspaper industry, violence and crimes, and the violation of human rights in the country.[64] In addition, the United States International Communications Agency (USICA), the propaganda arm of the State Department, hosted a conference for the editors of the major Caribbean newspapers in May 1981 where they were informed of a major buildup of Cuban troops and arms in Grenada. They were also offered financial assistance to collaborate with the U.S. to help isolate Grenada by means of adverse publicity.

The pattern of media propaganda against Grenada continued ceaselessly in some of the major newspapers and magazines in the United States. The *Boston Globe*, the *Washington Post*, the *New York Times*, the *Wall Street Journal*, *Time*, and *Newsweek* on numerous occasions ran some blistering headlines such as "No more freedom in Grenada," "Grenada has become the second Cuba in the Caribbean," "Soviet-made tanks found in Grenada," "Tourists fear for their lives as riots and violence erupted in Grenada." Similar allegations were made by a number of conservative newspapers in the Caribbean, including the *Trinidad Guardian* and the *Express*, *Barbados Advocate* and the *Sun*, *Voice of St. Lucia, Dominica Chronicle,* and the *Daily Gleaner* in Jamaica, all of which had distribution outlets in New York City, Washington, London, Toronto, Montreal, and Miami where most West Indians reside.

On September 20, 1981, identical front page editorials appeared in five Caribbean newspapers: the *Guardian* and the *Express* in Trinidad and Tobago, the *Advocate* and the *Sun* in Barbados, and the *Daily Gleaner* in Jamaica that called on Prime Minister Bishop and his colleagues in the government to restore freedom to the people of Grenada. The negative press reports were aimed at disrupting the tourist industry and undermined the economy. It was against this background that the regime moved swiftly to stifle internal opposition to its views. It closed the island's most popular newspaper, the *Torchlight*, in 1979, and the less popular *Catholic Focus* in 1980 for alleged slander and imperialist propaganda. In 1981, the PRG also closed the *Grenadian Voice* on the grounds that it represented the CIA in its effort to destabilize the revolution. Its publishers, the so-called "Gang of Twenty-Six" who were former owners of the *Torchlight*, were arrested for alleged implication in a CIA plot to overthrow the government.

The government's acute sensitivity to internal criticism stemmed from the persistent reports throughout 1981 and 1982 of an impending invasion by the "Patriotic Alliance," a group of Grenadians based in Trinidad and opposed to the revolution and to the PRG's dictatorial rule. To this must be added the role of the CIA, whose covert activities in Grenada were reported by three former CIA agents, John Stockwell, Ralph McGehee, and Bill Schaap in 1982.[65] Although based on circumstantial evidence, the juxtaposition of these two elements led Prime Minister Bishop to conclude that:

> We have to understand, Comrades, that this plan we are seeing now, the first element of which is this newspaper, is a different plan to all that went before, because this is not the type of plan in which local counters, local opportunists are being used, this is not the kind of plan where the ganga capitalists who are in the employment of the CIA are being used. To understand this plan fully you have to do a piece of magic in your heads, you have to forget the names of that 26 and instead you write one single word . . . the CIA. That is how you are going to understand this plan. . . . It is not the Committee of 26. It is the CIA. This is not about freedom of the press, it is about overthrowing the Grenadian revolution.[66]

President Reagan's determination to isolate Grenada diplomatically was carried out simultaneously with the buildup of U.S. military presence in the Caribbean. Indeed this was the final and ultimately determinant aspect of U.S. destabilization policy against Grenada. Between 1981 and 1984, the Reagan administration conducted sixteen military or training exercises in the region (table 8.6). The most notable of these was the U. S. military exercise code-named "Ocean Venture 81" which took place on the island of Vieques off the coast of Puerto Rico in August 1981. It had a large contingent of over 120,000 troops, 250 warships, and 1,000 aircraft. Within this operation was a separate training unit dubbed "Amber and the Amberines" which was seen by the Bishop regime as a direct provocation of Grenadians by design and intent in that it clearly referred to Grenada and its two sister islands in the Grenadines, Carriacou and Petit Martinique. Amber is in fact an area on the southern tip of Grenada near the site of the new international airport at Point Salines. Vieques like Grenada has a mountainous terrain and the combat unit involved in the training exercise was flown from the Norton Air Base in California nonstop to Vieques, covering approximately the same distance needed to invade the tiny island of Grenada. The objective of the military exercise in the Pentagon's fictional war-game scenario was for Amber to seize American hostages after which the U.S. would invade the island and set up a government that would not threaten the United States interest in the region. The Reagan administration denied this was the purpose for the exercise. It claimed that the exercise was for a variety of eventualities such as had been conducted by previous administrations under various code names although none was so reckless and overtly political. The military exercises instilled fear in the hearts of the Grenadian people and intimidated members of the Bishop regime and other socialist-inspired movements in the region.

The most blatant of all U.S. military exercises in the Caribbean occurred in March 1983, which once more singled out Grenada as a target. A total of 77 U.S. and allied warships assembled off the shores of Grenada; some used Barbados as their staging area while others sailed within six miles of Point Salines. President Reagan viewed the problems of the Caribbean strictly in terms of the East-West struggle, and therefore, U.S. policy toward Grenada was important for what he told the world about America's determination to confront communism in the region. He rebuked those who denigrated the importance his administration attached to Grenada because its best-known export is nutmeg. "People who make these arguments haven't taken a good look at a map lately . . . it is not nutmeg that is at stake in the Caribbean and Central America, it is the United States national security."[67]

This particular military exercise was condemned by Bishop as overt U.S. backyardism, that showed total contempt for the people of the Caribbean and an insult to all nations in the region, whether or not they were friendly to the Reagan administration. It also forced Bishop, who was attending the Non-aligned Summit in India, to cut short his visit and on his return declared a nationwide alert and warned the people of Grenada of an impending U.S. invasion of the island. Typical of his remarks, Prime Minister Bishop said:

> Such huge military manoeuvres, so perilously close to our shores . . . only demonstrate one more time the proximity of war and the blasé, imperial, and Monroe Doctrine-like attitude of the United States to our region and

Table 8.5
U. S. Military Assistance to the Caribbean Basin,
1980-1986[1] (in U.S. $ thousands)

	1980	1981	1982	1983	1984	1985	1986
Antigua-Barbuda	0	0	0	1,067	353	1,483	686
Barbados	30	30	56	55	70	192	344
Belize	0	0	20	48	204	919	612
Dominica	0	8	4	1,042	382	1,322	484
Dominican Republic	239	348	3,883	1,096	6,949	4,385	6,997
Grenada	0	0	0	0	2,335	3,450	464
Haiti	128	110	212	339	770	396	1,464
Jamaica	0	95	73	3,472	2,936	5,978	9,288
St. Kitts-Nevis*	N/A	N/A	N/A	N/A	32	2,704	451
St. Lucia	0	2	8	1,065	410	225	429
St. Vincent	0	0	1	31	44	85	2,992
Trinidad-Tobago*	0	15	0	5	0	39	50
TOTAL	**397**	**608**	**4,257**	**8,220**	**14,116**	**21,178**	**24,261**

Source: U.S. Department of Defense, Foreign Military Construction Sales and Military Assistance, Facts as of September 30, 1989 (Washington, D.C.: Department of Defense, 1989).

[1]Includes Foreign Military Sales agreements, Foreign Military Construction Sales agreements, Military Assistance Program, and International Military Education and Training Program.

*St. Kitts-Nevis became independent in 1983, and Trinidad and Tobago did not support the U.S. invasion of Grenada.

Table 8.6
U.S. Military Maneuvers in the Caribbean 1979-1984

1980 Solid Shield	Guantánamo and Puerto Rico, 20,000 troops, 42 ships, and 350 aircraft
1980 Readex	Guantanamo and Puerto Rico
1981 Ocean Venture	120,000 troops, 2,500 ships, and 1,000 aircraft
1981 Falcon's Eye	Puerto Cortés, Honduras
1982 No Name	Joint exercises with Canada in the Gulf of Mexico and the Florida straits
1982 Readex	War games, 39 ships, 200 aircraft and one British ship, with amphibian assault practice on Vieques Island
1982 Ocean Venture	45,000 troops, 60 ships, 350 aircraft; lasted one month, with Dutch forces participating
1982 Falcon Vista	Navy exercises with Honduras
1982 Safepass	War games north of Cuba, with 6 Western countries participating (NATO)
1983 Kindle Liberty	Training in Panama for defense of the canal, 3,000 U.S. troops and 7,000 Panamanian troops
1983 Readex	War games, 43 ships, including British and Dutch ships
1983 Universal Trek	Land and sea maneuvers, 5,000 U.S. troops and National Guard
1983 Unitas	Joint exercises between navy and Latin American countries carried out in the Caribbean, 2,000 U.S. troops and 12,000 Latin American
1983 No Notice Exercise	Navy exercises after Grenada invasion, with 8 ships
1984 Ocean Venture	Guantánamo, Florida straits, and the Gulf of Mexico, 30,000 troops and 350 ships
1984 Unitas	Navy exercises in the Caribbean and Latin America with U.S. ships
1984 Composite	Navy exercises in the Atlantic Ocean and Caribbean Sea, near Puerto Rico, with 250 U.S. ships (Training Unit I-85)
1984 No Name	Eastern Caribbean, with U.S. destroyer and Eastern Caribbean states' coast guards

Sources: "Proyecto Caribeño de Justicia y Paz," Puerto Rico, June-July 1982, and R. Escobar, "Cronología de las Maniobras Militares Norteamerianas en América Latina," in *Cuadernos de Nuestra América* 2, no. 4 (1985).

Note: Only exercises in the West Indies and Panama have been taken into consideration.

waters. . . . It was another classic example of the arrogance, contempt and insensitivity by the U. S. administration of Ronald Reagan for the peoples of the Caribbean.[68]

The U.S. destabilization of Grenada, particularly the economic sanctions and military exercises, have had a profound impact on the Bishop regime, whose aspirations to construct a new society independent of foreign influence and domination and to reduce Grenada's external dependence had become tenuous by late 1982.

The Effects of U.S. Destabilization of Grenada

The destabilization of Grenada, combined with widespread inefficiency at all levels, shortage of skilled personnel, personal shortcomings on the part of the PRG leadership, particularly their obsession with Marxist-Leninist philosophy, and the problems posed by the country's small size and limited resource base contributed to the collapse of the revolution. On the political front, the Bishop regime's anti-imperialist rhetoric isolated Grenada from its traditional tourist markets and from some of its Caribbean neighbors, notably Barbados, Dominica, St. Lucia, and Trinidad and Tobago up to the time of Prime Minister Eric Williams's death in 1981. Only Guyana and Jamaica, prior to Manley's defeat at the polls in October 1980, and a few leftist movements in the region supported the PRG and its radical position.

On the economic front, the tourist sector performed dismally under the PRG administration. A close examination of the figures for tourist arrivals in the Caribbean indicated that Grenada fared worst among eight OECS members. Only two countries within this group, St. Lucia and St. Vincent, showed a marked decline, but it was not as steep as Grenada's. During the first three years of the revolution, overnight tourists to Grenada fell from 32,000 in 1979 to 30,100 in 1980, to 25,000 in 1981, and to 23,200 in 1982. The dramatic decline was particularly pronounced in the U.S. segment of the tourist market. For example, there were 9,100 American overnight visitors to Grenada in 1979 compared to only 5,000 in 1982, a loss of 45 percent.[69] The virtual dislocation of the tourist industry was due mostly to the adverse publicity by the television and print media and by the propaganda campaign waged by the United States against Grenada as well as the PRG's socialist policies, which exposed the fundamental flaw in its economic development strategy. The new international airport which was constructed to boost the tourist industry could not automatically solve the country's development problems, since tourism itself was incompatible with the PRG's radical anti-imperialist and overtly pro-socialist stance. The decline in Grenada's share of the tourist market attests to the unreliability of the tourist industry as a vehicle of development. It casts serious doubts on the viability of the PRG's development strategy. Furthermore, the regimes close ties to Cuba and the socialist bloc made a bad situation worse in the view of American tourists.

The decline in the tourist industry had a detrimental effect on the island's economy. This is not surprising given the importance of the tourist sector to the island's economy. It is estimated that tourism contributes as much as 50 percent of Grenada's foreign exchange earnings and, in addition, has spillover effects on employment and tax revenues. Despite the high level of foreign borrowing and the large amount of foreign aid, by mid to late 1982, Grenada was in dire need of foreign reserves. Combined export earnings from the island's three major export crops fell by more than 40 percent, from U.S. $18.4 million in 1979 to U.S. $10.5 million in 1983.[70] In the same period, private sector investment declined from U.S. $5.4 million to U.S. $2.6 million.[71] Another setback was hurricane and flood damages which destroyed 40 percent of the island's banana crop, 27 percent of its nutmeg, and 19 percent of its cocoa production, for an estimated total cost of U.S. $27 million between 1979 and 1982. This was accompanied by a 22 percent decline in world market prices of Grenada's main products that resulted in a further loss of approximately U.S. $15 million in total export earnings.[72]

By early 1983, the Grenadian economy was engulfed in a severe economic crisis that resulted in a budget deficit and balance-of-payment problems. The shortage of funds forced the Bishop regime to suspend construction of the new airport, restrict imports, reduce public spending, and increase taxes on a number of government services. There were also major cutbacks in social services, especially in the areas of health and education. These problems were compounded by an almost total collapse in the public sector, such as unrepaired roads, schools, and other public buildings, electrical outages, a deterioration in public transportation services, and the retrenchment of state workers, many of whom were staunch supporters of the revolution and the Bishop regime.

Meanwhile, fear had gripped the entire Grenadian population as the U.S. increased its military exercises in the region and its threats to invade the island. Grenadians were alarmed at the Reagan administration's claim that their tiny island was a security threat to the United States. Despite Reagan's belligerence, most Grenadians did not believe his rhetoric and could not fathom a U.S. invasion. It did not seem possible to them that the U.S. would risk the international criticism that would result from bullying such a small nation. And even those who did not support the regime viewed the threats of an impending U.S. invasion as the strong and powerful taking advantage of the weak. A sense of unreality touched all aspects of life in Grenada. As fear turned to paranoia, the PRG mobilized the population into militias to protect itself from a likely U.S. invasion and diverted much needed resources from the economy to the military and paramilitary forces. But no matter how many people mobilized and how well they were trained, and no matter what the regime did, there existed the underlying realization that the Grenadian armed forces could not stand up to the military power of the United States. As a result, Prime Minister Bishop and some moderate members of the PRG softened their socialist rhetoric and sought rapproche-ment with the Reagan administration. Their primary goal was to prevent an invasion by the U.S.

But as the economy continued to deteriorate and U.S. threats to invade Grenada intensified, there developed a siege mentality within the PRG leadership, most of whom viewed all opposition to their socialist policies as being, at the very least, CIA inspired. This approach manifested itself into an internal power struggle as the radical elements of the PRG deepened their commitment to the revolutionary process and Marxism and purged Bishop and his supporters who attempted to retreat from the socialist philosophy. Bishop and his supporters were deemed traitors to the Marxist-Leninist principles who were about to turn the revolution over to imperialist America. Their deaths were marked with the slogan, "Towards a Higher Discipline in the PRA." The events of 19 and 25 October 1983 are well documented. Suffice to say that U.S. destabilization measures have played a major role in the collapse of the Bishop regime and revolutionary socialism in Grenada.

It is clear that neither the American medical students nor Washington's need to honor a request from the Organization of Eastern Caribbean States (OECS) was the true reason for the invasion. The invasion had more to do with the U.S. desire to maintain its hegemony in the hemisphere and to stamp out the remnants of a popular socialist experiment in Grenada. The timing could not have been better for the Reagan administration. The regime had killed off the popular leader of the revolution and in doing so left a dispirited population no longer ready and willing to resist a U.S. invasion. What Grenadians had wanted in their revolution were better schools, jobs, health care and educational facilities, and the right to organize. But they quickly found out that their tiny island had suddenly become embroiled in a new Cold War conflict of which neither the people nor their leaders were prepared to handle that kind of pressure.

Notes

1. Michael Manley, *Jamaica: Struggle in the Periphery* (London: London University Press, 1982), 7; Thomas G. Paterson, Gray Clifford, and Kenneth J. Hagan, *America Foreign Relations: A History since 1895,* vol. 11, 4 ed. (Lexington, Mass.: D. C. Heath, 1995), 55.

2. President Lyndon B. Johnson's speech cited in J. Pearce, *Under the Eagle: U.S. Intervention in Central America and the Caribbean* (London: Latin American Bureau, 1982), 64.

3. Anthony Payne, *The International Crisis in the Caribbean* (London: Croom Helm, 1984), 40-41.

4. Mir Zohair Husain, *Global Islamic Politics* (New York: Harper Collins, 1995), 218-20.

5. George P. Shultz, Speech to the "Annual Conference on Trade, Investment and Development in the Caribbean Basin," Miami, Florida, December 6, 1984.

6. Manley, *Jamaica,* 138.

7. Chris Searle, *Grenada: The Struggle against Destabilization* (London: Writers and Readers Publishing Comparative Society Ltd., 1983), 34.

8. Cited in *North American Congress on Latin America (NACLA) Report,* July/August (1981): 30.

9. Cited in Anthony Payne, Paul Sutton, and Tony Thorndike, *Grenada: Revolution and Invasion* (New York: St. Martin's Press, 1984), 58.

10. Percy Hintzen, *The Costs of Regime Survival: Racial Mobilization, Elite Domination, and Control of the State in Guyana and Trinidad* (Cambridge: Cambridge University Press, 1988), 185.

11. Clive Thomas, "Guyana: The Rise and Fall of Cooperative Socialism," in *Dependency under Challenge: The Political Economy of the Commonwealth Caribbean,* ed. Anthony Payne and Paul Sutton (London: Croom Helm, 1984), 94, 97.

12. Macdonald Scott, "The Future of Foreign Aid in the Caribbean after Grenada: Finlandization and Confrontation in the Eastern Tier," *Inter-American Economics Affair* 38, no. 4 (1985): 65.

13. Special Drawing Rights (SDR) established by the IMF was a checking account that countries could use to supplement their foreign reserves and settle international accounts.

14. Thomas, "Guyana," 97; Tyrone Ferguson, *Structural Adjustment and Good Governance: The Case of Guyana* (Georgetown, Guyana: Public Affairs Consulting Enterprise, 1995), 53-55.

15. Tom Barry, Beth Wood, and Deb Preusch, *The Other Side of Paradise: Foreign Control in the Caribbean* (New York: Grove Press, 1984), 326.

16. Anthony Payne, *Modern Caribbean Politics* (Baltimore: Johns Hopkins University Press, 1993), 117.

17. Ferguson, *Structural Adjustment and Good Governance,* 1.

18. Clive Thomas, *The Poor and the Powerless: Economic Policy and Change in the Caribbean* (New York: Monthly Review Press, 1988), 257.

19. *World Bank Report No. 5592, GUA,* Washington, D.C., 15 May 1985.

20. Ibid.

21. Ferguson, *Structural Adjustment and Good Governance,* 34.

22. Thomas, "Guyana," 98.

23. Ferguson, *Structural Adjustment and Good Governance,* 34.

24. Carl Stone, "Jamaica in Crisis: From Socialist to Capitalist Management," *International Journal* (Spring 1986): 288.

25. Barry et al., *The Other Side of Paradise,* 344.

26. Manley, *Jamaica,* 109.

27. Barry et al., *The Other Side of Paradise,* 342.

28. S. Keith and R. Girling, "Caribbean Conflict: Jamaica and the U.S.," *NACLA* 12, no. 3 (1978): 28.

29. Jay R. Mandle, *Patterns of Caribbean Development* (London: Gordon and Breach, 1982), 100.

30. Norman Girvan, "Swallowing the IMF Medicine in the Seventies," *Development Dialogue* 2 (1980): 62.

31. Manley, *Jamaica,* 140.

32. Fitzroy Ambursley, "Jamaica: From Michael Manley to Edward Seaga," in *Crisis in the Caribbean,* ed. Fitzroy Ambursley and Robin Cohen (New York: Monthly Review Press, 1983), 84; Anthony Payne, "Jamaica: The Democratic Socialist Experiment of Michael Manley," in *Dependency under Challenge,* ed. Payne and Sutton, 31.

33. Manley, *Jamaica,* 149.

34. Manley, *Jamaica,* 223-32; Evelyn H. Stephens and John D. Stephens, *Democratic Socialism in Jamaica* (Princeton, N.J.: Princeton University Press, 1986), 135.

35. Manley, *Jamaica,* 133.

36. Manley, *Jamaica,* 143-44.

37. Manley, *Jamaica,* 136-37.

38. Stephens and Stephens, *Democratic Socialism in Jamaica,* 128.

39. *Jamaican Tourist Board Travel Statistics,* Kingston, Jamaica (1976): 2.

40. Saul Landau, *Washington Post,* 25 August 1976, 6.

41. Payne, "Jamaica," 31.

42. Don Bohning, "Charges of Destabilization Grow in the Caribbean," *Miami Herald,* 22 June 1976, 5.

43. Thomas, *The Poor and the Powerless,* 232.

44. Ambursley, "Jamaica," 85.

45. *Gleaner,* 1 July 1976, 4; Barry et al., *The Other Side of Paradise,* 343.

46. Ambursley, "Jamaica," 84.

47. For a good discussion of IMF policies toward Jamaica, see Stephens and Stephens, *Democratic Socialism in Jamaica*; Payne, "Jamaica;" and Manley, *Jamaica.*

48. Manley, *Jamaica*, 151; Payne, "Jamaica," 35; Thomas, *The Poor and the Powerless*, 225-26.

49. T. Lacey, *Violence and Politics in Jamaica, 1960-1970* (Manchester: Manchester University Press, 1977), 159; L. Williams, "Ganja: A Billion Dollar Operation," *Weekly Gleaner,* 15 July 1981.

50. Alan Gabbidon, " Probe Tinson Pen as Ganja Centre," *Weekly Gleaner*, 9 September 1981.

51. Maurice Bishop, "Organize to Fight Destabilization," in *Selected Speeches 1979-1981*, ed. Maurice Bishop (Havana: Casa de las Americas, 1982).

52. Payne et al., *Grenada,* 49-50.

53. Searle, *Grenada*, 71-72.

54. Searle, *Grenada*, 56-57; Gregory Sandford and Diane B. Bendahmane, *The New Jewel Movement: Grenada's Revolution, 1979-1983* (Washington, D.C.: Foreign Service Institute, U.S. Department of State, 1985), 131.

55. Payne et al., *Grenada,* 50.

56. Payne et al., *Grenada,* 63; Searle, *Grenada*, 55.

57. Searle, *Grenada*, 55-56; Payne et al., *Grenada,* 50.

58. Payne et al., *Grenada,* 62; Searle, *Grenada*, 56-57.

59. Maurice Bishop, "Imperialism is the Real Problem," in *Selected Speeches,* ed. Maurice Bishop, 191.

60. Searle, *Grenada*, 57; Tony Thorndike, "Grenada: The New Jewel Revolution," in *Dependency under Challenge*, ed. Payne and Sutton, 119.

61. Cited in Payne et al., *Grenada,* 64-65.

62. Maurice Bishop, "Three Years of the Grenada Revolution," in *Forward Ever! Three Years of the Grenada Revolution*, ed. Maurice Bishop (Sydney: Pathfinder Press, 1982), 275-76.

63. Searle, *Grenada,* 60.

64. Government of Grenada, *Ministry of Information, Film Division,* St. George's, Grenada, 1983.

65. Searle, *Grenada*, 79-80.

66. Maurice Bishop, "Freedom of the Press versus CIA Destabilization," in *Forward Ever*, ed. Bishop, 185.

67. President Reagan's speech on 10 March 1983 to the National Association of Manufactures cited in Payne et al., *Grenada,* 67.

68. Prime Minister Maurice Bishop's address to the First Conference of Journalists from the Caribbean Area (St. George's, Grenada: People's Revolutionary Government, 17 April 1982); also cited in Payne et al., *Grenada,* 66-67.

69. *Department of Tourism,* St. George's, Grenada, 1978-1982.

70. Wallace Joefield-Napier, "Macroeconomic Growth under the People's Revolutionary Government: An Assessment," in *A Revolution Aborted: Lessons of Grenada,* ed. Jorge Heine (Pittsburgh: University of Pittsburgh Press, 1991), 97.

71. *World Bank Report on Grenada* (Washington, D.C., 1984), 42.

72. Searle, *Grenada*, 58; Payne et al., *Grenada,* 23-24.

Chapter 9

Conclusion: Dependency, Socialism, and Superpower Intervention in the Caribbean

From emancipation to the present, the hopes and aspirations of the leaders and peoples of the Caribbean have suffered persistent setbacks in their efforts to improve their living standards which, in some cases, have led to development strategies that moved away from the status quo at worst or have maintained it at best. As products and exploits of the European colonial powers and of the plantation economy, the territories of the Caribbean are almost immune to fundamental change that could lead to economic growth and development and thus reduce their dependence on the core capitalist states. One of the main reasons for the region's dependency and under-development is that the territories of the Caribbean like most other former colonies are mired in a colonial mold and that their small size and limited resource base have severely inhibited their development to the point where almost every consumer item is imported. Virtually everything, from goods, equipment, services, ideas, culture, and fashion, to economic and political ideologies are imported from the outside world, especially the United States.

Over the last four decades or so the whole Caribbean region and society have been drastically changed by the sociocultural impact of American cultural imperialism, in the mass media of newspapers, magazines, tele-vision, and movies, in the tourist industry, in commercial advertising, in American popular cults and religion, and even in educational patterns. The region's elites, in their general lifestyles, live more like their counterparts in New York and Miami. Their children develop life patterns shaped by the U.S. technologies of fast food, videocassettes, and American pop and rock music, all of which reflect the pleasure-seeking drives of a pervasive American materialistic hedonism. This cultural Americanism has convinced many in the Caribbean and elsewhere that their destiny, political or otherwise, now lies with the American empire. What all this means is that the Caribbean has become the psychological content of the new American cultural imperialism. The key reason for this is the Caribbean long history of retarded growth through colonialism, dependence, and imperialism, which have left a legacy of an undeveloped productive region, and a people not believing in them-selves, their own culture and identity. As already indicated, colonies were not permitted to be self-sufficient; what was consumed locally was imported and what was produced was exported to the metropolitan centers.

During the 1970s, internationally transmitted recessions and inflation generated by steep increases in the price of imported oil and manufactured goods led to shortages in foreign currency, huge budget deficits, and heavy borrowing by the countries of the Caribbean. These developments not only contributed significantly to the region's inability to develop its economy and control its own destiny, but also to the subordination of the Caribbean people.

Highly resistant to change with high rates of unemployment and double digit inflation, and with great inequalities in income and wealth within and between countries, most Caribbean societies lack a firm sense of identity rooted in Caribbean mores and values. The territories of the Caribbean share with a number of other Global South societies one of the worst income distributions in the world, Guyana, Jamaica, and Trinidad and Tobago being the worst offenders in this category. In these countries, the top 5 percent of the population account for approximately 30 percent of the total national income while the bottom 20 percent earned a meager 2 percent.[1] Similar numbers can be found in some of the smaller Eastern Caribbean islands, where over 50 percent of the wealth is concentrated in the hands of a few. This inequality in income distribution and wealth has and continued to be one of the major barriers to change and a promoter of instability in the region. This instability, according to Eric Williams, has made the Caribbean one of the most unstable areas in an unstable world.[2]

The resistance of Caribbean societies to undergo fundamental structural transformation, combined with their growing socioeconomic problems of poverty, unemployment, emigration, and racial tension, as well as violence, have added to the region's unstable position. Furthermore, the post-World War II development strategies of industrialization by invitation and import substitution industrialization discussed in chapter 2 did not improve the region's economy and reduce its dependence on the developed nations. The small open economies of the Caribbean continue to be as they have been during the twentieth century, vulnerable to the vagaries of the international capitalist system dominated and monopolized by the core capitalist states, especially the United States. Several reasons accounted for this scenario. One is that there was stiff competition among the various governments of the Caribbean to provide incentives in order to induce foreign capital. A second reason is that the surplus generated in the capitalist sector was not ploughed back into domestic investment but siphoned into banks and other financial institutions or luxury lifestyles in the home country of the multi-national corporations. A third reason is that most of the industries developed were capital intensive rather than labor intensive and, as a result, could not absorb the region's high unemployment. These factors not only reinforced the region's dependency on the developed countries, but are more likely to influence development and survival prospects in the Caribbean and other underdeveloped regions of the world than ideology, socialist or capitalist.

Cognizant of the fact that very little by way of development could take place in the Caribbean unless there are fundamental socioeconomic changes in the societies, the leaders of the region have made various efforts to break out of the confines of the capitalist management system and to embrace varieties of socialist practice and policy. The experiences of Guyana in the 1970s and early 1980s, Jamaica in the 1970s, and Grenada between 1979 and 1983 are three notable efforts in this direction. The interest in socialist transformation and its potential has generated considerable attention during this period because of the deeply rooted socioeconomic problems in the Caribbean under the capitalist managed system. These problems include high levels of unemployment, extreme concentration of income, distressing poverty levels among the bottom 40 percent of the population, extreme dependence on and vulnerability to trade, financial, and fiscal trends within the Western capitalist system, weak production structures, reliance on one or two main products for foreign currency earnings, low production in agriculture, extensive foreign ownership, and the massive export of capital and skills through emigration.[3]

The results of socialist development have not been favorable insofar as to reduce these countries' dependence on the international capitalist system. If anything, the failure of the socialist development strategies in the region highlighted the complexity of dismantling the colonial relationship, infra-structure, and dependency arrangements (trade, aid, and loans) with the West. In both Guyana and Jamaica, the patterns of economic growth under socialist management during the 1970s and early 1980s were among the worst in the Caribbean. In both countries, per capita income levels declined rather than increased due partly to lower bauxite demand and prices on the international market. In a period of downturn in production and real income, the governments in both countries increased public spending and borrowed heavily from foreign sources to sustain employment and government services and to increase transfer payments to the poor through price subsidies and state ownership of enterprises. Grenada strenuously tried to avoid the problems encountered by Guyana and Jamaica in that it minimized state ownership of foreign corporations and implemented a more stringent fiscal management policy. Although Grenada managed to avoid the negative economic growth rate and a prolonged economic recession, shortages of skilled personnel, weak organizational structures, and an overworked political leadership led to poor management of public projects and a massive waste of funds. By 1982, it too, like Guyana and Jamaica had the highest budget deficits in the region. These developments raise a very important question: Was socialism or the noncapitalist path of development a viable alternative to the capitalist road to development in the Caribbean?

Contrary to the views of several Caribbean dependency and development theorists, the body of literature presented in this study suggests the negative. For one reason, the small economies of the Caribbean, which emerged from colonialism with its attendant legacies of slavery, capitalism, exploitation, exports, and profits, have produced consolidated forms of underdevelopment and dependency in the region. For another, Caribbean societies remained linked and tied to the Western capitalism through a network of financial, commercial, banking, and military relationships, the benefits of which could not be matched from available resources in the socialist countries. Whatever trade or aid the three countries obtained from the Soviet Union, Cuba, and the socialist governments in Eastern European was certainly not enough to permit a rupturing of ties with the core capitalist countries. In this sense, diversification of trade and other forms of economic relationships were not a viable option for the three socialist regimes in the Caribbean.

Despite these facts, the truth is neither capitalism nor socialism has provided an easy path towards economic development or transformation of the productive forces and structures in the English-speaking Caribbean. Therefore, in Guyana, Jamaica, and Grenada there was definitely a need to adjust ideology and politics to the practical requirements of development and its constraints, both internal and external. One set of development constraints originated from poor management, shortages of foreign capital and skilled labor, extensive corruption, and political nepotism as well as small size and limited resources. Another set of constraints is that conventional capitalist economic strategies are borrowed and combined with socialist strategies that led to the promotion and development of a mixed or a trisector economy which is contradictory, internally inconsistent, and confusing to the leaders and the population, particularly the capitalist class. This intermediary or middle position did not appear to be consistent with socialist development strategy, or a gradual but decisive political and economic step toward the so-called noncapitalist or third path to development. A third set of development constraints apparently emanated from the socialist development strategies that have been accompanied by anti-imperialist and anti-American rhetoric which came into conflict with capitalist principles and antagonized the United States government, multinational corporations, and the capitalist class in and out of the region. As emphasized earlier, this conflict resulted in a series of destabilization measures inspired and led by the United States that contributed to the demise of socialism in the Caribbean in particular, and the hemisphere as a whole.

Perhaps the worst of these constraints stemmed from the region's long history of colonialism and imperialism which were and continue to be a form of domination by the transnational structures of power. These structures at the time constituted the epitome of nondemocratic rule, direct exploitation of labor and the region's resources, the lack of representative government based on universal suffrage, and the establishment of a slave plantation system dominated by white Europeans comprised of the planter class and the commercial and bureaucratic elite. One cannot, of course, underemphasize the role of racism in this period, which legitimized the exclusion of blacks from the political and economic decision-making process and instead singled them out for harsh treatment and injustice. This racist ideology justified treating blacks in the Caribbean differently from the white population there, and from those in the British settler colonies in North America, even in the period after slavery. The perception of the Colonial Office was that the black masses were not fit or qualified for full citizenship and, as a consequence, were considered inferior to whites, and the colonial educational system, in assuming so, reinforced this negative perception. Although a little more subtle, this attitude still exists among many whites and continues to haunt blacks throughout the world, particular in the United States, which has the second largest black population in the world after Africa.

There are, however, some positive aspects of colonial rule in the region. In the anglophone Caribbean, colonialism provided the base for the respect for the rule of law, the emergence of a civil society, the establishment of democratic principles, and the introduction of a competitive political system. It has bequeathed democratic institutions to the people of the region where internal conditions were favorable, and prevented the landed upper class from using the state to repress protests and organizational attempts of the subordinate classes. This is in sharp contrast to the repression exercised by large landlords in Central and South America. The argument that the transfer

of British institutions to the Caribbean contributed to the democratic outcome in the region does hold because early representative institutions such
as political parties and unions generally specified suffrage rights similar to
those prevailing in Britain and other democratic societies. Although these
institutions came in the early to mid-twentieth century, the legacy of British
colonialism in the Caribbean helps to explain why the region developed in a
democratic direction.

The general conclusion that colonialism is the primary reason for underdevelopment and dependency in the Caribbean and elsewhere is indeed an
accurate representation of the historical process by which the economy of the
region evolved. However, this tells very little about how and why the leaders
of Guyana, Jamaica, and Grenada have chosen socialism over capitalism as a
development strategy for their respective economies. Precisely what is meant
by socialism must first be clarified since sharp controversy exists over
whether the concept appropriately describes different political economy
structures or regimes claiming allegiance to the socialist ideology as broadly
defined. Some neo-Marxists in the Caribbean and elsewhere have claimed
that the experiments by the Manley regime in Jamaica in the 1970s or the
Guyana experience under Forbes Burnham between 1970 and 1985 were not
genuine socialist practice; only the political leadership in Grenada was
genuinely Marxist in its political and ideological objectives.

Socialism involves commitment to specific objectives, such as large-
scale redistribution of wealth, assets, or income in favor of the majority
classes, and a dominant role by the state to manage the economy on behalf of
the masses to improve their living standards, and to reduce or eliminate the
power and influence of the capitalist class. On the whole, socialist theory and
practice diverge on how to achieve these objectives and the political
structures necessary to accomplish socialist economic development. Social
democrats operate within the framework of the capitalist system and sought
to improve the quality of life of the poor through reforms and redistribution
of resources and social welfare policies. More radical socialists aspire to
overturn the capitalist system, both domestic and international, and replace it
with a political economy controlled by the state on behalf of the people.
Derived from this latter approach, repeated arguments of some Caribbean
authors, particularly those from the neo-Marxist school, are that the
historical options of Caribbean economies were limited to a comprehensive
socialist strategy for transforming the productive structures and liberating the
political and social order. Development theorists, on the other hand, claimed
that this approach by the neo-Marxists has more to do with challenging the
status quo rather than the pursuit of an alternative logic and credible path to

economic development. But as this study's theoretical framework suggests, and the analyses in chapter 2 bear out, neither modernization nor dependency theory provided a framework or an adequate explanation as how to overcome or eradicate underdevelopment and dependency in the Caribbean and other developing areas of the world.

Modernization theory attempts to apply ideas and solutions drawn from the experience of the advanced developed countries of Western Europe and North America to the underdeveloped regions of the world. This approach assumed that the underdeveloped countries possessed the relative abundance of natural resources and the necessary skills, structures, and productive forces conducive to development. This, in fact, limits the theory's ability to find adequate solutions to resolve the problems associated with dependency and underdevelopment in the Caribbean and elsewhere. As stated at the end of chapter 2 but bears repeating, dependency theory shifts the emphasis away from internal obstacles, such as natural variables, class struggle, weak infrastructure, lack of appropriate technology, foreign exchange, and skills in the underdeveloped countries to external causes. It also exaggerates the constraints placed on these countries by the international capital and political systems, and posits that development in the Global North resulted in underdevelopment in the Global South. This zero-sum approach leaves little room for the Global South countries to develop their economies within the present international structures and the accelerated pace of globalization. Some even supported the realists' claim that globalization is the Americanization of the world because the current institutions and rules that sustain and promote the global economy are under American control.

Having made these points, however, it is clear that both modernization and dependency theories have their own limitations. As argued here and elsewhere, dependency theory, because of its leftist thrust and ideology, is biased towards the Western development models, whereas, a major problem with modernization theory has been its Eurocentric focus and its attempts to view development in that particular perspective. Its essentially Western European focus has no basis when applied to regions in the Global South like the Caribbean where the main development task lies in building a strong and viable production base to overcome centuries of dependency and underdevelopment. On the whole, both theories pretend to rationalize and provide solutions that could lead to development in the Global South.

In the sections below, we will evaluate the main themes that have been used throughout the study to address the problems of socialist development as they apply to Guyana, Jamaica, Grenada, the Caribbean, and other underdeveloped regions.

Socialist Formulation in Guyana, Jamaica, and Grenada

Although both socialist and capitalist economies are susceptible to some of the same international economic forces, the societies of the Caribbean are particularly vulnerable to falling exports and prices on the world market; inflation; chronic balance of payment problems; currency devaluation and shortages of hard currency; high dependence on imports, due partly to small size and partly to a legacy of economic dependence; weak infrastructures; and the lack of appropriate technology. Furthermore, Guyana, Jamaica, and Grenada, because of their socialist ideology and anti-American rhetoric, had to face additional economic and political pressures from the United States and the capitalist elite. The three socialist regimes did not have the resources to offset the sanctions imposed on them by the U.S., or to train and retain managerial and technical personnel to solve the problems that emanated from the sanctions, and to effectively manage the day-to-day and long-term operations of an expanded state and/or private sector economy. In fact, their efforts to expand trade, create new export markets with the socialist bloc, improve the quality of the labor force, and earn and retain hard currency have met with very little success. This is also true for a number of socialist countries outside the Caribbean region.

The adoption of socialist development strategies in Guyana, Jamaica, and Grenada during the 1970s and early 1980s had been associated with the objective of reducing or eliminating their dependence on the United States and the apparent increasing monopolization of the global economy by the core capitalist states. The leaders of the three regimes embraced theories and articulated policies that diverged considerably from their actual practice. In theory, their socialist strategies hinged on the commitment by the state to take control of the productive forces created by capitalism and used the surpluses generated from the economy to provide social and welfare benefits such as free education and free health care as well as the redistribution of wealth in favor of the masses. They were also involved in the building of a strong and viable production base to replace the colonial structures, which they claimed had inhibited growth and development in the Caribbean. Their goals were to improve the life chances of the masses, reduce the power of the capitalist class, and hence their countries' external dependence.

In practice, socialist strategies of development in the three countries had several objectives. One was the consolidation of power by the state in favor of the ruling parties (see table 9.1). This was particularly true of Guyana and Grenada, where political power was heavily concentrated in the hands of party leaders and policy makers. The PNC regime in Guyana had a well-established and consolidated power structure, while in Grenada the PRG was in the process of strengthening its power when the regime collapsed. The consolidation of power in Guyana and Grenada involved the use of the state coercive apparatus to stifle internal strife, freedom, and to repress demands from the masses for political inclusion or for material concessions. In both countries the state and the party asserted control and direction over all aspects of economic, social, and political activities. This was facilitated by the regimes' control of the media, the merging of party and governmental functions, political control over the civil service, and state control of the economy. In neither case were there any checks and balances or constitutional constraints to limit the exercise of this enormous use and abuse of power. In both countries power was highly personalized rather than mainly institutional and each leader wielded enormous power over the bureaucracy and policy decisions while in office. As Carl Stone wisely remarked:

> This concentration of power enabled politics effectively to take command as the party-states asserted control, direction, and guidance over all spheres of economic and social life. This was facilitated by tight control of the mass media, the merging of party and governmental functions, political control over the civil service, and extensive growth of the state's policy leadership and control over the economy.[4]

The consolidation of political power in the hands of party leaders did take root in Jamaica, but not to the extent as it did in Guyana and Grenada. In part, this was due to Manley's beliefs in social democratic principles and a strong right-wing opposition party in the JLP. In sharp contrast to Guyana and Grenada, the Manley regime operated within the framework of the Westminster constitutional system of liberal democracy primarily because of the power of the relatively strong capitalist class, an influential and articulate middle class, a competitive media, and the constraints of the legal and constitutional limits to power.

Other socialist development strategies included the use of appropriate technology, mobilization of the masses with the aim to promote and increase political awareness and class consciousness, organizational development, and state ownership of foreign assets by Guyana and Jamaica. In Grenada there were no large corporations for the state to nationalize; therefore, there was no strong state ownership in the country. Generally speaking, the leaders of the three socialist regimes sought to reorganize the forces of production to meet the social welfare needs of the masses in areas such as food, shelter, clothing, health, and education. On the one hand, these practical approaches

were designed to reduce most of the deeply rooted poverty and unemployment found among the bottom 40 percent of income earners. On the
other hand, they would have nothing much to offer the top 60 percent of
income earners except for drastically reducing their living standards and
imposing upon them a lifestyle of austerity. This group would have to
consume less to accommodate greater equality in income and consumption.
In other words, the goal was to take from the rich to give to the poor. It is
important to point out, however, that this type of Robin Hoodism has not
been implemented successfully, not even in the core socialist states, let alone
in the Caribbean.

   Another aspect of the socialist strategy was a commitment by the three
regimes to a radical foreign policy based on non-alignment, anti-imperialism,
and collectivity aimed to redefine their power status and role in the international system, and to develop and pursue policies consistent with the
interests of other Global South countries. It was in this context that Guyana
and Jamaica initiated the formation of the International Bauxite Association
which, in the words of Prime Minister Manley, was to pursue a "common
economic diplomacy" to strengthen their position vis-à-vis the advanced
industrialized states and the multinational corporations. Among the IBA
objectives were the elimination of price competition between and among
bauxite producing countries, the exchange of important information, and the
harmonization of policies relating to all aspects of mining, processing, and
marketing of bauxite and its by-products. None of these goals was realized.
From the beginning the IBA did not achieve a high level of congruence and
capability which inhibited its ability to confront the industrialized countries
and the MNCs. Furthermore, the IBA was not designed as a cartel along the
lines of OPEC; rather, it was generally to raise consciousness among bauxite
producing countries about the need for change and the possible avenue of
pursuing that change.

   However, during the 1970s, the recession in developed economies led to
a lower demand on the world market for bauxite. As a result, Australia and
Guinea increased bauxite production and lowered their prices, thus
undermining the principal objective of the IBA. The IBA solidarity on price
and control of domestic production had conflicting effects among the bauxite
producing countries of the Caribbean. The overproduction of bauxite by
non-Caribbean countries, such as Australia, Guinea, and Sierra Leone and by
non-IBA members forced Jamaica and Suriname to reduce their taxes in
order to induce countries and companies to purchase their bauxite. Guyana,
which had nationalized its bauxite industry, had to compete directly with the
MNCs to gain a foothold in major markets and, as a consequence, found it

necessary to offer competitive prices. The result was that the buyer countries and the MNCs gained considerably at the expense of Guyana, Jamaica, and Suriname.

This situation highlights another important factor that affected IBA unity and solidarity among its members. There was no clear agreement on markets or a marketing strategy of bauxite among the producing countries. In a sense, therefore, the existence of the IBA assisted those countries which induced MNCs to purchase their bauxite and those that maximized investments, even on terms that undermined other IBA members. Thus government inducement and MNC co-optation in this situation were complementary. To these must be added that the aluminum companies transferred a large amount of bauxite and alumina production from Guyana and Jamaica to other countries because of those countries' nationalization and tax policies. Although the recession of the 1970s did reduce world production of bauxite, Jamaica and Guyana suffered a disproportionate, overtly political cutback in bauxite production. As the empirical evidence in chapter 8 reveals, Jamaica, the number one bauxite producer country in the world in 1970 lost its status to Australia in 1975. These factors proved that Manley's "common economic diplomacy" strategy had not worked effectively, particularly for Jamaica and other IBA members in the Caribbean in the areas of production and price control of bauxite.

Ideology

As argued in chapters 5 and 7 and shown in table 9.1, both Guyana and Grenada projected official doctrines supportive of Marxist notions of socialist development. In Guyana, this resulted from the fact that all the opposition parties in the country except the United Force espoused leftist ideologies, and in Grenada, the de facto one-party state of the PRG suppressed capitalist principles and anti-Marxist sentiments among segments of the political community. Evidence presented in chapter 6 indicates that the Manley regime in Jamaica, in contrast to the PNC government in Guyana and the PRG in Grenada, disavowed either explicitly or by implication, any Marxist-Leninist notions of class struggle and proletarian dictatorship in favor of social democracy. The reason for this was twofold. First, Manley was a social democrat with typically Fabian views, especially on issues such as equality, justice, and the role of social organizations in society. Second, Manley and the PNP were constantly attacked for their socialist philosophy and close ties with the Castro regime in Cuba by the opposition anti-Marxist forces, including the conservative JLP leadership. These groups not only conducted a smear campaign against the PNP government, but also exposed its corrupt practices at every step of the way.

In Guyana, the official ideology of cooperative socialism was by no means a serious attempt to overcome or reduce its economic dependence on the core capitalist countries. Rather, it was an ideological rationalization for the development of state capitalism in Guyana, which provided a base for the creation of a new class of indigenous capitalists that benefited from the state industries. In the scheme of things an elaborate patronage system evolved in which policy and political favors were exchanged for unquestioned political loyalty to the party and regime support. In this regard, cooperative socialism was designed more for self aggrandizement rather than as a guide to policy and practice in Guyana.

The PRG leadership adopted a genuinely Marxist political objective that included the struggle to overcome structural, economic, psychological, and cultural dependency through the diversification of trade, foreign aid, and the establishment of diplomatic relations with Cuba, Russia, and the socialist bloc in Eastern Europe. The goal was to bolster Grenada's sovereignty and reduce substantially the impact of U.S. economic and political pressure that had engulfed the island. Surrounded by anticommunist regimes and the major superpower in the region, the United States, it was only natural for the PRG to seek protection from the socialist bloc not only to reduce Grenada's economic dependence on the core capitalist states and Western financial institutions but also to guarantee against external threat. Although Grenada received a significant amount of assistance from Cuba and Eastern Europe, it was not enough for the PRG to sever ties with the Western industrialized nations. The regime's strong ties with Cuba and the Eastern Europe made Grenada vulnerable to U.S. aggression and destabilization measures which severely disrupted its economy. Neither Cuba nor the Eastern European states could have challenged the U.S. inspired and led invasion that Grenada was so powerless to resist. Revolutionary socialism was intended to dispose of the limitation of small size, and to reverse for Grenadians all visions of permanent mendicancy by posing radical solutions to development problems with the objective to overcome dependency. Most of the solutions, however, were incompatible with the fact of U.S. hegemony and its backyard theory of the Caribbean.

The general phenomenon of dependency in the modern world as it relates to underdeveloped societies is of course complex and multifaceted. Earlier passages in this book have discussed political, economic, structural, and psychological dimensions of dependency as they applied to Grenada in particular, and the Caribbean in general. But it is perhaps not too much to say that the psychological dimension of dependency is the most difficult for anyone to overcome for the simple reason that it is the most intractable. It is much easier to change economic structures and political attitudes than it is to change mental habits, that is, the ways people think. Two examples will suffice to support this. In the United States, the Civil War changed the American South economically almost overnight, yet it took a century or more for the ingrained mental habits of white prejudice to begin to disappear in the U.S. Most men and women, under pressure, will change their jobs or join another political party, but most of them find it more difficult to change or modify their perception of the world for the reason that those perceptions rest on psychological elements of human nature and are much more immune to the ability to change. It is not surprising then that the mental habit of psychological dependency on the part of former colonial peoples of the Caribbean is an even more stubborn problem. This, in a nutshell, is at the root of Caribbean dependency, which the PRG tried but failed to change in Grenada. Tony Thorndike has argued that the Grenadian revolutionaries, by taking over the Russian party model as their own, fell into the precise trap they had been so anxious to avoid—that of a psychological dependence upon external modes of government and assumptions developed for quite different societies and problems.[5]

As an ideology, revolutionary socialism blended policies which were inwardly reformist and outwardly nationalist to transform both the spirit of the masses and the material circumstances in which they live. Its goals were to build a true socialist state and society based on justice, equality, and unity, and to break out of the confines of the capitalist system, dependency, and the mold of a colonial past. In all fairness though, the regime did not survive long enough for revolutionary socialism to change centuries-old economic and political patterns.

In Jamaica, the declaration of democratic socialism was guided by the desire of Manley and the PNP leadership to find a third path, a noncapitalist path of development to distinguish from the neocolonial capitalist model of the Puerto Rican type and Marxist-Leninist model of the Cuban type. Both models were rejected by Manley for their respective dependence on the two superpowers. For Manley, the third path offered Jamaica the option of real independence and to create an egalitarian society in which people felt that they were of equal worth and value. "Surely," he writes, "there was another path, a third path, a Jamaican way rooted in our political experience and values, capable of providing an economic base to our political independence and capable of some measure of social justice for the people."[6] Democratic socialism constituted a serious aspiration for change by a large number of

Jamaicans aimed to restructure the country's political economy and to reduce its economic dependence on the core capitalist countries and institutions, eliminate social inequalities that had existed for centuries, and to deepen the political process. It comprised of a series of economic and social welfare reforms designed to ensure maximum opportunities for the middle class and to improve the living standards of the downtrodden classes. Underlying these proposals was a firm commitment to use public funds to increase the level of egalitarianism in Jamaica. Unlike Guyana and Grenada, which adopted Marxist principles, the Manley regime denied any Marxist commitments and upheld the principles of democracy which were deeply entrenched in the country's political culture and became the sine qua non of securing popular support.

Superpower Alignment

As discussed earlier, during the 1970s, the socialist strategies of Guyana, Jamaica, and Grenada were combined with certain foreign-policy initiatives which included non-alignment, the condemnation of U.S. imperialism and domination of the Caribbean, the establishment of diplomatic relations with Cuba, the Soviet Union, China, and other socialist states, and the promotion of a Global South economic strategy designed to increase collective self-reliance among developing countries. This was evident in the role played by Guyana and Jamaica in the NAM and the G-77 in the 1970s and early 1980s.

Despite their international socialist posture, both Guyana and Jamaica remained relatively isolated from any superpower connections. Having failed to diversify trade away from their traditional partners and establish close ties with the Eastern bloc, Guyana and Jamaica remained friendly with Cuba. Their radical Third World linkages, combined with their non-aligned stance and anti-imperialist positions on international affairs, strained their relations with the U.S. Both Burnham and Manley associated their respective govern-ments with the active thrust of the non-aligned movement which questioned much of the Western ideology and, in the spirit of and cooperation with Cuba, challenged U.S. supremacy in the Caribbean Basin. This, along with their nationalization of foreign assets, resulted in strong U.S. government and multinational corporations' action against the two regimes during the 1970s and early 1980s. In the case of Guyana, the U.S., prior to the election of Reagan in 1980, adopted a slightly hands-off policy against the Burnham regime because the political alternative was the Marxist PPP.

In Jamaica the situation was not the same. Democratic socialism was undermined by the U.S. government and the capitalists through adverse economic policies and political destabilization in support of the pro-U.S. and anticommunist JLP. In the Grenadian case, it was alleged that from the early days of the revolution, open hostility by the United States pushed the Bishop regime into a search of close economic and political ties with Cuba and the Eastern bloc after the United States, Britain, and Canada refused to recognize it. This set the PRG onto a foreign policy course which increasingly stressed the importance and positive aspects of socialism and the negative effects of the capitalist system. Forewarned by the U.S. not to seek assistance from Cuba, the PRG stood up to the Reagan administration and carried out its socialist experiments. But by 1983, its politics collided with U.S. policy in the Caribbean. The leaders of the NJM did not know whether to blame the collapse of the economy on their own shortcomings or on CIA destabilization efforts.

Political Support

Although espousing Marxist philosophy, the Burnham regime in Guyana obtained its mass support on the basis of racial mobilization of blacks in opposition to East Indian dominance. Following the split between Burnham and Jagan in 1955, the Guyanese society became highly polarized along racial lines which caused two dominant ethnic groups in the country, Afro-Guyanese (blacks) and Indo-Guyanese (East Indian) to become segregated. As mentioned in chapter 5, blacks, who predominate in the urban areas, the civil service, and in the police and security forces made it difficult for the Indian-dominated PPP to rule once the black population felt threatened by its policies, as was the case during the early 1960s. The vast majority of PPP supporters are predominantly farmers and owners of small and medium-size businesses, some of which are located in the cities while others are in the rural areas of the country. The turn to racial mobilization for political support in Guyana can be attributed to the leadership of the PPP who relied heavily on the East Indian support to form a majority government.

Unlike the racial divide in Guyana, the PNP's base of political support in Jamaica during the 1970s came mainly from a class alliance of urban and rural poor blacks, most of whom were unemployed and rallied behind the PNP's socialist reforms and commitment to improve their living standards. However, the Manley regime completely alienated the middle class and the capitalists, who through their terror of socialism aided in the destabilization of the country's economy and, at the same time, supported the conservative JLP. As indicated in table 9.1, in Grenada, the PRG anchored its base of support mostly on the youths who, with very little reservation, identified with the party efforts to build a revolution and transform the country and society along socialist lines. In all three countries, the majority of middle and upper income wage owners did not support the socialist policies of the regimes. Given the low productive capacity and income level of these countries' economies, it was almost impossible for the regimes to provide extensive social welfare benefits to attract solid working-class support for a long period of time. Much of their social policy was directed towards the poor, the unemployed, small farmers, and artisans. In Jamaica and Grenada the link between socialism and the working class was a weak one, and in the case of Guyana, it was racial ethnicity rather than class that established the PNC's base of support.

Political Style

The political and leadership styles of the three regimes were quite different. As mentioned at the beginning of the chapter, one of the positive aspects of the legacy of colonialism was the establishment of democracy in the English-speaking Caribbean, but democracy did not survive the first postindependence decade in all the countries of the region. The electoral processes in both Guyana and Grenada were corrupt to the point where it was very unlikely or almost impossible for the opposition to win an election and displace the governments in those countries. Virtually all observers of elections in Guyana have agreed that the division between two main ethnic groups contributed to the rigging of national elections and the development of authoritarianism in the country to maintain the PNC hold on power. The Burnham regime was brought to power by relying not only upon the support of the black and mixed races but, perhaps more importantly, upon the fact of black domination and preeminence in the colonial and postcolonial state bureaucracy, including its armed forces.

After the 1968 general election, the PNC dominated the state through racial mobilization, control of the electoral process, a highly politicized army and police, and support from a loyal bureaucracy. This was achieved mostly through patronage, which was an extremely important element of the PNC's ability to guarantee its support and power. The dispensing of patronage to party supporters and loyalists was greatly enhanced by the regime's socialist polices which involved the takeover of all foreign assets and control of most of the domestic economy. In 1980, state authoritarianism was consolidated through a new constitution, which bestowed absolute powers on Burnham. Fear of the opposition and the possible increase in political dissent led to a climate of political repression and curtailment of individual freedom, which was extended to all opposition groups, including the church and all social and political parties. Participation was discouraged except in limited areas subject to tight PNC party control. This was buttressed by a series of antidemocratic measures, including the suppression of human rights, trade union rights, the rule of law, and the traditional independence of the judiciary. These were the only mechanisms through which the Burnham regime was able to maintain its grip on power in Guyana for almost three decades.

The development of authoritarian rule in Grenada originated from the Bishop regime's preoccupation with security, the suspension of the country's constitution and the judicial system, and the establishment of a system called People's Power. Mass participation was opened up for those who supported the PRG and its socialist policies, while those who opposed were detained without trial for long periods of time. Genuine efforts were made by the regime to harness the energies of the Grenadian people towards building a socialist society. But like Guyana, fear and the possible increase in political violence and destabilization led to the harassment of opposition groups and political repression that were justified in the name of the revolution.

People's Power contributed to the violation of human rights, the rule of law, and parliamentary democracy in the country. Authoritarian rule in Grenada facilitated political control over the state bureaucracy, the economy and civil society, manipulation of the army and the police, and the abuse and corruption of power by officials of the PRG. These were perhaps some of the most disturbing features of the Grenadian revolution and the PRG. Here was a government with considerable economic and social achievements to its credit, which enjoyed genuine popular support among the masses in the country, yet was behaving illiberally out of a growing sense of insecurity and fear from a small segment of the population. There was no reason for the PRG not to hold elections; in fact, if an election had been held, especially in the first few months of the regime, the NJM would have won a very handsome victory. Even those who disliked the abundant rhetoric of the PRG and refused to participate in the revolution often expressed appreciation that the government was improving social services and creating jobs for the people. For many, Bishop was the hero of the revolution and he had touched the popular spirit of the vast majority of Grenadians.

In both Guyana and Grenada, repression and denial of individual rights and freedoms to a large section of their populations created a system that was antithetical to the interests of the poor and the working class. Authoritarian rule was imposed on the people of Guyana and Grenada despite their widespread acceptance of the inherited Westminster model of parliamentary democracy which, from the very beginning of the revolution in Grenada, was discarded and discredited by the Bishop regime as undemocratic.

In Jamaica, the situation was quite different. Despite the introduction of democratic socialism as a means for development, Prime Minister Manley and the PNP had less control over the society, the economy, the army, and the police than the PNC in Guyana and the PRG in Grenada. Much of the mass mobilization was directed towards the containment of political attacks from opponents of the PNP regime. The fear of strong antisocialist and anti-populist tendencies and the constraints of the legal and constitutional limits of power led to a more cautious and defensive style of leadership in Jamaica by the Manley regime.

Furthermore, antisocialist sentiments came under severe harassment from a militarized activist group in Guyana and Grenada. In Jamaica the situation was one of violent contestation for power between socialist and antisocialist forces. This contributed to the participatory management style of political leadership adopted by the Manley regime. This style of leadership derived from Manley's intellectual background as a Fabian socialist and a deep respect for democracy by the PNP in particular, and Jamaicans in general. Neither the PNP nor the JLP during the postindependence period attempted to manipulate the electoral process. Not surprisingly, Manley lost power through elections, Bishop was assassinated, and Burnham lost power only when he died from natural causes.

Individual Freedom

In Guyana and Grenada, political freedom was curtailed and opposition forces silenced, while in Jamaica individual political freedoms were protected and were under less assault by the government. There were fewer political prisoners, detentions without trial, or unrestrained imprisonment of political adversaries in Jamaica than in Guyana and Grenada. For example, Grenada had more than 300 political prisoners, some of whom were detained without trial for the entire period of PRG rule. The Bishop regime also took control of the only radio station in the country, Radio Free Grenada, and allowed the publication of only one independent newspaper. Political detainees and control of the media and the armed forces became the norm for the Burnham regime in Guyana. The PNC bore the scars of political assassinations of some prominent figures, including Walter Rodney, leader of the WPA, a Jesuit priest, Father Bernard Drake, Vincent Teekah, a respected minister in the government, and other individuals who disappeared without any apparent reason. In Jamaica elections were held on a regular basis since independence in 1962, and there has been no attempt by the two main parties to suppress individual freedom or form a one-party state. Whereas in Guyana, elections have been rigged between 1968 and 1986 to perpetuate the Burnham regime in power, and in Grenada, the de facto PRG could only be removed from power at gunpoint. At the core of this belief lies the brutal murder of Prime Minister Bishop and five cabinet ministers and the U.S. invasion of Grenada. Given the above, few, if any, would disagree that political repression and denial of individual rights and freedoms in Guyana and Grenada were far greater than the medium level that existed in Jamaica during the period of PNP rule (table 9.1).

Economic Features

Despite efforts by Guyana, Jamaica, and Grenada to create an economy to meet basic domestic consumption needs, the socialist strategies adopted by the three governments did not lead to the development of a basic needs economy. Carl Stone has stressed that the development of the basic needs socialist economy requires a dominant one-party state, a strong Marxist ideology, and a mass party or movement with a highly developed capacity for mobilization and distribution.[7] For a while, Grenada was headed in that direction before its economy collapsed under the weight of U.S. economic pressures in 1983. Grenada's pattern of economic growth between 1979 and 1982 was exceeded only by Barbados, Trinidad and Tobago, and Dominica in the Caribbean.

However, a much closer look at Grenada's economy revealed that the main growth sector was in government services, which expanded from 9 percent of GDP in 1975 to over 20 percent in 1982. Most of the government resources were directed at raising adult literacy, cooperative food production, and improving access to health care and educational services. Tourism, manufacturing, and most areas of agriculture recorded declines rather than growth over this period. Like Grenada, the Manley government in Jamaica did not make any serious efforts to dismantle its capitalist market economies. It adopted a policy of selected nationalization of some industries, and levied taxes on others. By 1980, state ownership in Jamaica accounted for only 15 percent of the economy, whereas in Guyana the state had control of over 80 percent of that country's economy but most of these institutions operated and functioned on ordinary capitalist principles with profit making as their primary goal. In Grenada, the PRG embarked on limited nationalization because it did not have the manpower or the resources to run the private sector. Thus, state ownership of the economy in Guyana was relatively high compared to the medium and low levels that had existed in Jamaica and Grenada respectively (table 9.2).

Meeting the basic needs of the majority classes was not the primary focus of significant economic efforts by the leaders of the three socialist regimes. In Grenada, the PRG was preoccupied with the consolidation of political power and national self-defense against U.S. hostility. As such, economic policies were designed to minimize dislocation and to create public sector employment for the youths without disrupting the existing pattern of ownership and distribution. In Jamaica, modest social democratic reforms of the capitalist economy and income redistribution were the principal goals of democratic socialism which, unlike Guyana, the primary goal of cooperative socialism was state ownership and control of the production forces.

While state ownership in Guyana merely replaced private foreign and local ownership, it was in no way premised on a fundamental alteration of capital-labor relation, either internally or internationally. Here political power was the principal instrument for the creation of economic wealth for the new capitalist class that supported the Burnham government. This factor, which is crucial for understanding the ideological and structural functions of the state in Guyana, flies in the face of the socialist policies articulated by the leadership of the PNC. In no case was significant progress made towards the implementation of socialist economic management or any major efforts to transform the productive base of these economies. In fact, the three regimes maintained a capitalist economic system with strong economic ties with the core capitalist states, which provided most of their aid and foreign exchange.

Despite their socialist and anti-imperialist position, Guyana, Jamaica, and Grenada borrowed heavily from the World Bank, the IMF, and other Western banks and institutions to ease their balance of payment problems. The IMF-World Bank group had the upper hand on the three countries because there was no socialist or noncapitalist equivalent in the Eastern bloc of either the IMF or the World Bank for short-term or long-term development loans. Their hope for economic recovery was pinned to financial assistance from the U.S., the IMF, and other Western financial institutions. Without formal commitments of aid or loans in any significant quantities from the socialist countries, particularly from the former Soviet Union, the people and governments of Guyana, Jamaica, and Grenada could not have escaped the effects of U.S. destabilization measures.

In response to these measures, the regimes turned to Cuba, the Soviet Union, and the socialist bloc for economic and financial assistance and for some degree of protection against the West. The substitution of the East for the West met with little success. It was problematic in that the economies of Guyana, Jamaica, and Grenada are highly integrated into the international capitalist system. Their limited resource base and fragile economies have, over the years, increased their economic dependence on their traditional allies for imports, financial assistance, and markets for their products. Furthermore, the legacy of colonialism meant a high degree of penetration of

Western beliefs, values, and institutional arrangements in the social, cultural, political, and economic systems of the three countries.

In exchange for the economic assistance from the West, the governments of Guyana and Jamaica had to scale down their anti-Western rhetoric and acquiesce to the demands of the U.S. and the IMF, and to become subject to their influence. They had to abandon their socialist economic strategies and adopt the free market economic system as part of the austere monetarist and fiscal policies of the IMF loan agreements. The so-called "rescue missions" of the IMF-World Bank group have contributed to the denationalization of foreign assets, a high unemployment rate and, in some instances, political instability, which have been extremely painful for the people of Guyana and Jamaica. They also led to the collapse of democratic socialism in Jamaica, revolutionary socialism in Grenada, and cooperative socialism in Guyana. Thus dependence on the capitalist West for financial assistance served to retard socialist economic advances in Guyana, Jamaica, and Grenada.

Dependence on the world capitalist countries and institutions by these countries could have been avoided if the core socialist states had developed policies that were more outward looking toward the Global South countries and had less of a hard currency problem as well as a larger share of world trade, financial resources, production, and services. The domination of the global economy by the core capitalist countries has increased the indebtedness of the Global South countries and widened the economic gap, which currently stands at sixty to one between the rich and poor states. It has also made the small socialist states in the Caribbean vulnerable to international capitalist pressures to either change direction or abandon the socialist path. These developments pointed to the difficulties encountered by the three regimes to implement socialist policies in the Caribbean. They also suggest that prospects for socialist development in the region are not very promising principally because they are bedevilled with geopolitical hazards.

Furthermore, efforts to pursue socialist politics in Guyana, Jamaica, and Grenada far outweighed efforts to reorganize their economies along socialist lines. The socialist strategies adopted by Guyana, Jamaica, and Grenada in the 1970s and early 1980s have not produced the structural transformation of their economies in favor of the masses, as articulated by the leaders and by the left intelligentsia in the Caribbean. However, their socialist efforts to manage the economy and to reduce their external dependence have not been significantly worse than traditional capitalist approaches. Neither ideology has provided a solution that could lead to economic development and reduce poverty and dependency in the Caribbean. The fact is that both capitalist and socialist models of development in the region have encountered political leadership failures and have overburdened the bureaucracy. The blending of socialist strategies with the existing market economies through regulation and state ownership, while grounded in good intentions, had produced less satisfactory results than anticipated. Put bluntly, politics and ideology cannot provide solutions to problems that are deeply rooted in the structure of underdeveloped economies.

While the socialist strategies described herein reinforced the political and economic profiles of Guyana, Jamaica, and Grenada projected in tables 9.1 and 9.2 respectively, they did not, and could not have, overcome these countries' economic dependence. The social and economic conditions and

Table 9.1
Political Profile of Guyana, Jamaica, and Grenada

Political Features	Guyana (1970-1985)	Jamaica (1972-1980)	Grenada (1979-1983)
Ideology (Marxist or Social Democracy)	Marxist	Social Democracy	Marxist
Superpower Alignment (West, East, or Non-aligned)	Non-aligned	Non-aligned	East
Political Support (Racial, Class, or Youth)	Racial	Class	Youth
Power Structure (Liberal Democracy, Party State)	Party State	Liberal Democracy	Party State
Political Style (Participatory, Authoritarian)	Authoritarian	Participatory	Authoritarian
Individual Freedom (High, Medium, Low)	Low	Medium	Low
Political Parties (Socialist, Nationalist, Marxist)	People's National Congress (PNC) (Socialist)	People's National Party (PNP) (Nationalist)	New Jewel Movement (NJM) (Marxist)

Table 9.2
Economic Profile of Guyana, Jamaica, and Grenada

Economic Features	Guyana (1970-1985)	Jamaica (1972-1980)	Grenada (1979-1983)
State Ownership (High, Medium, Low)	High	Medium	Low
Economic System (Market Economy, Basic Needs)	Market Economy	Market Economy	Market Economy
Economic Policy (Production, Redistribution, State Ownership)	State Ownership	Redistribution	Redistribution
External Economic Ties (Core Capitalist, Socialist, Periphery)	Core Capitalist	Core Capitalist	Core Capitalist
Foreign Aid (West, East)	West	West	East

dependency relations that led to the adoption of socialist developments in Guyana, Jamaica, and Grenada in the 1970s remain essentially the same in the 1980s, the 1990s, and beyond. The same dynamic of producing what was not consumed domestically and consuming what was not produced locally in the three countries and the entire Caribbean continue to prevail, despite the expansion of state property during the 1970s. These countries did not have the resources to eliminate most of the deeply rooted poverty and un-employment, to break out of dependence on plantation agriculture and mineral exports, and to develop autonomously of the world capitalist economy. As small Global South countries, their fortunes continued to be depended upon and dictated by developments in the core capitalist states of Western Europe and North America, particularly the G-7 that are beyond their control.

Finally, despite the U.S.-led destabilization measures, the socialist strategies implemented by the three regimes did provide, for a brief period, improvements in the economy and in social services such as health and education as well as strengthening the regimes' hold on power. This approach is similar to what Samuel P. Huntington (1968) described as the crisis model of political change, which stressed the choices made by a political leadership in the quest to gain and maintain control of the state. It subscribed to the notions put forth by D. A. Rustow (1970) and Barrington Moore (1966) that the conditions for conquest of power are different from those necessary to maintain that power.

Notes

1. David Lowenthal, *West Indian Societies* (New York: Oxford University Press, 1972), 298-318.

2. Ibid., 76.

3. Carl Stone, "Whither Caribbean Socialism? Reflections on Jamaica, Grenada, and Guyana," in *The Troubled and the Troubling Caribbean*, ed. Roy Glasgow and Winston Langley (Ontario, Canada: Edwin Mellin Press, 1989), 128-29.

4. Ibid., 134.

5. Tony Thorndike, "Revolution and Reform: The New Jewel Movement in Theory and Practice" (paper presented at the Conference on the Grenada Revolution, 1979-1983, University of the West Indies, St. Augustine, Trinidad, 24 May 1984), 46.

6. Michael Manley, *Jamaica: Struggle in the Periphery* (London: London University Press, 1982), 38.

7. Stone, "Whither Caribbean Socialism," 141.

Bibliography

Abbott, George C. "The Associated States and Independence," *Journal of Inter-American Studies and World Affairs* 23 (1981): 69-93.

Agnew, J. *The United States in the World Economy: A Regional Geography.* Cambridge: Cambridge University Press, 1987.

Ambursley, Fitzroy. "Grenada: The New Jewel Revolution," in *Crisis in the Caribbean*, ed. Fitzroy Ambursley and Robin Cohen. New York: Monthly Review Press, 1983.

———. "Jamaica: From Michael Manley to Edward Seaga," in *Crisis in the Caribbean*, ed. Fitzroy Ambursley and Robin Cohen. New York: Monthly Review Press, 1983.

———. "Jamaica: The Demise of Democratic Socialism." *New Left Review*, 128 (July-August 1981).

Ambursley, Fitzroy, and Robin Cohen, eds. *Crisis in the Caribbean.* New York: Monthly Review Press, 1983.

Amin, Samir. *Unequal Development: An Essay on the Social Transformation of Peripheral Capitalism.* New York: Monthly Review Press, 1976.

———. *Accumulation on a World Scale: A Critique of the Theory of Underdevelopment.* New York: Monthly Review Press, 1974.

Anderson, Thomas D. *Geopolitics of the Caribbean: Ministates in a Wider World.* New York: Praeger Publishers, 1984.

Axline, W. Andrew. *Caribbean Integration: The Politics of Regionalism.* New York: Nichols Publishing Co., 1979.

Bahadorrsingh, Krishna. *Trinidad Ethnic Politics: The Persistence of the Race Factor.* London: Institute of Race Relations, 1968.

———. *The Racial Factor in Trinidad's Politics in readings in Government and Politics of the West Indies*, eds. Trevor Munroe and Rupert Lewis. Mona, Jamaica, UWI.

Baran, Paul. *The Political Economy of Neocolonialism.* London: Heinemann Publishers, 1975.

Barry, Tom, Beth Wood, and Deb Preusch. *The Other Side of Paradise: Foreign Control in the Caribbean.* New York: Grove Press, 1984.

———. *Dollars and Dictators: A Guide to Central America.* New York: Grove Press Inc., 1982.

Beckford, George, ed. *Caribbean Economy.* Kingston, Jamaica: Institute of Social and Economic Research, UWI, 1978.

————. *Persistent Poverty: Underdevelopment in Plantation Economies of the Third World.* New York: Oxford University Press, 1972.

Beckford, George and M. Witter. *Small Garden; Bitter Weed: Struggle and Change in Jamaica.* Jamaica: Marion Publishing Co., 1980.

Bender, Gerald J. "Angola, the Cubans and American Anxieties." *Foreign Policy* 31 (Spring 1978).

Bender, L. D. *Cuba vs. United States: The Politics of Hostility*, 2 ed. San Juan: Inter-American University Press, 1981.

Benedict, Burton. *Problems of Small Territories.* London: The Athlone Press, 1967.

Benn, Dennis. "The Commonwealth Caribbean and the New International Economic Order," in *Dependency under Challenge: The Political Economy of the Commonwealth Caribbean*, ed. Anthony Payne and Paul Sutton. Manchester: Manchester University Press, 1984.

Bernal, R. "The IMF and Class Structure in Jamaica 1977-1980." *Latin American Perspectives* 11, no. 3 (1984).

————. "The Struggle for the Old International Order: The Caribbean Basin Plan and Jamaica" (paper presented at the Conference of the Caribbean Studies Association in Kingston, Jamaica, May 1982).

Best, Lloyd. "Size and Survival," in *Readings in the Political Economy of the Caribbean,* ed. N. Girvan and O. Jefferson. Mona, Jamaica: New World Group, 1971.

————. "Independent Thought and Caribbean Freedom," *New World Quarterly*, 3 (4), 1967; reprinted in *Readings in the Political Economy of the Caribbean*, ed. N. Gervan and O. Jefferson. Mona, Jamaica: New World Group, 1971.

————. "Outlines of a Model of Pure Plantation Economy," *Social and Economic Studies* (September 1968).

Best, Lloyd, and Kari Levitt. "Character of Caribbean Economy," in *Caribbean Economy: Dependence and Backwardness*, ed. George L. Beckford. Kingston, Jamaica: The Herald Ltd., 1975.

————. "Studies in Caribbean Economy," vol. 1. Kingston, Jamaica: ISER, UWI, 1974.

————. *Externally Propelled Industrialization and Growth in the Caribbean.* Montreal, Mimeo, 1969.

Biddle, William J., and John D. Stephens. "Dependency and Foreign Policy: Theory and Practice in Jamaica" (paper presented at the Conference of the Latin American Studies Association, Boston, October 1986).

Bishop, Maurice. *Forever Ever! Three Years of the Grenadian Revolution.* Sydney, Australia: Pathfinder Press, 1982.

————. "Imperialism Is the Real Problem," in *Selected Speeches 1979-1981*, ed. Maurice Bishop. Havana: Casa de las Americas, 1982.

————. "Education Is a Must," in *Education Is a Must*, ed. M. Bishop and C. Searle. London: Education Committee of the British Grenadian Friendship Society, 1981.

Bodenheimer, Susanne J. *The Ideology of Developmentalism: American Political Science's Paradigm Surrogate for Latin American Studies.* Beverly Hills, Calif.: Sage Publishers, 1971.

Boeke, J. H. "Dualistic Economies," in *Leading Issues in Economic Development: Studies in International Poverty,* ed. Gerald M. Meier. New York: Oxford University Press, 1970.

Bohning, Don. "Charges of Destabilization Grow in Caribbean." *Miami Herald,* 22 June 1976.

Boodhoo, Kenneth. "The Economic Dimension of U. S. Caribbean Policy," in *The Caribbean Challenge: U. S. Policy in a Volatile Region,* ed. H. Michael Erisman. Boulder, Colo.: Westview Press, 1984.

Boswell, Terry. "Colonial Empires and the Capitalist World-Economy: A Time Series Analysis of Colonization, 1640-1960." *American Sociological Review* 54 (April 1989): 180-196.

Bradley, C. Paul. "Mass Parties in Jamaica: Structure and Organization." *Social and Economic Studies* 9, no. 4 (1960): 375-416.

Braveboy-Wagner, Jacqueline. "The Politics of Developmentalism: U. S. Policy toward Jamaica," in *The Caribbean Challenge: U. S. Policy in a Volatile Region,* ed. H. Michael Erisman. Boulder, Colo.: Westview Press, 1984.

————. "Changes in the English-Speaking Caribbean: An International Systems Perspective with Implications for the United States." *Caribbean Monthly Bulletin* (October 1981): 50-64.

Brewster, Havelock. "Economic Dependence: A Quantitative Interpretation." *Social and Economic Studies* 22 (1973).

Brewster, Havelock, and Clive Thomas. *The Dynamics of West Indian Economic Integration.* Kingston, Jamaica: Institute of Social and Economic Research, UWI, 1967.

Brizan, George. *Grenada, Island of Conflict: From Amerindians to People's Revolution, 1498-1979.* London: Zed Books, 1984.

Brown, Lester R. *World without Borders.* New York: Vintage Books, 1972.

Bryan, Anthony. "The CARICOM and Latin American Integration Experience: Observations on Theoretical Origins and Comparative Performance," in *Ten Years of CARICOM. Inter-American Development Bank.* Washington, D. C., 1984.

Burnham, Forbes. *Towards the Socialist Revolution.* Georgetown: Guyana Printers, 1977.

————. *Economic Liberation through Socialism.* Georgetown: Guyana Printers, 1977.

————. *In the Cause of Humanity.* Georgetown: Guyana Printers, 1975.

————. *Declaration of Sophia.* Georgetown: Guyana Printers, 1974.

————. *Breakthrough.* Georgetown: Guyana Printers, 1973.

————. "A Vision of the Cooperative Republic," in *Cooperative Republic: A Study of Aspects of Our Way of Life,* ed. Lloyd Searwar. Georgetown, Guyana: Guyana Printers Ltd., 1970.

————. *A Destiny to Mould*. London: Longman Group, 1970.

————. *Birth of the Cooperative Republic in Guyana*. Georgetown, Guyana: Ministry of Information, 1970.

Caldwell, Malcolm. *The Wealth of Some Nations*. London: Zed Press, 1977.

Caporaso, James A. "Introduction to the Special Issue of International Organization on Dependence and Dependency in the Global System." *International Organization* 32, no. 1 (Winter 1978).

Caporaso, James A., and Behrouz Zare. "An Interpretation and Evaluation of Dependency," in *From Dependency to Development: Strategies to Overcome Underdevelopment and Inequality*, ed. Heraldo Munoz. Boulder, Colo.: Westview Press, 1981.

Cardoso, Fernando, H. "The Consumption of Dependency Theory in the United States." *Latin America Research Review* 12, no. 3 (1977).

Cardoso, Fernando H., and Enzo Faletto. *Dependency and Development in Latin America*. Berkeley: University of California Press, 1979.

Chen-Young, Paul. "Commentary" *Economic Report*, Jamaica 2, no. 11 (January 1977): 1-11.

Chernick, Sidney E. *The Commonwealth Caribbean: The Integration Experience*. Baltimore: Johns Hopkins University Press, 1978.

Chilcote, Ronald. *Theories of Comparative Politics*. Boulder, Colo.: Westview Press, 1994.

————. "Dependency: A Critical Review of the Literature." *Latin American Perspective* 1, no. 1 (1974).

Chilcote, Ronald, and Joel Edelstein, eds. *Latin America: The Struggle with Dependency and Beyond*. New York: John Wiley and Sons, 1974.

Chubin, Shahram. "Southern Perspectives on World Order," in *The Global Agenda*, 5 ed., ed. Charles W. Kegley, Jr., and Eugene Wittkopf. New York: McGraw-Hill, 2001.

Clark, Sebastian. *Grenada: A Workers and Farmers Government with Revolutionary Proletariat Leadership*. New York: Pathfinder Press, 1980.

Coard, Bernard. *To Construct from Morning: Making the People's Budget in Grenada*. St. George's, Grenada: Fedon Publishers, 1982.

————. "The Meaning of Political Independence in the Commonwealth Caribbean," in *Independence for Grenada: Myth or Reality?* St. Augustine, Trinidad: UWI, Institute of International Relations, 1974.

Cohen, Benjamin J. *The Question of Imperialism*. New York: Basic Books, 1973.

Coll, Armando Lopez. *La Colaboracion y la Integracion Economicas en el Caribe*. Havana : Editorial de Ciencias Sociales, 1983.

Collin, R. H. *Theodore Roosevelt's Caribbean: The Panama Canal, the Monroe Doctrine, and the Latin American Context*. Baton Rouge: Louisiana State University Press, 1990.

Cox, Robert W., and Harold K. Jacobson. "The United States and World Order: On Structures of World Power and Structural Transformation" (paper presented at the International Political Association Conference, Rio de Janeiro, Brazil, August 1981).

Cross, Malcom. *Urbanization and Urban Growth in the Caribbean*. Cambridge: Cambridge University Press, 1979.

Daly, Vere T. *A Short History of the Guyanese People*. London: Macmilan, 1975.

Danns, G. K. *Domination and Power in Guyana*. New Brunswick, N.J.: 1984.

———. "Militarization and Development: An Experiment in Nation Building." *Transition 1*, no. 1 (1978).

———. "Militarization and Development: An Experiment in Nation Building in Guyana." *Transition Guyana* 1, no. 1 (1978): 23-44.

Deere, Carmen Diana. *In the Shadows of the Sun: Caribbean Development Alternatives and U. S. Policy*. Boulder, Colo.: Westview Press, 1990.

Demas, William G. "Consolidating Our Independence: The Major Challenge for the West Indies." Lecture Series, University of the West Indies, Institute of International Relations, Trinidad and Tobago, 1986.

———. "The Caribbean and the New International Economic Order." 20, no. 3 (1978).

———. "The Caribbean Community and the Caribbean Development Bank." Speech delivered at a Seminar on Management in the Caribbean, Port-of-Spain, Trinidad: mimeo, 1975.

———. *The Economics of Development in Small Countries with Special Reference to the Caribbean*. Montreal: McGill University Press, 1965.

de Silva, Leelananda, "The Non-Aligned Movement: Its Economic Organization and NIEO Perspectives," in *The Challenge of South-South Cooperation*, eds. Brenda Palvic, Raul R. Uranga, Boris Cizely, and Marian Svetlicic (Boulder, Colo.: Westview, 1983), 76.

Despres, Leo A. *Cultural Pluralism and Nationalist Politics in British Guiana*. Chicago: Rand McNally, 1967.

Devas, Raymond. *Conception Island*. London: Sands & Co, 1932.

De Young, Karen. "U.S. vs. Cuba on Caribbean Isle of Grenada." *Washington Post*, 27 April 1979.

Dookman, Isaac. *A Post Emancipation History of the West Indies*. London: Collins, 1982.

Dos Santos, Theotonio. "The Structure of Dependence." *American Economic Review* 60, no. 2 (May 1970): 231-236.

Eaton, George E. *Alexander Bustamante and Modern Jamaica*. Kingston, Jamaica: Jamaica Publishers, 1975

Eisenstadt, S. N. *Modernization: Protest and Change*. Englewood Cliffs, N.J.: Prentice Hall, 1966.

Emmanuel, P. *Crown Colony Politics in Grenada, 1917-1951*. Bridgetown: Barbados Printers Ltd., 1978.

Erisman, H. Michael. *Pursuing Postdependency Politics South-South Relations in the Caribbean*. Boulder, Colo.: Lynne Rienner Publishers, 1992.

———. *The Caribbean Challenge: U. S. Policy in a Volatile Region*. Boulder, Colo.: Westview Press, 1984.

————. "Cuba and the Third World: The Nonaligned Nations Movement," in *The New Cuban Presence in the Caribbean*, ed. Barry B. Levine. Boulder, Colo.: Westview Press, 1983.

Essien-Udom, E. U. *Black Nationalism*. London: Penguin Books, 1966.

Evans, Peter B. "Dependency," in *The Oxford Companion to Politics of the World*, ed. Joel Krieger. New York: Oxford University Press, 1993.

————. *Dependent Development: The Alliance of Multinational, State, and Local Capital in Brazil*. Princeton, N.J.: Princeton University Press, 1979.

Fanon, Frantz. *The Wretched of the Earth*. New York: Grove Press Inc., 1961.

Feinberg, Richard E. "Central America: No Easy Answers." *Foreign Affairs* 59, no. 5 (Summer 1981).

Feinberg, Richard E., Richard Newfarmer, and B. Orr. "The Battle over the CBI: The Debate in Washington." *Caribbean Review* 12 (1983).

Ferguson, Tyrone. *Structural Adjustment and Good Governance: The Case of Guyana*. Georgetown, Guyana: Public Affairs Consulting Enterprise, 1995.

Frank, Andre Gunder. "The Development of Underdevelopment," in *Dependence and Underdevelopment*, ed. James D. Cockcroft, Andre Gunder Frank, and Dale L. Thompson. New York: Doubleday and Company Inc., 1972.

————. *Development and Underdevelopment in Latin America*. New York: Monthly Review Press, 1968.

————. *Capitalism and Underdevelopment in Latin America: Historical Studies of Chile and Brazil*. New York: Monthly Review Press, 1967.

Frederick, Edward. *From Camerhogue to Free Grenada: A Brief Introduction to the History of Grenada*. St. George's: Grenada National Museum, 1974.

Gabbidon, A. "Proble Tinson Pen as Ganja Center." *Weekly Gleaner*, 9 September 1981.

Garvey, Amy Jacques. *Philosophy and Opinions of Marcus Garvey*, 2 Vols. New York: Atheneum Press, 1967.

Gilpin, Robert. *War and Change in World Politics*. Cambridge: Cambridge University Press, 1981.

Girvan, N. "Swallowing the IMF Medicine in the Seventies." *Development Dialogue* no. 2 (1980): 55-74.

————. "The Development of Dependency in the Caribbean and Latin America: Review and Comparison." *Social and Economic Studies* 22 (1978).

————. *Foreign Capital and Economic Underdevelopment in Jamaica*. Kingston, Jamaica: UWI, ISER, 1971.

————. "Multinational Corporations and Dependent Underdevelopment in Mineral-Export Economies." *Social and Economic Studies* 19, no. 4 (1970).

————. "The Caribbean Bauxite Industry." *Institute of Social and Economic Research,* UWI, 1967.

Girvan, Norman, R. Bernal, and W. Hughes. "The IMF and the Third World: The Case of Jamaica, 1974-80." *Development Dialogue* 2 (1980): 113-155.

Girvan, N., and O. Jefferson. *Readings in the Political Economy of the Caribbean*. Kingston, Jamaica: New World Group, 1971.

Glean, C. A. "Reaching beyond the Grasp: A Revolutionary Approach to Education." *Bulletin of Eastern Caribbean Affairs* 7, no. 1 (1981).

Gonsalves, R. E. *The Non-Capitalist Path of Development: Africa and the Caribbean*. London: London Press, 1981.

———. "The Importance of the Grenada Revolution to the Eastern Caribbean." *Bulletin of Eastern Caribbean Affairs* 5 (March-April 1979).

Gonzalez, Heliodoro. "The Caribbean Basin Initiative: Toward a Permanent Dole." *Inter-American Economic Affairs* (1982).

Grant, C. H. "Political Sequel to Alcan Nationalization in Guyana: The International Aspects." *Social and Economic Studies* 22 (1973): 249-269.

Greaves, Ida. "Plantations in World Economy," in *Plantation Systems of the New World*: Washington, D.C., Pan American Union, 1959.

Greene, J. Edward. "The Ideological and Idiosyncratic Aspects of U. S.-Caribbean Relations," in *The Caribbean Challenge: U. S. Policy in a Volatile Region*, ed. H. Michael Erisman. Boulder, Colo.: Westview, 1984.

———. *Race vs. Politics in Guyana*. Kingston, Jamaica: ISER, UWI, 1974.

Greene, James and Brent Scowcroft. *Western Interests and U. S. Policy Options in the Caribbean Basin*. Boston: Delgeschlager, Gunn and Haim, 1984.

Greenwood, R., and S. Hamber. *Development and Decolonization*. London: Mcmillan, 1980.

Haggard, Stephan, and Robert Kaufman. *The Political Economy of Democratic Transitions*. Princeton, N.J.: Princeton University Press, 1995.

Haq, Mahbub Ul. *The Poverty Curtain*. New York: Columbia University Press, 1976.

Harden, Sheila, ed. *Small Is Dangerous: Microstates in a Macroworld*. London: Francis Pinter Press, 1985.

Harrod, J. *Trade Union Foreign Policy*. London: Macmillan Press, 1972.

Hayes, Margaret Daly. "United States Security Interests in Central America in Global Perspective," in *Central America: International Dimensions of the Crisis,* ed. Richard E. Feinberg. New York: Holmes and Meier, 1982.

Hearne, John. *A Search for Solutions: Selections from the Speeches and Writings of Michael Manley*. Ottawa: Maple House Publishers, 1976.

Heine, Jorge, ed. *A Revolution Aborted: The Lessons of Grenada*. Pittsburgh: University of Pittsburgh Press, 1991.

Heine, Jorge, and Leslie Manigat. *The Caribbean and World Politics: Cross Currents and Cleavages*. New York: Holmes and Meier, 1988.

Hendrickson, Embert. "In Pursuit of the Cooperative Republic: Guyana in the 1970s." *The World Today* (May 1979): 214-222.

Henrigues, Fernando. *Family and Colour in Jamaica*. London: MacGibbon and Kee Publishers, 1968.

Higgins, Benjamin, and Jean Dowing Higgins. *Economic Development of a Small Planet*. New York: Norton Press, 1979.

Hintzen, Percy. *The Costs of Regime Survival: Racial Mobilization, Elite Domination, and Control of the State in Guyana and Trinidad*. Cambridge: Cambridge University Press, 1989.

Hobson, John A. *Imperialism: A Study*. Ann Arbor: University of Michigan Press, 1965.

Hoyte, Desmond. "Making the Quantum Leap: Imperatives, Opportunities, and Challenges for CARICOM," *Caribbean Affairs* 2, no. 2 (April-June 1989).

Huntington, Samuel P. "The Change to Change." *Comparative Politics*, April 1971.

————. *Political Order in Changing Societies*. New Haven, Conn.: Yale University Press, 1968.

Hurwitz, Samuel, and Edith Hurwitz. *Jamaica: A Historical Portrait*. New York: Praeger Publishers, 1971.

Hussain, Mir Zohair. *Global Islamic Politics*. New York: Harper Collins, 1995.

Jackson, Robert L. *The Nonaligned, the U. N., and the Superpowers*, New York: Praeger Publishers, 1983.

Jacobs, W. R., and I. Jacobs. *Grenada: The Route to Revolution*. Havana: Casa de Las Americas, 1980.

Jagan, Cheddi B. *The West on Trial: The Fight for Guyana's Freedom*. Berlin: Seven Seas Publishers, 1966.

James, C. L. R. *A History of Pan African Revolt*. Washington, D.C.: Drum and Spear, 1969.

Jankowitsch, Odette, and Karl P. Sauvant. "The Initial Role of Non-Aligned Countries," in *Changing Priorities on the International Agenda: The New International Economic Order,* ed. Karl P. Sauvant. New York: Pergamon Press, 1981.

————. *The Third World without Superpowers: The Collected Documents of the Non-Aligned Countries*. Dobbs Ferry: Oceana, 1978.

Jefferson, Owen. *The Post-War Economic Development in Jamaica*. Mona, Jamaica: ISER, UWI, 1972.

Johnson, Louis. "Hemisphere Defense." *Atlantic Monthly* 166 (July 1940).

Joseph, Rita. "The Significance of the Grenada Revolution to Women in Grenada." *Bulletin of Eastern Caribbean Affairs*, no. 1 (1981).

Karol, K. A. *Guerillas in Power*. New York: Hill and Wang, 1970.

Katzenstein, Peter J. *Small States in World Markets: Industrial Policy in Europe*. Ithaca, N.Y.: Cornell University Press, 1985.

Kegley, Charles W. Jr. and Eugene Wiltkopf. *World Politics: Trend and Transformation*. 8 ed. New York: McGraw-Hill, 2001.

Keith, Nelson, W. Keith, and Z. Novella. *The Social Origins of Democratic Socialism in Jamaica*. Philadelphia: Temple University Press, 1992.

Keith, S. and R. Girling. "Caribbean Conflict: Jamaica and the U.S." *NACLA* 12, no. 3 (1978).

Kirton, C. D. *Public Policy and Private Capital in the Transition to Socialism: Grenada 1979-1983*. Mimeo, 1985.

————. "A Preliminary Analysis of Imperialist Penetration and Control via the Foreign Debt: A Study of Jamaica," in *Essays in Power and Change in Jamaica*, ed. C. Stone and A. Brown. Kingston: ISER, UWI, 1977.

Krasner, Stephen D. "Transforming International Regimes: What the Third World Wants and Why." *International Studies Quarterly* 25 (March 1981): 119-148.

Kwayana, Eusi. "Pseudo-Socialism." Paper presented to a Seminar of the University of the West Indies, Trinidad, 1976.

Lacey, T. *Violence and Politics in Jamaica 1960-1970*. Manchester: Manchester University Press, 1977.

Lagos, Gustavo. "The Revolution of Being: A Preferred World Model," in *From Dependency to Development: Strategies to Overcome Underdevelopment and Inequality*, ed. Heraldo Munoz. Boulder, Colo.: Westview Press, 1981.

Lairson, Thomas D., and David Skidmore. *International Political Economy: The Struggle for Power and Wealth*, 2 ed. New York: Harcourt Brace College Publishers, 1997.

Landau, Saul. "What Future for Jamaica." *Washington Post*, 25 August 1976.

Langley, L. D. *The United States and the Caribbean in the Twentieth Century*. Athens: University of Georgia Press, 1985.

Langley, Winston E. "From Manley to Seaga: Changes in Jamaican Foreign Policy," *Transition* 8 (1983).

Lautka, Cestmire. "Ethno-Linguistic Distribution of South American Indians." *Annals of the Association of American Geographers*, Map Supplement 8, 57, (June 1967).

Levitt, Kari. "Old Mercantilism and the New." *Social and Economic Studies* 12, no. 4 (1970).

Lewis, W. Arthur. "The Industrialization of the British West Indies." *Caribbean Economic Review* 2 (1950): 1-61.

———. *Labor in the West Indies: The Birth of the Workers' Movement*. London: Fabian Society, 1939.

Lewis, Gary P. "Prospect for a Regional Security System in the Eastern Caribbean." *Millennium* (1986).

Lewis, Gordon K. *Grenada: The Jewel Despoiled*. Baltimore: Johns Hopkins University Press, 1987.

———. "The Lessons of Grenada for the Caribbean Left." *Caribbean Contact* 12 (July 1984): 7-8.

———. *Main Currents in Caribbean Thought*. Baltimore: Johns Hopkins University Press, 1984.

———. *The Growth of the Modern West Indies*. London: MacGibbon & Lee, 1968.

———. *Puerto Rico: Freedom and Power in the Caribbean*. New York: Harper and Row, 1963.

Lewis, Vaughan. "Commonwealth Caribbean Relations with Hemispheric Middle Powers," in *Dependency under Challenge: The Political Economy of the Commonwealth Caribbean,* ed. Anthony Payne and Paul Sutton. Manchester: Manchester University Press, 1984.

Linowitz, S. "The Americas in a Changing World." *Commission on United States-Latin Americans Relations,* Washington, D.C., 1974.

Lowenthal, Abraham F. "The Insular Caribbean as a Crucial Test for U. S. Policy," in *The Caribbean Challenge: U. S. Policy in a Volatile Region*, ed. H. Michael Erisman. Boulder, Colo.: Westview Press, 1984.

———. "The Caribbean Basin Initiative: Misplaced Emphasis." *Foreign Policy* 47 (1982).

Lowenthal, David. *West Indian Societies.* New York: Oxford University Press, 1972.

Lowy, M. *The Politics of Combined and Uneven Development.* London: New Left Books, 1981.

Lutchman, Harold A. *From Colonialism to Cooperative Republic: Aspects of Political Development in Guyana.* Puerto Rico: Institute of Caribbean Studies, University of Puerto Rico, 1974.

Macpherson, John. *Caribbean Lands: A Geography of the West Indies,* 3 ed. Trinidad: Longman Caribbean, 1973.

Magid, Alvin. *Urban Nationalism: A Study of Political Development in Trinidad.* Gainesville: University Presses of Florida, 1988.

Maingot, Anthony P. *The United States and the Caribbean: Challenges of an Asymmetrical Relationship.* London: Macmillan Press, 1994.

———. "Caribbean International Relations," in *In the Modern Caribbean*, ed. F. W. Knight and C. A. Palmer. Chapel Hill: University of North Carolina Press, 1989.

———. "The United States in the Caribbean: Geopolitics and the Bargaining Capacity of Small States." Paper presented at the Colloquium on Peace, Development and Security in the Caribbean Basin; Perspectives to the Year 2000, Kingston, Jamaica, 1987.

———. "The Difficult Path to Socialism in the English-Speaking Caribbean," in *Capitalism and the State in U. S.-Latin American Relations*, ed. R. R. Fagen. Palo Alto, Calif.: Stanford University Press, 1979.

Mandle, Jay. "Ideologies of Development." *Transition 2*, no. 1.

———. "Continuity and Change in Guyanese Underdevelopment." *Monthly Review* 21, no. 2 (September1979).

Manigat, L. F. *The Caribbean Yearbook of International Relations*; Leyden: A. W. Sijthoff, 1976.

Manley, Michael. *Up the Down Escalator, Development and the International Economy: A Jamaican Case Study.* Washington, D.C.: Howard University Press, 1987.

———. *Jamaica: Struggle in the Periphery.* London: University of London Press, 1982.

———. *The Politics of Change: A Jamaican Testament.* London: Andre Deutsch Publishers, 1974.

Manley, Robert H. *Guyana Emergent: The Post-Independence Struggle for Nondependent Development.* Boston: Schenkman, 1979.

Marcus, Bruce, and Michael Taber. *Maurice Bishop Speaks: The Grenada Revolution 1979-1983.* New York: Path Finder Press, 1983.

Martin, J. Bartlow. *U.S. Policy in the Caribbean.* Boulder, Colo.: Westview Press, 1978.

McGowan, Patrick. "Imperialism in World-System Perspective." *International Studies Quarterly* 25 (1981).

McIntyre, Alister. "Some Issues of Trade Policy in the West Indies," in *Readings in the Political Economy of the Caribbean*, ed. N. Girvan and O. Jefferson. Kingston, Jamaica: New World Group, 1971.

McPhail, Thomas L. *Electronic Colonialism: The Future of International Broadcasting and Communication*. Beverly Hills, Calif.: Sage Publications, 1981.

Mill, John Stuart. *Principles of Political Economy with Some of Their Applications to Social Philosophy*. London: Longmans, 1878.

Millet, Richard. "Imperialism, Intervention and Exploitation: The Historical Context of International Relations in the Caribbean," in *Restless Caribbean: Changing Patterns of International Relations*, ed. R. Millet and Marvin W. Will. New York: Praeger, 1979.

Millett, Richard, and Marvin W. Will. *The Restless Caribbean*. New York: Praeger, 1979.

Mintz, Sidney W. "The Caribbean as a Socio-Cultural Area," in *Peoples and Cultures of the Caribbean: An Anthropological Reader*, ed. M. M. Horowitz. New York: Natural History Press, 1971.

———. *Sweetness and Power: The Place of Sugar in Modern History*. New York: Viking Press, 1985.

———. *Sugar and Society in the Caribbean: An Economic History of Cuban Agriculture*. New Haven, Conn.: Yale University Press, 1964.

Moon, Bruce E. "Consensus or Compliance? Foreign Policy Change and External Dependence," *International Organization* 39, no. 2 (1985).

Moore, Barrington, Jr. *Social Origins of Dictatorship and Democracy: Lord and Peasant in the Making of the Modern World*. Boston: Beacon Press, 1966.

Morissey, Marietta. "Imperial Designs: A Sociology of Knowledge Study of British and American Dominance in the Development of Caribbean Social Science." *Latin American Perspective* 3, no. 4 (1976).

Mortimer, Robert A. *The Third World Coalition in International Politics*. New York: Praeger, 1980.

Moss, Alfred G., and Harry N. M. Winton. *A New International Economic Order: Selected Documents, 1945-1978*. New York: UNITAR, 1978.

Munoz, Heraldo. *From Dependency to Development: Strategies to Overcome Underdevelopment and Inequality*. Boulder, Colo.: Westview Press, 1981.

Munroe, Trevor. *The Politics of Constitutional Decolonization: Jamaica 1944-1962*. Kingston, Jamaica: ISER, UWI, 1972.

Naipaul, V. S. *The Middle Passage*. New York: Macmillan, 1963.

Napier, Wallace Joefield. "Macroeconomic Growth under the People's Revolutionary Government," in *A Revolution Aborted: The Lessons of Grenada*. Ed. Jorge Heine. Pittsburgh: Pittsburgh University Press, 1991.

Nath, Dwarka. *A History of Indians in Guyana*. London: Oxford University Press, 1970.

Nettleford, Rex M. *Caribbean Cultural Identity*. Kingston, Jamaica: Institute of Jamaica, 1972.

———. *Norman Washington Manley: Manley and the New Jamaica*. New York: Africana, 1971.

Newfarmer, Richard. "Economic Policy toward the Caribbean Basin: The Balance Sheet." *Journal of Inter-American Studies and World Affairs*, no. 1 (February 1985).

Newman, Peter. *British Guiana: Problems of Cohesion in an Immigrant Society*. London: Oxford University Press, 1964.

Newson, Linda. "Foreign Immigrants in Spanish America: Trinidad's Colonialisation Experiment." *Caribbean Studies* 14, nos. 2 and 3 (April-July 1979).

Nkrumah, Kwame. *Neo-Colonialism: The Last Stage of Imperialism*. New York: International Publishing, 1965.

O'Brien, Donald C. "Modernization, Order, and the Erosion of a Democratic Ideal." *Journal of Development Studies* (8 July 1972): 351-378.

O'Shaughnessy, Hugh. *Grenada: Revolution, Invasion, and Aftermath*. London: Sphere Books, 1984.

Palma, Gabriel. "Dependency and Development: A Critical Overview," in *Dependency Theory: A Critical Reassessment*, ed. Dudley Seers. London: Frances Pinter Publishers, Ltd., 1981.

Pantin, Dennis. "The Plantation Economy Market and the Caribbean." *Institute of Development Studies*, Bulletin 12, 1980.

Payne, Anthony. *Modern Caribbean Politics*. Baltimore: Johns Hopkins University Press, 1993.

———. "Whither CARICOM? The Performance and Prospects of Caribbean Integration in the 1990s," *International Journal* 40, no. 2 (Spring 1985).

———. *The International Crisis in the Caribbean*. London: Croom Helm, 1984.

———. *Change in the Commonwealth Caribbean*. London: Royal Institute of International Affairs, 1981.

———. *The Politics of the Caribbean Community, 1961-1979: Regional Integration among New States*. New York: St. Martin's Press, 1980.

———. "From Michael with Love: The Nature of Socialism in Jamaica." *Journal of Commonwealth and Comparative Politics* 14, no. 1 (March 1976): 82-100.

Payne, A. J., and Paul K. Sutton. *Dependency under Challenge: The Political Economy of the Commonwealth Caribbean*. Manchester: Manchester University Press, 1984.

Payne, Anthony, Paul K. Sutton, and Tony Thorndike. *Grenada: Revolution and Invasion*. London: Croom Helm Ltd., 1984.

Pearce, J. *Under the Eagle: U. S. Intervention in Central America and the Caribbean*. London: Latin America Bureau, 1982.

Pearcy, G. Edzel. *The West Indies Scene*. Princeton, N.J.: Van Nostrand, 1965.

Perkins, Dexter. *The United States and the Caribbean*. Cambridge, Mass.: Harvard University Press, 1966.

Persaud, Thakoor. *Conflicts between Multinational Corporations and Less Developed Countries*. Austin: University of Texas Press, 1980.

Phillips, Dion. "The Increasing Emphases on Security and Defense in the Eastern Caribbean," in *Militarization in the Non-Hispanic Caribbean*, ed. Alma Young and Dion Phillips. Boulder, Colo.: Lynne Rienner, 1986.

Plischke, Elmer. *Microstates in World Affairs: Policy Problems and Options*. Washington, D.C.: American Enterprise Institute for Public Policy Research, 1977.

Polanyi, Karl. *The Great Transformation: The Political and Economic Origins of Our Time*. Boston: Rinehart, 1944.

Post, Ken. *Arise Ye Starvelings: The Jamaican Labour Rebellion and Its Aftermath*. The Hague: Martinus Nijhoff, 1978.

Pottinger, George. "A New Look at Development and Social Change in the English-Speaking Caribbean," in *The Troubled and the Troubling Caribbean*, ed. Roy Glasgow and Winston Langley. Ontario: Edwin Mellen Press, 1989.

Prebisch, Raul. *Towards a Dynamic Development Policy for Latin America*. New York: United Nations, 1963.

————. *The Economic Development of Latin America and Its Problems*. New York: UN, Social and Economic Affairs, 1950.

Premdas, Ralph R. "Guyana, Socialism and Destabilization in the Western Hemisphere." *Caribbean Quarterly* 25, no. 3 (1980).

————. "Guyana: Socialist Reconstruction or Political Opportunism." *Journal of Inter-American Studies and World Affairs* 20, no. 2 (May 1978): 133-163.

————. "The Rise of the First Mass-Based Multiracial Party in Guyana." *Caribbean Quarterly* 20, nos. 3 and 4 (January 1975).

Premdas, Ralph R., and R. Hintzen. "Guyana: Coercion and Control in Political." *Journal of InterAmerican Studies and World Affairs* 24, no. 3 (August 1984): 337-354.

Pryor, Frederic L. "Socialism via Foreign Aid: The PRG's Economic Policies with the Soviet Bloc," in *A Revolution Aborted: The Lessons of Grenada*, ed. Jorge Heine. Pittsburgh: University of Pittsburgh Press, 1991.

Ramsaran, R. "The U. S. Caribbean Basin Initiative." *The World Today* 38, 1982.

Reid, S. "An Introductory Approach to the Concentration of Power in Jamaica Corporate Economy and Notes on Its Origin," in *Essays in Power and Change in Jamaica*, ed. Carl Stone and A. Brown. Kingston: Jamaica Publishing House, 1977.

Reno, Philip. *The Ordeal of British Guiana*. New York: Monthly Review Press, 1964.

Richardson, Bonham C. *The Caribbean in a Wider World, 1492-1992: A Regional Geography*. New York: Cambridge University Press, 1994.

Rippy, J. Fred. *The Caribbean Danger Zone*. New York: J. P. Putnam & Son, 1940.

Roberts, W. Adolphe. *The Caribbean: The Story of Our Sea of Destiny*. Indianapolis: Bobbs-Merrill, 1940.

Rodney, Walter. *The Struggle Goes On!* Georgetown, Guyana: Working People's Alliance, 1979.

————. *How Europe Underdeveloped Africa*. Washington, D.C.: Howard University Press, 1972.

————. *The Groundings with My Brothers*. London: Bogle-L'Ouverture, 1969.

Rostow, Walt W. *The Stages of Economic Growth*. Cambridge: Cambridge University Press, 1960.

Rothstein, Robert L. "New International Economic Order," in *The Oxford Companion to Politics of the World*, ed. Joe Krieger. New York: Oxford University Press, 1993.

Rottenberg, S. "Labour Relations in an Underdeveloped Economy." *Caribbean Quarterly* 4, no. 1 (1977)

Rueschemeyer, Dietrich, Evelyne H. Stephens, and John D. Stephens. *Capitalist Development and Democracy*. Chicago: University of Chicago Press, 1992.

Russett, Bruce, and Harvey Starr. *World Politics: The Menu for Choice*. New York: W. H. Freeman and Company, 1996.

Rustow, D. A. "Transitions to Democracy: Toward a Dynamic Model." *Comparative Politics* (April 1970).

Ryan, Selwyn. *Race and Nationalism in Trinidad and Tobago*. Toronto, Canada: University of Toronto, 1972.

Sachs, Ignacy. "The Logic of Development." *International Social Science Journal* 24, no. 1 (1972): 37-43.

Sackey, James A. "Dependence, Underdevelopment, and Socialist Oriented Transformation in Guyana," *Inter-American Economic Affairs* 33, no. 1 (1979).

Sandford, Gregory, and Diane B. Bendahmane. *The New Jewel Movement: Grenada's Revolution, 1979-1983*. Washington, D.C.: Foreign Service Institute, U.S. Department of State, 1985.

Schlesinger, Arthur. *A Thousand Days: John F. Kennedy in the White House*. New York: Houghton Mifflin, 1965.

Schoenhals, Kai P., and Richard Melanson. *Revolution and Intervention in Grenada: The New Jewel Movement, the United States and the Caribbean*. Boulder, Colo.: Westview Press, 1985.

Scott, Macdonald. "The Future of Foreign Aid in the Caribbean after Grenada: Finlandization and Confrontation in the Eastern Tier." *Inter-American Economics Affair* 38, no. 4 (1985).

Seabury, Paul, and Walter A. McDougall, ed. *The Grenada Papers*. San Francisco: Institute for Contemporary Studies, 1984.

Searle, Chris. *Words Uncharmed*. London: Zed Books, 1984.

————., ed. *In Nobody's Backyard: Maurice Bishop's Speeches, 1979-1983*. London: Zed Books, 1984.

————. *Grenada: The Struggle against Destabilization*. London: Writers and Readers Publishing Comparative Society Ltd., 1983.

Searwar, Lloyd. "Non-Alignment as a Viable Alternative for Regional Cooperation." Paper presented at a Seminar on Geo-Political Change in the Caribbean in the 1980s, Georgetown, Guyana, March 1982.

Seers, Dudley. *Dependency Theory, A Critical Reassessment.* London: Frances Pinter Publishers Limited, 1981.

Serbin, Andres. *Caribbean Geopolitics: Toward Security through Peace?* Boulder, Colo.: Lynne Rienner Publishers, 1990.

Shannon, Thomas Richard. *An Introduction to the World-System Perspective.* Boulder, Colo.: Westview, 1989.

Sheridan, R. B. *Sugar and Slavery: An Economic History in the British West Indies, 1623-1775.* Baltimore: Johns Hopkins University Press, 1973.

———. *The Development of the Plantations to 1750: An Era of West Indian Prosperity, 1750-1775.* Barbados: Caribbean Universities Press, 1970.

Sim, R., and J. Anderson. "The Caribbean Strategic Vacuum." *Conflict Studies* 121 (1980).

Simmons, David. "Militarization in the Caribbean: Concern for National and Regional Security," *International Journal* 40 (1985).

Singham, A. W. *The Hero and the Crowd in a Colonial Polity.* New Haven, Conn.: Yale University Press, 1968.

Smith, Anthony. *The Geopolitics of Information: How Western Culture Dominates the World.* New York: Oxford University Press, 1980.

Smith, M. G. *Plural Society in the British West Indies.* Kingston, Jamaica: UWI, 1965; reprinted by the University of California Press, 1974.

Smith, Raymond T. *British Guyana.* London: Oxford University Press, 1962.

Smith, Tony. "The Underdevelopment of Development Literature: The Case of Dependency Theory." *World Politics* 31 (January 1979): 247-288.

Smith, W. S. "Dateline Havana: Myopic Diplomacy." *Foreign Policy* 47 (1982).

Spinner, Thomas J. *Political and Social History of Guyana 1945-1983.* Boulder, Colo.: Westview Press, 1984.

Steele, Beverly A. "Grenada, an Island State: Its History and Its People." *Caribbean Quarterly* 20 (March 1974).

Stephens, Evelyne Huber, and John D. Stephens. *Democratic Socialism in Jamaica.* Princeton, N.J.: Princeton University Press, 1986.

Stewart, Robert. "The 1872 Diary of James Splaine, S. J., Catholic Missionary in Jamaica: A Documentary Note." *Caribbean Quarterly* 30, nos. 3-4 (September and December 1984): 99-109.

Stone, Carl. "Whither Caribbean Socialism? Reflections on Jamaica, Grenada and Guyana," in *The Troubled and the Troubling Caribbean,* ed. Roy Glasgow and Winston Langley. Ontario, Canada: Edwin Mellen Press, 1989.

———. *Power in the Caribbean Basin: A Comparative Study of Political Economy.* Philadelphia: Institute for the Study of Human Issues, 1986.

———. "The 1976 Parliamentary Election in Jamaica." *Journal of Commonwealth and Comparative Politics* 15 (1977): 250-265.

———. *Electoral Behaviour and Public Opinion in Jamaica.* Mona, Jamaica: ISER, UWI, 1974.

———. *Class, Race, and Political Behavior in Jamaica.* Kingston, Jamaica: ISER, UWI, 1973.

————. *Stratification and Political Change in Trinidad and Jamaica.* Beverly Hills, Calif.: Sage Publications, 1972.

Sunshine, Kathy. *The Caribbean: Survival, Struggle and Sovereignty.* Washington, D.C.: EPICA, 1985.

Sutton, Paul. "Living with Dependency in the Commonwealth Caribbean," in *Dependency under Challenge: The Political Economy of the Commonwealth Caribbean*, ed. Anthony Payne and Paul Sutton. Manchester: Manchester University Press, 1984.

Targ, Hary. "Global Dominance and Dependence, Post Industrialism and International Relations Theory." *International Studies Quarterly* 20, no. 3 (September 1976): 461-486.

Thomas, Clive Y. *The Poor and the Powerless: Economic Policy and Change in the Caribbean.* New York: Monthly Review Press, 1988.

————. "The Rise and Fall of Cooperative Socialism," in *Dependency under Challenge: The Political Economy of the Commonwealth Caribbean*, ed. Anthony Payne and Paul Sutton. Manchester: University of Manchester Press, 1984.

————. "State Capitalism in Guyana: An Assessment of Burnham's Cooperative Socialist Republic," in *Crisis in the Caribbean*, ed. Fitzroy Ambursley and Robin Cohen. London: Heineman Publishers, 1983.

————. "From Colony to State Capitalism: Alternative Paths to Development in the Caribbean." *Transition* 5 (1980).

————. "The Non-Capitalist Path as Theory and Practice of De-Colonization and Socialist Transformation." *Latin American Perspectives* 17 (1977): 10-28.

————. "Bread and Justice: The Struggle for Socialism in Guyana." *Monthly Review* 28, no. 4 (1975): 23-35.

————. *Dependence and Transformation: The Economics of the Transition to Socialism.* New York: Monthly Review Press, 1974.

————. "Monetary and Financial Arrangements in a Dependent Monetary Economy." Mona, Jamaica: ISER, UWI, 1965 (Master's thesis, 1964).

Thorndike, Tony. *Grenada: Politics, Economics, and Society.* Boulder, Colo.: Lynne Rienner, 1985.

Tipps, Dean C. "Modernization Theory and the Comparative Study of Societies: A Critical Perspective." *Comparative Studies in Society and History* 15 (March 1973).

Todaro, Michael P. *Economic Development in the Third World*, 4 ed. New York: Longman Press, 1989.

Turner, Mary. *Slaves and Missionaries: The Disintegration of Jamaica Slave Society, 1787-1834.* Urbana: University of Illinois Press, 1982.

Valenta, Jiri. "Soviet Policy and the Crisis in the Caribbean," in *Colossus Challenged: The Struggle for Caribbean Influence*, ed. H. Michael Erisman and John D. Martz. Boulder Colo.: Westview Press, 1982.

Valenzuela, Samuel, and Arturo Valenzuela. "Modernization and Dependency: Alternative Perspectives in the Study of Latin American Underdevelopment," in *From Dependency to Development: Strategies to Overcome Underdevelopment and Inequality*, ed. Heraldo Muniz. Boulder, Colo.: Westview Press, 1981.

Vincent, Theodore G. *Black Power and the Garvey Movement*. Palo Alto, Calif.: Ramparts, 1976.

Waddell, David A. *The West Indies and the Guianas*. Englewood Cliffs, N.J.: Prentice Hall, 1981.

Wallerstein, Immanuel. *The Modern World-Systems*. New York: Academic Press, 1980.

————. "The Rise and Future Demise of the World Capitalist System: Concepts for Comparative Analysis." *Comparative Studies in Society and History* 16 (September 1974): 387-415.

Watty, William. *From Shore to Shore*. Barbados: Cedar Press, 1981.

West, Robert C., and John P. Augelli. *Middle America: Its Lands and People,* 2 ed. Englewood Cliffs, N.J.: Prentice Hall, 1976.

Williams, Eric. *From Columbus to Castro: The History of the Caribbean 1492-1969*. London: Andre Deutsch, 1970.

————. *Capitalism and Slavery*. London: Andre Deutsch, 1964.

Williams, L. "Ganga: A Billion Dollar Operation." *Weekly Gleaner*, 15 July 1981.

Williams, William Appleton. *The Tragedy of American Diplomacy*. New York: Dell Publishers, 1962.

World Bank Report, "Guyana: A Framework for Economic Recovery," no. 5592, GUA, Washington, D.C. (15 May 1985).

World Bank, Economic Memorandum on Grenada, Washington, D.C., 1982.

Zorinsky, Len S. *Miami Herald*, 26 March 1982, 18 (A).

Index

About the Author

Euclid A. Rose received his doctorate from the State University of New York at Albany. Currently he is an assistant professor at Siena College. Rose has held appointments at SUNY Albany and at Palm Beach Community College.